Meals to Come

CALIFORNIA STUDIES IN FOOD AND CULTURE
Darra Goldstein, Editor

MEALS TO COME

A HISTORY OF THE FUTURE OF FOOD

Warren Belasco

UNIVERSITY OF CALIFORNIA PRESS
BERKELEY   LOS ANGELES   LONDON

The publisher gratefully acknowledges the generous contribution to this book provided by the General Endowment Fund of the University of California Press Foundation.

University of California Press, one of the most distinguished university presses in the United States, enriches lives around the world by advancing schol-arship in the humanities, social sciences, and natural sciences. Its activities are supported by the UC Press Foundation and by philanthropic contributions from individuals and institutions. For more information, visit www.ucpress.edu.

University of California Press
Berkeley and Los Angeles, California

University of California Press, Ltd.
London, England

Library of Congress Cataloging-in-Publication Data
Belasco, Warren James.
    Meals to come : a history of the future of food / Warren Belasco.
        p.   cm.—(California studies in food and culture ; 16)
        Includes bibliographical references and index.
        ISBN-13 978-0-520-24151-0 (cloth : alk. paper)
        ISBN-10 0-520-24151-7 (cloth : alk paper)
        ISBN-13 978-0-520-25035-2 (pbk. : alk paper)
        ISBN-10 0-520-25035-4 (pbk. : alk. paper)
        1. Food—History.   2. Food supply.   I. Title.
    II. Series.
TX353.B455   2006
641.3009—dc22   2005036472

Manufactured in the United States of America
15   14   13   12   11   10   09   08   07   06
10   9   8   7   6   5   4   3   2   1

This book is printed on New Leaf EcoBook 50, a 100% recycled fiber of which 50% is de-inked post-consumer waste, processed chlorine-free. EcoBook 50 is acid-free and meets the minimum requirements of ANSI/ASTM D5634-01 (Permanence of Paper).♾

CONTENTS

PREFACE

Food is important. In fact, nothing is more basic. Food is the first of the essentials of life, our biggest industry, our greatest export, and our most frequently indulged pleasure. Food means creativity and diversity. As a species, humans are omnivorous; we have tried to eat virtually everything on the globe, and our ability to turn a remarkable array of raw substances into cooked dishes, meals, and feasts is evidence of astounding versatility, adaptability, and aesthetic ingenuity. Food is also the object of considerable concern and dread. What we eat and how we eat it together may constitute the single most important cause of disease and death. As psychologist Paul Rozin puts it, "Food is fundamental, fun, frightening, and far-reaching."[1]

Probably nothing is more frightening or far-reaching than the prospect of running out of food. "A hungry stomach will not allow its owner to forget it, whatever his cares and sorrows," Homer wrote almost three thousand years ago. Even in good times, we are not allowed to forget our deeply rooted heritage of food insecurity. "When thou hast enough," Ecclesiasticus warned circa 180 B.C., "remember the time of hunger."[2] Designed to take advantage of any surplus, our bodies store up fat for the next famine—hence the current obesity crisis—and our prophets warn us against complacency. Given the mounting environmental concerns about population growth, global warming, soil erosion, water scarcity, agrochemical pollution, energy shortages, diminishing returns from fertilizers, and so on, it does seems justified to wonder whether the current banquet is over. Will our grandchildren's grandchildren enjoy the dietary abundance that most of us take for granted? And how on earth will we feed a rapidly growing, urbanized population in the Third World?

As policy analysts debate possible scenarios, starkly different forecasts and proposals emerge. Some futurists predict unprecedented affluence and convenience—a world of "smart" technologies providing a cornucopia of nutritious, tasty, and interesting foods. Others worry about global shortages, famine, and ecological degradation. Some are confident that the current way of producing and distributing food will take care of the future. Others see the status quo as a sure route to disaster. While many in government, academia, and industry look to new tools—especially genetic engineering—to feed us tomorrow without any modification of our modern high-consumption values, others propose low-tech alternatives organized around smaller scale, localized food systems dependent on a return to more traditional appreciation of limits.

Students in my university courses on the food system and on the future always want to know how I think it'll all turn out. I usually duck that question, for as a historian, and thus mindful of life's quirks and uncertainties, I am uncomfortable making predictions. What I can do, however, is illuminate the discussion by tracing its historical evolution. Given our historical amnesia, it is all too easy to forget what has already been predicted. My research has found that little in the latest forecasts is really new. Western culture has maintained a long-standing romantic fascination with extravagant technology alongside a rich tradition of skepticism and alarm. For example, in the current controversy over genetic engineering, some scenarios resemble the feverish extrapolations offered in response to earlier proposals to streamline the conversion of solar energy to food through synthetic chemistry, irradiation, and yeast cultivation. Similarly, the debate over whether bioengineering is compatible with agrarian ideals sounds quite a bit like earlier arguments over the use of hybrids, tractors, and chemical pesticides.

In this study I look at the way the future of food has been conceptualized and represented over the past two hundred years. When the economist/parson Thomas Malthus (1766–1834) published his *Essay on the Principle of Population as It Affects the Future Improvement of Society* (1798) in response to the "speculations" of the French mathematician the Marquis de Condorcet (1743–94) and the English radical William Godwin (1756–1836), he crystallized a three-way debate about the future of the food system. In *How Many People Can the Earth Support?*

(1995), demographer Joel Cohen articulates the same enduring positions on the question of how we might feed the future: (1) bake a bigger pie, (2) put fewer forks on the table, or (3) teach everyone better table manners.[3] Seeing no limits on human ingenuity and creativity, Condorcet predicted that science and industry could always bake bigger *and better* pies for everyone. Dismissing such techno-cornucopian optimism, Malthus took the "fewer forks" position: humanity's capacity for reproduction would always outrun the farmer's capacity for production and the scientist's capacity for miracles, so prudence dictated a more conservative, less expansive approach to the future. Pessimistic about human nature, Malthus also doubted Godwin's "better manners" stance, which held that in an egalitarian society with altruistic values, people would figure out ways to share nature's bounty. Godwin's democratic optimism was elaborated upon by nineteenth-century socialists and liberals alike, who promoted resource redistribution as the solution to hunger.

The same three-way debate continues today, albeit with more statistics and less elegant prose. Citing two centuries' worth of miraculous productivity gains, Condorcet's cornucopians at the World Bank and Monsanto maintain hope for more of the same through free-market capitalism and biotechnology. Citing two centuries' worth of environmental disaster and resource depletion, neo-Malthusians like Paul Ehrlich and Lester Brown worry about the limits to growth. Meanwhile, noting that at least a billion people remain hungry amidst mounting agricultural surpluses, the Godwinian neosocialists at Food First argue that only with a more equitable economic system can the poor feed themselves.

The outlines of this controversy may be familiar to those versed in issues to do with the relationship between food and population, which have long engaged scholars of demography, agronomy, and political science. But discussion of these issues has not been confined to the realm of agricultural economics. Despite our recent agricultural surpluses, worries about the future of food are embedded in an array of expressive, prescriptive, and material forms: utopian and dystopian fiction and film, refereed scientific journals, USDA yearbooks, mass journalism and advertising, agriculture school syllabi, nutrition textbooks, Victorian fantasies of a meal-in-a-pill, world's fairs, Disney amusement parks, chain supermarkets, communal gardens, market research, "kitchens of tomorrow," space food, the recent rebirth of organic farmers' markets, and current debates over genetic engineering and other "smart" technologies. Taking an integrative, interdisciplinary approach, I examine these varied sources for their underlying positions on the question of whether we face a future of scarcity or abundance, firm limits or boundless expansion, decline or progress.

This book situates food at the center of the debate. While there are many noteworthy histories of the future[4]—and I am greatly indebted to them—previous scholars have sometimes underestimated the importance of basic belly issues in speculative discourse. At the same time, if historians have overlooked food, food writers and activists have sometimes lacked a historical perspective on their causes. Thus some advocates of the "limits to growth" paradigm appear unaware of the racist, nativist elements of earlier Malthusian population control and resource conservation ideas. Similarly, cornucopian proponents of biotechnological food production seem unaware that they are repeating the hyperbole once voiced in favor of foods synthesized from coal, wood pulp, and algae. By giving food issues a deeper historical context, this book hopefully improves current policy analyses and discussions. Also, as a history of the future, this study enriches the relatively new discipline of future studies. We need to examine previous forecasts and predictions in order to reveal basic patterns and possible fallacies in the art and business of futuristic projection. What makes for good forecasts, and when do forecasts go off track? This perspective seems especially useful in the wake of the Y2K hyperbole, when we were bombarded by a mind-numbing array of millennial images, statistical extrapolations, and highly touted "expert" scenarios.

Like history, futurism is a narrative-based medium. Futurists construct dramatic scenarios to portray how they think things will, or should, turn out. This book examines three different ways of dramatizing the future—policy debates, speculative fiction, and stories about products.

Part I, "Debating the Future of Food," constructs a chronology of two hundred years of worrying by the food policy establishment—the "think tanks"—comprised largely of white, professional, European and American males working in mainstream institutions. Their debates seem to have gone through cycles, becoming more pressing at particular periods—for example, the 1890s, 1920s, late 1940s, 1970s, and 1990s. In chapter 2, I identify the conditions and events that have precipitated food security scares, namely, food price inflation, spikes in birth rates, environmental stresses, and acute cultural anxieties about human migration and rapid demographic change. Then in chapter 3, I analyze what might be called the enduring deep structure of the policy debates: the questionable statistics, logical fallacies, recurrent archetypes, manipulative rhetorical devices, and, above all, the strongly subjective, often moralistic assumptions about diet and culture buried beneath an avalanche of seemingly objective calculations. Why do most forecasts fail? And why do forecasters keep recycling the same metaphors and faulty assumptions?

Part II, "Imagining the Future of Food," examines speculative fiction—a more vibrant and dissident forum for conceiving of the future than the white-paper futurism of part I. Whereas think tank forecasters have had considerable difficulty conceptualizing beyond their own establishment values, paradigms, and experiences, speculative-fiction writers have freely allowed for radical discontinuities, wild cards, surprise turns, near misses, lucky breaks, unexpected decisions, and even chaos when they create futuristic scenarios. My argument is that the fantasies of utopian and dystopian fiction have served to both reflect and shape the policy debate over the future of food. Speculative stories have also given greater voice to those who are not well represented by mainstream policy analysis—especially radical environmentalists, socialists, and feminists.

Chapter 4 looks at food production, distribution, and consumption as depicted in the technological utopian fiction of the Progressive Era, a period of heightened expectation that industrial agriculture and scientific nutrition could be harnessed to radically egalitarian ends. Chapter 5 examines food systems envisioned in the darker, dystopian stories of the later twentieth century. Unlike the Progressive utopians, who believed that Enlightened Evolution was on their side and that they could have it all—technology, order, and democracy—these jaundiced followers of Aldous Huxley offered radical critiques of consumer capitalism, technocratic efficiency, and corporate globalization; concerns regarding the unintended consequences of cornucopian science; and a strongly Malthusian fear of congestion and crowding.

From the vantage point of both the impassioned policy debates (part I) and the mostly dystopian fantasies of the past half century (part II), tomorrow's dinner prospects look rather dismal. Yet some hope persists, for even though front-page news stories may tend toward pessimistic and alarmist predictions, modern American life—and much of life in the world generally—is in fact infused with products, symbols, and markers that speak not just of a bountiful today but also explicitly of a thriving tomorrow. In part III, "Things to Come," I examine these material assertions of optimism as found in world's fairs, restaurants, stores, and kitchens—as well as in the upbeat feature stories that function largely to sell the cornucopian future.

Tolstoy notwithstanding, not all happy stories are the same.[5] In chapters 6, 7, and 8, I discuss three cornucopian futures: classical, modernist, and recombinant. The classical future is a continuation and elaboration of the progress of the past—a future of ever bigger and better things made available largely through materialistic, quantitative, often imperialist expansion. In the classical vision, the new evolves seamlessly out of the old. The classical future means the expansion of frontiers—overseas and under the seas, into deserts and tropical forests, underground and in outer space. Such expansion is often justified as a sign of steady evolution from savagery to civilization. For illustration I draw examples mainly from the world's fairs of the late nineteenth and early twentieth centuries.

The modernist future, representing a distinct break with the past, is a radically new vision based on the very latest technologies and scientific breakthroughs, often producing a seemingly more efficient result. The modernist future is one of unprecedented needs, drives, and breakthroughs. If the classical future eyes the visible riches of untapped frontiers, the modernist looks for wealth in the invisible—nitrogen from air, protein from microbes, energy from atoms. Aiming to streamline production, consumption, and evolution itself, modernism came of age in the 1920s and peaked at the Depression-era world's fairs in Chicago (1933) and New York (1939).

While culinary modernism has been favored most by pure scientists, it tends to scare off consumers wary of extreme discontinuities. The recombinant future is perhaps the most palatable and marketable, as, in a cultural version of genetic engineering, it splices the classical with the modern. It envisions a world of neotraditional foods mass-produced by modernist means—microwavable stir-fries, aseptically packaged chai, "fifties-style" low-fat hamburgers cooked on automated grills. Recognizing the human need for "authentic" tastes, NASA's dieticians have abandoned tubed food in favor of interplanetary meals that include fajitas, pad thai noodles, barbecued tofu, and curried lentils. Less confident in the new than modernism, more eclectic and multicultural than classicism, the recombinant (or postmodernist) menu may reflect how many of us actually approach and experience the future: one foot forward, the other planted in an imagined, decontextualized past. For case studies I examine the multicultural foodscape of the 1964 New York World's Fair, food displays and service at the Disney theme parks, the evolution of space food, new versions of the "smart" kitchen (a combination of high-tech gadgetry and artisanal ideals), and the recent enthusiasm for "functional" foods (which purport to engineer scientific nutrition into familiar forms).

Historically, each of these futures has had a heyday of sorts—the classical before 1920, the modernist between 1920 and 1964, and the recombinant since 1964—but there has also been considerable overlap and blurring. At any one time or site—dining room, restaurant, or fair—one might simultaneously experience *several* futures. Furthermore, while each vision of what is to come can theoretically support a corporate-capitalistic version of the future, a more subversive reading is also available. With such contested, porous categories, there are considerable stakes in the classification, as the advocates of genetically modified foods have discovered. While some defenders of genetic engineering attempt to present it as a seamless continuation of ten thousand years of agricultural progress (the classical vision), its strongest critics seek to relegate it to the scary, ultramodernist realm of Frankenfoods and Brave New Pharm. Meanwhile, its most able advocates have been staking out the more complicated, and perhaps more marketable, recombinant category, framing biotechnology as a truly "green" revolution that will strengthen sustainable agriculture and retain traditional foodways. As of this writing, it is by no means clear which position will prevail in an increasingly contentious and globalized public debate.

But one thing *is* certain. For an informed public discussion, we need to resist using worn clichés that obscure what the struggle over the future is really about: power. And to highlight that fact, we start in chapter 1 with a brief overview of a recurring theme in food futurism—the concern that an overpopulated world might not be able to afford the food most closely associated with male Anglo-American hegemony: meat.

PART I

DEBATING THE FUTURE OF FOOD

The Battle of the Think Tanks

ONE

THE STAKES IN OUR STEAKS

Stories about the future tend toward large abstractions. In part this is simply because the future *is* an abstraction; it has not happened yet. And it is also because futurists like to think about major dynamics and drivers: population growth, demographic variables, renewable resources, carrying capacity, economic development, industrialization, and so on. Similarly, food forecasts involve big generalizations and theoretical concepts: abundance, scarcity, total caloric demand, potential agricultural yields, hydraulic cycles, global warming, hybridization, to name a few. This book delves into many of these big-picture abstractions. But we should not forget that a book about food also deals with meals—intensely localized food events that require personal choices by real people. Everyone eats. Everyone has tastes and distastes. Everyone is picky. When it comes to deciding what to eat, the most abstract theorizers may be as picky as four-year-olds. Indeed, lurking behind their abstractions may be food prejudices and preferences formed when *they* were four years old. Mindful that deep-seated food values can influence how we see the world, I am struck by how much of the Anglo-American discussion of our future prospects has really been about our right and ability to eat meat, especially beef. And yet until the recent boomlet in academic food studies, few scholars dared to put such an explicitly carnivorous spin on their analyses of future demography, environment, and politics.[1]

Long before I became a food historian, I already knew that meat had much to do with politics, ecology, population, and the future. This idea came not from classes but from student life, when I temporarily gave up meat in favor of grains and beans.[2] Like many converts to the counter-cuisine—the natural foods revival of the late 1960s and early 1970s—I started worrying about the future of the food supply when I read Frances Moore Lappé's *Diet for a Small Planet* (1971). For Lappé the meat-centered diet favored by most Americans clearly threatened the ability of future generations to feed themselves. Labeling the typical grain-fed farm animal "a protein factory in reverse," Lappé argued that it took 21.4 pounds of feed-grain protein to produce one pound of beef protein. Other livestock were only marginally better, with feed-to-food conversion ratios of 8:1 for pork, 5.5:1 for poultry, and 4.4:1 for milk. Feed crops occupied one-half of all harvested agricultural land in the United States, which served almost 80 percent of its grains to animals. Tapping countercultural images of addiction, Lappé labeled Americans "protein heads" who hogged the world's protein resources while millions elsewhere starved. Reducing U.S. livestock by half would meet the Third World's "caloric deficit . . . almost *four times over.*"[3] In later editions, Lappé zeroed in on the class aspects of diet: Americans drove Cadillacs while much of the world barely walked. The well-fatted steak took food out of the mouths of others while it clogged our own arteries. It also de-graded our agricultural resources, for the heavily industrialized farming that produced this meat consumed more energy than it yielded, "mined" the topsoil for nutrients, and polluted the water with runoff chemicals and manure. In short, a meat-centered diet was unhealthy, unfair, and unsustainable.[4]

Like many young people just awakening to the world's ecological crises after the first Earth Day (1970), I assumed that Lappé's analysis was radically new. After thirty years of further study, I am still persuaded by her argument,[5] yet I now see that meat has affected population growth, conquest, and resource issues for quite a long time. Over 2,400 years ago, Socrates argued that domesticated meat's lavish land requirements inevitably led to territorial expansion and war with neighbors. In *Guns, Germs, and Steel* (1997), Jared Diamond suggests that Eurasia was the origin of so many expansionist empires precisely because it harbored such an abundance of domesticated mammals. According to medievalist Massimo Montanari, invasion of the declining and still largely vegetarian Roman Empire by northern, meat-eating "barbarians" brought widespread deforestation and consolidated landholding to accommodate larger herds of livestock. And since 1492, European livestock may have done more to destroy Native American ecosystems than all the human invaders combined. In *The Conquest of Paradise: Christopher Columbus and the Columbian Legacy,* Kirkpatrick Sale writes, "Cattle reproduced so successfully on Española [Hispañola] that, it was said, thirty or forty stray animals would multiply to three or four hundred in a couple of years. . . . All these voracious animals naturally dominated and then destroyed native habitats, rapidly and thoroughly, with human help and without." Jeffrey Pilcher observes in his history of Mexican foodways: "The introduction of livestock proved to be the greatest success story in the culinary conquest of America. . . . Herds [of cattle] overran the countryside, driving Indians from their fields."[6]

By the late eighteenth century, calculations of livestock's ecological and political costs had become a staple of British vegetarian literature, as in William Paley's 1785 *Principles of Moral and Political Philosophy:* "A piece of ground capable of supplying animal food sufficient for the subsistence of ten persons would sustain, at least, the double of that number with grain, roots, and milk." In 1811, radical publisher Richard Phillips argued that British farmers could potentially feed forty-seven million vegetarians "in abundance" but "sustain only twelve millions *scantily*" on animal products. Similarly, poet Percy Bysshe Shelley's "Vindication of a Natural Diet" (1813) blasted the meat eater who would "destroy his constitution by devouring an acre at a meal."[7]

Both Phillips and Shelley had supped at the table of the renowned romantic radical William Godwin (Phillips as Godwin's publisher, Shelley as his future son-in-law). While the utopian socialist Godwin would never have dined with the conservative economist Robert Malthus, on one point they did agree: the ecological wastefulness of meat production. Malthus, in his *Essay on the Principle of Population* (1798), cited "an acknowledged truth, that pasture land produces a smaller quantity of human subsistence than corn land of the same fertility. . . . The present [grain-based] system of grazing, undoubtedly tends more than the former system to diminish the quantity of human subsistence in the country." Unchecked population growth, Malthus warned, would necessarily require a reduction of meat—this in fact had already happened as the European population boomed after the seventeenth century.[8] While the rich could always afford meat, the inherent extravagance of livestock production reduced the grain available for direct consumption.

Malthus disagreed loudly with Godwin's circle over what to do about this. Godwin's followers were willing to cut back on or even give up beef in order to feed more people, for a larger population would, as they put it, increase "the aggregate of human happiness."[9] But Malthus was not.

While Malthus did offer an abstract agronomic rationale for raising cattle—that manure made excellent fertilizer—I suspect that taste also guided his reasoning, for his countrymen simply loved beef, especially the "fatted" and ecologically costly grain-fed variety that British herdsmen had just begun to produce in the 1790s.[10] Malthus thus discounted the voluntary asceticism suggested by Godwin's circle. Oh yes, he allowed, a frugal, all-vegetable diet modeled after that of China or India *could* sustain a growing population, but he thought such a drab cuisine would surely chill the utopian's "spirit of benevolence," which, "cherished and invigorated by plenty, is repressed by the chilling breath of want." Why try to stretch the grain supply to accommodate more people when a less crowded planet's diet would be so much tastier? As for the optimum human population, neo-Malthusian ecologist Garrett Hardin suggests: "There should be no more people in a country than could enjoy daily a glass of wine and a piece of beef with their dinner."[11] Such a high standard of living would clearly require fewer forks—a point that neo-Malthusians have made consistently when advocating birth control. Against this restrictionist credo stood the more-the-merrier faith of Godwin's followers. By foregoing livestock production, agriculture could sustain at least four times as many "human beings in life, health, and happiness," American vegetarian crusader William Alcott argued in 1848. Indeed, Alcott suggested—anticipating right-to-life arguments to come, albeit organized around matters of food choice, not reproductive rights—a food production system organized around "flesh-eating" amounted to the murder of future generations, for "we prevent their coming into the possession of a joyous and happy existence, and though we have no name for it, is it not a crime?"[12]

As this book shows, this argument has been going on, more or less steadily, for the past two centuries. But so far, neither the egalitarian/ vegetarian nor the Malthusian view has prevailed. Rather, the dominant position has been that of Malthus's *other* opponent, the Marquis de Condorcet, an Enlightenment philosopher who insisted that we do not have to give up anything—babies *or* steaks. A consummate cornucopian, Condorcet confidently predicted that scientific research could increase agricultural yields indefinitely. With proper encouragement of the agricultural "'arts' . . . a very small amount of ground will be able to produce a great quantity of supplies of greater utility and higher quality." And even if some upper limit were reached in the distant future, there were no theoretical obstacles to "manufacturing animal and vegetable substances artificially." For Condorcet, "the perfectability of man is indefinite"—especially *if* good science was supported by good government. As I argue later, this is a significant "if"—an enormously utopian caveat. Doubting the "if," Malthus urged a more "sober" look at human history that seemed to disprove such "elate and giddy" fancies. Perhaps mindful that Jacobinic excesses had recently killed many French intellectuals, including Condorcet, Malthus questioned the ability of humans to devise the wise political institutions needed to subsidize truly democratic scientific research. Godwin, on the other hand, firmly agreed with Condorcet's humanistic confidence in an infinite creativity capacity— "Man is a godlike being. We launch ourselves in conceit into illimitable space and take up our rest beyond the fixed stars"—but his faith rested less on technological ingenuity than on egalitarian, democratic reform; in other words, the political half of Condorcet's "good science + good government" equation.[13]

With all these appeals to ultimate goals and credos, the stakes in this argument clearly extend far beyond our taste for steaks. As Frances Moore Lappé and almost every debater before and after her has known, the anxieties, hopes, and assumptions expressed about the meaning and future of meat reflect a larger debate about the meaning of progress itself. The rest of this book details some of the more important forecasts, especially the recurrent predictions about animal foods. But before recounting these speculations, it seems reasonable to ask why so much expectation has been embodied, as it were, in such fleshy issues. Why such an extended and weighty discourse about the future of meat eating? To paraphrase Byron, why *does* so much depend on dinner, especially the meat-and-potatoes kind?[14]

The assumption that there is something inherently essential about a carnivorous diet often surfaces when meat eaters are challenged by moralistic vegetarians. For example, I ask each of my food studies students to share the following highly incendiary passage by novelist Isaac Bashevis Singer with five people and to track their reaction:

> I watched someone at the next table working away at his plate of ham with eggs. I had long since come to the conclusion that man's treatment of God's creatures makes mockery of all his ideals and the whole alleged humanism. In order for this overstuffed individual to enjoy his ham, a living creature had to be raised, dragged to its death, tortured, scalded in hot water. The man didn't give a second's thought to the fact that the pig was made of the same stuff as he and that it had to pay with suffering and death so that he could taste its flesh. I've more than once thought that when it comes to animals, every man is a Nazi.[15]

Having taught this course for many years, I have read thousands of responses. It is telling that when confronted so aggressively, many people do not feel satisfied defending their food preferences on the basis of taste, convenience, or even nutrition alone. Rather, they seek the higher ground of a timeless archetype that seems to stand beyond disproof. In Western culture, Biblical references often serve that function, and most of my students' respondents seem confident that if (according to Genesis 1:28) God gave us dominion over animals, sent us into the land of milk and honey (Exodus 3:8), and then told us to sacrifice the fatted calf (Luke 15:23), their cheeseburger stands sanctified by holy writ.

However, think tankers engaged in the food security debate have mostly been secular modernists well aware that our meat-centered diet is a relatively novel luxury. In *Feeding the World*, geographer Vaclav Smil observes that "per capita means of meat consumption remained low during the whole preindustrial era, averaging usually no more than 10 kg/year." Well through the mid-nineteenth century the bottom half of French and British societies consumed less than 20 kilograms of meat a year, and not until after World War II did Europe's richest countries reach the levels of meat consumption that Americans had enjoyed one hundred years earlier. Less affluent countries have lagged far behind. For example, in 1995 the average Filipino ate 20 kilograms of meat a year, compared with 80 kilograms per capita in Western countries. And feeding grain to livestock—Lappé's bugbear—is even *more* modern. According to Smil, only about 10 percent of the world's grain was fed to animals in 1900; by 1950 it was 20 percent, and by 1990, 45 percent. Feedlots accounted for 43 percent of the world's beef in 2003—and for well over half of the world's poultry and pork. The percentages were much higher in the richer countries, of course, and that may be exactly the point: to the extent that meat eating increases with affluence, it has been associated with Progress, a highly contested ideology. If there is a common thread linking the dietary assumptions, hopes, and fears of those who have pondered the future of food, it has to do with the meaning of "growth," "evolution," "improvement," "modernization," "development."[16] And with that come issues of power—the stakes in steaks.

For the nineteenth century's dominant class, Progress meant the expansion of Civilization, which in turn meant the hegemony of carnivorous Europeans. Numerous historians have quoted American neurologist George Beard, an influential Victorian health advisor: "In proportion as man grows sensitive through civilization or through disease, he should diminish the quantity of cereals and fruits, which *are far below him* on the scale of evolution, and increase the quantity of animal food, which is nearly related to him in the scale of evolution, and therefore more easily assimilated." In Beard's evolutionary hierarchy, those closest to apes—"savages"—could more easily follow the apes' vegetarian diet. In other race-based schema, however, "savages" were slurred as cannibals, who, in a sense, ate a *lot* of meat but of the inappropriate variety. Conversely, a grain-based diet was associated with declining regimes whose starved peasantry needed liberation by enlightened Westerners. From Columbus onward, European colonial ventures were often justified as progressive crusades against both primitive cannibalism and feudalistic vegetarianism. Just as Europe's classical heritage valued moderation, the Spanish steak and Anglo-American roast seemingly occupied a robust middle ground between the extremes of wildly uncivilized cannibals and decadently *over*civilized, rice-eating Orientals. And few imperialists doubted that red meat would trump white rice and all starch-based societies. "The rice-eating Hindoo and Chinese, and the potato-eating Irish are kept in subjection by the well-fed English," Beard observed.[17]

The association of beef with colonial subordination goes back to the seventeenth century, as when Rhode Island founder Roger Williams urged natives to keep cattle as a sign of their move "from Barbarism to Civilite"; it was fitting that Native Americans who refused to be so "civilized" fought back by attacking the settlers' cows. But the steak-eating "races" did ultimately triumph, as a 1909 medical text trumpeted: "White bread, red meat, and blue blood make the tricolor flag of conquest." Such overtly racist sentiments were heard well through mid-century, as in a 1939 text sponsored by a meat company: "We know meat-eating races have been and are leaders in the progress made by mankind in its upward struggle through the ages." Eating grain-centered "natural foods," a chemist warned in 1957, would mean a reversion to "cave man days." These attitudes were effectively reinforced by immigration to the Americas, where a meat-based diet was taken as a sign of having arrived in a truly better future of market-based "freedom of choice." In a 1906 essay, "Why There Is No Socialism in the United States," German sociologist Werner Sombart concluded that to the extent that immigrants ate more meat, especially beef, they became more American—and less likely to become subversive radicals: "All socialist utopias come to nothing on roast beef and apple pie." On the other hand, those who persisted in their grain-based Old Worldish ways were somewhat suspect for their resistance to a classic cornucopian perquisite—the expansion of appetites and waistlines.[18]

Vegetarians also accepted the savage-to-civilized spectrum, albeit in reverse. Some, like George Bernard Shaw, simply inverted the evolutionary ladder and put vegetarians on top in terms of "cultivation," or refinement. "A hundred years hence a cultivated man will no more dream of eating flesh or smoking than he now does of living, as Pepys' contemporaries did, in a house with a cesspool under it." Implicitly likening genteel beef-eaters to primitive man-eaters, Shaw quipped that meat eating was "cannibalism with its heroic dish omitted." Feminist temperance leader Frances Willard agreed that the advance of civilization would preclude eating meat: "The enlightened mortals of the 20th century surely will be vegetarians."[19]

Others allowed that meat might very well be part of Civilization, but like Huck Finn fleeing his genteel Aunt Sally, they would just as soon light out for what they argued were more robust territories. Historian James Whorton writes: "One of the pillars of the [nineteenth-century] physiological argument against meat eating was the contrast between the vigorous vegetarian races of the world and the puny flesh eaters. Time and again, the [carnivorous] Eskimo and Laplander were humiliated by being lined up against the [vegetarian] natives of the South Seas and of central Africa, the peasantry of Ireland, Spain, and Russia, even the slaves of the American South, whose 'bodily powers are well-known.'" "The brave and vigorous Spartans never ate meat," domestic reformer Catharine Beecher argued. "Most of the hardiest soldiers in Northern Europe seldom taste of meat. . . . Except in America, it is rare that the strongest laborers eat any meat."[20]

Others allowed that carnivores had powers, too, but of the wrong kind. Sylvester Graham warned that meat eating unleashed "despotic, vehement, and impatient" forces. While Western culture commonly attributed such characteristics to older, more primitive societies, for Graham such carnal appetites and excesses belonged to modern urban life. This countercultural critique, rooted in the romantic vegetarianism of the early nineteenth century, blamed mankind's fall from innocence on Prometheus, who, by stealing fire from the gods, enabled men to roast meat. With the taste for flesh came modern greed, lust, and ambition. Godwin's son-in-law Shelley doubted "that had Buonaparte descended from a race of vegetable feeders, that he could have had, either the inclination or the power to ascend to the throne of the Bourbons." Similarly, in *Frankenstein* Mary Shelley's misbegotten Creature adopted a vegetarian diet in his search for an existence more peaceful and virtuous than that led by his unscrupulously ambitious human creator.[21] Accepting this basic belief that vegetarians were more tranquil, many utopian novelists envisioned future societies that conspicuously eliminated—or greatly reduced—the role of animal foods. In all, these romantics revalued the dominant evolutionary scheme. Most agreed that most "primitive" peoples ate less meat (especially beef) than more "advanced" ones; the difference was over whether one *liked* the results of such "progress."

At the end of the nineteenth century, these ethnocentric theories of progress became mixed with somewhat more scientific-sounding appeals to efficiency. Adopting the time-management calculations of what historian Harvey Levenstein calls the New Nutrition (1890–1930), many experts endorsed animal products as the most efficient way to ingest nutrients, particularly calories and protein. For these Progressive-Era theorists, nutrient-dense animal foods had the key quality of all-in-one "smartness" that would characterize many futuristic products of the twentieth century, such as vitamin pills, diet shakes, power bars, nutraceuticals, and other "functional foods." Understandably, such notions were especially appealing to the livestock industry, which heavily subsidized and publicized much nutritional science research.[22] During the Second World War, American scientific consensus recommended unprecedented proportions of red meat as "a fighting food." "It's an important part of a military man's diet," one Office of Price Administration pamphlet proclaimed, "giving him the energy to outfight the enemy." It was assumed that American troops "could not do their job on a diet of beans," nuts, figs, and berries.[23] While Americans on the home front cut back temporarily for the sake of the fighting men, they assumed that victory would mean more meat in their diet than ever. Modern economic historians reinforced meat's evolutionary/progressive gloss by noting that humans usually eat more animal foods as they prosper. This observation was not new, as one of the few points of agreement between Malthus and Marx was that workers would immediately spend pay raises on more meat. Elaborating on this tidbit of economic history in 1941, M. K. Bennett propounded what came to be called Bennett's Law: with more industrialization people inevitably eat more meat, dairy, alcoholic beverages, and processed foods, and fewer "starchy staples"—a rather dreary, ideologically loaded term for what vegetarians considered a rich array of grains and legumes. The axiom that economic development—the modernist equivalent of the Victorians' Higher Civilization—would automatically move people "up the food chain" was repeated through all the food security debates of the late twentieth century.[24]

In a 1990s version of this "nutrition transition," Adam Drewnowski has proclaimed as "inevitable" and "irreversible" the developing world's adoption of Western dietary patterns, saturated fats and all. Dismissing as "naive" the Lappé-style hope that "the affluent will ever voluntarily adopt a diet of poverty"—in other words, a "Chinese-style" diet based in carbohydrates, with meat as a spare condiment—Drewnowski seemed to accept what neo-Malthusian Lester Brown, in *Who Will Feed China?* (1995), deplored: the wealthier Chinese are now consuming more meat, fat, and sweets. While Brown worried that China might drain world grain supplies to support its expanding appetite for animal foods, Drewnowski did not say how the world would sustain this "nutrition transition."[25] In 1998, Monsanto president Robert Shapiro offered biotechnology as the solution. Since people will automatically *"move up the protein ladder"* as they prosper, Shapiro reasoned, genetically engineered corn and soy offer a "sustainable" and "equitable" alternative to conventional, chemical-dependent feed grain production, which may have fed 1 billion people well, but with "colossal wastefulness."[26] Shapiro's rhetoric shows how the more savvy marketers might attempt to straddle agendas of all three contenders: Malthus (sustainability), Godwin (equity), and Condorcet (greater yields).

Whether posed in racial, economic, or nutritional terms, these evolutionary tales usually locate utopia in the meat-eating West and dystopia in the grain-based East. While some romantics have valued peasant cuisine for its healthy vitality and ecological sustainability, in most forecasts Asia has stood for a despotic, hungry past and also for an undesirably overcrowded future. Both Condorcet and Godwin worried that the spread of Oriental despotism to the West might hinder the scientific innovation and political reform needed to combat hunger. For Malthusians, Asia has been an object lesson in how population could outpace food production. In 1924 plant scientist Edward M. East predicted: "The China and India of today will be the world of tomorrow when the world as a whole reaches the same population status." In this Asiatic world, "food is scarce. Man works from sun to sun. When crops are good there is unrest but no rest, there is privation and hardship; when crops are bad there is mass starvation." Similarly, a 1951 *Atlantic Monthly* article recommended studying famine-plagued India "as a corrective to complacency," for, with the population increasing faster than the food supply, "the world is moving toward the condition that India has already reached." And forty years later, David and Marcia Pimentel warned that "as our population escalates, our resources inevitably will experience pressures similar to those now experienced by China," including a largely vegetarian diet imposed by a shortage of land, water, and energy.[27]

A professor at the East India Company's training school for colonial bureaucrats, Malthus established the theme of Asia as harbinger of the future early on with references to China and India as worst-case scenarios of unchecked growth: China represented overpopulated places "where people are habituated to live almost upon the smallest possible quantity of food," mainly rice and "putrid offals" (the last an image likely to create far more repugnance among British readers, Stephen Mennell suggests, than among French cooks, who might actually savor such entrails). And the "famines of Indostan," Malthus continued, offered a tragic example of nature's "checks" in action; in short, a total breakdown of a food production system that, at best, provided bare-bones subsistence.[28] To simplify the axiom: China = little food, India = no food. Only a few radicals noted that European intervention and corrupt government had much to do with modern food system failures in both countries (or that the same politics had produced numerous famines in the West as well). In most Malthusian discourse, India and China's ills were the unfortunate result of an inherent propensity to multiply. Ever the materialist, Malthus blamed rice agriculture for Asia's overpopulation precisely because it was so much more productive than meat or wheat: "Corn [British for 'wheat'] countries are more populous than pasture countries, and rice countries are more populous than corn countries." With more food, the Malthusian law went, came more babies—until the next famine restored a temporary balance.[29]

According to one 1928 iteration, because Asians were stuck in this overpopulation-famine trap, the vegetarian nations of the Orient were more fatalistic. Warning in 1955 of a population crisis wrought by the birth of "80,000 Hungry Mouths a Day," biologist Paul Henshaw detected an Oriental "self-abnegation—a suppression of the ego-centered desires [such as a taste for meat?]." Then there were frequent commentaries on India's perplexing refusal to eat its abundant if somewhat scrawny cattle. What else but self-abnegating fatalism could explain this inability to exploit such a ready source of protein? Reflecting Western blindness to vegetarianism—and to the important ecological functions performed by India's cows—the pseudoanthropological phrase "sacred cow" came to stand for a misplaced, self-defeating superstition, or, as Merriam-Webster puts it, a belief "that is unreasonably immune from criticism or opposition."[30]

Malthus also argued that one check on population growth was emigration out of the crowded country—a frightening prospect for those whose countries would be "invaded" by these environmental refugees.

As long as Europeans could flee overpopulated homelands to their colonies, few whites complained, but when the flow went the other way, nativist sentiments multiplied. When East Asian immigration to the United States increased in the late nineteenth century, the "Yellow Peril" took visceral, culinary forms. Although many Asian immigrants worked in agriculture—and indeed helped to supply America's cheap and abundant produce and meat—their own cuisine was caricatured vividly and often viciously. People joked that Chinese food was just "cooked grass and noodles" and that it was so insubstantial that you always felt hungry an hour later. Worse, rumors circulated that the residents of congested Chinatown (a Malthusian microcosm) routinely consumed rats, dogs, and other "offal." Westerners also found significance in what Asians did *not* eat. Thus in 1953 a professor of medical geography could cite the "Chinese contempt for milk"—as well as the Indians' refusal to kill their allegedly nonproductive sacred cows—as evidence of a lower standard of living. Only in the late twentieth century, with growing interest in multicultural foodways, could a Chinese-American literature professor take pride in "how poor the masses of ordinary Chinese have been for millennia and how inventive hunger has made them. How from the scraps, offal, detritus, and leftovers saved from the imperial maw peasant Chinese have created a fragrant and mouth-watering survival."[31]

For much of the twentieth century, the preferred epithet for Chinese food was "coolie rations," which reflected the charge by white labor unions that competing Chinese workers were enslaved, subhuman "coolies"—even though most immigrants to the United States came freely and unencumbered. Given such sentiments, one wonders how receptive most Americans were to Pearl Buck's 1945 praise for the Chinese way of treating meat as a condiment rather than as the main dish: "We have known, abstractly, that the Chinese people is one of the oldest and most civilized on earth. But this [Chinese cook]book proves it. Only the profoundly civilized can feed upon such food." Although such a dietary shift would have conformed with official advice to conserve meat, it is telling that the U.S. government classified production of the tepidly Americanized Chinese food by La Choy as "nonessential" to the war effort, and the company was induced to sell out to budding food conglomerate Beatrice Foods in 1943. If the food of our Chinese allies was treated so indifferently, Japanese fare was considered repulsive refuse. According to a 1945 cookbook, "Every Jap[anese soldier] is outfitted with a tiny portable stove and a can of Nipponese 'Sterno.' In a small pouch he carries raw rice. He makes a stew of the dirty kernels and if he's lucky, embellishes it with fish heads and tails. These are canned or salted down and, according to GIs, taste like preserved garbage."[32]

Academics engaged in the food-population debate often reinforced such stereotypes. In *Must We Fight Japan?* (1921), Columbia professor Walter Pitkin attacked those who would accept an "Asiatic standard of living" for the sake of a larger population. Noting that few Americans had cut back on meat (or wheat) during the recent war, Pitkin doubted the appeal of "universal vegetarianism, such as we now see all over Asia." Nor would "the white man" accept the way densely populated Asians often worked their tiny farms without animals. "Any white man who has observed the day's work of an Oriental who farms with few or none of the beasts of burden cannot honestly say that the Oriental is civilized. He has dispensed with the beasts only by making himself, his wife, and his children beasts." Pitkin's bestial analogy echoed popular Yellow Peril novels, which, Mike Davis shows, likened the Asian "invaders" to "swarming," grain-devouring locusts. Such Malthusian images of Asia endured in late-twentieth-century dystopian fiction, which frequently associated a Malthusian future with "fishy" synthetics, grilled "offal," and grainy gruels. For example, in the 1982 film *Blade Runner,* the Los Angeles of 2019 resembles a nightmarish Tokyo—Davis calls it "mongrel masses on the teeming ginza"—where ordinary people subsist on artificial sushi and cheap noodles.[33]

Since, until fairly recently, more South Asians migrated to British lands than to the United States, India has remained a sad but less threatening abstraction for most Americans, except perhaps as a dinnertime goad to "clean your plate" for the sake of the "starving Indians," whose pictures frequently found their way into travelogues, news reports, documentaries, and popular books on hunger and population issues. In addition to encouraging the expansion of American waistlines, such images served all three debating positions. Altruistic descendants of Godwin exploited guilt-inducing famine photos to gin up support for everything from charity to revolution. (Thus the first line of Lappé's *Diet for a Small Planet* invokes the clean-your-plate-for-India cliché.) Malthusians used descriptions of an Indian famine, often conflated with other images of "swarming" Calcutta, to dramatize warnings about population saturation. Cornucopians, too, employed visions of the nightmare Asian alternative in their appeals for more agricultural research funding. Noting in 1913 that "economists prophesy a deficiency in the world's food supply," the president of the Society for Horticultural Science urged stepped-up efforts to discover new food plants as a way to forestall "the problems that will

confront us when people swarm on the land, as now in India or China."
A 1928 editorial in *World's Work* hoped that research on higher food
yields would head off the "menace" of an Oriental, vegetarian future.
Working that same row twenty-five years later, *Farm Quarterly*'s editor
urged more fertilizer research "if we want to continue eating our high-
protein meat diet and not slip to the cereal diet of the Orient."[34]

Self-interest also guided the Cold War's Green Revolution: improving
the supposedly abject Asian diet through the use of better seeds and chemicals would keep Asians from migrating here or, worse, going Communist. Inevitably, stories about the Asian economic "miracle" of the 1980s
and early 1990s were accompanied by images of McDonald's restaurants
in Beijing. After almost two hundred years of unrelenting contempt for
"coolie rations," the thought of people lining up for Big Macs in Tianan-
men Square was a miracle indeed! But quasi-Malthusian environmentalists like Lester Brown of the Worldwatch Institute were more worried
than enchanted by the prospect of Asia's growing demand for animal
protein. And a more nuanced, anthropological view might reveal that in
much of the region a McDonald's meal was viewed as only a snack because it lacked rice and had *too much* bread and meat—the twin cornucopian staples of the Anglo-American diet.[35] Still, there was no doubt
that Asian prosperity meant more meat consumption than before, and with
that shift came the maladies of affluence, especially obesity, diabetes, cancer, and heart disease. Reporters seeking famine-stricken "basket-case"
stories now headed away from Asia and toward sub-Saharan Africa.[36]

The need to have a dysfunctional Other against which people can
measure their vitality suggests that something more than race or geography has been involved in the perennial contrasts between meat eaters
and vegetarians: gender matters, too. In *Meat: A Natural Symbol*, Nick
Fiddes links the prestige of meat, which has been growing since the seventeenth century, to the theme of *domination*—domination over nature,
over animals, over resources, over other people. "Meat has long stood
for Man's proverbial 'muscle' over the natural world." For Fiddes, that
domination has included the patriarchal control of women, who have
often been treated *as* meat and who historically tend to eat a lot less meat
than men do.[37]

The gendered nature of meat production and consumption has deep
roots—ranging from the sexual division of labor between male hunters
of meat and female gatherers of everything else to the persistent distinction between male-associated red meat and female-associated salads. Such
differences became institutionalized during the nineteenth century—the

same period when so many of our futurist themes were established. For upper-class Anglo-American women of the Victorian era, Joan Jacobs Brumberg has shown, the estrangement from meat became quite extreme: "No food (other than alcohol) caused Victorian women and girls greater moral anxiety than meat." For these women at least, Civilization meant less red meat, not more: "Meat eating in excess was linked to adolescent insanity and nymphomania." Similarly, Laura Shapiro attributes the genteel fetish of the decorative salad to "the assumption that women were averse to red meat." In the most popular late Victorian cookbooks, meat was to be disguised, and even frankfurters were to be blanketed in a "purifying" (and feminizing) white sauce. Meanwhile, back in the British metropole, Sidney Mintz observes, nineteenth-century working-class women were getting by on cheap calories from bread, jam, and sugar while their men demanded their daily meat ration. Reflecting the same dichotomy, American food policy during the Second World War assumed that fighting men deserved red meat, while women could make do with protein substitutes. After the war, Amy Bentley suggests, American women were more favorable to the continuation of meat and flour rationing if it helped to alleviate hunger elsewhere. The postwar boom also gave birth to the fast food industry, which entangled women as low-paid workers serving beef to a predominantly male clientele, while female customers favored salads, chicken, and other "lighter" fare.[38] Clearly, for much of history men have had a greater stake in steaks. Also, most futurists were (and still are) men. Putting these two factors together—the male slant in meat-eating and futurism—I wonder if it is their gender that has made male futurists more prone to worry about a meatless future, while female futurists may have been somewhat less fazed by the prospect of a "peasant" diet. It does not seem coincidental that, from Mary Shelley and Charlotte Perkins Gilman to Frances Moore Lappé and Marge Piercy, those utopians most comfortable with a more vegetarian future have usually been feminists too.

Though hard to prove—and by no means universal—the gender variable is worth remembering when assessing the direst forecasts discussed here. In addition to being more committed to meat, men have traditionally been less involved in cooking. Conversely, as improvisers, scroungers, and self-sacrificers, women have been managing scarcity for a very long time. Hunger expert Ellen Messer writes that women act as the "'shock absorbers' of the household, who absorb shortfalls in income or consumption, often at some nutritional cost to themselves." Along the same lines, geographers Peter Atkins and Ian Bowler report that Brazilian women are "far better geared up [than men] for a household food emergency because of their closer involvement with day-to-day coping strategies."[39]

Perhaps men's remove from daily food preparation has made them somewhat more alarmist as they contemplate scarcity and famine. Anthropologist Carole Counihan suggests that in cultures where food is scarce, boys tend to suffer from greater "hunger anxiety" than housebound girls, who because they are held closer to their mothers' cooperative networks are better situated to find and prepare food. This shows up particularly in children's stories about hunger. "Girls seem more successful in their stories at resolving neediness," Counihan observes, "and are perhaps less threatened by it than boys." While girl writers devise practical ways to satisfy hunger, boys' stories end more violently, with a tendency toward moral abstraction. Could the same be said for some of the adult tales recounted here? In "Hedge Nutrition, Hunger and Irish Identity," Marie Smyth writes that for British Malthusian politicians the Irish famine was a highly theoretical exercise in overpopulation, but for Smyth's matriarchal ancestors it was an identity-shaping opportunity to learn how to scramble for berries, bake rough corn bread over peat fires, and feed a family. When Smyth's mother taught her to scrounge free food in hedges, "we were learning that a woman's work is to feed others, whether they are hungry or not." All over the world and throughout time, women have struggled and sacrificed to feed others, while men philosophize—and also eat better than women. Ironically, a nutritional case can be made that women should eat more meat (especially for iron), while men, who suffer more from heart disease, should eat a lot less.[40]

Although the Malthusians have sounded the loudest alarm about a meatless future, the cornucopians have not been silent either. At the risk of overdoing the point about gender, I would suggest that those cornucopians pushing high-tech "smart farming" tools and methods to produce more meat (again, for the sake of Progress) have been reenacting one of the earliest gender coups in history—the shift from a sustainable subsistence horticulture controlled or at least shared by women to a livestock-dependent, market-oriented monoculture controlled by men (i.e., husbandry). Carolyn Merchant estimates that female gathering, horticulture, and fishing produced 85 percent of the calories consumed by precolonial New England Indians, but this agricultural system, dominated by "corn mothers," soon gave way to the export-oriented, feed-grain-and-livestock economy of the "Puritan fathers." In Mexico, too, a corn-bean-squash system managed by women was violently suppressed by Spanish settlers anxious to cash in on the European hunger for meat and wheat. Inevitably, in the mythologizing of Spanish cowboy culture in twentieth-century Anglo-American westerns, women had virtually no role at all—except perhaps as prudish schoolteachers hindering men from their blood-letting. If the main reason to Go West was to produce "good beef for hungry people," as the cattle-driving bachelor-hero of Howard Hawkes's *Red River* (1948) puts it, no wonder women were irrelevant. Similar gender transformations have occurred worldwide and have been viewed as essential to modern industrial "development." But not everyone has benefited equally from such "progress," which Indian eco-activist Vandana Shiva calls "maldevelopment." While industrial agriculture has boosted overall yields, it has often displaced women into subordinate service jobs and tasks. Similarly, on the domestic front, when modern husbandry, refrigeration, and, marketing greatly increased the meat supply in the late nineteenth century, the result may have been more roast beef for Father but "more work for Mother," who was now expected to prepare much more elaborate meals that she herself might not even share.[41] And when nutritional science put a higher value on protein derived from animals than from vegetables, or prized beef over poultry, or wheat over corn, it also reinforced that gendered realignment of status and power.

These, then, have been the many stakes in steaks: race, gender, health, purpose, progress, profit, power. This struggle for control of the food supply is an old tale, to be sure—as are so many of the stories we tell about the future.

TWO

THE DEBATE

Will the World Run Out of Food?

The Anglo-American debate about future food supplies has gone through several spikes or cycles, becoming more pressing at particular periods—for example, the 1790s, 1890s, 1920s, late 1940s, 1960s and 1970s, and 1990s. Why has anxiety about food running out been higher in certain periods? What events and crises have aroused such worries? How has the debate changed over the years? And how has it stayed the same?

This chapter outlines the evolution and context of the debate—the way each period's social, cultural, political, and ecological concerns have sparked worries about the future of food. The next chapter analyzes ongoing continuities, patterns, themes, and fallacies—the deep structure of the debate. Examining these changes and continuities in the discourse on food futurism helps us understand the futuristic controversies of the early twenty-first century, notably, the prospects of genetic engineering, functional foods, and other "smart" technologies.

As for the answers to the big question itself—will there be enough food?—Malthusians say no. Since population growth will eventually outrun food production, a balance can be achieved only through either the preventive, discretionary "checks" of birth control and voluntary conservation or nature's more onerous checks, primarily hunger, famine, and resource wars. Meanwhile, in the more immediate future, while these forces come into play, we may be dining on less meat (which is resource-intensive) and more grain. Voicing techno-optimism, cornucopians believe we can have our babies and our steaks, too. Following Condorcet, they believe scientific and technological ingenuity can feed many more people. For the past two hundred years the futurists of these two schools have been mainly white, upper-middle-class British and Euro-American men working at top universities, corporations, foundations, and government agencies—the collective think tanks housing those closest to the food policy establishment. Meanwhile, the egalitarians, relegated to the policy-making sidelines, have struggled to be heard. In part II, we will look at a highly provocative but less established forum, speculative fiction, which has often voiced their dissident perspectives.

THE FIRST CENTURY

Among historians it is almost axiomatic that predictions of the future reflect contemporary problems.[1] And predictions about future food supplies seem to be prompted by any of the following conditions: (1) *sudden inflation* in food prices; (2) *environmental stresses,* such as urban congestion, bad weather, bad harvests, or a degradation of agricultural resources; (3) *scary demographics,* such as an unexpectedly high spike in population growth; and (4) *cultural anxieties* about sexuality, working-class unrest, unruly immigrants, or the ominous Other.

Many of these systemic common denominators came into play in the revolutionary 1790s, the decade of the Malthus-Condorcet-Godwin debate. Personal factors also played a role. Studies of these famous futurists suggest that, for Condorcet and Godwin at least, their optimistic projections compensated for their private travails. Writing his famous *Esquisse (Historical Table of the Progress of the Human Spirit)* while hiding from Jacobin zealots in 1793–94, Condorcet trumpeted the Enlightenment's extraordinary pride in rational discourse, industrial capacity, and democratic consciousness even as the Terror threatened the whole rationalist/utopian project—and his own life. Even before the French Revolution, this "philosophical historian of human progress," Frank Manuel writes, "was an anxious man, always expecting catastrophe." In *The Prophets of Paris,* Manuel observes: "Condorcet leads one to reflect on the strange paradox of a modern man whose inner emotional anguish [thanks, largely, to a tempestuous romantic life] is accompanied by a compensatory historical optimism which knows no limits." Despite his personal woes, Condorcet ardently believed that, in the light of long-run scientific progress, "nature has set no limit to the realization of our hopes."[2] Similarly, William Godwin's faith in the possibility of building a rational, democratic community helped him withstand his own difficulties, which included the early death of his partner, Mary Wollstonecraft; parenting a rebellious child; social notoriety; and mounting debt. Even near the end of his life, with his life in shambles and his idealism soundly attacked by Malthus and Co., Godwin could still assert: "Man is a godlike being. We launch ourselves in conceit into illimitable space, and take up our rest beyond the fixed stars." Godwin's faith in human perfectability extended to the most material needs. Although he sometimes went hungry and borrowed heavily from friends, this "prince of spongers" seemed confident that a progressively managed modern agriculture could provide everyone an adequate (if largely vegetarian) diet for many centuries to come.[3]

Malthus's upbringing and family context were far more tranquil than that of Condorcet or Godwin, yet his "serene and happy life" did not deter his gloomy predictions about the human prospect. Robert Heilbroner suggests that the young Malthus's famous *Essay on Population* originated as a friendly but serious private refutation of his father's utopian tendencies. While the avuncular and optimistic Daniel Malthus admired both Rousseau and Godwin, his son took a decidedly negative view of turn-of-the-century economic, demographic, and social trends. Like Benjamin Franklin and John Adams, Malthus was struck by the recent doubling of the North American population in twenty-five years (and every fifteen years in backwoods areas)—a warning of what could happen, he argued, when food was bountiful and general conditions "wholesome" *(scary demographics)*. That the English population had also doubled during his youth did not surprise Malthus, for "England is certainly a more healthy country than the back settlements of America." Given previous famine cycles—Fernand Braudel's "biological *ancien regime*"— Malthus could feel reasonably confident that such population surges would inevitably be followed by food shortages. In fact, as British food prices soared at the end of the century, Britain was forced to import grain for the first time, and meat was even more scarce, especially for the very poor—a reiteration of what Braudel calls the "vegetable supremacy" of overpopulated places.[4]

Doubting that modern agricultural science could overcome the "constancy of the laws of nature," Malthus warned against "giddy" cornucopian extrapolations of recent scientific advances. "The present rage for wide and unrestrained speculation seems to be a kind of mental intoxication, arising, perhaps from the great and unexpected discoveries which have been made of late years, in various branches of science." Especially in light of the revolutionary excesses of the time—which eventually claimed Condorcet's life *(cultural anxieties)*—Malthus expressed considerable doubts about human "perfectability." The ongoing Napoleonic wars, combined with bad domestic harvests, escalated grain prices to "famine prices," according to Heilbroner *(dramatic inflation)*. Given the deteriorating conditions throughout Europe in the late 1790s, Malthus hoped that the optimists could "be persuaded to sober themselves with a little severe and chastised thinking." While Malthus's skepticism certainly suited the counterrevolutionary agenda of the British ruling class, the *Essay*'s final paragraph nevertheless held out hope for the human ability to overcome adversity, even the weight of numbers: "Evil exists in the world not to create despair but activity. We are not patiently to submit to it, but to exert ourselves to avoid it."[5] This sober but essentially positive conclusion was often overlooked by his followers. Similarly, Malthus himself was unfairly attacked as a sexual prude and heartless misanthrope.

A crude version of Malthusianism guided British social policy for much of the ensuing century—with horrific consequences for Ireland, India, and the poor at home, who were denied food relief lest they be "encouraged" to reproduce.[6] But for the most part the nineteenth century was firmly cornucopian, at least for Western empires who pursued a cheap food policy by seizing distant lands, importing foods, and modernizing food production and distribution. Such expansion was partly motivated by the Malthusian specter, as fear of what James Madison and Thomas Jefferson called demographic "concentration" and "condensation" drove public investment in overseas and frontier settlements, agricultural research, and an elaborate transportation infrastructure to allow the easy flow of people and food. In North America, where abundance was considered an entitlement, the reigning ethic of providentialism rationalized the appropriation of Native American lands as God's will. Reversing the founding fathers' worries about overpopulation, American boosters during the mid-nineteenth century welcomed the population boom as a spur to further invention, conquest, and economic growth.[7]

The cornucopian ethos infused popular culture in myriad shapes, arenas, and texts. For example, Jean Anthelme Brillat-Savarin's world-spanning gastronomic exuberance was formalized in French restaurant menus that, according to Rebecca Spang, "promised the universe on a platter." (In tacit confirmation of the Malthusian axiom that abundant food encouraged sexual reproduction, early nineteenth-century French restaurants also offered private cabinets for illicit rendezvous.) In line with the gendered dynamics of the Anglo-American meat religion, Victorian material culture trumpeted a carnivorous patriarchy. In *Death in the Dining Room,* Kenneth Ames argues that upper-middle-class Victorian dining room sideboards—ornamented with slaughtered game—celebrated Western man's Darwinian control over nature. Sculpted cornucopias overflowing with imported tropical produce reinforced the sense that abundance came through "alimentary imperialism." Similarly, in *Advertising Progress: American Business and the Rise of Consumer Marketing,* Pamela Walker Laird describes Victorian food ads full of plump, overfed babies; harvest goddesses holding cornucopias; and bountiful breads, corncobs, and cakes—often proudly backed by impressively large factories, complete with smoke, which was glorified as an emblem of technological progress. Lavish industrial expositions and world's fairs linked industrial food production with liberated consumption by juxtaposing the latest agricultural and processing machinery with mountainous displays of corn, butter, chocolate, coffee, and exotic fruits.[8]

While they expressed doubt that a capitalist market could distribute the benefits of mass production equitably, radical egalitarians sounded much like Condorcet in extolling the potential of industry, combined with the expansion of agricultural lands, to meet future food needs. In a late treatise, Godwin noted that mankind had only just begun to cultivate "the four quarters of the world." Praising "the monuments of human industry," Godwin had little doubt about the outcome of any contest between "the face of the earth and the ingenuity of man." "If art and the invention of the human mind are exhaustless," he exulted, "science is even more notoriously so." "Science increases at least as fast as population," Friedrich Engels agreed in 1844, and, in a clear swipe at Malthus, he asserted that scientific knowledge could grow "in geometrical proportion" to the birth rate. Along the same lines, Karl Marx seconded Justus Von Liebig's belief that scientists could overcome soil depletion—a mounting anxiety in the nineteenth century—through the invention of artificial fertilizers, although he also argued that communal farms would treat soil more responsibly than capitalist operators. The belief that industrial means could be organized for socialistic ends was a central tenet of nineteenth-century utopian thought.[9]

Despite the general hopefulness of mid-Victorian-era culture, however, the Malthusian dread that too much food and sex would be mankind's eventual undoing persisted. In particular, Malthusian doctrine hindered efforts to help the poor and primed worriers to view even the slightest increases in food prices as harbingers of Malthus's impending "checks" on overpopulation. In *The Ecology of Fear,* a history of apocalyptic thought, Mike Davis suggests that the mid-nineteenth century was the "sunny afternoon of bourgeois optimism" in Europe and America, but the spell was broken after 1870 by a rash of economic depressions, environmental disasters, cultural clashes, and political violence. American anxieties about crowding and decay were aggravated by the growth of filthy industrial cities inhabited by non-Protestant immigrants who were routinely portrayed, according to Mary Ryan, as "vast hordes," the "human tide," and the "huge conglomerate mass" *(scary demographics).*[10] Worse, these new arrivals seemed to be out-reproducing native-born "Anglo-Saxons." Alarm about "race suicide"—or what demographers dubbed the "differential fertility rate"—underlay the Victorian anxiety about health and diet, including whether eating more (or less) meat affected sexual vitality and reproductive viability. It also prompted a "strenuous life" movement with consequences ranging from a health food revival to a more "muscular" American foreign policy that seized Cuba, Panama, the Philippines, and other places on the globe to establish calorie- and meat-exporting colonies. Mounting conservationist recognition that Americans were using up resources too fast furthered the sense that the late-nineteenth-century Gilded Age might be testing the continent's natural limits.[11]

The global picture worsened such fears. In the 1870s, widely reported Indian and Chinese famines killed over 25 million people and stimulated speculation about similar disasters in the West. Prominent Darwinist William Graham Sumner worried that "earth hunger" resulting from overpopulation might spark more war, famine, tyranny, and other Malthusian checks. Francis Walker, director of the 1870 U.S. census, ridiculed optimistic estimates of 350 million Americans by 1950, as he doubted, in an Orientalist allusion, that Americans would ever adapt to "the use of dogs, cats, and mice as food, upon such short notice."[12]

Fears of shortage stimulated agricultural expansion, which in turn led to inevitable gluts and cornucopian I-told-you-so boasts, such as the one voiced by economist Simon Patten in 1885: "There never was a time in the world's history when the population was as well supplied with food and with so little outlay of labor as at the present time." In what has been the great paradox of modern industrial agriculture, gluts led to still more surpluses as farmers sought to maintain income amid falling prices by modernizing and expanding production. And on the related labor treadmill, expanding agricultural production, especially in the American West, stimulated demand for migrant farm workers, particularly from Asia, and this in turn provoked more nativist agitation for legislation to reduce "coolie" competition. The consolidation of farms also meant fewer farmers, which heightened concerns about an agricultural decline. Without farmers, asked turn-of-the-century populists, agrarians, and country-lifers, who would grow our children's food? Even more serious, what would happen when there were no new lands to farm? Frederick Jackson Turner's widely shared 1893 lament for the "official" closing of the American frontier reflected the general fin de siècle dread of losing a primary safety valve for population pressures.[13]

THE 1890s

As if to prove the vulnerability of a globalized, consolidated food system, wheat crops failed worldwide in the 1890s—perhaps due to the El Niño weather pattern, Mike Davis suggests—and rising grain prices sparked a new round of Malthusian warnings and cornucopian reassurances.[14] Future Americans would face considerable stress, according to mathematician H. S. Pritchett, who extrapolated that the U.S. population would surge from 63 million in 1890 to 1.1 billion by 2100. Popular naturalist Felix Oswald doubted that the United States would house more than 300 million people in 2000, but even that lower (and in fact accurate) figure would necessitate an agricultural transition to perennial crops, such as "breadstuffs" derived from tree fruits. Growing competition for land would also bring conflicts between northern "Caucasian races" and southern "aborigines and Ethiopians." Voicing similar fears, former British official Charles Pearson foresaw a losing battle with the more vigorously reproductive races of the East and South. American historian Henry Adams agreed "that the dark races are gaining on us. . . . In another fifty years, at the same rate of movement, the white races will have to reconquer the tropics by war and nomadic invasion, or be shut up, north of the fortieth parallel." But Pearson doubted that the "higher races" could even survive in the tropics—long considered a food reserve for overpopulated Europe. Agreeing with Pearson, British geographer E. G. Ravenstein, in his much-cited 1891 paper, "Lands of the Globe Still Available for European Settlement," estimated that the world would reach its ultimate carrying capacity of just under 6 billion people by 2072. But, with world population at only 1.5 billion in 1890, Ravenstein still saw room for further agricultural intensification in the so-called temperate zones, and he dismissed widespread Anglo-American worries that a more crowded future would be mostly vegetarian. The famous economist Alfred Marshall praised Ravenstein's paper but fretted that even if the world could accommodate four times as many, it might soon "be over-populated by people who were less careful, and whom, for that very reason, perhaps, the world would less care to have."[15] According to this common variation on a Malthusian theme, the *quality* of future populations mattered more than the mere *quantity* of people.

Ravenstein and Marshall received the attention due such academic heavyweights, but the most-quoted pronouncement of doom was delivered by Sir William Crookes in his 1898 presidential address before the British Association for the Advancement of Science: rising wheat prices, coupled with an impending nitrates shortage, signaled that "England and all civilised nations stand in deadly peril of not having enough to eat." Even if all the wheat-growing nations used all the available land, Crookes feared that an "increase of population among the bread-eaters" would mean major shortfalls after 1931. Yet Crookes, an eminent scientist, also hoped that "the Chemist will step in and postpone the day of famine." Crookes no doubt knew of synthetic chemist Marcelin Berthelot's famous boast that by 2000 the "wheat fields and corn fields are to disappear from the face of the earth, because flour and meal will no longer be grown, but made" in the laboratory. American pioneer nutritionist W. O. Atwater agreed that chemistry could defeat Malthus, although the more cautious Atwater predicted that future gains in yields would be achieved through better fertilizers, pesticides, genes, irrigation, transportation, storage, and management—the basic industrial agriculture package that surviving farmers would soon adopt en masse. Similarly, in 1893 the first U.S. Secretary of Agriculture, Jeremiah Rusk, predicted that improvements in conventional farming could increase production sixfold—perhaps enough to feed even a billion Americans by 1990.[16]

Rusk's assessment was part of a series of nationally syndicated newspaper columns designed to transmit the largely cornucopian spirit of the 1893 World's Columbian Exposition in Chicago. Most of the series' seventy-four experts confidently assumed that modern technologies—ranging from conventional seed selection to that science fiction favorite, the meal-in-a-pill—could easily feed the 150 million Americans expected in 1993 (actual: 256 million). In light of the gender dynamics discussed in chapter 1, it is telling that the meal-in-a-pill was advocated by one of the six women in the series, Kansas activist Mary E. Lease, who saw the pill as a way to liberate both women and animals. With food synthesized in laboratories, there would be no need for women to be enslaved in kitchens, and "the slaughter of animals—the appetite for flesh meat that has left the world reeking with blood and bestialized humanity—will be one of the shuddering horrors of the past." In Lease's vision of 1993, slaughterhouses would be converted into "conservatories and beds of bloom." The only overtly vegetarian author in the 1893 newspaper series, Lease was not particularly alarmed by the arrival of "coolie" labor. On the contrary, Lease predicted, as the center of population moved westward to the grain-rich prairies, "the almond-eyed Mongolian from the Orient will meet, in the tide of humanity pouring westward the Aryan brother from whom he separated on the plains of Asia 6000 years ago."[17] While no one else in the series was as sanguine about the imminent mixing of races on the prairies, most did agree that western agricultural expansion and intensification was the solution to future food needs.

As Donald Worster has shown in *Dust Bowl,* the "scarcity howlers" encouraged a massive plowing up of the Great Plains. But the transition took time. Until world agricultural production caught up with rising world demand, farm prices rose between 1900 and 1919, which meant good times for farmers—the "golden era of American agriculture," according to Gilbert Fite. Wheat prices were so favorable, having more than doubled between 1914 and 1919 alone, that they later became the baseline for attempts to set parity. Food inflation also encouraged professional forecasters to ponder food scarcity in the future. In "Population: A Study in Malthusianism," his 1915 Columbia University doctoral dissertation, Warren S. Thompson, one of the leading demographers of the twentieth century, pointed to rising cereal and meat prices as clear evidence that a more crowded future world would rely mostly on cereals, pulses, and root crops, not animal products. This suggests an important refinement in the correlation between food prices and dreary forecasts: When commodity prices are low and farmers are suffering, city people benefit while cries of doom tend to come from farmers and their immediate allies. When prices are high and farmers are prospering, the doomsayers tend to be more urban—including most demographers, food analysts, and big-city reporters.[18]

THE 1920s

Food price inflation was not the sole variable, however, for conditions in American cities in the years following World War I showed how many other social, political, and technological trends might combine to precipitate a sense of crisis. Unmanageable auto traffic, crowded downtown sidewalks, the proliferation of pushcarts in packed immigrant ghettoes, the spectacular increase in organized crime, the growing hegemony of mass culture, particularly movies and jazz—all signs of modern "concentration"—combined with a postwar baby boom to reinforce fears that the United States was becoming far too congested, especially by people of the wrong class, ethnicity, or genetic "stock."[19] This sense of overcrowding created a sympathetic mass audience for neo-Malthusian interpretations of the recent war, which seemed an inevitable result of the same European imperialist expansion that had bought time (and calories) for a crowded Continent in the nineteenth century. "The real harrier of the dove of peace is not the eagle of pride nor the vulture of greed, but the stork!" sociologist Edward A. Ross wrote in a *Scribner's* piece on "Population Pressure and the War." Similarly, in *The Economic Consequences of the Peace* (1920) John Maynard Keynes identified population growth as a "fundamental" cause of wars and an inexorable strain on resources that Europeans could no longer afford. While few expressed sympathy for desperate Germany, the almost equally depressing situation in shattered, hungry, superinflationary Britain haunted Anglos everywhere. Looking for additional checks besides high grain prices, neo-Malthusians could also point to the worldwide flu epidemic, which was most deadly among undernourished populations, and the Bolshevik Revolution, which succeeded because so many Russians were desperately hungry. And for those looking ahead to overpopulated hot spots elsewhere in the world, Asia seemed especially menacing, particularly well-armed, land-hungry Japan.[20]

While the Old World's future looked bleak enough, prospects did not look much better for North America, according to the Department of Agriculture. Noting that the U.S. population was growing faster than crop acreage or yields, the USDA's top agricultural economists warned in 1923 that Americans might soon need to shift to German dietary standards: more calories from grains, fewer from animal products. And even at the unenviable standard of its land-hungry former enemy, the United States might feed 350 million people at most. Two years later, the prospects still looked grim to USDA economist Oliver Baker, who estimated that feeding an unthinkably overcrowded 190 million Americans in the year 2000 (actual: 275 million) would entail even less meat. Hopefully, Baker added, the United States would never descend to the low-meat diet of Japan—a "condition of poverty" that "would weaken rather than strengthen the nation." But a grain-based European-peasant standard of living would be bad enough, Edward M. East warned in *Mankind at the Crossroads* (1924). If the world population reached 3.5 billion by 2000 (actual: 6 billion), "we shall turn steadily toward vegetarianism. Legumes and nuts will furnish an ever greater proportion of our proteids. And we shall pay, pay heavily, when even these luxuries are vouchsafed to us." As evidence that overpopulation was already debasing living standards, East compared a 1850 hotel menu, which offered over fifty kinds of meat and game, with one from 1925, with "only" a half dozen. Even more striking, East asserted that per capita American meat consumption had already dropped from 184 pounds a year in 1890 to just 138 pounds in 1922.[21]

Future USDA secretary and U.S. vice president Henry A. Wallace agreed that even if farmers were 30 percent more efficient in 2025—a very generous increase by contemporary forecasts—a U.S. population of 200 million would necessarily live "largely on foods of cereal, vegetable, and dairy origin." Applying the same calculations to meat's requisite accouterments—wine and beer—the president of the agricultural section of the British Association for the Advancement of Science found a temperate, vegetarian future unthinkable, for "the race . . . which cuts out meat and alcohol in order to multiply is of the permanent slave type destined to function like worker bees in the ultimate community." Summarizing all these polemics in *The Shadow of the World's Future* (1928), esteemed Australian statistician Sir George Handley Knibbs had "little doubt" that future humans would be far more vegetarian in their eating habits, which Knibbs, like almost everyone else engaged in this discussion, equated with Oriental deprivation.[22]

To be sure, not *all* population-controllers were so averse to an Asian diet. "Everyone in the world need not feed on the celebrated Anglo-Saxon roast beef," French businessman Henry Brenier argued at the World Population Conference held in Geneva in 1927. Why not consider the "ubiquitous soya bean," which produced protein quite efficiently on tiny Chinese and Japanese farms? Along the same lines, opportunistic California farmers attempted to market tropical avocados as protein-rich substitutes. But peasant imports—whether horticultural or human—offered little hope in the view of nativist sociologist E. A. Ross, whose *Standing Room Only?* (1927) wondered why Westerners should forego meat and other luxuries to accommodate more people. More than steak was at stake. "Mankind may indeed double in number and redouble if tasty dishes be given up for coarse and ill-flavored fare; if flesh disappears from the week-day diet; if groves, orchards and vineyards become truck patches; if dooryards, playgrounds, commons, and parks are set to growing beans and cabbages . . . if the typical working day is from dawn till dark. . . . With small holdings and more hand labor, school attendance could not be expected of the farm children after they were old enough to help. So, among people living thickly upon the land, as now in the Orient, ignorance, superstition, and peasantism would finally prevail." Rather than cutting out the steaks, Ross, like most Malthusians, preferred reducing the number of steak eaters, mainly through immigration restrictions and birth control.[23]

Those eugenicists and nativists who strongly advocated birth control supported Margaret Sanger, who sounded Malthusian warnings about food shortages to support her more controversial goal of expanding women's sexual freedom.[24] For those who for one reason or another could not mention or accept the still-dangerous subject of birth control, the alternative was definitely a somewhat less carnivorous future, although not necessarily a completely vegetarian one. Alonzo Taylor, director of Stanford University's Food Research Institute, represented mainstream nutritional opinion in 1926 when he projected a U.S. population of 175 million in 1980 (actual: 226 million) and forecast a likely reduction of per capita beef consumption from 68 pounds in 1926 to 50 in 1980 (actual: 95), and a reduction of pork consumption from 90 lbs to 64 (actual 55). While such intakes were more than adequate, he concluded, even further livestock reductions would be required if the U.S. population ever reached an unimaginable 200 million.[25]

All of these themes were marshaled by the two most widely quoted Malthusians of the decade, Raymond Pearl and Edward M. East. Pearl had been a biostatistician at the U.S. Food and Drug Administration during the war and then worked at Johns Hopkins University. In "The Biology of Death" (1921) Pearl argued that "it can not be doubted that the underlying cause of the great war through we have just passed was the ever-growing pressure of population upon subsistence." Noting the ongoing reduction in death rates, Pearl estimated that the U.S. population would reach 197 million by 2000 (up from 106 million in 1920). Based on an average daily (male) consumption of 3000 calories, the United States would require by then almost twice the calories that U.S. farmers had produced during the wartime boom years. In light of diminishing agricultural returns, Pearl doubted that farmers could do it. And the prospects for feeding our European allies, who were dependent on surplus American calories, were much worse. Mindful that "hunger is a potent stimulus to Bolshevism," Pearl's book reflected Red Scare fears that European-style radicalism would spread to America's own displaced "peasantry" and hungry working classes.[26]

Pearl's gloom was seconded and expanded by Harvard University plant geneticist East, who doubted that U.S. agricultural research could meet the challenge. His *Mankind at the Crossroads* opens starkly: "The facts of population growth and the facts of agricultural economics point severally to the definite conclusion that the world confronts the fulfillment of the Malthusian prediction here and now." With world population having doubled (to 2 billion) in one hundred years, East warned, current growth rates threatened complete "saturation" of all habitable parts of the earth by the end of the twentieth century. Estimating that it took an average of 2.5 acres to support one person, East calculated that virtually all of the arable new land might provide, at best, a peasant-style, that is, vegetarian, diet for 5 billion people—and food at the "American dietary standard" for far fewer. Remarkably, although East had done pioneering work on the hybridization of corn, which would soon revolutionize grain-fed meat production, he thought it "highly improbable" that science could substantially increase yields of existing lands. And even if scientists did improve yields, East insisted that all gains in food production would soon be devoured by the increased population. "Where more food is provided, more people will appear to consume it." In all, if the present demographic trends continued, East warned, the babies of 1924 would live to see a world in 2000 "filled with people without faith or hope, a seething mass of discontented humanity struggling for mere existence."[27] Pearl and East's basic statistics took on a life of their own and, echoed by the USDA's own pessimistic estimates, they influenced futuristic calculations for two decades.

No cornucopian spokesman equaled Pearl or East in charismatic quotability, but the technological optimists did have the highly visible facts of consumer culture on their side. After all, once-unbelievable wonders like electricity, telephones, cars, X-rays, airplanes, and radio had became commonplace. Encouraged by the early successes of rayon, plastics, margarine, coal-tar dyes, saccharine, and artificial nitrates, science journalist Edwin Slosson pitched synthetic food as mankind's best hope. "The history of civilization," Slosson wrote in *Creative Chemistry* (1919), "details the steps by which man has succeeded in building up an artificial world within the cosmos." Writing during the shortages of 1917, Sir William Crookes was quite upbeat: "Starvation will be averted through the laboratory." While Henry Ford asserted that a mechanical cow would be less "wasteful" of grain and hay, the main bets were on high protein yeast—a nutritious wartime substitute used in Germany. In 1928 the president of the American Chemical Society boasted, "Thirty men working in a factory the size of a city block can produce in the form of yeast as much food as 1000 men tilling 57,000 acres under ordinary agricultural conditions."[28]

Other cornucopian plans were somewhat more conventional. Enthused by the recent discovery of vitamins, nutritionists joined food processors in boosting "fortification" as a key weapon against malnutrition. Also, in what Jack Kloppenburg has called the Golden Age of the Plant Hunters, horticultural explorers searched the globe for new genetic stock and unconventional food sources. In a "plea for the expansion of the vegetable kingdom" as a way to prevent the dire scenarios of Pearl and East, botanist Vernon Kellogg praised Luther Burbank for "ransacking the world to find edible plant kinds that are not already grown here." In response to Crookes's much-repeated warnings about impending wheat shortages, Columbia University geographer J. Russell Smith suggested substitution of underutilized "minor cereals" such as quinoa, buckwheat, rice, and corn, as well as "tree crops" such as acorns, chestnuts, olives, and nuts. Smith also hoped that yields of "primary" grains (i.e., wheat) could be increased greatly through higher inputs of machinery, chemistry, and genetics.[29]

Smith's hope is largely what happened over the following ten years, albeit with devastating economic and ecological effects. Enriched by botanical "ransacking," genetic research flourished. Meanwhile, Malthusian anxieties spurred further speculative, unsustainable exploitation of dry lands using the latest implements, especially tractor-drawn disk plows and combines. Belying Crookes's original prophecy, the world's wheat farmers expanded acreage *and* yields much faster than the growth in the number of bread eaters. Similarly, fears of famine drove public subsidies for major irrigation and reclamation projects. U.S. Commerce Secretary Herbert Hoover supported California's Central Valley water projects because, with 40 million more Americans expected by 1950, "our future supplies of food must come from just such projects as this." The result was further expansion and intensification of California's "factories in the fields," its highly industrialized system of vegetable production. In almost every modernizing area, farmers replaced horses with tractors, holdings grew larger, and marginal, small-scale farmers lost out. The elimination of horses also released feed grains to other livestock, thereby diminishing fears of an imminent meat shortage.[30]

Some modernizers welcomed the concentration and industrialization. In *Too Many Farmers: The Story of What Is Here and Ahead in Agriculture* (1929), journalist Wheeler McMillen took the "get big or get out" approach later advocated by Richard Nixon's USDA secretary, Earl Butz: giant-scale "corporation farming" was the best way to equalize agriculture and industry; to free small farmers from "enslavement" to primi-

tive animals, endless toil, and marginal soil; and to foster overall economic development. "Let agriculture itself become a big business and
take its place amongst the enterprises that make America a phenomenon
of the earth." Agrarians might worry about the threat to rural communities and values, but to little avail. With the inevitable overproduction
came lower food prices, thereby reducing the food security fears voiced
in the urban-oriented press but also speeding up the technological treadmill. As European farmers recovered from the war, more American farmers found themselves overextended, particularly in marginal western areas.
By the decade's end, as supply outstripped demand, USDA's Oliver Baker
reversed his earlier warnings: "Instead of population pressing on the food
supply, as was feared a few years ago, the food supply is pressing on population." Economist Joseph Davis, writing in 1932, agreed: "Threat of
coming dearth is not the central food problem." "Demand, not resources,
is the major factor limiting the food supply for the world of commerce."
As prices plunged, chemists pondered not how to make up food deficits
but how to invent new, nonfood uses for mounting surpluses. Along the
same lines, farm supporters like Baker wondered how to get Americans
to eat *more* meat, not less.[31]

THE 1930s

Fears of overpopulation almost disappeared during the Depression. Instead, as birth rates dipped along with overall consumer demand, some
economists and demographers even wondered if the United States—and
the West in general—might be *under*populated. How much had changed
in ten years, demographer Enid Charles marveled in a much-cited analysis of population decline: whereas in 1923 J. M. Keynes had lamented
having too many mouths to feed as a major obstacle to a higher, meat-
based standard of living, by 1933 farmers were routinely slaughtering livestock, dumping milk, and destroying surplus grain to slow disastrous
deflation. Tapping the well-established racial motif, Winston Churchill
suggested that agricultural surpluses were due to the fact that while the
"civilized" races could "produce or procure" more food than they could
eat, the "yellow men, brown men, and black men" had not yet "learned
to demand and become able to afford a diet superior to rice." Revised
calculations by Warren Thompson (the author of that firmly Malthusian
1915 dissertation) suggested that the U.S. population might peak at 136
million by 1950 and then decline by 1980 to 126 million, which was the
population in 1930. Metropolitan Life Insurance statistician Louis

Dublin predicted further U.S. shrinkage after the year 2000, to around 70 million people by 2100. Yet even while it seemed unlikely that American population would keep doubling, food supply concerns persisted. For one thing, if agricultural surpluses bankrupted more and more farmers, who would be left to grow tomorrow's food? Even more troublesome, food was *already* very short for many people, *despite* the surpluses. This "paradox of plenty"—that millions went hungry even as farmers were forced to destroy unmarketable grain, milk, and meat—made the socialist position almost respectable during the Depression and certainly gained support for government efforts to redistribute food through "surplus disposal."[32]

Topping off the insecurity was the ecological devastation left by speculative overproduction, as seen most dramatically in the Dust Bowl. While some hoped that the Depression and apparent baby bust would relieve pressure on overworked lands, Baker argued that population decline and falling prices might actually increase soil erosion, for surviving farmers would be driven to grow even more grain to make up for lower incomes. "In a population declining more rapidly than the natural resources, land may be abundant and abused." So even if concerns about overpopulation slowed, worries about overuse of resources, especially soil, did not. With nowhere left to run, Americans—and human "civilization" in general—needed to take much better care of what it already had, mainly through soil conservation and land-use planning. Blending Malthusian and Godwinian themes, advocates of centralized resource management, according to Donald Worster, portrayed America as "an *overdeveloped* country, violently pressing on the earth's marginal lands to make greater profits, while already producing enough food to go around if it were not wasted or hogged by a few."[33] For leftist New Dealers, the word "planning" had the same cachet as "rational" did for utopians of the Enlightenment, but unlike Condorcet, the new conservationists of the 1930s believed that the earth's resources were limited. Like Godwin, however, they valued cooperative social experiments. In a preview of the organic/sustainable agriculture movement of the 1970s, USDA's Baker, Lewis Gray, and M. L. Wilson joined Ralph Borsodi, Helen and Scott Nearing, the Nashville Agrarians, and other back-to-the-land advocates in supporting a controversial program to resettle displaced workers and bankrupt farmers on subsistence homesteads. In addition to enabling the poor to grow their own food using low-tech, ecologically sustainable methods, these homesteads might also provide part-time labor for decentralized "village industries," which would revitalize rural economies.[34]

Cornucopians addressed the same problems of underpopulation, overproduction, hunger, and erosion, but for solutions they tended to agree with McMillen's advocacy of corporate-scale, "scientific" food production. For these futurists, rational planning meant highly rationalized planning. "The independent farmer as we now know him probably is doomed," Yale chemical engineer C. C. Furnas pronounced in *America's Tomorrow* (1932): "The march of machinery is driving him out; machinery means capital, and capital means big business." Continuing the progression, Furnas argued that business means efficiency, which might even mean going off the land altogether. "Plants and animals are laboratories where chemical compounds are made. Man is learning chemistry very rapidly, and he is also learning to put nature out of business." Dow Chemical's William Hale agreed that "chemurgy"—the fullscale application of synthetic chemistry to all phases of the food chain—was "the key to human happiness." Like many engineers, Hale believed that food shortages—and indeed the whole economic collapse—resulted from excessive reliance on outdated, inefficient techniques and institutions, especially the independent farmer, grocer, and cook. Hale's suitably boosterish books, *Chemistry Triumphant* (1932) and *The Farm Chemurgic: Farmward the Star of Destiny Lights Our Way* (1934), envisioned a handful of giant farms supplying processors with more than enough grain, meat, and produce to meet all future food needs. Agricultural surpluses could be converted to fiber, cellulose, levulose, glucose, and other raw materials needed by the chemical industry, or they could be stored indefinitely as insurance against bad harvests. This radical reorganization would free most farmers to work in factories and would return their overworked land to nature.[35]

While revolutionary, Hale's vision of a better world through chemistry seemed moderate compared to that of the British Secretary for India, Frederick Edward Smith, Earl of Birkenhead, whose *The World in 2030 AD* (1930) envisioned a world virtually without agriculture, "at least in civilised lands." Like everyone involved in food security debates, Birkenhead was quite familiar with the inefficiencies of raising livestock. Instead of the "wasteful and round-about method" of using plants to convert solar energy into cellulose, which was then converted by animals into meat, giant food factories would synthesize nutrients directly from sunlight. "By 2030 starch and sugar (two of our most valuable foods) will be as cheap as sand or salt to-day." Eventually proteins, too, would be synthesized directly, and these would be converted into self-reproducing

THE DEBATE / 37

steaks. "It will no longer be necessary to go to the extravagant length of rearing a bullock in order to eat its steak. From one 'parent' steak of choice tenderness, it will be possible to grow as large and as juicy a steak as can be desired. So long as the 'parent' is supplied with the correct chemical nourishment, it will continue to grow indefinitely, and, perhaps, internally." Not to be outdone by his political rival, Winston Churchill looked "Fifty Years Hence" in 1932 and envisioned synthetic foods, concocted from "microbes" in "vast cellars," and "practically indistinguishable" from the natural variety. Like Birkenhead, Churchill saw in the future self-replicating meat portions grown directly from elementary nutrients. "We shall escape the absurdity of growing a whole chicken in order to eat the breast or wing, by growing these parts separately under a suitable medium." Common to such modernist reconstructions was an effort to solve dirt farming's perennial inefficiencies by doing away with conventional agriculture entirely. By 2030, Birkenhead glowed, farming would be relegated to "a rich man's hobby," "a charming old-world fancy," and the stuff of "historical romances." Similarly, Churchill predicted that "parks and gardens will cover our pastures and plowed fields," leaving lots of room for cities to expand if population increased again.[36] The assertion that hyperindustrialized food production would enhance soil conservation and convert unsightly farms to decorous parks was a central tenet of technological utopians, ranging from the great nineteenth-century chemists Liebig and Berthelot to Monsanto's genetic engineers at the end of the twentieth century.

While it was only a few futurists who went so far as to abolish the family farm, faith in "science at the helm" was a reflection of 1930s modernism, as captured in the 1933 Chicago Fair's motto, "Science Finds—Industry Applies—Man Conforms." One of the remarkable features of Depression culture is how a cornucopian faith in abstract Science and Industry outlasted the failures of actual scientists and industries to feed, clothe, and house millions. The USDA's back-to-the-land subsistence homesteads aside, for the most part federal agricultural policy favored further modernization and industrialization of food production, albeit somewhat restrained by the new consensus regarding soil conservation. As Farm Security Administration photographers and John Steinbeck's *Grapes of Wrath* (1939) captured the plight of the poorest victims of this latest round of enclosures, the survivors "adjusted" by working larger farms using more chemicals, hybrids, electricity, machines, and irrigation—the basic elements of the technological treadmill.[37]

THE 1940s TO THE 1950s:
COLD WAR JITTERS

The "creed of maximization" enabled American farmers to meet the challenges of the Second World War, but neo-Malthusian anxieties returned afterward. Severe postwar food shortages and inflation raised fears of famine not only in Europe but also in the Third World, where life-saving medicines and pesticides brought about what was called the population "explosion" or "bomb," which some saw as a greater threat to world peace than the atomic bomb. From the standpoint of the new baby boom, the birth dearth of the 1930s seemed a momentary lull in the inexorable dynamic of human doubling and redoubling. Whereas Depression-era demographers and economists had fretted about the economic implications of a world population dipping below 2 billion, postwar forecasters revived Pearl and East's alarms about a world population that could top 3.3 billion by 2000. "Growth of the population to 3.5–4.0 billions in the early twenty-first century will be prejudicial to the welfare of the bulk of the world's population," venerable Duke economist Joseph Spengler concluded in 1948. Noting that the earth's population had tripled between 1750 and 1950 (to about 2.35 billion), some alarmists were even forecasting a global population to exceed 5 billion by 2000—an absolutely astounding idea at the time (although the reality eventually exceeded 6 billion).[38]

The United States, too, seemed to be resuming unsustainable growth patterns as the American birth rate increased at twice the predicted rate and the population approached the 150 million mark—twice its 1900 number—the prospect that had seemed so ominous to Pearl and East. In fact, statisticians could not keep up with the American baby boom. In 1948 the U.S. Census Bureau forecast a 1950 population that was 5 million above the 1946 forecast. Writing in 1949, Joseph Davis, director of Stanford's Food Research Institute, suggested that the U.S. population might reach 160 million by 1955 instead of 1970, and perhaps even 300 million by 2000—far more than Pearl's once-alarming 197 million. Noting that "able scholars" of the 1930s had predicted a U.S. "peak" of 135 million, Davis urged demographers to be far more humble: "Surely the time has come for us to admit that our best population specialists cannot make dependable forecasts of our population for 5 or 10 years ahead. We must quit demanding the impossible of them." In other words, given the surprises of the 1940s, all bets were off when it came to population predictions.[39]

If demographers were humbled, conservationists felt affirmed. The environmental jeremiads of the late 1940s and early 1950s combined Dust Bowl lessons with a resurgent Malthusianism. Ecological doomsaying peaked in 1948, which saw the publication of both William Vogt's *Road to Survival* and Fairfield Osborn's *Our Plundered Planet*—the latter dedicated "to all who care about tomorrow." Recycling and tweaking many of Pearl and East's statistical calculations, Vogt and Osborn reached much the same conclusion: the earth could not feed many more people. The best lands were already taken, soil was eroding at an alarming rate, and, despite wartime increases, yields were topping out. Both doubted that scientists could squeeze more food out of existing farms or, even more far-fetched, synthesize food in factories. Ridiculing the hubris of chemists like Hale, the zoologist Osborn wrote: "Is he not nature's 'crowning glory'? . . . He has seemingly 'discovered' the secrets of the universe. What need, then, to live by its principles?" The most developed countries were living off capital borrowed—or "plundered," in Osborn's title—from overseas colonies and from Mother Nature.[40]

Once again, anxieties about future diets were often reduced to meaty terms, especially after beef prices soared during the "beefsteak election" of 1946, when Republicans won back Congress partly on a promise to repeal the price controls that they blamed for the meat crisis. Two years later, President Harry Truman won reelection by blaming his opponents for the lingering inflation. Similarly, Vogt skillfully reaped considerable media attention by linking future meat shortages to the ecological effects of population growth and imperial conquest. Thanks to the pillage of distant continents, Vogt observed, erosion was now a global problem. Only a farsighted campaign to reduce population and restore topsoil would preserve the cherished meat-and-potatoes family feast. "We must develop our sense of time, and think of the availability of beefsteaks not only for this Saturday but for the Saturdays of our old age, and of our children and grandchildren's youth."[41]

Vogt at least offered some hope that birth control and conservation would save the family roast. Fellow Malthusians Frank Pearson and Floyd Harper were considerably grimmer in *The World's Hunger* (1945), which estimated that, even with modest improvements in farm management, the world could support a maximum of 3 billion at an "Asiatic standard" (little or no meat), 2.2 billion at a continental European standard (some meat), and 902 million at a North American standard (a lot of meat). Barring "revolutionary discoveries" worthy of Jules Verne, a significant "nutrition upgrade" for the world would require either vast depopulation (Malthus) or a wholesale redistribution of nutrients (Godwin) in which North America would have to give up two-thirds of its animal foods. A better solution, according to demographer P. K. Whelpton of Scripps Population Research, was to *reduce* the U.S. *population* by two-thirds, thereby guaranteeing more "beefsteak and milk for everybody."[42]

Even the less alarmist forecasts of the postwar decade routinely doubted whether the world could afford much more meat, especially the grain-fed variety. Since "man and animals compete for nature's food," observed Frederick Stare, head of Harvard's Department of Nutrition, "the production of animal food products must certainly be curtailed"— except perhaps for skimmed milk, which was more economical to produce. Stare's recommendations resembled those of Frank Boudreau, head of the Milbank Memorial Fund, a prominent population think tank: feeding 3 billion people in 2000 would require eating more "skim milk, wheat and barley, soy bean and peanut products" and shifting grains used for livestock "into direct human use as food." The normally hyper-cornucopian *Life* magazine agreed that American farmers should stop feeding grain to animals. Moreover, *Life*'s editors commented, in light of current projections "we now stand very close to discovering that Malthus was a true prophet," and, in an unusual gesture toward the Godwinians, they hinted that the world's grains might stretch further if Americans started "going easy on the toast, not to speak of the prime ribs."[43]

Long-range government forecasts supported such anxieties. The USDA's top soil scientist, Robert Salter, calculated that if Americans continued to grow feed grains at the current level of intensity, the resultant soil exhaustion would mean rapidly rising meat and milk prices by 1960. Even with heavy use of fertilizers and with erosion controls, a world population of around 3 billion by 2000 might not be able to afford significantly more meat and milk. A 1950 presidential commission on U.S. water resources predicted that even effective soil conservation *and* expansion of cultivated land would meet America's extravagant dietary needs by only "a rather narrow margin," and after 1975 the United States might need to reduce its livestock consumption. Translating such forecasts into familiar racialist terms, one Canadian agricultural periodical lamented that "perhaps never again—unless an unforeseen miracle occurs—will the white people of the world be able to enjoy the extremely high level of food that was available to them in 1938 and 1939. The white races . . . will have to adapt themselves . . . to a gradual change in their diet, consuming less livestock products and more cereals"—grim prospects indeed if one had to look back longingly to the recent Depression as the lost banquet days![44]

However dire the United States' circumstances might be, the poorest nations were much worse off, as booming populations ruined marginal soils and then streamed to intolerably overcrowded cities. Vogt essentially wrote off Latin America ("biological bankruptcy"), India ("the demographic nadir"), and Africa ("the dying land"). Dividing the world by economic stages, some experts differentiated doomed "Malthusian" countries from more "developed" ones, but for Vogt there were no bright spots, as the whole world was overpopulated and verging on ecological collapse. "By excessive breeding and abuse of the land mankind has backed itself into an ecological trap," Vogt wrote. In a now-familiar formulation, Vogt doubted that the world of 2000 could "support three billion people at any but coolie standards."[45] Repeating Malthus's critique of charity, Vogt dismissed foreign aid as an "international WPA" that would only increase population. But public support for development—a moderately liberal version of Godwinian redistribution—was strengthened by dreary annual reports from the U.N.'s Food and Agriculture Organization (FAO), which estimated that two-thirds of the world was hungry or malnourished and drew startling contrasts between projected world needs and likely production. Assessing the FAO's goal of doubling the food supply by 1970, Kansas State University's president Milton Eisenhower wrote in 1948: "I say in all earnestness that it is an open question whether food production, for all our science, can be increased that much."[46] Coming from the head of a mainstream agricultural college, such pessimism had considerable weight.

The emerging Cold War added fears that Communists would now exploit the growing hunger in the overpopulated Third World. With China "lost" in 1948–49, would India, with an even higher birth rate and with its well-known famines, be next? And if India went, according to this dietary domino theory, could the rest of Asia be far behind? The neo-Malthusian case for population control thus took on a national security dimension. *Science News Letter* declared in 1947: "Cutting down the birth rate is a better way to insure peace than reduction of armaments." If the "under-developed" nations did not curb their population growth, the British president of the U.N. Security Council warned in 1950, "either there will be an outburst of anarchy, or some attempt will be made to solve their problems on Stalinist lines." The following year, *Senior Scholastic* boiled this "lesson" down for its captive audience of American school children: "Politically, overpopulation creates a breeding ground for communism. Communist propaganda thrives on poverty and discontent."[47]

National defense became the rationale behind pleas for greater spending on agricultural research, alongside similar requests for increasing the budgets for education, highways, and space exploration. Thus the head of the Soil Conservation Service advocated more "conservation technology" that would "reduce the hunger and discontent among peoples which so frequently leads to discord, dictatorships, and war." "Better grass will give more food for defense," USDA experts argued as they urged more research to improve pasture quality. As John Perkins shows in *Geopolitics and the Green Revolution* (1997), Cold War competition warranted massive research and the development of new seeds that would eventually increase grain yields in poor countries. "Agitators from Communist countries are making the most of the situation," the Rockefeller Foundation's Warren Weaver wrote in *The World Food Problem* (1951). Better seeds might help the hungry "to attain by evolution the improvements, including those in agriculture, which otherwise may have to come by revolution."[48]

While the Green Revolution—directed by Weaver—did not begin to yield real gains until the late 1960s, there was no shortage of assertions in the 1940s and 1950s that Western science, technology, and trade could head off the catastrophe forecast by Vogt and others. If anything, faith in scientific wonders seemed confirmed by the population boom, which, according to the cornucopian paradigm, was a result of Western science's life-extending conquest of diseases. Pointing to the spectacular effects of pesticides and antibiotics, the president of the British Association for the Advancement of Science concluded, "It is the advance of science that has made [population growth] possible."[49] Within this self-congratulatory perspective, which seemed to relegate all progress to the realm of sanitized Science, rather than of messy politics, the same miracles would inevitably expand the food supply and thus defeat hunger. As in earlier cycles, those pondering how to do so scanned the whole range of yield-boosting possibilities—from the conventional (more machines, more chemicals, more water, better genes) to the far-fetched (hydroponics, synthetics, yeast, algae, and nuclear-powered farms in the Arctic, tropics, oceans, and space).

We will look more closely at these cornucopian proposals in part III. Here, while still sketching the debate's chronology and context, it is important to note the distinctions between views with shorter and longer time frames. Those contemplating just the next few years—mainly farmers, food producers, and their allies in the USDA—worried more about gluts than shortages.[50] Having stepped up production during the war, industrial agriculture continued to overproduce once the war was over. Food prices generally fell after 1948, but given the familiar treadmill— the need to grow and raise more commodities just to net the same income—production did not slow down. Surplus-wary USDA economists encouraged each American to eat forty more pounds of meat and two hundred more pounds of milk a year. If Americans did not keep eating more meat, the founder of Cornell University's nutrition school warned in 1947, farmers might reduce grain production, forcing us to eat cereals directly rather than via animals—"a step toward a coolie diet." Similarly, every postwar *Yearbook of Agriculture* included proposals by USDA scientists to expand the nonfood uses of agricultural products. Yet highlighting the "paradox of plenty" in turn heightened public sensitivity to the persistence of hunger across the globe.[51] And the more people contemplated the extent of world hunger, the tougher the problem seemed.

Cornucopians looking past 1970 or 1980 tended to expect the productivity of industrial farming to level off eventually. With the population increasing much faster than previously thought, and with growing recognition of the soil erosion crisis, it seemed prudent to contemplate more unconventional food resources. After reviewing all the ways to increase production using the known technologies, M. K. Bennett, head of Stanford's Food Research Institute in the late 1940s, felt compelled to consider off-land possibilities: "Land is not all. One cannot dismiss as inconceivable the profitable use of the plankton of the oceans as food or feed; and ways and means of utilizing solar radiation to provide the energy for artificial synthesis of the food elements remain to be speculated about." John Boyd-Orr, first FAO chief and a Nobel Peace Prize winner, thought conventional farming could feed 5 to 6 billion people— a very high estimate for 1950—but after that it might be necessary to "call in the chemists, who can synthesize nearly all the constituents of food except the mineral elements, of which there is no shortage." Many analysts were much taken by the case made in *The Coming Age of Wood* (1949) by Egon Glesinger, former forestry director for the FAO, who championed the high protein and B-vitamin virtues of torula yeast cultured in fermented sawdust.[52]

If mainstream policy makers were willing to consider such science fiction scenarios, the synthetic chemists were even more enthusiastic. For example, in *The Road to Abundance* (1953), chemist Jacob Rosin followed the "chemurgic" path set out by William Hale twenty years earlier in deploring the inefficiencies of even the most modernized farms. With population doubling every seventy years, and with mankind already woefully short of the "six trillion calories a day that it requires," it was time "to recognize that our dependence for food upon the dilatory and inefficient plant is a cruel bondage. We have given the plant almost the entire 'floor space' of our planet, and devoted to it by far the largest part of our energies. And in return we have not gotten enough food to go round." Like many chemists, beginning with Liebig and Berthelot, Rosin framed industrial synthesis as conservationist reform. If compact chemical machinery is replaced by sprawling farms, "the surface of our earth will be freed from its dedication to food production. A new way of life will emerge. Crowded cities will disappear, and the earth will be transformed into a Garden of Eden." Other visionaries rhapsodized about the untapped protein potential of the oceans, tropics, rooftop gardens, and the Arctic.[53]

The postwar cornucopians also revived one of Condorcet's often overlooked caveats: that, to gain its maximum benefits, science needs democratic social conditions. This good science + good government equation made Condorcet as utopian as Godwin. In turn, Condorcet was simply reiterating the conditions suggested by the arch-cornucopian Francis Bacon (1561–1626): scientific mastery of nature would be realized only in the conducive political context of a *novum organum,* which could take significant upheavals to achieve. Similarly, even the most elated high-tech optimists of the postwar period usually allowed that there was no limit to what humans could accomplish—*if* they could get along equitably. After hyping virtually every technological innovation, journalist Robert Brittain, in *Let There Be Bread* (1952), added this reservation: mankind can "create abundance *if we will.*" This "will" involved at least two other utopian provisos: a "world-wide effort" to develop backward countries and, in a bow toward the egalitarians, a reduction in American opposition to radical land reform. While Brittain claimed "sober confidence" that these conditions could be realized, these were in fact what Malthus had branded "giddy" stipulations. Similarly, after resolutely countering the "hysteria" of Vogt and others with numerous technological possibilities, the president of the American Association for the Advancement of Science suggested that "scientific realism" would feed the future *only if* combined with "true justice" and a "One World" perspective. Along the same lines, Victor Cohn's *1999—Our Hopeful Future* (1956) outlined the myriad ways that "science gets dinner"—ranging from rooftop algae ponds to fully automated push-button farms—but ended by observing that ending hunger also required international peace, considerably more foreign aid, and the end of the McCarthyite suppression of free thought.[54]

Surveying a host of such cornucopian proposals, historian Whitney Cross observed:

> All such prospects depend on an immense *if*. We have to reckon with human cussedness. Suppose scientists learn all the answers. How can the world's farmers, a numerous and ignorant lot, possibly be educated in time? And how can the world's industrialists, a selfish lot when not also ignorant, be pushed into line? This is the crux of the problem. This is where the whole question of conservation descends from the utopia of science to the earthy level of human policy. . . . Science and technology can undoubtedly feed us. But they cannot function unless social action conforms to what they require.[55]

Amid the grandiose expectations of postwar reconstruction, however, altruistic social action did not seem so far-fetched. Citing such successful cooperative endeavors as the Manhattan Project, the Marshall Plan, and the founding of the United Nations, cornucopians bet that humanity could indeed muster a One World perspective to beat world hunger. In this faith, some even sounded like Godwinians in their calls for land reform, decolonization, women's rights, democratic elections, and other elements of a just community.

The Malthusians were less sanguine about human benevolence, much the way Malthus himself had doubted Condorcet's ideas in light of the postrevolutionary malaise of 1798 in France. For proof they cited the dropping of the atomic bomb, the spread of Communist dictatorships in Europe, and the outbreak of civil wars in the Middle East, India, and Korea. "Belief in Utopia dies hard, especially among Americans!" Vogt exclaimed in dismissing "a spate of 'if' books" that based their optimistic projections on assumptions of enduring peace and cooperation. For weary veteran demographer Warren Thompson, too, the latest round of technological hyperbole was a bit too much, in light of the persistent inability of modernizers to reform land tenure or "to get the new types of cooperation among farmers that are essential to the successful application of scientific achievements." Having "lived through three flutters of excitement on the part of the public because of its misunderstanding of the difficulties of translating science into food production," Thompson thought it wiser if humans "learned how to control our own conduct as regards the rate of reproduction."[56]

Cal Tech scientist Harrison Brown was even more dubious in his elegant conservationist/Malthusian synthesis, *The Challenge of Man's Future* (1954). While it might be possible "in principle" to double world food production using all the known conventional techniques plus a few lucky breakthroughs in genetics and algae research, Brown doubted that governments could get along well enough to pitch in the $100 billion the research and worldwide implementation might take. Stating what might be called the *dys*topian caveat, Brown suggested that only a Big Brother dictatorship could manage a densely populated world of 4.8 billion (by 2000). "It seems clear that the first major penalty man will have to pay for his rapid consumption of the earth's non-renewable resources will be that of having to live in a world where his thoughts and actions are more strongly limited, where social organization has become all pervasive, complex, and inflexible, and where the state completely dominates the actions of the individual."[57] If optimists were willing to invoke speculative fiction scenarios in their search for ways to feed the future, so, too, were pessimists—and as we shall see in part II, the dystopian motif largely prevailed in postwar futurist fiction.

Dystopia actually wrought utopia, however—at least in the short run. The dire forecasts after both world wars spurred enough agricultural research and investment to accomplish what had seemed quite difficult, if not totally improbable, in 1925 and 1950: a major boost in conventional agricultural production of feed grains and livestock.

Ironically, it was the work on hybrid corn conducted by two of the gloomier forecasters of the 1920s—East and Wallace—that yielded some of the highest gains later on. By 1949, all Corn Belt acreage was planted in hybrid seed, leading to a doubling of average corn yields between 1935 and 1955 (and a sixfold increase between 1935 and 1985.) Appropriately enough, Wallace's company—Pioneer Hi-Bred—also led the way in genetic research on higher-yielding chickens and cattle. Mindful that increased livestock production was a major postwar priority, advocates of large-scale research programs for industrialized agriculture generally did a skillful job of exploiting public fears of diminished meat supplies. Arguing that an "adequate diet at moderate cost" derived at least 45 percent of its calories from animal products (a questionably high ratio), one presidential commission warned of major cutbacks in animal foods in the absence of a substantial increase in funding for water projects. Similarly, the FAO's chief economist asserted that since "the best-fed peoples are consuming more meat and milk" (at least 35 to 50 percent of total calories from animal foods), the world needed a major development program to bring "the techniques of modern science" to the three-quarters of the world's farmers still laboring at subsistence levels. By this standard only "a handful of nations" were well-fed; conversely, Mediterranean countries like Italy, Tunisia, and Egypt, with only 10 percent of total calories from animals, were considered malnourished, while China, Japan, and India—with 95 percent of calories from grain—were "desperate."[58]

Given this apparent protein deficit, cornucopians heralded virtually every new technology as a way to increase the global supply of animal foods—although, characteristically enough, such breakthroughs seemed most likely to benefit those already quite well fed. In 1952, *Fortune* celebrated drug company research on antibiotics that, when added to animal feed, promised "to supply U.S. dinner tables with more chicken, turkey, and pork at a lower absolute cost than ever." Also promising, *Science Digest* reported that same year, was Swedish work on "chromosome multiplication" that could potentially exceed the capabilities of mere hybridization, yielding "hogs as hefty as horses, and cattle as big as elephants"—a hopeful prospect considering the "skyrocketing" meat prices. And if science could devise ways to convert surplus sugar wastes into beefsteaks, the president of the Sugar Research Foundation suggested in 1954, "it will be possible to feed the people of the world adequately for the first time in human history." To bolster their case for increased funding, supports of this view reiterated the two equally distasteful alternatives: "coolie rations" and "ersatz" foods. Rare were those who protested, as did MIT's Robert Harris, that "people can be well nourished on a diet that is rich in cereals. There is no indispensable food and it is now obvious that there are many ways to compound a good diet."[59]

But dietary expectations clearly discouraged any serious consideration of eating lower on the food chain. Armed with genetically improved seeds and animals, modern management, wholesale mechanization, subsidized irrigation, and an arsenal of chemicals, American farmers enabled *more* meat and dairy consumption. The American '50s came to be symbolized not by sautéed yeast cubes on rice—the synthetic-Asian nightmare—but by lavish backyard barbecues, fast food hamburgers, and extra-large milk shakes topped with whipped cream. Even in 1954, a year of exceptionally dismal long-term forecasts, the U.S. Department of Agriculture's animal research chief in Beltsville, Maryland, boasted that Americans consumed five times the animal foods available to the world's "average citizen." Thanks to agricultural research, a *Life* editorial exulted in 1955, "nearly all Americans not only enjoy a national diet but a *luxury* diet.

Their land is so increasingly productive that they can afford the luxury of using up 10 calories of corn and forage to produce *one* calorie of beef." In other words, a grain-to-meat conversion ratio long considered to be an unsustainable extravagance—indeed an invitation to war—was now praised as "America's biggest weapon in the cold war."[60] To be sure, most of these increases were benefiting only the more affluent part of the world, and at mounting environmental and political costs. As such, the table was being set for the revival of Godwinian outrage in the 1960s.

Even as supermarket shelves groaned with convenience products designed to add value to the land's mounting surpluses, Malthusian worries persisted. If demographers from the 1920s into the 1950s had been horrified by the prospect of a world population of 3 billion in 2000, in the late 1950s projections began to skyrocket way beyond previous worst-case scenarios, thereby keeping alive that recurrent stimulus to anxiety: scary demographics. Between 1954 and 1957, the United Nations' "high estimate" for 1980 jumped from 3.9 billion to 4.8 billion, with a truly frightening 6.9 billion possible for 2000. Feeding twice as many people in 2000 at *existing,* inadequate dietary levels, the FAO argued in 1958, would require a 150 percent increase of caloric production for the poor countries, and 120 percent for the world as a whole. At current rates, *Saturday Review*'s Edgar Ansel Mowrer fretted in 1956, the world of 2100 might have 20 billion people subsisting mainly on "sawdust, seaweed, and synthetics." Calculating the world's carrying capacity, a 1957 Cal Tech team headed by Harrison Brown estimated that even if the world adopted the best American agricultural practices, it might feed an "upper limit" of 4 to 5 billion people at moderate European standards, 7.7 billion at "Asiatic" levels. This was a relatively optimistic estimate compared to demographer P. K. Whelpton's speculation that only 4 to 5 billion people could be supported "on a level of living like that of India or China."[61]

The ominous Asiatic Other endured as the classic Malthusian basket case—a cliché replenished by postwar politics, travel, statistics, and hackneyed prose. For example, Mowrer illustrated his vision of an Orwellian synthetic "hive" with allusions to "the awful promiscuity of boat-dwellers on the Pearl River at Canton, China; or crowded Calcutta on a summer night during the monsoon." In 1959, two well-publicized reports put "teeming" Asia—and overpopulation in general—at the top of the news agenda. Just before Thanksgiving—well-timed in this "clean plate era"—a CBS Reports documentary titled "The Population Explosion" illustrated the worst Malthusian scenario with archetypal images of an Indian famine. With a record-breaking 9 million viewers, the documentary was the first national network news report to discuss contraceptives frankly. In doing so it reinforced the controversy sparked by the president-appointed Draper Committee, which had outlined the national security threats posed by Third World population growth and suggested a variety of mainstream think tank solutions, including more economic development assistance and support for international population planning programs. Appropriately enough, the committee's chair, investment banker William Draper, had been motivated to take such a strong stand by his visits to Asia.[62] Similar travels would also play a major role in the subsequent careers of leading neo-Malthusians Paul Ehrlich and Lester Brown.

THE 1960s TO THE 1970s

If all this history sounds repetitious, it is because the three-way debate fed on itself and endured through the decades: doubting science and reason, Malthusians predicted still more hunger; defying Malthus, cornucopians took steps to produce more food; pointing to mounting surpluses, egalitarians—not exactly an equal party during the Red Scare but heard nevertheless, partly through the foreign aid lobby—critiqued an economic and political system that fattened the rich with cheap meat while depriving the poor of basic grains and depleting the soil.

There was not much to add when the debate heated up again in the mid-1960s, except a stronger sense of imminent catastrophe. Scary demographics redux, the population was growing faster than anyone had foreseen ten years before. In 1967—just before Frances Moore Lappé visited the library at the University of California, Berkeley, to research *Diet for a Small Planet*—Harrison Brown lamented that at the current growth rate of close to 2 percent a year, the world population could exceed 7.5 billion in 2000 and might even top 25 billion by 2050—well ahead of Mowrer's hysterical extrapolations of 1956. Characteristically, worries about meat dramatized concerns about crowding, as when Brown's biologist colleague James Bonner decried the waste of "9000 of our daily calories on a gigantic cow and pig welfare program" and asked rhetorically, "Could we not all turn vegetarian?" Noting, as Lappé would emphasize later, that seeds, beans, and grains could be combined nutritiously, Bonner allowed that animal protein was *not* necessary for human welfare—a fairly significant admission for a mainstream, male American scientist. While Bonner believed that a massive economic development program for the Third World might stave off disaster, he doubted that governments had the "will and courage" to do so. His final sentence suggested the darkening mood of his time: "Horrified historians may record that, as the world sped on a collision course with starvation, its great powers fiddled with a war in Viet Nam, a crisis in Berlin, a contest in arsenal building, and a race to the moon."[63] No utopian caveat here! Coming from a consummate insider who routinely briefed top industry executives and engineers at exclusive Cal Tech symposia, such fatalism indicated a real loss of confidence in public leadership.

Whereas earlier Malthusians had fretted mostly about declining conditions over the long run, the population crisis seemed more immediate in the super-heated 1960s, when it was easy—perhaps too easy—to see overpopulation as the root cause of the world's myriad problems. With the news full of burning rivers, smog-choked air, gridlocked streets, asphyxiated birds, escalating insurrection in urban ghettoes and the Third World, and Western governments crippled by social and cultural conflict—and with much of this dramatized in dystopian stories that engaged so many young people—apocalyptic thinking seemed almost rational and mainstream. In their much-publicized scare book, *Famine 1975!* (1967), William and Paul Paddock moved the impending food crisis up from sometime after 2000 to the 1970s and 1980s. And while some egalitarians might have been willing to forego corn-fed meat to free up grain surpluses for food relief, the Paddocks took a harder line. With "the time of the famines" imminent, the United States would have to practice disciplined "triage" in deciding which countries to save and on what terms, for American taxpayers, deprived of their cheap meat at home, would be "dead serious" about "getting their money's worth" when sharing valuable grain overseas. India would be relegated to the "can't be saved" category or, better yet, allowed to become a "drag" on Russia and China's fragile food stocks.[64] These assessments came from a retired U.S. Foreign Service officer with twenty years of experience in Asia (Paul) and an expert in Latin American agricultural development (William).

Similarly, in his widely quoted and excerpted bestseller, *The Population Bomb* (1968), Stanford University entomologist Paul Ehrlich predicted a clear series of "eco-catastrophes" in the 1970s leading to worldwide famines: the end of all ocean life, growing domestic unrest leading to a breakdown of the basic infrastructure (water, electricity, roads, dams), mounting pest resistance to pesticides resulting in major harvest failures, and, thanks to continued political resistance to birth control, a world population growing at a rate of more than 70 million a year. For

Ehrlich, the more optimistic scenario was that worldwide famines might hold off until the mid-1980s. Doubting that Americans would sacrifice their meat, cars, or hot showers for the sake of a more equitable distribution of resources, Ehrlich suggested forced birth control, including child lotteries and "spiking foreign food aid with antifertility drugs." Despite being technically and politically infeasible, Ehrlich's case for proactive population control touched a radicalized audience well aware that a viable contraceptive pill was now available. A fixture on the campus speakers' circuit, Ehrlich founded Zero Population Growth, a major organizer of the first Earth Day in 1970, and he wrote the introduction for the paperback edition of Harry Harrison's 1966 novel *Make Room! Make Room!*, which in turn became the 1973 hit movie *Soylent Green*—a nightmare about a vastly overcrowded planet in 2022. Publishing twenty-four articles and three books in the late '60s and early '70s—and cited many other times—Ehrlich clearly got around. And his alarmist message received respectful treatment in the more conservative media, as in a 1970 *Life* cover article on Zero Population Growth titled "A Thoughtful New Student Cause."[65]

The neo-Malthusian gloom received quasi-official support in a USDA report by the young economist Lester Brown, who warned that the United States could fill the widening gap between grain demand and supply only through 1984, at which point the developing world faced a possible doomsday scenario. The darkened mood infected even the customarily boosterish USDA *Yearbook of Agriculture*. In the 1969 edition, the Economic Research Service's chief economist, Rex Daly, appeared to contradict the volume's title, *Food for Us All,* when he pondered whether conventional agriculture could feed 6 billion by 2000. Like Lappé two years later, Daly allowed that if Americans "ever chose—or were forced" to give up meat entirely, the United States could feed four to five times as many people. While Daly doubted the situation would come to that, he did suggest that even a reversion to 1930 U.S. levels of animal food consumption would free up a significant amount of grain resources. With synthetic foods and vegetable substitutes "more widely used" in the future, Daly cautiously predicted a leveling off in domestic meat and dairy consumption by 2000. Ending on a note of uncharacteristic uncertainty (at least for a top USDA official), Daly cautioned against an unrestrained cornucopian faith. "In planning for the future, the costs of being too optimistic are great indeed." If "the best and the brightest" who staffed Washington in the 1960s were so depressed about Progress, the devolutionary spiral of "overshoot and collapse"—a phrase soon to be popularized by the globalist think tank Club of Rome—seemed increasingly plausible.[66]

Similarly bracing was the massive 1969 report *Resources and Man* from another otherwise cornucopian stalwart, the National Academy of Sciences. Sounding almost like Harrison Brown, Ehrlich, and the Paddocks, the report suggested that, at current growth rates, the earth's population could eventually reach 30 billion, virtually all of them near starvation. While the earth might be able to feed 10 billion people at a "decent" quality of life (mostly vegetarian), a world of 30 billion would have to be "intensely managed" (the dystopian caveat). While the Green Revolution—the cornucopians' best hope in the 1960s—might "buy time," the National Academy of Sciences still recommended radical restraint of population growth and resource consumption: "The Malthusian limits are more likely to be extended by recognizing their validity and doing something about them than by uninformed ridicule."[67]

The "buy time" argument was just about the best argument mainstream cornucopians could offer at this point. Whereas the Green Revolution had seemed the ultimate solution back in the 1950s, by the late 1960s, with the population projections so disturbing, it seemed just a momentary stopgap. Accepting the Nobel Peace Prize in 1970 for his pioneering work on wheat breeding, Norman Borlaug cautioned, "The Green Revolution has won a temporary success in man's war against hunger and deprivation; it has given man a breathing space. If fully implemented, the revolution can provide sufficient food for sustenance during the next three decades. But the frightening power of human reproduction must also be curbed; otherwise the successes of The Green Revolution will be ephemeral only." Borlaug thus asserted a rather big Malthusian "if": agricultural technology would feed the future *only if* accompanied by strong population planning. Similarly, Lester Brown insisted that the Green Revolution had tremendous potential to end hunger, but *only if* coupled with "enlightened policies," international cooperation, equitable trade, accessible markets, human rights, land reform—the basic ingredients of the egalitarian package. Calling for acceptance of "the idea of an interdependent world, a 'global village'" where "rich and poor nations alike" worked together, the former USDA economist sounded more romantic than Godwin and his countercultural successors.[68]

But what about algae, yeast, pills, and synthetics—those chemical panaceas once taken seriously by many leaders, from Winston Churchill to John Boyd-Orr? Such dreams did persist, but more on the margins of respectability. For example, in *The Next 200 Years* (1976) the Hudson

Institute's Herman Kahn predicted that by extending existing best practices and by exploring unconventional food sources (including yeast and algae for animal feed), world agriculture should *theoretically* be able to provide enough grain to support an American-style diet for 15 billion people in 2176. Leaving theory aside, Kahn also offered a somewhat more realistic scenario in which future Americans ate less meat and more single-cell proteins (algae, yeast), "super cereals" (highly fortified grains), and soy analogues. Barbara Ford's *Future Foods: Alternative Protein for the Year 2000* (1978) supported more research on single-celled proteins as an efficient substitute for grain-fed beef, which Ford predicted would become "a rarity in the year 2000."[69] During the nostalgic, back-to-nature swing of the 1970s, however, the dominant consumer culture firmly recoiled from the dystopian algae diet of *Soylent Green* and Kurt Vonnegut's *Breakfast of Champions* (both 1973).

Indeed, of the periods discussed so far, the 1970s was the most skeptical concerning purely cornucopian, technological fixes. Had time travel been possible, both Malthus and Godwin might have felt quite at home here, as both had so many ardent followers. But Condorcet would have felt lost in an era with so little faith in modernistic solutions. What was going on? Of the four worry-precipitating conditions—sudden inflation, environmental stresses, scary demographics, and cultural anxieties—the first two were most spectacularly associated with the energy crisis that peaked when protesting Middle Eastern oil producers cut production following the Arab-Israeli war of October 1973. "No event of the period following the Second World War had so sharp and pervasive impact on the world economy," wrote Brookings Institution economists Edward Fried and Charles Schultz in 1975. The sudden tripling of oil prices undermined a cheap industrial food policy dependent on cheap petroleum. That threat was compounded when blight and bad weather raised world food prices in 1972–74. Unprecedented sales of surplus North American grain to China and the Soviet Union drove prices up further. While American consumers' complaints about food inflation led the Nixon administration to impose temporary price controls on beef, the crisis was much worse in poor countries dependent on imports of both grain and the oil needed to grow the Green Revolution's chemical-dependent seeds. This was the context for USDA Secretary Earl Butz's infamous call on American farmers to plant "from fencerow to fencerow"—an encouragement to overproduce that eventually led to declining prices, Grain Belt depression, and fatter consumers.[70] Another Middle Eastern oil stoppage in 1979 (after the Iranian revolution) again sent petroleum prices soaring and left Americans stuck in long gas station lines. In the heady aftermath of the first Earth Day in 1970, the resource crisis seemed clear evidence that a wasteful consumer economy was straining the world's carrying capacity.

In this setting, the Club of Rome's appeals to accept what it termed the "limits to growth" and to cut consumption had considerable resonance, especially in light of persistently dreary population projections. If the present population and consumption trends continued, *The Limits to Growth* (1972) concluded, the earth's natural limits might be reached within one hundred years, to be followed by a "sudden and uncontrollable decline." Boasting computerized "systems analysis" of the data, the book sold 9 million copies in twenty-nine languages—in part because it seemed to give state-of-the-art statistical support to so many other contemporary forecasts. Attempting to contradict the doomsayers, Roger Revelle, director of population studies at Harvard, suggested that the world might feed as many as 40 billion people, but Revelle's $700 billion price tag for the required investment in rural infrastructure was not likely to uplift many spirits, especially as the astounding bill would cater only a *vegetarian* diet. Moreover, the world was evidently not inclined to invest, as major donors cut agricultural development assistance by half over the following decade.[71] The cornucopians' utopian caveat notwithstanding, there was little collective will to fund a better future for all. The inability or unwillingness of central governments to take adequate steps furthered cultural anxieties about a world seemingly out of control. And with the American government stymied by political scandal (Watergate), defeated in Vietnam, and defied in the Middle East, it was easy to doubt that familiar hegemonic institutions could solve difficult problems.

But however bad things looked, events were *not* quite out of control. When catastrophic food wars and ecosystem collapses did not materialize, the apocalyptic mood of the 1970s diminished in the 1980s, whose political culture was dominated by the optimistic conservativism of Ronald Reagan and Margaret Thatcher. Energy and food prices stabilized after the spikes of the 1970s. Gains in world food production continued to outpace population growth, which actually slowed slightly (from 2.06 percent a year in 1965 to 1.74 percent in 1985.) The fact that viable birth control was now more acceptable and available may have helped to defuse worries about the population bomb. As birth rates fell even in those perennial "basket cases," China and India, the alarmist treatment of the "population problem" clearly tapered off in the popular press. At the same time, using more land, irrigation, tractors, and chemicals, the world's farmers produced more grain per capita in 1985 than in any year before or since. Thanks in part to such gains, world meat production nearly doubled between 1965 and 1985.[72]

And despite the appearance of chaos, some institutions did coalesce and respond even during the trying 1970s, which were fertile times for the formation of think tanks dedicated to studying food and population issues, sometimes with a clear ideological orientation. Neo-Malthusian environmentalists found their home in Lester Brown's Worldwatch Institute, founded in 1974. Heirs of Godwin's emphasis on egalitarian solutions for hunger were served by Frances Moore Lappé's Institute for Food and Development Policy (Food First), established in 1975 with the profits from *Diet for a Small Planet*. While the USDA continued to be the most productive source for cornucopian views, those seeking ultra-combative assertions of high-tech free market optimism could also read the numerous reports of CAST, the Council for Agricultural Science and Technology, founded in 1972. Somewhat more liberal were the sixteen research centers supported by CGIAR, the Consultative Group on International Agricultural Research (founded in 1971), whose approach to sustainable development might be characterized as humanistic technology guided by conscientious government and responsible capitalism— somewhat close to Condorcet's original formula. Perhaps the most influential of these centers inside the Washington Beltway was the International Food Policy Research Institute (1975), with its diverse mix of economic, agronomic, demographic, and anthropological analysis. The same period also gave birth to many university centers and programs in environmental studies, sustainable agriculture, nutritional ecology, population studies, and so on. The creation of such institutions may well have helped to diminish anxiety about the future, for even if the conservative governments of the 1980s were doing little or nothing to avert the apocalypse, at least these problems were being studied by organizations that provided safe cover for concerned activists.

It is unclear whether the relative lull of the 1980s reflected genuine, widespread belief in the Reagan-Thatcher version of the cornucopian future or simply exhaustion after the intensive worrying of the 1960s and 1970s. In any case, the lull was indeed temporary, for the 1990s saw a definite increase in futuristic angst, at least as measured by that decade's plethora of predictive books, reports, and journalistic articles—many written by the same think tankers who had been largely ignored in the myopic 1980s. Unlike earlier periods of concern, this one was not precipitated by an immediate food or population-related crisis. Energy and food prices were lower than ever when adjusted for inflation, population growth had slowed markedly, and "compassion fatigue" had reduced the press's attention to persistent Third World famines.[73] In part the speculative impulse was compelled by an artificial deadline—the approaching year 2000, long a target date for futuristic thought. But despite the hype, the much anticipated new millennium threatened to be something of a bust. As part III shows, when people in the 1990s glanced beyond New Year's Day 2000, surprisingly few forecasts took an unabashedly modernistic stance, even with the short-lived dot.com bubble. Dystopians ruled the science fiction market, and think tank discourse was not much more upbeat. Chastened by too many unintended consequences from high-tech panaceas—including the spectacularly costly failure of computer programmers to set post-Y2K dates properly—few now expected a push-button future of flying cars, meal pills, or chemurgic industrial farms. As numerous journalists observed, the Jetsons no longer captivated the imagination, except as a nostalgic example of the postwar "Populuxe" era, when many people *had* seriously believed in technological utopias.[74] Savvy marketers of the '90s knew that almost anything "new and improved" had to be cloaked in a familiar, preferably "traditional" wrapping—the "recombinant" formula favored by late-twentieth-century consumer culture.

In line with the jaundiced "retro" mood, many forecasts recycled familiar themes, especially those dealing with the prospects for animal foods. Malthusians were especially skillful at replenishing old ideas with new statistics. In the 1990s, the most unrelenting Malthusian was Cornell University entomologist David Pimentel. Crunching familiar rates of feed-grain conversion, energy use, resource depletion, and population growth, Pimentel calculated that the United States produced enough grain and soy in 1994 to feed 400 million people, but considering the ecological costs, this highly industrialized grain production was unsustainable. Looking ahead to 2050, Pimentel projected that a more "ecocompatible" (largely vegetarian) agriculture might support 210 million Americans—exactly half the likely U.S. population. Pimentel estimated that if Americans wanted to live sustainably at their *present* consumption level, with only slight reductions in meat and dairy, they would need to cut the U.S. population to under 100 million by 2080. As for the world, his most optimistic scenario for 2050 envisioned a world population stabilized at 7.8 billion people who might be adequately fed if the wealthy ate less animal food. Pimentel's more pessimistic "business as usual" scenario projected a 2050 population of 13 billion fed along lines already well explored by much neo-Malthusian science fiction: teeming dystopias reliant on synthetic and/or "coolie" rations (e.g., *Soylent Green, Blade Runner, Brazil*). But an "optimal" world population—with enough animal protein for all—would be less than 2 billion people.[75]

Many of these assumptions and fears were reiterated by another well-quoted pessimist of the 1990s, Worldwatch's Lester Brown. After venturing cautious optimism for the Green Revolution in his 1970 book, *Seeds of Change,* most of Brown's later papers, speeches, and books offered impressively documented variations on the old theme of ecological unsustainability, especially of meat. In *Full House: Reassessing the Earth's Carrying Capacity* (1994), Brown (with Hal Kane) had little doubt that the "availability [of meat] per person will decline indefinitely as population grows." And like all the eco-accountants before him, Brown based his assessments of carrying capacity on how much grain was converted to animal products. At the U.S. level, the world might adequately support 2.5 billion; at the Italian level, 5 billion; and at the Indian level, 10 billion. But in his often-cited *Who Will Feed China?* (1995) Brown recast the old fear of the Asiatic (i.e., meatless) diet by suggesting that China's overpopulation might threaten the future *not* because the country would be too *poor* (the old Yellow Peril) but because it would be too *rich* (the new Asian Miracle). As China, and East Asia in general, prospered, its citizens would move "up the food chain" to consume more animal products. With 1.2 billion Chinese, and the number still growing, that would be a lot of eggs, pork, and quarter-pounders. Brown doubted that the earth could supply enough grain to feed that hunger, especially given deteriorating agricultural resources and booming population in the world's poorest regions.[76]

If Pimentel and Brown were the most articulate and statistically savvy Malthusian heirs, it was Frances Moore Lappé's Food First that best maintained the Godwinian position. Like the neo-Malthusians, the egalitarians at Food First agreed that the world's ecosystems had limits, especially for producing environmentally luxurious red meat and tropical produce. In light of the Green Revolution's failure to help small farmers or the world's poorest consumers, Lappé's group questioned whether corporate agribusiness could feed a growing population equitably. Like the socialist utopians who followed Godwin, Food First argued that the world could produce more than enough food for everyone indefinitely if we shared it better. Achieving equity would require rejection of the dominant definition of freedom as the ability "to choose among thirty brands of breakfast cereal and twenty of shampoo." Rather, feeding the world entailed a "redistribution of decision-making power," and with that, "a redistribution of the economic, social, and political resources which make the exercise of such power possible." In practical terms, global social justice meant less cheap, grain-fed meat and fewer tropical imports for the rich.[77]

It is testimony to the strength of the carrying-capacity paradigm that even many cornucopians tacitly acknowledged limits to how much meat the world could afford if it became more crowded. While optimists still believed that modern agriculture could feed everyone *adequately,* few went so far as to claim that everyone in the future would eat *like Americans.* This was certainly the case for Paul Waggoner's *How Much Land Can Ten Billion People Spare for Nature?* (1994). Reporting for the resolutely pro-agribusiness Council for Agricultural Science and Technology, Waggoner offered one of the more widely quoted positive scenarios of the 1990s. Yet even after applying every "smart farming" technique currently "on the shelf," Waggoner concluded that industrial agriculture could presently support 10 billion *vegetarians.* With some scientific breakthroughs (especially in biotechnology) *and* a reduction in red meat consumption by some affluent Westerners, Waggoner hoped that the world of 2050 might be able to feed itself without a serious ecological breakdown. Such projections, while considerably less dreary than the worst Malthusian scenarios, did little to hearten the most ravenous carnivores. True, the world might not starve, but it might also be a good idea if we considered a few substitutes.[78] A similar sort of ambivalence pervaded the largely cornucopian projections of *2025: Scenarios of US and Global Society Reshaped by Science and Technology* (1997) by the widely respected futurist consulting firm Coates and Jarrett. While the affluent 1.3 billion of "World 1" would enjoy many benefits from "smart" technologies—including nutraceuticals, genetically redesigned low-fat animals, tasty synthetics, and highly automated kitchens—the less favored 5.1 billion of "World 2" would "get along" on a much more traditional, though generally adequate, food supply system. Worse, the poorest 2.0 billion of "World 3" would "strike a hard line" of hopeless, endemic famine. Dividing up the world this way—a segmentation found in the more sophisticated global forecasts—was a tacit acknowledgment that the cornucopian goodies lovingly described in 85 percent of the book might be reserved for just 15 percent of the world's people.[79]

Coates and Jarrett, along with Waggoner, thus seemed to accept considerable limits on the old cornucopian dreams of feeding everyone well.

Not so for economist Julian Simon, who marched resolutely toward the twenty-first century carrying the banner of nineteenth-century laissez-faire liberalism. For Simon there was no crisis as he marshaled numerous statistics suggesting that life had never been so good for so many people. As evidence, he argued that food prices, relative to wages, had actually fallen to a tenth of what they were in Malthus's day, despite massive population increases; thus, in real terms, American wheat was much cheaper in 1980 than in 1800, even as the U.S. population had soared from 5 to 225 million. Having won a famous 1980 bet with Paul Ehrlich that, despite population growth, metal prices would fall over ten years, the University of Maryland business professor went on to challenge virtually every tenet of the environmentalist litany: soil erosion, species extinction, water and air pollution, energy shortages, pesticide poisoning, diminishing agricultural returns, and so on. As for feeding the future, there was no problem that technological ingenuity, nurtured by a free market, could not solve. "We now have the technology to feed, clothe, and supply energy to an ever-growing population for the next 7 billion years," Simon proclaimed. And, contrary to conventional wisdom, population growth would actually increase the food supply, for with more people would come more ideas and inventions. "If population had never grown," Simon lectured environmentalist Norman Myers in 1994, "instead of the pleasant lunch you had, you would have been out chasing rabbits and roots."[80] Simon's use of historical statistics was so uniformly positive that even his admirers admitted to some skepticism, but legions still turned out to see the enthusiastic "Doomslayer" combat his foes. Like the Terminator, he seemed unfazed by overwhelmingly unfavorable odds. Or was he academia's George Jetson—admired for the irrelevance of his archaic views to fin de siècle troubles?

The future did pose new questions not entirely answered by Simon's breezy extrapolation of historic triumphs. In particular, the post-2000 era promised—or, depending on one's view, threatened—to be driven by three Gs: globalization, genetic engineering, and the greenhouse effect. As before, ideology influenced the interpretation of these drivers. Cornucopians applauded globalization as the extension of free trade and capitalism, celebrated genetic engineering as a way to feed the hungry, and either dismissed the evidence of global warming (the more conservative stance) or saw it as a great opportunity for a free market exchange of pollution credits (the more liberal one). Malthusians cited the greenhouse effect as evidence of world population saturation, ridiculed the giddy extrapolations of the biotechnologists, and worried that globalization might release a flood of ecological and economic refugees. And egalitarians blasted the corporate control of genes, viewed global warming as a reflection of worldwide economic inequities, and hoped for solutions through "globalization from below"—the spread of internationalized resistance. To be sure, not every forecast fell neatly into one of these familiar boxes, for as the next chapter suggests, the categories blurred somewhat during the 1990s. Still, the continuities in the debate are remarkable—and cry out for further analysis.

THREE

THE DEEP STRUCTURE OF THE DEBATE

Having identified the conditions that precipitate food security worries—inflation, demographic spikes, environmental crises, cultural anxieties—it is time to take stock of the enduring conventions and patterns, the deep structure, of the debate about the future of food. While many historians might hesitate to speak in generalities about a two-century period, such generalizations may be appropriate here. For one thing, in the long view of food production, the past two hundred years may be seen as a single modern era characterized by agricultural industrialization, consolidation, and globalization. For another, participants in this debate have created continuities by constantly citing or repeating arguments and data from previous cycles of the debate—the closed loop of cross-references that becomes apparent only when a debate is traced over several reiterations. Ideas persist well past their original context, Donald Worster argues in *Nature's Economy,* his multicentury survey of ecological thinking: "Once born, ideas tend to pursue a life of their own; they can extend beyond their origins to become shapes and molders of perception elsewhere. Sometimes they survive as anachronisms in their own environment." For example, Edward East's estimate that it takes 2.5 acres to support one person survived over several decades despite the changing agricultural realities. Another example is the enduring apocalyptic and utopian motif in Western thought—what I. F. Clarke calls the pattern of expectation. As Howard McCurdy demonstrates in his history of space policy, *Space and the American Imagination,* the strongest policy debates are a result

of the interaction between immediate crises—"precipitating events"—
and long-run archetypal fantasies, both positive and negative. The more
deeply rooted these expressions of "imagination," McCurdy argues, the
more vibrant and enduring the policy debate. While space fantasies are
quite deep seated, there is no concern more deeply rooted in the human
imagination than having enough to eat. "The struggle for food has always
been the chief preoccupation of mankind," John Boyd-Orr observed in
1953.[1]

COMMON DENOMINATORS

We can begin our examination of these long-lasting patterns with several enduring points of agreement among the contenders. Here again,
the primary actors are the Malthusians and the cornucopians, with the
egalitarians angling for entry into the fray but not generally winning equal
time on the floor.

Urgency

To the extent that people have worried at all about the future, they have
been unusual. Most have been well-credentialed, often highly acclaimed,
experts in a particular field who at a crucial midpoint in their careers became concerned about the world's ability to feed itself in the future. Frus-
trated with the myopic specialization characteristic of the academy, corporations, and bureaucracies, they sought an interdisciplinary, generalist
perspective on global problems. In one of the earliest calls for a more in-
clusive social history, Malthus blamed scholarly inattention to population
cycles on the narrow, upper-class, courtly biases of conventional historians, who routinely ignored what ordinary people were experiencing.
Condorcet, too, thought elite state politics to be an insignificant historical driver compared to the role of basic human needs, particularly the
pursuit of personal convenience and utility. Just after World War I, economist John Maynard Keynes asserted that understanding "the great
events of history" requires more study of "secular changes"—such as a
growing population's need for food—and less focus on "the follies of
statesmen or the fanaticism of atheists."[2] Such claims are echoed today
among those who advocate a "bottom-up" approach to the study of history and society.

Contemplating the complexity of the world food system, most futurists have agreed with William Vogt's 1948 call for a "holistic approach"

to replace the "static, mechanical, piecemeal" methods of conventional analysis. Vogt's willingness to cross boundaries produced many bold connections, as when he noted what would later be called the "ecological wake"—the downstream consequences—of expanded wheat consumption: "Today's white bread may force a break in the levees and flood New Orleans next spring." And to illustrate the interconnectedness of the global food chain, Vogt observed: "The famous steaks and chops at Simpson's carried with them the nitrogen, potassium, phosphorus, and other soil minerals from half the world." Seeing such links was necessary to overcome consumer "obliviousness" regarding the "globe-girdling" food system, Edward East argued in 1924. "Our daily life is a trip around the world, yet the wonder of it gives us not a single thrill." East worried about this lack of wonder, for, like William and Paul Paddock writing in 1967, he attributed the lack of concern about impending worldwide famine to the plodding narrowness of mainstream science. Likewise, in *Tough Choices: Facing the Challenge of Food Scarcity* (1996), Lester Brown argued that understanding global ecological constraints required a comprehensive, interdisciplinary approach far beyond the limited, linear assumptions of conventional economics.[3] In fact, in all of these tracts the reader is treated to an ingenious and mind-expanding integration of demography and nutrition, politics and agronomy, sociology and chemistry, science fiction and classical mythology.

Much like Plato's utopian philosopher king, these futurists felt obliged to employ their expertise in the public arena. Or as another thinker, Francis Bacon, put it, "In the theatre of human life it is only for Gods and angels to be spectators." As public intellectuals and science popularizers, they wrote essays geared for an educated middle class audience—sometimes risking the scorn of their more narrowly focused colleagues for making their ideas so accessible. Leaving aside their think tank credentials, some even fit the Frank Capra–esque version of the idealistic scholar-citizen—eccentric, rumpled, ever-ready to upset deans and politicians for the sake of the greater good. Take, for example, Harrison Brown. Before conducting atomic research for the Manhattan Project during World War II, Brown worked his way through graduate school by fronting a dance band and tending bar, then went on to quick tenure at prestigious Cal Tech, where he started "brooding" about the dual threats of the nuclear and population bombs. He wrote *The Challenge of Man's Future* "on a porch overlooking Ocho Rios Bay, Jamaica," and after its publication spent the next thirty years organizing symposia and teach-ins about humanity's future for several generations of scientists, students, and policy-oriented businessmen. In a 1954 interview with *Saturday Review*, Brown expounded the missionary, interdisciplinary credo common to most futurists: "I believe that our [educational] system turns out far too many narrow specialists who have difficulty communicating with their fellow men." One of Brown's goals at Cal Tech was to encourage scientists and engineers to think comprehensively about the future, and a 1986 tribute credited Brown with laying much of the academic groundwork for environmental studies.[4]

Similar examples of the prophetic public intellectual pattern abound, starting with Malthus, Godwin, and Condorcet themselves, all of whom departed from established niches to take risky, even life-threatening positions on big questions. The pioneering chemist Justus von Liebig frequently angered fellow scholars with his willingness to extrapolate way beyond the scope of his laboratory, as did his successor, Marcelin Berthelot, whose extravagant predictions for synthetic foods frequently found their way into the popular magazines. The primary players in the 1920s cycle—Keynes (economist), East (geneticist), Raymond Pearl (entomologist), Oliver Baker and Lewis Gray (agricultural economists), and Edwin Slosson (science journalist)—were all formally trained academics whose concern about population trends induced them to venture outside safe institutional cocoons to speculate about long-run prospects and solutions. Like Vogt, who moved from ornithology to environmentalism, and Harrison Brown, who shifted from geology to world systems theory, most of the post–World War II analysts also outran their professional training when they took on public prophet roles. Julian Huxley (biologist), John Boyd-Orr (nutritionist), Samuel Ordway (lawyer), Karl Sax (botanist), Georg Borgstrom (plant physiologist), Paul Ehrlich and David Pimentel (entomologists), Lester Brown (agricultural economist), Julian Simon (economist), the Paddocks (agronomists), and Frances Moore Lappé (social work student) all sought public roles as policy agenda setters and claims makers.[5]

Even as these thinkers discarded disciplinary constraints, previous professional prestige often lent considerable weight to their new publicist/visionary roles, even if they did not always know what they were talking about. In what might be called the Nobel Laureate syndrome, spectacular success in one field sometimes led them to make unsupported claims in others. Cornucopian chemist Liebig's missionary zeal to defy Malthus induced him to back numerous doomed experiments with artificial food products. Sir William Crookes's scientific reputation enhanced the impact of his dire wheat projections, which, however, were based on unfounded assumptions about diet, agriculture, and economics. In *The Geography of Hunger*, FAO official Josue de Castro made imaginative connections between Third World hunger and Western imperialism, and also offered dubious generalizations about a link between protein deficiency and sexual drives. After winning the Nobel Peace Prize as the first FAO director, John Boyd-Orr spent some of his cultural capital supporting flaky proposals to develop synthetic and microbial foods. And Garrett Hardin's undisputed skills in evolutionary biology did not always transfer to his Darwinist dismissals of medical intervention in poor countries as self-defeating "death control."[6]

Because these professionals-turned-publicists often wrote their best-known books, articles, and speeches as new converts to the public cause, what they had to say carried a profound sense of mission, certainty, and urgency. Choosing what Phyllis Piotrow calls the "activist" path, they expanded, simplified, and sometimes exaggerated an issue in order to gain attention. In addition to defying their colleagues, they also had to battle a public complacency that was encouraged, in the United States at least, by agricultural gluts and relatively cheap food. Perhaps the best way to get on the policy-setting agenda was to claim an emergency, or, as Harvey Brooks puts it, turn a slowly evolving, barely noticeable "creeping crisis" into an imminent "traumatic crisis" that could not be ignored.[7]

The titles of their works often suggest this sense of impending emergency: for example, "Shall the World Starve?" (J. R. Smith), *Deserts on the March* (Paul Sears), *The White Man's Dilemma* (John Boyd-Orr), *Standing Room Only* (Karl Sax), and—from perhaps the best recent practitioner of the "wake-up call"—Lester Brown's *Saving the Planet, Full House, Who Will Feed China?* and *Tough Choices*.[8] Urgency led to an "either/or" millennium or apocalypse outlook: either we choose to go the way I advocate or disaster awaits. We are at the crossroads, the great divide, the watershed. There is no middle ground, and no time to lose. When Oliver Baker wrote that Americans of 1923 were "at the turning point" in their nation's history, he could just as well have been speaking the mind of Harrison Brown in 1954 or Lester Brown in 1994. And these prophets would have agreed with Baker that present policy decisions will "affect not only our agricultural progress but also our national welfare for a century to come."[9] Exacerbating this crisis sensibility, as always, was the perennially perceived threat to a meat-based diet.

The rhetoric of mobilization took several forms. Malthusians frequently posed the forced choice: either we can choose to reduce births and conserve resources or, as Pimentel put it in 1997, "the harsh reality of nature will impose a drastic solution for us." East phrased it just as sharply in 1924: "This [birth] rate will be cut down. The only question is whether it will be cut down because we wish it or because we cannot help it." "Make no mistake about it," Ehrlich warned in 1968, "the imbalance will be redressed." Recent disasters—droughts, famines, riots, wars—could then be cited as harbingers of even worse "checks" to come. Egalitarians agreed on the inevitability of violent revolution if social inequities were not addressed soon. Cornucopians, too, favored militant metaphors, speaking of the "war" against malnutrition, hunger, erosion, Marx, and Malthus himself. Liebig set the tone in 1862 when he warned that unless Europeans adopted his soil replenishment ideas immediately, all-out food warfare was imminent: "In their self-preservation nations will be compelled to slaughter and destroy each other in cruel wars. These are not vague and dark prophecies nor the dreams of a sick mind, for science does not prophecy, it calculates. It is not if, but when, that is uncertain." So also, a 1934 *Popular Science Monthly* likened white-uniformed food chemists—Liebig's progeny—to a "crack army that fights in the laboratory," "stands guard over the nation's food supply," and "is winning the battle for better foods for us all."[10]

Jeremiads also served well to overcome consumer complacency, as in William Vogt's 1948 pronouncement that "The Day of Judgment is at hand. There are too many people in the world for its limited resources to provide a high standard of living." And in light of the world population's rapid doubling rate—as Malthus knew well, compound rates multiply quickly—policy makers could not wait for the population growth to level off on its own. Noting that the world had gained as many people between 1950 and 1990 as had existed in the millions of years before 1950, cornucopian agricultural scientist Derek Tribe read "the writing on the wall": "Any dispassionate analysis of the increases now occurring [in 1994] in the world's population must inevitably result in consternation and a degree of alarm." Tribe's solution was a second and even third Green Revolution. Enlisting the rhetoric of urgency, biotechnology advocates asserted that genetic engineering techniques could dramatically shorten the time needed to develop the miracle seeds and magic bullets ("functional" foods) needed to win the war against overpopulation and hunger. And given the pressing need for immediate and unprecedented responses, all sides freely used the word "revolutionary" to describe their proposed solutions, whether political or technological.[11]

The Battle of Statistics

If metaphors of military mobilization framed the contest of opinions, statistics were the primary ammunition as combatants sought to subdue opponents (and civilian bystanders) with a barrage of extrapolations based on current tendencies—especially estimates of unused arable land, maximum yields, likely birth and death rates, grain-to-meat conversion ratios, and per capita intake of calories, vitamins, and protein. Global carrying capacity was voiced as the ultimate bottom line, as in geographer E. G. Ravenstein's 1891 estimate that the "total possible population" of the world was 5,994,000,000, and C. T. De Wit's more hopeful 1967 calculation that, based on "total photosynthetic potential," the earth could support a trillion people. While optimistic biochemist William Reville heralded a 30 percent increase in overall "global caloric availability" between 1930 and 1990, Ehrlich's far more pessimistic accounting of the "human appropriation of the products of photosynthesis" concluded that the earth could not support much more than the existing population of 1986. Such attempts to account for every unit of energy and organic matter illustrate what Joseph Amato identifies as the quintessentially modern obsession with "the small and the invisible." And with increased scientific attention to ever more minute particles—especially microbes and atoms—came ever more precise instruments to measure and count them. Since the late nineteenth century, Amato argues, scientists have successfully identified civilization with "the control of miniature things"—Alfred North Whitehead's "manufactured unseen."[12] Control of the microbe enabled the population explosion of the twentieth century. For nutritionists, ecologists, and economists assessing the impact of this demographic revolution, the preferred units of measurement were the kilocalorie and milligram.

Agriculture is not physics or microbiology, however, for its measurements are less precise, its assumptions and variables maddeningly complex and subjective. And the range of variation is worsened by misuse of the dangerous caveat, "if present trends continue." Reading current statistics as tea leaves—choice harbingers of things to come—oracles confidently touted their own projections as based on solid, long-term trends while belittling their opponents' numbers as momentary, short-term fluctuations. Distinguishing between the two was not easy, for as Garrett Hardin quipped, "sequence" was all too easily extrapolated into "trend," which is "half brother to Destiny." Impressed by the alarming growth spurt since the 1950s, one 1970 analysis might conclude that world population could top 30 billion by 2500, while an extrapolation from the less fertile 1930s might forecast under a billion by the same date. Malthus—the consummate catastrophist—projected infinite doubling rates and unlimited food inflation based on late-eighteenth-century anomalies. Similarly, when grain prices spiked in the mid-1990s, Lester Brown announced the arrival of a new century of food shortages. Cornucopians did much the same. When farmers responded by overproducing wheat in the late 1990s, editorials at *The Economist* and *Wall Street Journal* touted one year's low prices as proof of perennial abundance.[13]

With the dominant culture so bonded to the gods of calculation, the press often presented these questionable numbers as scientific gospel. Hunger policy analyst Peter Eisinger observes that issues are more likely to make the news agenda if they are "countable"—a fact of public-policy life that encouraged even that most romantically based of disciplines, ecology, to become increasingly quantitative by the mid-twentieth century. Yet even as forecasters sought the high ground of the undisputed long-term trend, the brief shelf-life of most news stories may have given greater attention to short-term fluctuations—especially the negative turns. Thus, one year of sharply higher food prices due to drought or war might make a greater impression than five years of glut. Similarly, photos of babies with bloated bellies in a famine-stricken region had far more weight than images of well-fed children in a neighboring province.[14]

Eisinger also questions the value of statistics that lack a clear historical baseline for comparison—and in the case of food production and consumption, there are few reliable long-term numbers. If we did not have reliable counts of U.S. hunger until the 1990s, how accurate were earlier estimates of *world* hunger? So also, in judging overall trends one must read the fine print carefully. While optimists might point to spectacular increases in *yields per acre* between 1950 and 2000, pessimists might bemoan a decline in the *rate of increase*. Conclusions also differed based on the historical periods being compared. Touting progress, cornucopian Julian Simon boasted that the ratio between food prices and wages in 1990 was one-tenth of what they were in Malthus's time—an interval of almost two hundred years—while his Malthusian antagonist Norman Myers lamented an apparent plateau in grain production since 1985, a much shorter time frame. Even with identical time frames, judgments can vary sharply based on *what* is being counted. In the late twentieth century, cornucopians celebrated the continued decline of *grain* prices, while Malthusians worried about a simultaneous spike in *seafood* prices. In the 1920s, Malthusians, concerned that population was outpacing agriculture, cited a slight leveling off in grain production between 1900 and 1920, while optimists pointed to the rapid rate of technological innovation over those same years.[15] Each side, moreover, prized one set of important indicators while dismissing the opponents' set as anomalies. Thus Malthusians assumed that population increases would continue ad infinitum while rates of technological innovation would not. For cornucopians the opposite seemed self-evident: technology would keep improving indefinitely while birth rates would surely stabilize. So much of the debate surrounded the general *direction* of things—up or down—but it was not always clear *which things, compared to what,* and *since when.*

Questionable Assumptions

Behind the statistics lurked subjective, often moralistic assumptions about diet, human adaptability and creativity, the nature of the good life, and political change. Even the most interdisciplinary think tankers rarely ventured much beyond their own values, paradigms, and experiences. This tendency to generalize and universalize one's own worldview was well-established by the original debaters, as when Malthus asserted that the "passion between the sexes" would *always* outpace the ability to produce food, or when Condorcet argued that the search for convenience would *inevitably* lead humanity in the direction of greater rationality and democracy. As fiction writers know well, reality is much messier than such absolutes suggest. Malthus might not know what to make of a world that has more sexual passion *and* grain than it can safely handle, nor would Condorcet be able to comprehend a world where the proliferation of fast foods—the cutting edge of convenience—has outrun the development of rational democracy.

As chapter 1 suggests, deep-seated prejudices against grain-based cuisines have shaped basic views of progress and development. While the priority accorded to animal foods may have some scientific rationale, there is no doubt that the animal industry has also had a hand in shaping both dietary advice and the income-based "nutrition transition" to meat and other luxury foods. Yet few forecasts factored in the way special interests could influence a particular outcome. Moreover, in the social construction of what constituted real food, certain grains, particularly wheat, were prized over others, such as corn, rice, rye, and potatoes. Such prejudices directly shaped the estimates of the earth's carrying capacity, for some of the less-favored grains actually yield more calories per acre and per unit of energy than wheat. While Sir William Crookes venerated wheat as "the most sustaining food grain of the great Caucasian race," critic Joseph Davis observed that "excellent foodstuff though it is, wheat merits no such encomium." Writing at the start of the "Dirty Thirties," Davis well knew that the Western wheat fetish may even have *reduced* the earth's carrying capacity, as it encouraged a feverish overexpansion of dry farming into marginal areas at great cost to native ecosystems and economies. Similarly, modern grain-fed meat was more ecologically extravagant than traditional free-range, just as the modern American fetish for "fresh" milk disadvantaged smaller but often more sustainable farms that produced cultured dairy products.[16]

Calculations based on minimal caloric (and protein) requirements are also questionable, as they might favor males over females, young over old, large over small, field laborers over office clerks. By exaggerating daily needs, some assessments have overestimated the extent of hunger in the world. Here again, political considerations have inflated requirements, as many interests—governmental, industrial, scientific, and professional—have gained from overstated claims of malnutrition, particularly after World War II, when modern farmers produced more grain than they could sell and their governments looked for ways to gain power by giving it away to the hungry Third World. The variability of such standards is demonstrated by the steady decline in recommended daily intakes, from an average of 3,500 to 4,000 calories in 1900 to just over half of that today.[17]

Furthermore, while calories do matter, all calories are not equal in either production requirements or nutritional benefits. Thanks to increased sugar production, many more calories became available to the British working class, but they were not particularly good calories. Similarly, as vegetarians have insisted for centuries, it takes many more calories of agricultural input to produce five hundred calories of steak than the same calories of bean burritos. Furthermore, as egalitarians have argued, estimates of total availability do not account for actual distribution or consumption. Yet ending hunger is not *just* a matter of redistributing calories. Even if the earth can physically feed everyone, agribusiness lacks the incentives to do so. In practical terms, the food industry profits mainly by concentrating calories into highly processed, value-added steaks and snacks. But once these calories are bundled into more profitable products for an affluent market, they are less available to the poor. Such value-added processed products also waste many calories as they are moved from farms to factories and then to kitchens and beyond. Joel Cohen notes: "As much as

40 percent of food may be lost between production and consumption, including a loss of 10–15 percent after food leaves retail establishments." In short, calculations of the total food supply require a comprehensive audit of the global food chain. Production of calories is only the start.[18]

Per capita estimates of available agricultural land have been equally simplistic. Cornucopians have often inflated the earth's carrying capacity by arguing how little land is actually used by the current population, without taking into consideration the quality of the land. For example, in a recent critique of the environmentalist "litany," Bjorn Lomborg argues that, with only 68 people per square kilometer, Egypt is not at all overpopulated but this means ignoring the fact that most of those square kilometers are desert. On the other hand, Malthusians might come to the opposite conclusion by factoring in only the very best land, as in John Bongaarts's counter that Egypt has "an extraordinary" 2,000 people per square kilometer of *irrigated* land. When East estimated that the optimal (i.e., North American) lifestyle required 2.5 acres per capita (and thus the earth's carrying capacity was 5.2 billion people), he dismissed more labor-intensive societies as "slavish." Racism aside, such calculations ignored the myriad variables that actually determine yields, especially the availability of water, fertilizer, better seeds, pest control tools, and cheap labor. While overestimating farmland requirements, East also underestimated the real estate needed for American-style housing, transportation, leisure, clothing, and such. According to Garrett Hardin, such "ghost acreage" totaled as much as nine acres per person. Similarly, Hardin calculated that if all energy inputs are included, the average American needed not 2,300 calories a day but more like 230,000. The food supply was only one of many restraints on the planet's carrying capacity.[19]

Built into the predictions of many of these forecasters is the assumption that modern consumer capitalism cast the mold for the optimal Good Life. Thus they had difficulty imagining radical alternatives except as negative and dystopian. Unwilling to sacrifice an affluent lifestyle for a larger population, Hardin dichotomized the options into either the nightmare of Calcutta or the paradise of an affluent California suburb: "Should we just drift toward a world population of, say, 30 billion people . . . in which everyone walks or rides a bicycle and is often hungry; or should we strive for a lesser population (perhaps half a billion) in which a large minority can enjoy motor cars and plenty of gourmet food?" In this, Hardin echoed fellow Malthusian Edward A. Ross, who in 1927 worried that overpopulation would force the West back to a simpler, "Oriental" life of "ignorance, superstition, and peasantism."[20] Until 1970 or so, only a few stray conservationists and vegetarian socialists resisted such all-or-nothing thinking and were willing to forego *some* modern conveniences and comforts in order to make *some* resources stretch further.

Channeling expectations and hopes along narrow lines has obscured the actual alternatives, which are in fact complex. As Cohen ably demonstrates, determining how many people the earth can support requires consideration and sorting out of numerous value-laden questions, almost all of them fiercely contested. For example:

- *How many at what average level of material well-being?* People live at widely variable levels of comfort, ranging from simple straw houses with mud floors to five-bedroom penthouses with Persian carpets.

- *How many with what distribution of material well-being?* As vegetarians have pointed out, the world can support far more people if the available calories are distributed evenly in the form of a simple grain-based diet for all.

- *How many with what technology?* A world of SUVs obviously supports far fewer people than a world of bicycles and footpaths.

- *How many with what domestic and international political, economic, and demographic institutions?* The nature, structure, and competence of human organizations affect the earth's carrying capacity. Well-organized, democratically governed agencies that care about ordinary people may deal more effectively with crises than do authoritarian kleptocracies.

- *How many with what variability or stability?* Do we want a steady, predictable food supply or are we willing to tolerate cycles of boom and bust? Stability requires greater resources.

- *How many with what risk or robustness?* We could probably handle more people if we were willing to tolerate greater risks— as, for example, settlement in flood plains and other hazardous zones.

- *How many for how long?* We can plan for twenty years or a thousand. The latter figure might reduce the carrying capacity, as we would be more cautious—as in the old Iroquois injunction to consider the next seven generations when making decisions.[21]

Few forecasts have accounted for even a handful of these "soft" variables. Most mainstream analysts have assumed there is one "objective" answer to the carrying capacity question, ignoring the possibility, for instance, that some of us might want to scale back for the sake of the future generations, or that, under the pressure of events, humans might adapt more quickly than assumed. Those desiring to consider such scenarios have generally had to look to the marginal realms of the debate: to utopian radicalism or speculative fiction.

Wrong Predictions: Things (Not) to Come

Inevitably, given the uncertain variables, rigid assumptions, and inadequate data, forecasts have generally proved wrong, particularly those concerning the prospects for the start of the new millennium, which had long been the focus of so many predictions. Few projections imagined the year-2000 reality of about 6 billion people on the planet, of whom "only" one-fifth would be malnourished. Well through the early 1960s, futurists of all stripes generally underestimated the gains in both world population *and* food supply. While predictions of the U.S. population for 2000 were sometimes fairly accurate (actual: 280 million), most forecasters assumed that we would have a much smaller world population than we now do, or that if we actually did hit 6 billion it would mean near starvation for at least half, and considerable hardship for the rest of us.

Indeed, many predicted that conventional field agriculture would not be able to feed many more than 3 to 4 billion people in 2000. They differed primarily over how we should deal with these gloomy prospects: Malthusians advocated mandatory birth control and soil conservation, while cornucopians hoped that conventional farming might improve enough to "buy time" before the arrival of the ultramodernist breakthroughs that would save us: atomic power, algae and plankton, climate control, floating ocean platforms, the resources of outer space, and so on. Yet even though the population increased much faster than generally expected, widespread, sustained food shortages did not materialize—thanks largely to unprecedented, unglamorous, and largely underestimated improvements in conventional dirt farming: higher-yielding plants and animals, bigger tractors, stronger chemicals, smoother roads, broader irrigation, and the like. Also instrumental were enormous government subsidies for the cheap energy (calories) that powered much of this modernization.[22]

Consider, for instance, the surprising productivity increases in corn farming—the major link in the petrochemical-driven conversion of sunlight into grain-fed livestock. In 1924, East had estimated that his own hybrids might improve corn yields by 20 percent. Adding up all the likely technological improvements—not just genetics—a 1923 USDA report considered a 50 percent increase by 1950 to be "roseate." In reality, average Iowa corn yields more than tripled between 1930 and 1980. World agriculture also outdistanced population growth, as total agricultural output more than doubled and overall per capita grain production jumped 38 percent between 1950 and 1984. Daily consumption of calories per capita in the Third World increased 27 percent between 1963 and 1995.[23] Such results surpassed all but the most glowing expectations. Most forecasters before 1980 might have been quite surprised to see a world of 2000 that had managed to muddle through without either major food wars or science fiction miracles. They would also have been amazed by the decline in food prices. Traditionally, Malthusians viewed food inflation as an inevitable result of population growth, while most cornucopians believed prices would need to rise to spur technological innovation. They would have found the cheaper meat prices even more startling, as many analysts routinely supposed that a world of 6 billion would inevitably be vegetarian.

To summarize what these debaters had in common: most were idealistic, interdisciplinary missionaries who used reductionist statistics based on questionable assumptions to make inaccurate predictions.

DIFFERENCES

Now on to the key differences among the think tankers, which, in keeping with the generalist tenor of the discussion, involved disagreement concerning such basic issues as the rise and fall of civilizations, the essential nature of humans, and faith or lack thereof in human ingenuity.

The Outline of History

For one thing, the debaters of the future conflicted sharply in their interpretations of the past. Pointing out that the Malthusian nightmare had not yet come true, cornucopians argued that modern history was on their side. While the population had boomed in the West since 1800, food production had increased even faster. By the mid-nineteenth century it was already clear that international trade had greatly expanded the food supply, as British economist William Jevons boasted in 1865: "The plains of North America and Russia are our cornfields; Chicago and Odessa our granaries; Canada and the Baltic our timber forests; Australia contains our sheep farms, and in South America are our herds of oxen; the Chinese grow tea for us, and our coffee, sugar, and spice plantations are all in the Indies." The resultant bounty seemed a clear refutation of Malthusian doomsayers. "What a curious commentary it is on the danger of prophecy," J. W. Cross wrote, "to consider that in this year 1888, when Mr. Malthus would have proved to us that population was bound to have outrun the means of subsistence, the fact is that the means of subsistence were never in greater abundance in proportion to the population, than they are in England to-day." Thirty-eight years later, agricultural economist Robert McFall dismissed the alarmist prophecies of East, Keynes, and Pearl: "Pessimistic utterances on this question are not new . . . yet this last century has seen what is probably the greatest development of the human race in history. Man has an uncanny faculty of surmounting obstacles and making the prognostications of the pessimists appear ridiculous in the light of subsequent history." By the late twentieth century, with the world having apparently dodged the Malthusian bullet so many times, *The Economist* exulted that the "headline grabbing . . . doomsters" kept having to "eat their words." Asserting in 1994 that 5 billion people were living and eating far better than ever before, Julian Simon concluded that "the Malthusian theory . . . runs exactly counter to the data over the long sweep of history." Among Simon's very last words before his death in 1998 were "Life has never been better."[24]

To this, the Malthusians (and many radical egalitarians) replied that the West had temporarily lucked out, since it had free colonial lands to exploit for food and resources and to absorb excess population. Malthus had predicted as much in 1798, when he noted that emigration offered momentary relief for overcrowded homelands. Sharpening this point in a supplement thirty years later, he observed that emigration to less populated regions entailed "much war and extermination"—a fact well known to Britain's colonies in America, Africa, and India. In a common refrain, Malthusians likened Europeans and Americans to bandits who had, in Edward Ross's words, "set their table with food from all over the globe." As "contented parasites," Vogt wrote in 1948, modern consumers treated the rest of the world as a "raw material colony." In 1973, Georg Borgstrom likened the Europeans' "big grab" to a "swarming" of hungry locusts. Historian Fernand Braudel observed that colonization both relieved "the weight of numbers" and also contributed to further population growth. For Hardin, all of human history constituted a single, catastrophic progression: "colonize—destroy—move on."[25]

The party was now over, Malthusians warned; there was nowhere to run. Announcing the end of the frontier in 1893, Frederick Jackson Turner voiced widely shared fears about the future of democracy. But while Turner drew a somewhat abstract and idealized link between open land and democratic institutions, others made more material connections to impending food shortages, as in 1909, when the president of the American Society of Animal Nutrition warned that, with "no more 'new worlds'" and "little more 'out west,'" rapid American population growth and failing soil fertility threatened an imminent "struggle for land and the food it will produce such as the world has never yet beheld." The ensuing world war seemed ample proof to East that the imperial "globe-trotting" of the past was just a "temporary escape from Nature's Laws." He warned that while the "flow of good things" into the West during the nineteenth century had "caused staid old economists to applaud the cleverness of humanity in stealing out from under the hand of fate," the "Belshazzar's feast" of the Victorians was an aberration in a more long-term process of population growth, diminishing returns, and resource depletion. Having "plundered all the available soils," Europeans could no longer count on "boarding a large proportion of their people at the long distance hotels" overseas. The colonies were becoming overpopulated, too, and the colonized were rebelling. This sense that the era of Good Times was a fleeting and morally tainted anomaly pervaded later Malthusian analyses as well. "Our ancestors skimmed the continent's cream," wrote Vogt in 1948. "We are rapidly separating out the butterfat that is left." Ehrlich observed in 1970: "We've always had what you might call a 'cowboy economy,' where you fouled up our nest and then moved on westward to find a new one. But we've reached the limits of westward movement a long time ago, and now we're stuck with our waste."[26]

History proves, Malthusians warned, that complacent civilizations fall when too many people crowd onto too little good land. Malthus himself ranged the world widely, from China to Mexico, in pursuit of classical precedents for ecological collapse—a reflection of his own era's fascination with the decline and fall of great empires into picturesque ruins. "The shadows of former civilizations cross the stage like ghosts in Macbeth—Egypt, Assyria, India, China, Persia, Greece, Rome, Arabia," an anonymous "eminent biologist" warned in *Harper's Monthly* in 1928. "Will America also join in this ghostly procession?" Unless we wake up soon, Vogt warned twenty years later, "we shall be slipping toward the oblivion of Ur, of Timgad, of Angkor Wat, of the North Chinese, the ancient Mayans." Of the last, Hardin noted in 1993 that "unsustainable agriculture" produced an 85 percent decline in the Mayan population almost overnight: "As Will Durant put the matter (with only a slight exaggeration), 'From barbarism to civilization requires a century; from civilization to barbarism needs but a day.'"[27] Clearly, this story has had legs.

But cornucopians had their historical precedents, too, especially for the human ability to respond ingeniously to scarcity. For every Malthusian reference to the Irish potato famine, cornucopians could respond with hybrid corn. For every wasted Mesopotamian garden there was a California desert converted to lush paradise. For every Gibbon tracking the decline of previous civilizations there was a Burbank helping to build new ones. Given the unexpected innovations of recent centuries, cornucopians felt confident in expecting even more unimaginable discoveries. "A hundred years ago, who could have foretold photography or the telephone?" chemist Berthelot asked in 1894. "The long evolution" proved that anything was possible, especially from chemists. Using chemistry, mankind had mastered fire, invented an astounding array of cooking tools, and processed "an indefinite number of compounds"—from the simple, like sugar, to the complex, like saccharin. Given such a record, Berthelot concluded, a "tablet of factory-made beefsteak" seemed virtually around the corner.[28] The same sort of reading of history inspired later proponents of genetic research—whether hybrid corn in the 1920s or cloning in the 1990s—to celebrate the chronicle of human discovery and mastery as one-directional and seamless.

Looking at that same record, Malthusians were less sanguine. There are limits to invention, they argued: we still can't live to be two hundred, walk on Mars, or cure the common cold. Not every problem has been or *can* be solved. Noting that the ancient Greeks erected temples for the unknown gods they might have overlooked, the Paddocks labeled the hope that "something would turn up" the "panacea of the unknown panacea." Similarly, forty years earlier, Malthusian J. O. P. Bland ridiculed "economists of the Micawber type who . . . predict that something will assuredly turn up in time to prevent mass starvation."[29] For Bland, such sentiments encouraged a complacent attitude of "eat, drink, and be merry"—another classical allusion. Battling over the correct historical interpretation, debaters sought the higher ground of the archetype—an extension over centuries, and even millennia, of the contest between trends and fluctuations.

Population Trends and Human Nature

These differences inevitably extended to long-term population projections. All agreed that the human population could double at least once. But then what? Cornucopians generally expected the population to stabilize as the world developed economically. Condorcet argued that as increasing prosperity reinforced "the progress of reason," people would want to make their children happier and would therefore voluntarily reduce family size. This belief became a staple of liberal economic thought. Egalitarians tended to agree that development would reduce fertility rates, but they expanded "development" to include greater equity and liberty. For example, socialist economist Scott Nearing explained that nineteenth-century workers stopped having so many children because democratization told "the men at the margin that they were free and equal to every other man and had a like right to rise." To this equation of freedom with population stabilization feminists added that an increase in women's rights, education, and opportunities would reduce family size—especially if birth control were made available to those who needed it.[30]

In the mid-twentieth century, many cornucopians adopted the demographic transition paradigm: economic and political development would eventually lower birth rates, but there might be a lag between the initial stages of improvement—especially the use of life-saving sanitation and medicine—and the more substantial, birth-reducing stages of economic and political modernization. With "death control" preceding birth control, a lot of children were going to survive, and the population would boom, perhaps for several generations. Acknowledging that the world might not be able to afford even a short-term population explosion, proponents of the demographic transition hypothesis seconded the Malthusian call for birth control. But they were considerably more hopeful that economic progress would *ultimately* tame population.[31]

While agreeing on birth control, Malthusians doubted that economic and political development was the ultimate answer. As the American baby booms of the 1920s and 1950s demonstrated, rising affluence did not always reduce rates of reproduction. And even if birth rates did eventually slow down, a higher standard of living could further deplete resources and strain the carrying capacity. As we have seen in chapter 1, the demographic transition brought a nutritional transition to more luxurious dietary standards. Could the world really afford more two-car families eating grilled steaks and imported salads on redwood decks behind four-bedroom suburban homes? Indeed, could the global environmental manage even a few extra eggs, a beer or two, and an occasional Big Mac for everyone? Multiplied by several billion, the ecological bill of adding even a few simple pleasures could be huge.

Doubting the rationalist assumptions of the demographic transition scenario, Malthusians held a fundamentally different view of human nature that was deeply rooted in biological metaphors. Following Malthus's belief that the atavistic need for food and "passion between the sexes" would always overcome nobler aspirations toward "perfectability," Malthusians firmly insisted that natural laws applied to people too. While cornucopians and egalitarians thought humans would control themselves when it was in their economic interest to do so, Malthusians often likened humans to rabbits, sardines, or ants, who would keep breeding and feasting until they simply ran out of food and room. Given that "nature's explosive fecundity is as awesome as the power of the atom," one *Saturday Review* writer feared the earth might soon be "covered with a writhing mass of human beings much as a dead cow is covered with a writhing mass of maggots." Raymond Pearl's much-quoted population projections in *The Biology of Death* were in fact based on the exponential population growth curves of fruit flies.[32]

It is no accident that some of the most outspoken Malthusian scientists, like Pearl, have been entomologists who used insect models to describe population growth as "teeming" or "swarming." Observing that flour beetles did not fare well when forced to compete for food and space in overcrowded glass jars, zoologist Thomas Park, retiring president of the American Association for the Advancement of Science, issued a "Warning to Mankind" in 1963: "If man does not manage his biology, it will manage him." Extending Park's analogy, *Time* magazine spelled out nature's "own subtle systems for choking off excessive breeding. . . . Horrible things happen among jammed-up flour beetles. Females destroy their eggs, they turn cannibalistic and eat one another. Males lose interest in females, and though plenty of flour is left for food, the beetle population reaches a statistical plateau." Locust analogies were used to illustrate the waste-laying potential of mass consumption, as well as Southern California's seeming fall from pastoral paradise to overpopulated nightmare. Occasionally an insect analogy might be used positively, especially by utopians invoking bee hives or ant colonies as natural models of happy cooperation.[33] But on the whole such altruistic insect analogies did not appeal to a culture so easily frightened by the "bug-eyed monsters" of pulp science fiction.

In another naturalist metaphor, the indiscriminate sprawl of modern metropolises such as Los Angeles and Calcutta was termed a cancerlike metastasis. And then there was Gregg's Law, proposed in 1955 by physician Alan Gregg. Branding humanity "a cancer of the Earth," Gregg medicalized the familiar Malthusian axiom that bountiful food encouraged population growth: "Cancerous growths demand food; but they have never been cured by getting it." Gregg's well-publicized doubts about growing more food for the poor were particularly subversive, as he was about to retire from his position as vice president of the Rockefeller Foundation, the cornucopian funder of the Green Revolution.[34]

Such biological images echoed late nineteenth-century fears of urbanization, with its "motley multitude, "huge conglomerate mass," "alien hordes," "human tide," and "vast hordes who swarm here to make a living." According to Mary Ryan, "urban chronicles of the postwar period placed poor families and prostitutes in dens and herds where they came together by animal instinct." One reporter attacked Chinese and Jewish New Yorkers who "herd together without the decency of cattle." In line with the insect motif, immigrant neighborhoods were routinely described as "infested," and early public health educators mounted "swat the fly" campaigns that, in effect, targeted two sorts of "invaders"—bugs and the immigrants who were thought to harbor them. Reversing the imagery, proponents of chemical pesticides likened invasive insects to unwanted immigrants; both threatened the food supply of the native-born. Asians in particular were often associated with insects, whether as the swarming locusts of Yellow Peril hysteria, the beetlelike Japanese of World War II propaganda cartoons, or the fly-covered famine victims of India and Bangladesh. But such imagery was also used to dehumanize outcast Europeans, as when a 1849 British news report described how desperate Irish famine victims lived in shallowly dug holes roofed over with sticks and pieces of turf. Called a scalp, such a shelter "resembles, though not quite so large, one of the ant-hills of the African forests."[35]

Decrying these beastly caricatures, cornucopians reasserted Enlightenment faith in the human ability to control natural drives. We are not termites, demographer Enid Charles argued in 1934; we can adapt and change, for there is no inherent "biological necessity." "Men and women are not vinegar flies, however useful the latter may be for population studies," FAO Director Norris Dodd insisted in 1948. "The development of great modern industrialized nations tends to show that human beings, endowed with the ability to understand and to weigh values, can modify the dictates of that simple biological law which compels procreation, insectlike, up to the uttermost limits of the available food supply." Yet the insect analogy persisted even in mainstream environmental rhetoric, as in the title of a 1994 article in National Wildlife Fund's *International Wildlife*: "Putting the Bite on Planet Earth: Rapid Human Population Growth Is Devouring Global Natural Resources."[36]

Such oral images bespoke radically different ways of embodying demographic trends. For Malthusians, population growth meant more mouths to feed, while for cornucopians it promised more brains and hands. While Malthusians viewed the "teeming masses" as passive, parasitic consumers, cornucopians saw them as active, creative producers. James Gibson notes in *Americans versus Malthus* that nineteenth-century expansionists viewed population growth as a "spring" toward greater ingenuity in "the arts"—the collective instruments of human domination over nature. "Man's creative genius is in truth more vigorous than his demon of destructiveness," science journalist Robert Brittain proclaimed in 1952. Contrary to the "Malthusian fallacy" that curing diseases brought more food shortages, Brittain argued, "masses of healthy people" were an essential resource for more food production. Forty years later, the economist Simon agreed: population growth improved the food supply because it encouraged innovation. "On average, human beings create more than they use in their lifetimes."[37] The idea that human activity might actually increase resources, rather than just use them up, was a staple of cornucopian thought.

Limits to Growth?

For the optimists—cornucopians and egalitarians alike—the only limits to growth were those set by human social and political arrangements, not by nature. As Condorcet insisted, "Nature has set no limit to the realization of our hopes." In potential, "man is a godlike being," Godwin exulted at the start of the nineteenth century. "Nature never made a dunce." And Lappé wrote at the end of the twentieth: "Famines . . . are not natural disasters but social disasters"; "our capacity to help end world hunger is infinite." Such assertions of boundlessness also predated Condorcet and Godwin, but so too did the counterparadigm of natural boundaries. Tracing the origins of "the idea that there are strict limits to the population capacity of any area," Worster cites Swedish botanist Linnaeus's seminal essay, "The Oeconomy of Nature" (1749), which in turn had ancient roots. What Malthus brought to the debate were statistics—"the ironclad ratios"—and his passionately apocalyptic prose. For Malthus, any observation of plants, animals, and even humanity rendered the notion of "unlimited progress" a "gross absurdity," "unphilosoph-ical" and "totally unwarranted." Yes, nature allowed variation, expan-sion, and even growth, but its laws were fixed and constant. Moreover, the notion that humans could be counted on to act creatively and in-geniously in times of crisis seemed belied by history. Thus, to the cornu-copian cry "The sky's the limit!" Malthusians replied, "Don't hit your head on the ceiling!" Paradoxically, the space program of the 1960s gave greater legitimacy to the Malthusian small-is-beautiful paradigm even as it allowed mankind to reach toward the stars. Photos of the earth taken from space emphasized the beauty and fragility of the planet and de-limited its "wholeness." Economist Kenneth Boulding's "spaceship earth" metaphor conveyed that the earth was a closed system with finite re-sources, and much in need of a disciplined, cooperative crew. Contrary to the "open earth" fantasies of "cowboy economics," Boulding urged a "spaceman economy, in which the earth has become a single spaceship, without unlimited reservoirs of anything . . . and in which, therefore, man must find his place in a cyclical ecological system."[38]

To the Malthusians' zero-sum model of the earth's carrying capacity, cornucopians responded with liberal market theory: If a particular re-source item became scarce, market forces would make it profitable to grow more food and even to develop substitutes, such as high-protein yeast grown on wood by-products. Shortages invited inventions and even-tual gluts. "To make manufactured products abundant and cheap, large demand has been necessary," W. O. Atwater wrote in 1891. "It may seem paradoxical to say that the dense population which the older economy told us was to be the precursor of starvation will be actually the an-tecedent condition of a cheap and abundant food-supply." For precedent, Atwater noted how the mass market had recently brought about enor-mous decreases in the cost of clothing. To this faith in supply and de-mand cornucopians added a call for free trade to distribute the fruits of technological innovation more efficiently and equitably. "It is by sea trade that an enriched future must be fed," wrote geographer J. Russell Smith in 1919. Voicing the view of many liberal cornucopians, Smith added that it was the *absence* of free markets and open trade—in other words, an inefficient distribution system—that created hunger. Equating a cap-italist market with freedom was an enduring trope of cornucopian thought. "The world's problem is not too many people," Julian Simon declared in 1993, "but lack of political and economic freedom." And for business professor Simon, it was clear that "market-directed economies" distributed food far more efficiently than "centrally planned economies."

While socialists concurred that efficient distribution was essential to feed the hungry, they argued that real-world capitalism better served those in power than those in need—class instead of mass. Some liberal cornucopians agreed, hence their support of land reform, liberalized voting, and an end to the strong agricultural subsidies that protected Western farmers while glutting the world market with cheap grain.[39]

Malthusians might agree that the economy was often unfair, but they have been less sanguine about mankind's ability to equalize the market. Here, as elsewhere, the dispute boils down to different views on human nature, especially people's ability to overcome deeply ingrained tendencies and prejudices. To say that hunger is a matter not of carrying capacity but "only" of distribution is, in a sense, to dismiss a time-old, perhaps innate, shortage of what Joel Cohen calls "human caring capacity."[40] Considering the colossal nexus of enduring political and economic forces that have created and maintained global inequities, it is easy to believe that such oppressive power relations are, in fact, a part of nature, almost as fixed as the genetically programmed tendencies of other animals. Claiming the conservative position of tough realism, Malthusians have urged us to focus on what humans *did* do, rather than on what they *could* do. And these political and social limits can be even tougher in some ways than the physical ones.

Faith versus Doubt

The preference for the actual over the potential shaped the Malthusian perspective on scientific and technological solutions. Cornucopians argued that if less-productive farmers adopt known technologies already available "on the shelf"—better fertilizers, tractors, seeds, trucks, and so on—and if the current rate of innovations persist, the world should have enough to eat. This may be true in theory, Malthusians replied, but in the real world different conditions apply. As the great Liebig discovered firsthand when farmers misapplied his ideas and failed miserably, just because a scientist invents it does not mean a farmer can use it. Warren Thompson likewise observed: "What science can do is one thing; what it is feasible for a farmer to do is quite another." Vogt, too, distinguished the "theoretical" from the "practical," while Harrison Brown drew a line between the "conceivable" and the "feasible." Such problems were long known as well to those most dedicated to agricultural modernization. In the 1920s, the USDA noted that while the latest technologies promised some productivity increases, actual field results were always lower due to the "inertia of large masses of the agricultural population, partly due to innate conservatism, partly to lack of information, partly to inadequate capital." Forty years later, the Paddock brothers were pessimistic about future famines in part because, as agricultural development workers, they had witnessed in person the difficulties of transferring First World technologies to Third World ecological, political, and social conditions.[41] Similar doubts surrounded proposals for synthetic food, algae, and so on. Yes, science might be able to invent such products, but would real people actually eat them?

As part III shows, cornucopians had high hopes for "smart farming"— clever, high-tech agricultural management—but some Malthusians tended to think there aren't enough smart farmers to do it right. Some clearly had a lower opinion of rural people, especially before 1960. Reflecting racist eugenics, Vogt blamed soil erosion on dumb farmers, whom he termed "Kallikaks of the land." (The Kallikaks were a poor New Jersey family whose inbreeding supposedly accounted for their criminality.) While many cornucopians of the colonial era agreed that Third World "coolie" farmers were incompetent, they held out hope for white overseers. Asserting the high agricultural productivity of British-ruled Jamaica, J. Russell Smith hoped that "the white man" would continue to "come in as the ruler, the capitalist, the plantation manager, the engineer, the sanitarian, the expert, and the professional man, but in these capacities he can make the framework and uphold the structure of tropical society—industrially, commercially, and politically." When colonialism collapsed after 1945, the white overseer was replaced by the white agricultural extension agent hoping to facilitate "technology transfer" to "developing" nations. In response, Malthusians voiced *Heart of Darkness* doubts that white outsiders could survive in tropical climates or navigate the treacherous shoals of native politics, while egalitarians detected a self-interested neocolonialism in such "benevolence" but also held out hope that radical democratization—even revolution—would unleash the ingenuity of native farmers.[42]

As realists, Malthusians also pointed out the negative by-products of miracle technologies such as tractors, irrigation, DDT, hybrid grains, and genetically modified corn. Since "nature bats last," every human advance potentially prompts some serious, even disastrous ecological "blowback." Pesticides and antibiotics have saved lives, but they also encouraged the growth of even more resistant pests and bacteria. International trade facilitated the exchange of food *and* diseases across borders. The disastrous social and environmental costs of the Green Revolution led populists to argue that traditional subsistence farmers are, in fact, much smarter than the technicians and agrichemical companies seeking to modernize them.[43]

While acknowledging the damage sometimes wrought by previous generations' high-tech solutions, cornucopians still believed that what humans have done, they can redo—rebuild soil, restore ecosystems, find better technologies. Similarly, egalitarians hoped to right previous wrongs by restructuring unjust societies. But Malthusians doubted what law professor Richard Falk calls the "anthropological fix"—a major overhaul of basic relationships, expectations, values, and perhaps even human nature itself.[44] Aren't these social engineering proposals as impractical—and scary—as the scientists' fantasies of synthetic foods and algae burgers? Down deep, the optimists keep reiterating that utopian caveat, the big "if": *if* we can cooperate, *if* we can be more generous, *if* we can think smarter, *if* we can be better people, *then* we can solve this problem. Wary of all the "ifs," the pessimists have their own dystopian caveat: even if we *could* remake human beings to be more "perfect," we might not like the results. For every *Looking Backward,* there is a *Brave New World.*

The Battle of the Metaphors

Futurist fiction aside, this battle between faith and doubt in many ways comes down to a war of classical metaphors and quotations. While cornucopians looked to Prometheus's empowering humans with technology (fire), Malthusians cited Sisyphus engaged in the cyclical futility of the technological treadmill, the superficial palliative, the temporary stopgap—as well as the tragic cost to Prometheus of his own hubris. Robert Brittain's 1952 paean to human ingenuity, *Let There Be Bread,* opens with extensive quotes from Sophocles' *Antigone,* including:

> He is master of ageless earth, to his own will bending
> The immortal mother of gods by the sweat of his brow . . .
> There is nothing beyond his power. His subtlety
> Meeteth all chance, all danger conquereth.

Malthusian Edward East dug even further into ancient mythology when he suggested that it was self-defeating to raise more food to raise more people, who would then need more food: "We plant like Cadmus, the mythical founder of Thebes, who slew the sacred serpent of Mars, and sowing its teeth brought forth a harvest of armed men who fought each other to the death."[45]

Edenic myths worked both ways: Malthusians decried the "paradise lost" to human greed and avarice, while cornucopians cited the "paradise regained" via human effort and creativity. Sunday-sermon syntax worthy of King James animated both sides: cornucopians cited the parting of the Red Sea (flood control), manna falling from heaven (algae), making the desert bloom (irrigation), resurrecting the dead (also irrigation), the miracle of the loaves and fishes (booming agricultural yields), and Ecclesiastes' injunction to "cast thy bread upon the waters" (international food aid), while Malthusians preached against "sowing seeds of destruction," "reaping a bitter harvest," worshiping "the false gods of cleverness," and ignoring "the writing on the wall." Was the peacetime use of synthetic nitrogen, pesticides, and nuclear power a fulfillment of Isaiah's call to convert "swords into ploughshares" or of Ecclesiastes' lament "He that increaseth knowledge increaseth sorrow"? Agronomists invoked Jonathan Swift's charge "to make two blades where one did before," while ecologists enlisted the Chinese proverb "One hill cannot shelter two tigers." "Be fruitful and multiply" (Genesis 1:27) countered "Thou has multiplied the nation and not increaseth the joy" (Isaiah 9:3). And "Waste not, want not" was a Malthusian call for conservation, an egalitarian plea to share scarce resources, and a cornucopian rationale for converting wood by-products to edible yeast. Caricaturing their opponents, cornucopians slurred Malthusians as Luddites, doomsayers, defeatists, boys crying wolf, Chicken Littles, "runaway environmentalists," and "nature-worshiping," science-doubting victims of "a collective inferiority complex." Malthusians maligned cornucopians as "blue sky dreamers" living in a "fool's paradise," Jules Verne addicts, tricky alchemists, pathetic magicians who hoped "to keep pulling rabbits out of hats," deceptive propagators of "the Emperor's New Crops," and deluded devotees of the sorcerer's apprentice and of Doctors Faust, Pangloss, and Demento. Overwhelmingly male, some debaters inevitably cast their opponents as too feminine—hysterical Cassandras (pessimists) or naive Polyannas (optimists). And in keeping with the prophetic urgency of their mission, all sides saw themselves as minority voices "crying in the wilderness."

The battle of the metaphors extended beyond the classics. Cornucopians invoked romantic images of westward expansion, adventure, and exploration, while Malthusians preferred sober analogies from banking, accounting, and gambling. To cornucopians, we would feed the future by conquering new frontiers—the deserts, seas, tropical forests, and space—or by embarking on new voyages to unlock the secrets of the atom, photosynthesis, and genetics. But to Malthusians the future was a high-interest mortgage to be paid by our children, who would have to foot the hefty bills left over from our reckless squandering of their inheritance. "The present generation, its children, and grandchildren must now begin to pay the bill for the population 'joy-ride,'" Guy Irving Burch and Elmer Pendell declared in 1945. "By a lopsided use of applied science," Vogt wrote, "[mankind] has been living on promissory notes. Now, all over the world, the notes are falling due." "We're committing grand larceny against our children," conservationist "archdruid" David Brower agreed in 1970. "Ours is a chain-letter economy, in which we pick up early handsome dividends and our children find their mailboxes empty." Yet financial metaphors have also suggested a better course, as when East anticipated the key tenet of the sustainable agriculture movement: "The only way to treat the soil is like a bank account; husband it carefully by proper farming and make a deposit once in awhile." Along the same lines, other conservationists spoke of "honest accounting" and paying the "true costs." Assessing the "Earth's Bottom Line" in 1994, Worldwatch's Sandra Postel advised: "Globally, the ecological books must balance."[46]

In a way, the debate boiled down to competing views of "smartness"— the sharpness of cutting-edge science versus the precautionary conservatism of aging parents. While cornucopians urged faith in the adventure of scientific research, Malthusians advised against taking risks, against betting the farm on unfounded speculation or on the assumption that past winnings could be replicated. Acknowledging that the nineteenth century had made astounding gains in food production, Ross cautioned, "It would be rash, however to assume such exploits in food-winning can be duplicated again and again. Rather they should be looked on as gifts of the gods, as buried treasure stumbled on." And to keep multiplying "carelessly," with the hope that the chemists will save us, "would be a pure gamble in human lives."[47] Along the same lines, critics of high-tech industrial foods have counseled consumers not to let themselves be "guinea pigs" in the reckless experiments of cornucopian science.

As in other highly contested arenas of debate—history, statistics, philosophy, the classics—each position strove to be seen as more "mature" than the others. Taking the side of "sober," "severe and chastised thinking," Malthus characterized the utopians' conceptions as "elate and giddy," "crude and puerile," "childish absurdities," and "vain and extravagant dreams of fancy." Following this lead, his successors cautioned us to start acting like responsible adults who, having outgrown our carefree adolescence, must settle down, accept limits, live "sustainably" within our means, take "precautions," and start making "prudent" plans for our children and grandchildren. The solution, East argued, was to give up the chemists' childish wish-fulfillment fantasies, "the air-castles of those credulous day-dreamers who expect all future troubles to be straightened out by the genius of the test-tube shaker." Similarly, Harrison Brown urged us to move beyond the cornucopian playthings of childhood: "Today we are children. . . . We have found wondrous toys which we have played with and fought over . . . but finally after a million or so years our childhood is about to end." In *Nature's Economy*, Worster adopted similar developmental analogies in differentiating the more youthful, "transformative" "homily of cornucopian expansion" from the more responsible "ethic of environmental self-restraint," "the exercise of a highly civilized, mature will and self-discipline." Scolding Green Revolution missionaries as "innocents abroad" who greatly underestimated the difficulties and complexities of social change, environmentalist Angus Wright called for a more sensible rejection of scientific "miracles": "Historically science and technology made their first advances by rejecting the idea of miracles in the natural world. Perhaps it would be best to return to that position."[48]

To be sure, cornucopians denied that they were stuck in an irresponsible, credulous adolescence. Instead, they depicted themselves as the more pragmatic adults—the people who, refusing to succumb to despair, roll up their sleeves and labor hard to solve problems. "Fatalism," Robert Brittain wrote, "whether it clothes itself in the mud and feathers of the witch doctor or in the solemn proposals of the philosopher, owes its perennial appeal to the fact that it permits us to avoid work." The Green Revolution's Warren Weaver praised the "imaginative and useful optimists" who "refuse to admit defeat" in their search for "constructive" solutions. Forty years later, advocates of genetically modified foods urged more research funding as a prudent, long-term "investment." Similarly, proponents of farm consolidation, chemurgy, and corporate-style technocracy based their arguments on the claim that America had now "come of age" and so needed more sophisticated management. The same aspiration for "evolution" guided utopian socialists like Edward Bellamy to urge the replacement of capitalist "prodigality" by a more cooperative system.[49] As with so much of the debate, maturity—like foresight—was in the mind of the beholder.

LESSONS

Before moving on to other forums of futuristic speculation, it would be useful to reflect on what can be learned from the battle of the think tanks. Several lessons come to mind.

First, to put it in political terms, those who believe "you ain't seen nothin' yet" are far more electable than those who seem to accept limits and boundaries, as Ronald Reagan proved in 1980 and 1984. That is, in the words of hunger analyst Peter Eisinger, there is a "presumption of abundance" in America. Or, as environmental economist Robert Costanza has commented, technological optimism is the default vision of Western culture. Significantly, at the 1999 annual meeting of the World Future Society, a downbeat session on future food security attracted an audience of ten while a giggly panel on robots attracted one hundred. The "gee whiz" almost always trumps the "bummer." Literary critic Tom Vargish observes that, given the Western heritage of "providentialism"—the strong belief that the "invisible hands" of God, the market, and Science destine us to infinite greatness—we feel like "orphans" when we are urged to accept limits to growth. In addition to alienating us from our heritage, the Malthusian perspective on reproduction also seems ungenerous, if not downright racist. Moreover, there are existential reasons to resist the notion of boundaries. While we all know that in the long run everything must end, in day-to-day practice we tend to live as if we are immortal. And to the extent that "growth" is associated with "growth in personhood and growth in the body social," sociologist Elise Boulding writes, the prospect of any *limits* to growth "equals death."[50] It should be noted, however, that even if the limits view of the think tanks has had less direct impact on policy, the Malthusian worldview as filtered through speculative fiction has profoundly influenced many young people, especially those born after 1950—a theme to be explored in part II. While technological utopianism may still control the ballot box, it has been seriously challenged at the box office.

Another lesson is that, for making predictions, it is best to brush up on one's classical metaphors, myths, and allusions. Command of the archetypes is in fact an essential prerequisite for framing news stories, capturing the public imagination, and setting the policy agenda.[51] Futurists have cannibalized, rearranged, and repackaged the past to support virtually any position. And thanks to the historical amnesia and scientific illiteracy of the audience, few have recognized the repetitiveness.

Third, if you are going to make predictions, you might as well be bold and confident about them. Whatever their position, the futurists who have received the greatest attention have been the ones with the loudest, most urgent and certain scenarios, even if they have turned out to be wrong. One reason why so many have been wrong is that in their determination to see the Big Picture, they missed the fact that life is always lived locally, on the ground, day to day, with great differences even among neighbors. There are as many futures as there are people—and maybe even more if one considers that each of us faces many options. Change occurs incrementally; in pace the agents of evolution are more like the unnoticed tortoise than the flashy hare. But in think tank discourse, it is the hare that gets the headlines. And headlines tend to reduce complexity even further—as when the *Literary Digest* boiled down Raymond Pearl's subtly hedged set of calculations, guesses, and inferences about population growth into a much starker lead, "When the World Gets Overcrowded," followed by an opening sentence far more assured than any of Pearl's own prose: "Our children's children will have to face a standard of living much below that which we enjoy." Exactly whose children, and which "we"? Overgeneralizing headlines like "Will the World Starve?"—a perennial favorite—ignore the fact that some might starve while, even in times of famine, some might get along just fine. The possible became the inevitable in a 1990 *Futurist* article in which some scientists merely speculated whether factory tissue culture *could* have a significant future in food production, but the headline announced, "Food without Farms." Another form of attention-getting abstraction is performed by editors of essay collections whose introductions are sometimes more definite in venturing predictions than the individual pieces buried inside. Since many reviewers, journalists, and general readers rarely stray beyond the first few pages, the editor's introduction probably makes more impact, though often at the expense of nuance and ambiguity. While the appearance of certainty has been a particularly strong asset for professional trend-spotters (and military generals), readers of a declarative forecast should consider Joel Cohen's "law of prediction": the more certain the scenario, the less you should believe it. [52] Here again, however, historical amnesia undermined such caution, as few tracked or remembered previous predictions.

Despite the redundancy of the debate, the fourth lesson is that it would be wrong to conclude that nothing changes. Santayana notwithstanding, history does not quite repeat itself, although, as others have said, it may echo loudly. While much of the deep structure of the earlier iterations of the debate persists, we do hear from more voices today, especially women, people of color, neo-agrarians, and non-Westerners. Analysis of the population problem has also become more nuanced and a bit less polarized. Today's Malthusians grudgingly allow that agricultural technology has produced wonders over the past fifty years, while today's cornucopians seem somewhat chastened by such technological disasters as DDT and Chernobyl. And even though egalitarians remain on the margins of the discussion, everyone allows for the need to equalize production and distribution. Reflecting a greater respect for diversity, today's Malthusians have moved decisively away from the more mean-spirited, racist attitudes of the pre-1960 period. Aware of today's skeptical food market, cornucopians are less likely to rhapsodize about steaks synthesized from sludge or coal dust. (Indeed, with all the concerns about health, few rhapsodize about real steaks, either.) From the 1950s on, cornucopians have been more willing to advocate technological *and* "anthropological" fixes—especially birth control, land reform, and democratization, while Malthusians are less likely to dismiss increased food production as a mere palliative. As Paul Ehrlich begins to sound more and more like Frances Moore Lappé, it has become harder to distinguish Malthusian birth-controllers from radical egalitarians. In fact, some recent analyses of the global food security issue are *so* ecumenical, so determined to cover *all* the complexities and variables, that it is hard to know where nuance becomes incoherence, confusion, or an all-things-to-all-people opportunism. At least in the earlier debates, with clear sides, it was easier to determine where to set one's priorities—more production, more conservation, *or* more justice. Today everyone claims to be an environmentalist, including the Rockefeller Foundation's president, who casts genetic engineering as a "double green revolution," and Monsanto, whose public relations department pitches biotechnology as a "sustainable" *and* "fair" way to feed a hungry world.[53] One wonders if being too complex—the ecumenical fallacy—is almost as specious as being too simplistic.

But fallacies aside, the fifth lesson is that long-run accuracy has not always been a major consideration anyway. For the most part, futurists have not really been discussing the future so much as they have been projecting contemporary events, worries, and hopes onto the future. It is really hard, maybe impossible, to conceive of anything beyond the immediate past and present. But accuracy is only one of many reasons why people make predictions. Another is to affect the present. There is a difference between a "correct" forecast (one that turns out to be accurate) and a "useful" forecast (one that changes present conditions in order to create a desirable future or prevent an undesirable one). Hoping to shape the current agenda, some succeeded. Environmentalist Hazel Henderson notes a feedback loop between the apocalyptic mood of the 1960s and the increase in environmental regulation in the 1970s. If Rachel Carson had not predicted a future without songbirds in 1962, the Environmental Protection Agency might not have banned DDT in 1972. Looking back from 1996, Paul Ehrlich allowed that his earlier predictions of imminent food wars may have been incorrect, but they were useful if they prodded international agencies to improve food production, distribution, and relief. In a 1986 tribute to Harrison Brown's long career as a futurist, environmental scientist John P. Holdren wrote, "The idea is not to be 'right,' but to illuminate the possibilities in a way that both stimulates sensible debate about the sort of future we want and facilitates sound decisions about getting from here to there."[54]

Despite their differences, the three sides of the debate have been de facto allies in attracting public attention and funding. The bolder the Malthusian cries of impending disaster, or the more imminent the socialist threat, the more generous the research subsidies for cornucopian labs and experimental stations. Just as Liebig and Berthelot depended on the fear articulated by Malthus and Marx to fund their synthetic chemistry research, at this moment Monsanto absolutely *needs* Lester Brown and Vandana Shiva to scare up support for its pledge to feed the world through "leading-edge agriculture." Conversely, scary cornucopian visions of algae burgers, factory farms, and Frankenfoods have motivated Malthusians to push for stepped-up resource conservation and population planning; Worldwatch *needs* Monsanto. And the inability of cornucopian capitalism to share surpluses fairly—the perennial paradox of plenty—fuels sympathy for egalitarian options. To finance its research into restructuring global trade and low-tech alternative agriculture, Food First exploits dissatisfaction with Archer Daniels Midland's "value-added, technology-based" solutions to world hunger and cleaning up the planet.[55]

Recognizing these feedback loops and symbiotic relationships should give some hope. At a time when global trends may seem to be pushing us toward disaster tomorrow, it is heartening to think that our best protection may be to predict it today. Of course, back in 1798, Malthus said pretty much the same thing about his own nightmare forecasts: "Evil exists in the world not to create despair but activity. We are not patiently to submit to it, but to exert ourselves to avoid it."[56]

FIGURE 1. The political locust, 1795. The original caption reads, "Caricature of a devouring insect [a common biological metaphor] nibbling at the remains of 'poor old England,' left destitute by high taxes, military setbacks, food shortages, and an influx of destitute French clergy." The image suggests the economic, political, and cultural anxieties behind Robert Malthus's 1798 *Essay on Population*. (Library of Congress, Prints and Photographs Division, LC-USZC2-629.)

FIGURE 2. Chinese famine victim, early twentieth century. China and India represented worst-case scenarios in Western discussions of overpopulation. (George Grantham Bain Collection, Library of Congress, Prints and Photographs Division, LC-USZ62-68803.)

FIGURE 3. Rice distribution during famine, China, 1946. Reliant on "coolie rations" for a bare subsistence, overpopulated Asia seemed ripe for revolution. (Photograph by Arthur Rothstein; Library of Congress, Prints and Photographs Division, LC-DIG-ppmsca-07586.)

FIGURE 4. "Junks laden with sea-weed, the Korean's table delicacy," Fusan, Korea, 1904. In Western eyes, overcrowded Asians ate bizarre, unpalatable foods. The association of seaweed with Malthusian hardship probably doomed modernist proposals to make algae the superfood of the future. (Library of Congress, Prints and Photographs Division, LC-USZ62-72713.)

FIGURE 5. East Side women discussing the price of meat during a meat boycott, New York City, April 1910. With cheap animal foods considered a universal entitlement in America, the inflation of meat prices sparked street protests, middle-class jitters, and Malthusian speculations. (George Grantham Bain Collection, Library of Congress, Prints and Photographs Division, LC-USZ62-55772.)

FIGURE 6. Cornucopian ideology, 1860: "The Union Must Be Preserved." This ad for Cuban tobacco illustrates the cornucopian paradigm: future abundance requires agricultural expansion, aggressive sea trade, and national unity. (Library of Congress, Prints and Photographs Division, LC-USZ62-90702.)

FIGURE 7. Cornucopian technology, Walla Walla, Washington, circa 1902. Modern American machines combined harvesting, cutting, threshing, and sacking. Industrial monocultures lowered bread prices and staved off Malthusian conditions, but at a great cost to rural communities and ecologies. (Library of Congress, Prints and Photographs Division, LC-USZ62-71471.)

FIGURE 8. Industrial agriculture: countless straight rows of lettuce extend almost to the horizon, with not a human in sight, in California's Salinas Valley, 1939. (Photograph by Dorothea Lange; Library of Congress, Prints and Photographs Division, LC-USF34-018899-E.)

FIGURE 9. The chemurgic future: U.S. Department of Agriculture Regional Laboratory, Peoria, Illinois, 1942. Perennial overproduction impelled a search for industrial uses of agricultural surpluses—in this case, butylene glycol from corn for automobile antifreeze and commercial solvents. (Photograph by William J. Forsythe; Library of Congress, Prints and Photographs Division, LC-USE6-D-005344.)

FIGURE 10. El Monte, California, federal subsistence homestead, 1936. An alternative agrarian future was envisioned in a brief utopian experiment by New Deal egalitarians. Here a family of eight grows food to supplement the father's wages as a streetcar conductor. (Photograph by Dorothea Lange; Library of Congress, Prints and Photographs Division, LC-USF34-T01-001715-C.)

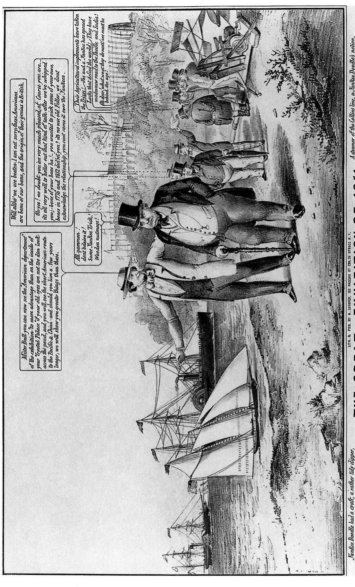

FIGURE 11. Crystal Palace Exhibition, London, 1851. The first great cornucopian world's fair displayed "Yankee superiority" in agricultural and transportation technology. As men gather around a grain harvester (right), the top-hatted Englishman (center) scowls, perhaps in disdain for America's lack of "artistic" achievement. (Image by Currier & Ives; Library of Congress, Prints and Photographs Division, LC-USZ62-10826.)

FIGURE 12. Statue of Liberty in cereals, Nebraska exhibit, New Orleans World's Fair, 1885. Cornucopian fairs celebrated abundance; the neoclassical version often took the form of massive mimetic sculptures composed of favored commodities. (Library of Congress, Prints and Photographs Division, LC-USZ62-60765.)

FIGURE 13. "The Man on Horseback." President Theodore
Roosevelt modeled in butter, Louisiana Purchase Exposition,
St. Louis, 1904. A proponent of the imperial future was
appropriately fashioned out of an animal product whose
continued abundance depended on territorial expansion.
(Stereograph, Library of Congress, Prints and Photographs
Division, LC-USZ62-78469.)

FIGURE 14. Igorots (Philippine natives) posed in front of thatched huts, Louisiana Purchase Exposition, St. Louis, 1904. The display of purported dog-eaters accentuated the classical version of progress as a steady evolution from barbarism to civilization. (Library of Congress, Prints and Photographs Division, LC-USZ62-80332.)

FIGURE 15. Visitors to the 1904 St. Louis World's Fair contemplate the contrasts between a "primitive" Filipino village and the neoclassical Agricultural Building in the distance. (Stereograph, Library of Congress, Prints and Photographs Division, LC-USZ62-111761.)

FIGURE 16. Headquarters, U.S. Department of Agriculture, Washington, D.C. Aspiring to the classical future envisioned by the great imperial fairs of Chicago and St. Louis, construction of this temple of corn, wheat, and meat began in 1905 and was completed in 1930, on the eve of the modernist fairs of the Depression. Appropriate to the importance of cheap, abundant food in the American Dream, the Department of Agriculture is the only federal department building located directly on the Mall, and only a last-minute intervention by President Roosevelt prevented it from being situated in the very middle (see Christopher Weeks, *AIA Guide to the Architecture of Washington* [Baltimore: Johns Hopkins University Press, 1994], 60). (Photo by author, 2005.)

FIGURE 17. A sanitary grocery of the 1920s in the proto-modernist style, featuring simple lines, uniformity, and the use of clear glass. Fordist agriculture could now deliver former luxuries—especially meat and tropical produce—safely and efficiently. (Theodor Horydczak Collection, Library of Congress, Prints and Photographs Division, LC-H814-T-2974-004-x.)

FIGURE 18. Grand Union Super Market, East Patterson, New Jersey, 1952. Populuxe style ascendant in the suburban supermarket— synthetic materials, recessed lighting, pale Moderne accents, and overflowing bins of denaturalized meat and produce. (Gottscho- Schleisner Collection, Library of Congress, Prints and Photographs Division, LC-G613-T-61187.)

FIGURE 19. Electric farm, New York World's Fair, 1939. Streamlined barn and outbuildings, spotless lawns and streets: the
"push-button farm" of the near future. (Gottscho-Schleisner
Collection, Library of Congress, Prints and Photographs Division,
LC-G612-T-35035.)

FIGURE 20. House of Glass, New York World's Fair, 1939. The modernist kitchen of tomorrow: a gleaming white laboratory. (Gottscho-Schleisner Collection, Library of Congress, Division of Prints and Photographs, LC-G612-T-35254.)

FIGURE 21. "Research into possibilities of using shortwave radio waves for internal heating of food products in dehydration process is being carried on at the regional agricultural research laboratory, Albany, CA," 1942 (from caption card, Farm Security Administration, Office of War Information Photograph Collection, Library of Congress). In the modernist future, nerdy "dreaming boys" would apply the very latest technologies to improve food production. This is also a good example of science following fiction, for Hugo Gernsbeck's *Amazing Stories* had predicted radio cooking a decade before. (Photograph by Russell Lee; Library of Congress, Prints and Photographs Division, LC-USW3-003844-D.)

FIGURE 22 (TOP). The recombinant future: downtown Silver Spring, Maryland, 2005. At the start of the new millennium, Washington, D.C.'s first shopping center—a deserted relic from the streamlined 1930s—was refurbished into a New Urban mall of moderately upscale franchises serving artisanal and ethnic foods (here, breads) in a retro-hip mood and with "smart" information systems. Barely visible around the corner on the left is the Silver Theater, a faded art-deco movie palace reborn as a chic multiplex featuring classic and independent films, as well as organic snacks from nearby Whole Foods. (Max Desfor, personal photograph.)

FIGURE 23 (LEFT). Recombinant café, Silver Spring, Maryland, 2005. At modernism's peak in the mid-twentieth century, who would have predicted that fifty years later Americans would line up to pay over three dollars for a cup of frothy gourmet coffee, served in a somewhat countercultural atmosphere—here with a dash of neo-deco—that almost obscured the chain's prominence in global capitalism? On the same block are franchised Tex-Mex, fusion noodles, Chesapeake, Lebanese, Thai, Indian, and roadhouse Texan food establishments. Perhaps only H. G. Wells could have predicted such instances of the "second-hand archaic." (Max Desfor, personal photograph.)

FIGURE 24. Ecotopia, D.C.? Beans and cabbages grow in Alice Waters's Edible School Yard on the Mall during the 2005 Smithsonian Folklife Festival. Did such scenes betoken a more sustainable future to come? With organic veggies sprouting at the foot of Republican Capitol Hill, anything seemed possible. (Photo by author.)

PART II

IMAGINING THE FUTURE OF FOOD

Speculative Fiction

FOUR

THE UTOPIAN CAVEAT

WHY STUDY UTOPIAS AND DYSTOPIAS?

While all forecasts aim to be self-fulfilling—to invent the future—not all forecasts are equally effective. For a forecast to make its mark, it needs to be communicated well. In the business of communication, it is the superior storytellers who can parlay their skills to gain power. Take Ronald Reagan or, even better, Walt Disney, whose "imagineers" literally engineered myths into a multi-billion-dollar fantasy conglomerate. The manipulation of myths, symbols, and stories is an essential means by which humans frame alternatives and focus aspirations. Mythmakers "provide dreams to live by," Donald Worster writes. The "ought to" often shapes the "is."[1]

The Disney Company has in fact had much to say about the future, and not through a think tank. The problem with think tank futurism is that it can be too disembodied, too abstract. People like to see and feel for themselves. For full effect, scenarios need to be dramatized, narrated in stories, embedded and embodied in places and people. Stories give life, "juice," to dry calculations. They show a lived future, complete with characters and plot lines, romance, love, hate, and all the messy human emotions that analytical white papers usually miss. Again, think Disney: not much analysis there, but lots of life.

Storytelling reaches a wider audience than think tank scholarship does.[2] More young people have experienced the Malthusian nightmare of overcrowding and environmental catastrophe through the dystopian dramas *Soylent Green* and *Blade Runner* than through the technocratic prose—however compelling—of Harrison or Lester Brown. Similarly, the egalitarian utopias of novelists Edward Bellamy, William Dean Howells, and Marge Piercy may have moved more Americans to action than the abstractions of Godwin and Condorcet.

Speculative fiction comes in two guises. Utopian stories inspire, motivate, dare us to dream of a better future. Dystopian stories wake us up with cautionary hints about the dangerous tendencies of our time. Both genres hope to set off a chain of events that will shape the future. By encouraging our aspirations, utopias hope to be self-fulfilling; by encouraging us to take preventive steps, dystopias hope to be self-defeating.

In short, futurist stories are overtly activist. Feminist Charlotte Perkins Gilman viewed her "pragmatopian stories" as important "cultural work" that could "introduce people to unexpected possibilities." H. G. Wells— perhaps the greatest professional futurist—prized "kinetic utopias" that would induce readers to resist the dead weight of the past and take special steps to achieve a better tomorrow. Similarly, science fiction novelist Kobe Abe hoped that a vivid dystopian tale would "make the reader confront the cruelty of the future" and discover "the abnormal in that which is closest to us." Harold Berger urges us to study dystopias "to resolve which paths must *not* be taken, which deeds must *not* be done."[3]

While some may protest that fantasy stories count for less than sober white papers, we should probably not draw too distinct a difference between the two. All futures are speculative and imagined. Where literary futures differ from, say, *USDA Yearbook* or *World Watch* futures is in the degree of license afforded the imagination. Fiction writers do have more freedom to stray beyond present trends and paradigms, to roam "outside the box." They can factor in wild cards, unexpected twists and turns, surprise decisions.

But the two forms—art and social science—do interact. Just as there has been a mutually sustaining symbiosis among the debaters discussed in part I, the genres of fiction and nonfiction engage in a constant dialogue and dialectic, a feedback loop of influence and reinforcement. Malthus's ultraserious *Essay on Population* was a response to the decidedly more playful, sometimes fictitious speculations of eighteenth-century utopians, who in turn had extrapolated the "real life" dynamics of New World exploration and colonization. Similarly, dystopian novelists wrote their stories in response to "serious" economic, scientific, and sociological analyses, starting with that of Malthus himself, whose themes of overpopulation, soil exhaustion, hubris, and social devolution found their way into innumerable apocalyptic tales. Indeed, Godwin's daughter, Mary Shelley, was one of the earliest and most influential spinners of quasi-Malthusian yarns with *Frankenstein* (1818), a warning against technological arrogance, and *The Last Man* (1826), a grim tale of plagues, famine, and impending human extinction. Such stories then influenced generations of think tank predictions. The rash of utopian and apocalyptic novels at the end of the nineteenth century animated Progressive and New Deal efforts to ameliorate the worst social and political effects of laissez-faire capitalism. In the area of food, such reforms included significant protection of farmers, food workers, and consumers. In a similar feedback loop, the spate of dreary forecasts spawned by think tanks and speculative fiction alike in the 1960s and 1970s contributed to the rush of environmental regulations that, if not preventing the End, have probably helped delay it somewhat. When Julian Simon boasted that the air, water, and food supply were significantly better in 1994 than in 1970, he was right—but it took a heavy dose of dystopian doomsaying in the interim to leverage those improvements. And at present, critics of biotechnology are employing familiar dystopian rhetoric—in names like "Frankenfoods," "Farmageddon," "Brave New Pharm"—to win political support for strong regulation of genetically engineered products.

There are many examples of the interaction between science and fiction. In *Space and the American Imagination,* Howard McCurdy shows how architects of the U.S. space program drew their inspiration from space operas and science pulps they had avidly consumed as children. Completing the loop, U.S. space policy gained public backing through the space stories and tourist sites constructed by Disney's imagineers in the 1950s and 1960s. Along the same lines, science fiction magazines inspired the streamlined design of the great techno-utopian world's fairs of the 1930s, which in turn influenced the ebullient roadside design of the postwar "Populuxe" era. Similarly, Edward Bellamy's 1888 *Looking Backward* inspired the builders of Chicago's 1893 White City, which then served as the model for public architecture throughout the country. But sometimes imagination can outrun feasibility. The New Deal's subsistence homestead program was an overt—and ultimately unsuccessful—attempt to convert arcadian utopian dreams into federally financed farms and homes. Similarly, while pulp space fantasies won initial support for NASA's extravagant public works program, they also raised expectations that could not be fulfilled in the real world of space science.[4]

Speculative fiction foregrounds the utopian caveat—the great "ifs" upon which so many rosy scenarios hinge. According to Jean Pfaelzer, utopian novels ask, "What if the world were good?"[5] What would such a world look like? And what if we *don't* act wisely, what if we don't co-operate or share our resources? While think tank futurism tends to understate those possibilities, utopian and dystopian stories explicitly spell out the consequences of our good and bad behavior.

First the utopias. By imagining places where people *do* act nobly, utopian stories can make leaps of faith far longer than those of William Godwin, Frances Moore Lappé, or Julian Simon. And because speculative stories are usually set in a remote time or place, they offer a distant perspective on daily life—including those most domestic activities, cooking and eating. Through creative "defamiliarization," literary analyst Daphne Patai writes, speculative fiction helps us "break through the crust of the obvious" and see our own world anew and more critically. Such estrangement subverts complacency, Pfaelzer suggests: "As utopia permits a glimpse at what life can be, we notice, hopefully or critically, what life is. In utopia's inversion of 19th century reality, the Gilded Age rather than utopia appears to be, at least for a moment, unnecessary and untrue."[6] By showing us how societies *could* be organized to feed everyone adequately and efficiently, utopias suggest that hunger, agro-ecological devastation, and domestic drudgery are neither inevitable nor eternal.

As entertainment, utopian stories certainly do have inherent attractions.[7] Ultracompassionate, they really worry about present suffering, injustice, unhappiness. Ultraoptimistic, they generally support the Age of Enlightenment's faith in rational thought, planning, and humanistically "appropriate" technology. They address the big problems of life—war, hunger, inequality, bigotry, passion, child-rearing, sickness, unhappiness, spiritual emptiness—and they propose comprehensive solutions. Concerned with root causes, not piecemeal palliatives, they offer blueprints, not minor tinkering. Utopias prize convenience, utility, and efficiency—but as wholesale social *systems,* not just retail consumer goods. At the archetypal level, utopias take us back to the womb, where life is stable, simple, calm, peaceful, orderly, balanced, and completely nurturing. In addition to updating the classical themes of Eden, the Golden Age, the Heavenly City, Arcadia, and Plato's *Republic,* utopias reinforce key American myths, especially the Virgin Land (the New World as a place to start over from scratch), the City on a Hill (a small "beacon" model for the world), and the Middle Landscape (an ideal balance between city and country, industry and nature).

Like all popular entertainment, speculative stories are highly formulaic. One common narrative device is the visitor from our troubled world who winds up in a very different one, usually through one of four different ways. In what might be called the Rip Van Winkle convention, the sleeping visitor wakes up in another time. In the Robinson Crusoe version, the voyager gets lost or shipwrecked in an unknown place. Or a Time Machine–type device bridges a time warp to the future. Finally, in the Odyssey format—most recently seen in the *Star Trek* series and films—the protagonist engages in an extended journey to distant places. Whatever the travel mechanism, upon arrival the visitor usually engages in lengthy philosophical conversations with local leaders, often while on tour or over extended, delicious meals. Since everything must be explained, speculative literature tends to be quite chatty. After initial disorientation, disbelief, and resistance, the visitor is converted to the ways of the new world. This may be signified by a romantic involvement with a native. The visitor then breaks the news to the folks back home via letters or a journal.

To these narrative conventions dystopian stories add their own special features. If a utopia is based on classical stories of Eden, Arcadia, and the Golden Age, a dystopia has even more archetypes: hubris (tragic arrogance), Babylon (the decadent imperial city), the Jeremiad (warnings of apocalyptic retribution for backsliding by the chosen people), Judgment Day, Armageddon. Dystopias tend to come in two basic varieties. The "hard" version may feature a Hobbesian war of all against all, a Malthusian struggle for the basics of life, a Darwinian survival of the fittest, or Garrett Hardin's "lifeboat ethics," where the strong throw the weak overboard. If it is set after a war or an ecological crash, the survivors inhabit the Wasteland, characterized by ruins, plagues, and deforestation. Sometimes just a tiny remnant of humanity is left—the Last Man motif. In the "soft" variant, life is too easy, with few struggles, so humans become weak, dumb, and vulnerable. This is the cornucopian dystopia in which abundance and security are achieved but at the cost of free will and thought—the totalitarian nightmare that most worried think tanker Harrison Brown as well as many fiction writers, especially after World War II.

As dismal as they may seem, dystopian stories are immensely popular—perhaps even more so than utopian ones. Like tragedies in general, they expose, project, and purge our worst fears. Delineating an "etiology of doomsday," Warren Wagar sees three kinds of fears: a basic dread of nature, our earliest childhood fears of powerlessness, and fear of what humans can do each other. Food certainly plays a role in all three. The harder, Malthusian dystopias project our archetypal dread that our natural, "animal" instincts will outrun the ability of the earth to feed us. In the softer, cornucopian dystopias, where abundance is produced at the cost of freedom, the diet is often synthetic, foul-tasting, and almost compulsory—a culinary symbol of the worst that humans can do to each other and also perhaps a recapitulation of children's distaste for meals imposed by dictatorial adults. But even the darkest visions offer some hope. Predictions of imminent catastrophe may give a sense of power to the powerless, as they can fantasize about the righteous punishment of those currently in control and the redemption of the worthy afterward, especially if the rebels or survivors succeed in rebuilding a better society. Wagar suggests that stories about such postcatastrophic survivors offer a refreshing simplicity, as daily life is reduced to the struggle for the very basics: food, shelter, companionship, and safety.[8] And as we will see, the "good" characters in these stories—the rebels, the survivors, the rebuilders—tend to prefer natural, healthy foods, with a strong dose of vegetarianism as well. As always, what you eat tells much about who you are.

In short, both utopian and dystopian stories are highly moralistic and inherently countercultural. Serving dissident interests, they are written by and for those who may not be heard in the mainstream debate. And yet these stories are not entirely outside the debate either, as they both reflect and shape the ongoing discourse. A steady regimen of utopian fantasies and dystopian nightmares has no doubt affected public expectations about current scientific developments—whether in aerospace (the outer frontier) or genetics (the inner frontier). Just as NASA's publicists must deal with popular hopes and fears shaped by space fiction and film, anyone wishing to convince a wary public of biotechnology's benefits needs to be aware of how science fiction has addressed humanity's efforts to control evolutionary biology. Similarly, anyone advocating foods that are highly processed, synthetic, or ultra-"functional" should understand that recent speculative fiction has not been kind to culinary modernism. In fact, today's modernizers might have had a more receptive audience in the late nineteenth century, when many utopian novels proposed to harness up-to-date cornucopian means (a general streamlining of food production and preparation) to egalitarian ends. But early in the twentieth century depictions of futurist foods turned negative, fostering suspicion of the modern and nostalgia for the premodern.

PROGRESSIVE-ERA UTOPIAS

Appearing toward the end of what might be considered history's most cornucopian century, late nineteenth-century utopian fiction certainly expressed much of that era's faith in progress. Given the enormous technological and imperial leaps enjoyed by Western elites, the culinary gains were indeed delicious. But while utopian writers shared the Victorian creed of "improvement," they also shared that era's darker concerns about whether this feast could be sustained indefinitely (that nasty Malthusian question) and whether this civilization could withstand the internal stresses resulting from a grossly inequitable distribution of the benefits (the egalitarian issue).

The social context was indeed grim. Hunger and famine seemed endemic in much of the world, including western Europe. Even in America, perhaps the most prosperous of societies, the inequities were stark. Millions of immigrants arrived from Asia and Europe, most of them impoverished. With factory automation, workers' skill levels dropped, as did wages. In the 1880s, the life expectancy for the average American was forty-five, the average unskilled worker made $1.50 a day, and one-sixth of all children between the ages of ten and fifteen held paid jobs. Rapid, unregulated economic growth produced equally spectacular collapses. The country experienced three major depressions in the late nineteenth century (all worse than the 1930s): 1873–77, 1882–85, and 1893–98. Many workers' strikes became violent as management brought in replacements and private armies. Radical socialist ideas spread, raising the specter of revolution. At the same time, the rich gorged themselves on ever more elaborate banquets served behind the high walls of their neomedieval castles. The strains of gross inequity took their toll on the affluent, too, as "neurasthenia" became a catch-all diagnosis for a complex of depression, hysteria, and nervousness. "Auto-intoxication" ("constipation with a college education") became a leading symptom of an overly civilized diet.[9] Suffocated by domestic confinement, feminists advocated for suffrage, birth control, equal property rights, and greater economic and educational opportunities for women.

Meanwhile, rapid technological innovation brought on a sense of future shock: steel, railroads, meatpacking, steam engines, telephone, electricity, pneumatic tubes, trolleys and subways, and synthetic chemistry all appeared during this era. As robber barons seized control of production, institutions of consumption also consolidated, as in the development of large department stores, full-service apartment houses, skyscrapers, land-grant state universities, art museums, and opera houses. While many Victorians felt that bigger was better, they also worried about the resultant loss of intimacy, control, and freedom. These anxieties played out in the era's richly ambivalent speculative literature—both apocalyptic and utopian. A distinctly dystopian strain of thought surfaced at the very beginning of the nineteenth century with the publication, soon after Malthus's original *Essay*, of Jean-Baptiste Cousin de Grainville's *Le Dernier Homme* (1805), in which medical advances foster overpopulation, which then leads to soil exhaustion, deforestation, the collapse of fisheries, and—to top it off—a dying sun. Grainville's story inspired Mary Shelley's own version, *The Last Man* (1826), which Mike Davis calls "the first truly secular apocalypse." Mounting fears later in the century fostered the literary destruction of familiar places—London, New York, California—by barbarous social and natural forces. Combining the insect and Asian images discussed in part I, California populist Pierton Doover's *Last Days of the Republic* (1880) describes an invasive "human ant colony of Chinese coolies"—low-wage farm laborers who get the vote, win a civil war against white militias, and take over Washington, D.C., where they raise the Chinese flag. English novelist William Delisle Hay's *Three Hundred Years Hence* (1881) forecasts Malthusian conditions of overpopulation (130 billion people), resource exhaustion, race war, and the extinction of most animals—as well as a dystopian-cornucopian response: totalitarian rule, submarine cities, synthetic foods, fungus farms, and the extermination of all nonwhite races. The xenophobic hysteria was repeated in many other fin de siècle novels, including John Mitchell's *Last Americans* (1889—the Irish conquer New York), Ignatius Donnelly's *Caesar's Column* (1890—a debased immigrant proletariat exterminates middle-class society), and King Wallace's *The Next War* (1892—blacks try to poison whites but are exterminated). Subversive worries that Nature might not be so easily dominated, or that it might even fight back, surfaced in novels detailing the revenge of natural forces over human ambition and arrogance, for instance, Mary Shelley's *Frankenstein* (1818), H. G. Wells's *Island of Dr. Moreau* (1896), Robert Louis Stevenson's *Dr. Jekyll and Mr. Hyde* (1885), and even Herman Melville's *Moby-Dick* (1851).[10]

Such nightmares motivated the utopians to rebuild a doomed society from scratch. Richard Jeffries's gloomy *After London, or Wild England* (1885)—capitalist greed, overpopulation, and agricultural bankruptcy turn London into a "vast miasmatic swamp"—inspired William Morris's sunny *News from Nowhere* (1891), which reconstructs post-apocalypse Britain into an ecologically sublime anarchist arcadia: the former Houses of Westminster have become compost bins, London's docks—once mighty depots of empire—have reverted to sleepy marsh, and "healthy and strong-looking" peasants breakfast on a "dark-coloured, sweet-tasting farmhouse loaf." Similarly, in W. H. Hudson's *A Crystal Age* (1887), the collapse of urban-industrial society is followed by a return to primordial forest life, where small groups of gardeners live in harmony with nature—a "Wordsworthian land of human regeneration through nature," I. F. Clarke writes. Given the strongly romantic roots of such stories, it is worth noting that after fleeing the disasters wrought by the overreaching scientist Dr. Frankenstein, Mary Shelley's forlorn Creature (often misnamed the Monster) attempts to regain purity by becoming a vegetarian—a standard trope in many English utopian redemption tales.[11]

Historians Kenneth Roemer, Neil Harris, and Howard Segal have studied over 150 utopian works published in the United States between 1880 and 1914—the genre's heyday. While most American utopian authors were white, male, middle class, Protestant, and often from New England, there were also many female utopians. Carol Farley Kessler has analyzed twenty-nine feminist utopian stories written by women between 1836 and 1920. Regardless of gender, most American utopian writers offered up a gentler middle-class socialism than that advocated by European Marxists. While not the most subversive voices around, they were perhaps more effective because they addressed a genteel culture that felt unheeded by either the urban "rabble" below or industrial plutocrats above. But unlike Henry Adams, whose revulsion for modernity turned racist and neofeudalistic, most American utopian writers offered modernistic solutions to overpopulation, civil wars, famine, and resource depletion. Relatively few Americans echoed the European romantics' love for handicrafts, dark breads, subsistence farming, and village-based communalism. William Dean Howells's Altruria (1894) came close—a pastoral "utopia of radical simplicity" where wood-chopping, mushroom-grazing villagers resist specialization and many modern comforts. Yet even Altruria has good roads, electricity, and a well-stocked library.[12]

The Morris/Hudson theme of a radical break with modernity would be more appealing later in the twentieth century. Most American utopians of the late nineteenth century hoped to build a just, sustainable, and urbane society using the latest technology. Unlike the utopians of a century later, the Victorians did not believe in either/or. Modernism *could* coexist with social justice and ecological balance. While they had much

to worry about, the Victorians also felt optimistic about many things—
great discoveries in chemistry, biology, and physics; advances in transportation and communications that promised to defeat ignorance and
alienation by bringing people together; and nearly revolutionary changes
in the organization of industry and business that promised to produce
more goods for more people at cheaper prices. The problem, most utopians believed, was not in these basic tools of science, technology, and industry but in how they were organized and for whose benefit. They sin-
cerely believed that cornucopian means and egalitarian ends could be
harmonized.[13] Perhaps the best way to understand this harmony is to
follow the food chain as envisioned by various late-nineteenth-century
American utopians, from field to fork.

THE UTOPIAN FOOD CHAIN

It makes sense, then, to start with agriculture, which is portrayed as fully
up to date, professionally managed, and, above all, neat. Upon their arrival or awakening, the visitors to utopia invariably describe the landscape
as a garden—a carefully cultivated, decorative, productive workplace that
also serves as a leisure forum for picnics, contemplation, and aesthetic
refinement. In this use of the word, "garden" suggests humanistic development, not primitivist retreat—a well-designed tool for the maximum
production of plants *and* pleasure. Production and consumption merge,
as do rural and urban landscapes. The farms in utopia have become more
suburban, with well-paved roads, architecturally decorative buildings,
greenhouses, fountainlike water supply systems, and effortless waste disposal. Rapid transportation and instant communications reduce the isolation of farm life. After cars appeared in the early twentieth century,
utopian farmers are described as living in town and motoring out to the
fields. This is a city dweller's fantasy of country life—a pastoral world
without sweat or refuse. Hence the lack of untidy, high-maintenance animals and the preference for minimal-care fruit trees, leaving considerable
time for reading, music, and chatty dinners. In the late nineteenth century
such "vine and fig" fantasies also propelled settlers toward Southern California, whose boosterish real estate ads promoted the ideal combination
of effortless horticulture and Mediterranean urbanity.[14]

If utopian farms have become more urbane, cities are more like farms,
as street trees bear fruits and nuts, rooftops yield vegetables, and park
ponds produce edible fish. Functioning as a horticultural cheap-food program, urban agriculture averts famine and elevates everyone's spirits. In

A. P. Russell's *Sub-Coelum: A Sky-Built World,* published in the terrible depression year of 1893, fruit trees line all the public roads, producing an aesthetic, nutritional, and political wonderland:

> The long lines of thrifty trees were a delight to see. In bloom, they filled the imagination. The bees made them musical. Filled with luscious fruit, they stimulated the palate and made happy the birds. Such walks and drives, bordered by fragrance and richness! Belonging to nobody, but to everybody! In full fruitage the bounty was in fruition. The Government, if a sentient, sentimental thing, might have realized the blessing, and led in the thanksgiving. Patriotism, under such conditions, was as natural as filial affection. . . . Generosity, too, was spontaneous. Easy supply was inseparable from free giving. . . . Better men and women were but the natural result of the never-ending munificence.

Appropriately, Russell's frontispiece quotes Shakespeare's *Coriolanus:*

> *Servant:* Where dwellest thou?
> *Coriolanus:* Under the canopy.

Life "under the canopy" is an agrarian pomological paradise, with a suggestion of infantile regression both in the effortless harvest—the fruits just appear—and in the taste, as Russell lingers on the soft, pulpy fruits, especially the native pawpaw, an "ambrosial . . . unsurpassable custard."[15] Such easily digested pap persisted in many utopias through the early twentieth century, perhaps a concession to the dental challenges facing middle-aged readers of these novels.

Unlike the ideal yeoman farm, however, most utopian farms are described as cooperative. In this sense they had less to do with Thomas Jefferson than with French socialist Charles Fourier (1772–1837), who argued that a highly disciplined communalism would achieve a balance between population and resources and thereby refute Malthus. One American Fourierist confidently predicted in 1851 that a fully "Harmonized" Europe could support four and a half billion people. Collectivization was also a way to defeat capitalist consolidation of agriculture. As early as the 1840s, Fourier's most enthusiastic American disciple, Albert Brisbane (principal writer for the short-lived periodical *The Future*), predicted that only through mechanization and cooperation could rural "Associationists" compete with the large-scale corporate "agricultural feudalism" of the near future. Acknowledging the economies of scale inherent in consolidation, American Fourierists proposed big industrial farms operated by hundreds of people living communally in neoclassical apartment blocks (located on suitably neoclassical campuses); such "phalanxes" would be linked to nearby urban consumers through good roads and clean, well-regulated public marketplaces. While Fourier himself—like William Morris later on—favored preindustrial-style crafts and subsistence, Carl Guarneri writes, "American Fourierists sought a greater role for technology in the phalanx, viewing it as an application rather than a repudiation of the principles of nature. Like the phalanx itself, mechanical invention extended man's mastery over nature, brought 'riches and abundance' that released humans to cultivate higher needs, and spread fraternity by increasing interchanges between peoples."[16]

Given their inclination toward technological agrarianism, utopian novelists adopted the latest proposals of the newly emerging agricultural experiment stations: soil rotation, careful genetic selection, specialization of functions and products, good brick housing for animals (raised for milk, eggs, and wool, not meat), close scrutiny for pests, wise recycling of wastes back into the soil, hothouses to extend growing seasons, and an overall intensification of production to feed more people on a limited amount of land. Thus the visitor/narrator in Charlotte Perkins Gilman's *Herland* (1915) marvels at how a Holland-sized "mighty-garden" easily feeds 3 million utopians by replacing wild forests with fruit-bearing trees and by practicing the latest methods of soil conservation—in stark contrast to the way profligate American farmers "skimmed the cream" of their own impoverished land. Some utopias include canning and manufacturing plants right on the farm to capture the value added by processing. As professionals, utopian farmers take courses (especially in botany and chemistry), write books, and retire while still healthy enough to travel.[17]

While some utopian writers addressed legitimate rural concerns—especially the isolation, hard work, and unfavorable markets—most were city people with an urban audience and urban prejudices. In some cases their interest in modernizing agriculture was not so much to help farmers as to eliminate the troublesome peasantry altogether. By 1999, Arthur Bird predicted in *Looking Forward* (1899), "all agriculturalists were 'gentleman farmers.' Their great slaves were electrical machines. They never groaned, complained, or knocked off work in the busy season to go on an excursion. The electrical farming implements could work all day without sitting under a shade tree with a jug of cider and a corn-cob pipe. They labored patiently and faithfully and performed their tasks with great accuracy." It is understandable that at a time of heightened populist agitation utopians might want to turn farmers into button-pushing masters of a technology that, driven by an unseen source, seemed "pure" and infinite. Utopian farmers are also envisioned as civil engineers—another emerging profession infused with cornucopian ideals—as they flood deserts, level mountains, shift ocean currents, alter weather patterns, tap the earth's core for heat to farm the tundras, and even slow the earth's rotation to lengthen the growing season. Embracing the artificial and synthetic, some utopian authors move food production indoors under glass and even underground—a move widely depicted as a triumph over climate, invasive pests, overpopulation, and messy organic life in general.[18]

In a few tales, farms become laboratories where chemists synthesize food directly from the elements—the ultimate in efficiency and purity. Domesticated animals were banished from the all-female Arctic utopia of Mary E. Bradley Lane's remarkable *Mizora* (1880), but the women ate "chemically prepared meat. . . . No wonder that they possessed the suppleness and bloom of eternal youth, when the earthy matter and impurities that are ever present in our food, were unknown to theirs." Reflecting the new dietetic dictates of the Gilded Age, such foods were considered well-balanced, sterile, and wholesome. Here again, modern utopians incorporate cornucopian means but with more egalitarian goals. Using chemistry "to solve the problems of cheap light, cheap fuel, and cheap food," *Mizora's* scientists outdid even Liebig and Berthelot in their invention of bread synthesized from limestone refuse (left over from all the marble used to construct the utopia's stately neoclassical mansions). "Bread came from the laboratory and not from the soil by the sweat of the brow. Science had become the magician that had done away with all that." But *this* lab was operated entirely by and for women. Kristine Anderson's introduction to the 1975 edition suggests that "*Mizora* is a woman's dream of total control—not only of her own body, mind, and soul, but of her whole environment," a world of "absolute female power in a world created by and for women."[19] These feminist goals permit one significant culinary anomaly: the use of *natural* fruits and vegetables. Since, following the gendered dietitics discussed in chapter 1, these are already classified within the female sphere of control—unlike meat and wheat—there is no reason to replace them. Only the male sphere has to be appropriated. While few utopias go as far as *Mizora's* elimination of men entirely, most do alter the conventionally gendered power structures. This essential difference in control of production made these stories seem so utopian at the time—and perhaps now, too.

As middle-class city people, utopian writers gave far more attention to food distribution, preparation, and consumption than to agriculture. Edward Bellamy's *Looking Backward* (1888)—the most important utopian novel of its time—barely mentions farming or farmers, except for the almost mandatory allusion to the gardenlike landscape and a passing mention of storing staples to insure against bad harvests. Bellamy describes the utopian Boston of 2000 in detail, however—the hassle-free shopping, pneumatic delivery system, public kitchens, gracious food service, and communal dining rooms. As the primary shoppers, women readers may have been particularly attracted to his progressive visions of congenial, safe, and honest marketing. The classically ornamented ward stores boast goddesses of plenty holding cornucopias—but no sneering clerks, ads, or bargaining. Similarly, Mizora's central market, with its glass roof, artificial heating and cooling, and lush flowers and shrubs, anticipates the year-round shopping mall, but without the manipulative commercialism. All foods are openly displayed, with ingredients and price (set at a "just value") on the label. There are no sellers; you just put money in the basket and take your own change. While different chemists produce foods of different tastes and even qualities, all foods are preserved "for years" without any loss of taste or safety. Mizora's vision of a pleasant shopping mall extends the one envisioned in 1836 by Mary Griffith, whose visitor to the Philadelphia of 2136 is enchanted by the all-brick, fireproof central market, with its rows of crockery, domestic wares, utensils, and seeds "all neatly arranged and kept perpetually clean." On the ground floor, cold stream water runs through "cool niches" to keep vegetables fresh. Food is displayed in tidy, neat rows, with no muddy residues. A visit to the butcher finds no sight of blood, no foul smells or grease. "In short, the whole looked like a painting." Market women sell delicious locally grown strawberries and green peas without hawking, begging, or haggling. Unlike the "coarse, vulgar, noisey, ill-dressed tribe" of real nineteenth-century markets, these saleswomen wear dress "appropriate to their condition and their bearing [has] both dignity and grace."[20]

Such sociological details reveal a hypercritical sensitivity to working-class pretenses—the "tawdry finery" and "sluttish, uncouth clothes"—as well as a strong desire to banish class conflict by, in effect, making everyone middle class. Service personnel—waiters, clerks, household servants—become equal partners committed to honesty and safety. At the butcher's stall, customers are described as merely requesting a piece of meat "and lo, a small door, two feet square, opened in the wall, and there hung the identical part." Meats are scrupulously weighed by law—no "butcher's thumb." Other utopian novelists shared Griffith's dream of "cleanliness, order, and cheerfulness" in the shopping environment. Some took their inspiration from the self-service, one-stop department stores that captivated the Progressive Era as models of cornucopian consolidation. Others introduced automated food delivery systems to save time and further reduce opportunities for troublesome class conflict. While many retailers today regularly offer what seemed inconceivable in the nineteenth century—even down to relabeling clerks "associates"—one key element of the Victorian stories remains as much a fantasy as ever: the lack of competition. Distressed by the unstable laissez-faire economy of the real world, most utopian writers eliminated the market in the interest of cutting wasteful duplication, dishonest marketing techniques, and the social disorder of the boom/bust cycle. In Edward Bellamy's Boston of 2000, central warehouses ship goods to large depots—one per ward—whose orders are based on long-term plans rather than on the messy vagaries of supply and demand. And consumers buy only what they need with credits issued equally to every citizen. In a way, then, the utopian distribution system came close to that of Soviet state socialism, and indeed the Bolsheviks experimented with Bellamy-like communal dining rooms soon after the 1917 Revolution.[21]

Perhaps the best illustration of the way these utopian stories join familiar elements of modern consumer society with radically egalitarian structures is their re-visioning of housework. Almost all of them anticipate key elements of the convenience-food complex that we in the twenty-first century now take for granted: packaged foods, labor-saving gadgetry, home delivery, and public restaurants. Underlying these conveniences is a democratizing desire to liberate women from household drudgery. Here Fourierism again prevails, for his communal "phalanx" featured a common dining room where cooking was streamlined through mass production, much the way the modern textile mill was democratizing cloth production. Along the same lines, in Jane Sophia Appleton's 1848 "Sequel to the Vision of Bangor in the 20th Century," community eating houses relieve men of the need to "buy" a wife to do housework, and so end the "absurdity" of one hundred housekeepers presiding over one hundred little ovens. For Appleton, private domesticity seemed as quaint and wasteful as the old-fashioned handloom, and her wonder at the efficiency and sanity of the communal kitchen would be repeated many times over the next seventy years:

> You would hardly recognize the process of cooking in one of the large establishments. Quiet, order, prudence, certainty of success, govern the process of turning out a ton of bread, or roasting an ox!—as much as the weaving a yard of cloth in one of our factories. No fuming, no fretting over the cooking stove, as of old! No "roasted lady" at the head of the

dinner table! Steam, machinery, division of labor, economy of material, make the whole as agreeable as any other toil, while the expense to pocket is as much less to man as the war of patience, time, bone, and muscle, to women.

Voicing similar hopes in 1870, Annie Denton Cridge dreamed of a large, mechanized cooking establishment that, by feeding one-eighth of Philadelphia's population at a single seating, would give housewives time to read, think, and discuss big ideas—and all at a cost lower "than when every house had its little, selfish, dirty kitchen."[22]

In *The Grand Domestic Revolution* (1981), Dolores Hayden shows how "material feminists" of the Progressive Era waged a multifront campaign for centralized, cooperative housekeeping arrangements in an ever-widening, mutually reinforcing circle of fiction, popular periodicals, nutritional journals, architectural designs, world's fair exhibits, and concrete business plans. For example, Bellamy's best-selling novels and follow-up articles in the popular press inspired the creation of Bellamy Clubs that, among other things, experimented with cooperative eating arrangements. H. G. Wells provided another bridge between speculative fiction and serious forecasting in *A Modern Utopia* (1905), which predicted the kitchenless home as an inevitable evolutionary advance: "The ordinary utopian would no more think of a special private kitchen for his dinner than he would think of a private flour mill or dairy farm." Promoting the progressive virtues of outsourcing and economies of scale, Charlotte Perkins Gilman argued that the idea of all domestic tasks being accomplished within the private home was "unevolved": scandalously wasteful, harmful to family members exposed to poor-quality cooking, and unfair to women. In *Herland,* Gilman's most futuristic novel, the socialization of all domestic tasks, including child-care, leaves women free to "mother" *all* citizens as members of one "sisterhood." Gilman likens this to the altruistic practices of worker ants and bees who nurture all offspring for the greater good of the whole colony—perhaps an intentional reframing of the Malthusian insect metaphor. Gilman acknowledged the difficulties of cooperation in the real world, however, and her "pragmatopian" stories sketch a somewhat less "evolved" modern world of kitchenless apartments serviced by home delivery businesses run by enterprising women.[23] Most utopians were more overtly socialistic than Gilman in their visions of public feeding establishments.

The utopian version of socialism was of a middle-class sort, of course, not a full embrace of proletarian culture and cuisine. Communal dining scenes in these novels often retain genteel etiquette, formal dress, fine china, and lengthy philosophical conversations. And, like the re-thinking of the shopping scene, it is not always clear whether women are being freed from kitchen drudgery or from lower-class kitchen drudges. In Annie Denton Cridge's 1870 dream of fully mechanized central kitchens complete with self-feeding pie machines (modeled after automated printing presses) and steam-powered "waiter wagons," the primary attractions are efficiency—no need to rely on the "small retail shop" of the private kitchen—and freedom from insolent immigrant servants: "No Bridget to dread now." In the cooperative utopia of Bradford Peck's 1900 novel, *The World a Department Store*, "all foods [in 1925] are prepared by skilled artists, on a very large scale, which saves the great waste of each private home running its own special culinary department." You phone a restaurant for a home-delivered meal and get a better dinner "at about one half the expense." Women are also spared having to deal with "incompetent and unintelligent servants." Instead they are served by "attendants" who come from the same class (thanks to the rotation of jobs) and who can be addressed as "brother" or "sister." Julian West, Bellamy's visitor to 2000, is similarly impressed by his well-dressed waiter, whose "tone" is neither "supercilious" nor "obsequious," more like a citizen soldier serving his country than a "menial" serving his betters. As Harvey Levenstein suggests, solving the "servant problem" was a primary attraction of these visions.[24] But genuinely altruistic impulses were involved as well, for the cooperative menial labor required in many stories—three years of compulsory national service in Bellamy's utopia—called for some self-sacrifice.

The same mixed purpose surrounded the fascination with labor-saving gadgetry—the pneumatic tubes, self-kneading bread machines, electric dishwashers, menuphones (for ordering takeout), conveyor belts (for automated table service), and so on. In "A Century Hence," a 1880 poem about 1980, it is hard to tell what is most attractive about instant delivery service—its convenience, its variety and abundance, or the speed of the deliveryman's performance and the distance he traveled:

An order for supper, by telephone now
Had scarcely been made, by my host,
When in sprang a servant, I cannot tell how
With coffee, ham, biscuit, and toast.
He'd come from St. Louis, three hundred miles out,
with dishes delicious and rare:
There were venison and turkey and salmon and trout
with pineapples, oranges, and pear.[25]

In Victorian utopias, such technological wizardry is by no means incompatible with progressive politics, for automation frees people for higher pursuits. Utopian leisure time is a serious, public-spirited enterprise—an opportunity to improve yourself and society.

Many utopian novels also feature socialized food preparation because it promises a more professional, modernized attention to nutritional needs and safety. Echoing the New Nutrition of dietary reformers like Wilbur Atwater and Edward Atkinson, utopian writers proposed a lighter, more "balanced" diet, with proper attention to the chemical fundamentals and a disdain for the wasteful excesses of the Victorian WASP diet. Central kitchens promise to produce a standardized, "wholesome" meal akin to that infamous gift of the home economics movement, the school cafeteria lunch, albeit much tastier. Explaining the theory behind such collectivism, Bellamy's Dr. Leete notes that when it rained in the individualistic nineteenth century, "the people of Boston put up three thousand umbrellas over as many heads," whereas in 2000—the "age of concert"—they simply cover the streets and thus "put up one umbrella over all the heads."[26] The centralized meal serves the same function by offering equal access to safe, cheap food—although recognizing that people also need privacy, it is also possible to eat home-delivered meals in your own dining room. In a way, utopians confronted the dietary issue much the way Henry Ford—a man said to be much influenced by utopian thinking—dealt with transportation: with an emphasis on utility, standardization, centralization, and an overall rationalization of basic processes.

Nineteenth-century vegetarianism was one of the products of rationalization, and its claims are aired more freely and fairly in utopian literature than elsewhere. Livestock raising is banished for ethical, ecological, and health reasons. For some utopians, foregoing animal products signaled solidarity with all living creatures, a commitment to nonviolence, and, given the identification of meat-eating with male power, an overt feminism. Others saw vegetarianism as an expression of human superiority over animalistic nature. In the all-female Mizora, artificially synthesized meat is considered "a more economical way of obtaining meat than by fattening animals." Similarly, in Gilman's Herland, eliminating livestock saves space, and the inhabitants are in any case outraged by the idea of eating flesh or robbing a calf of its milk to feed a human. Avoiding animal products also heightens purity, whether in the factory, kitchen, or colon. Herman Hine Brinsmade's Utopia Achieved (1912) offers perhaps the most complete set of arguments for vegetarianism—ranging from Sylvester Graham's theory that meat is overstimulating to an Upton Sinclair–style critique of meatpackers' excess profits and labor exploitation. Fulfilling the agenda of many Progressive-Era reformers, Brinsmade's New Yorkers of 1960 enjoy a "simple, nourishing diet" as instructed by the Federal Health Bureau's experimental stations, whose stated goal is to teach citizens how "to get the most nourishment, the maximum strength and health producing elements from the least amount of food." With food bills cut in half, citizens have more money to invest in education and the arts. Brinsmade's ascetic streak is also revealed in his description of a Lower East Side park dedicated to that "true pioneer" Horace Fletcher, "who unselfishly came among us when we were ahungered and athirst and pointed out to us the real way of living." Brinsmade thus aligned himself with Fletcher's wildly popular system of "thorough mastication," but it is doubtful that he won many new converts with the ideal daily menu for a middle-aged male utopian: a 2,000-calorie balance of "carbohydrates, fats, proteids":

> breakfast: gluten gruel, soft-boiled egg, creamed potato, zwieback, malt honey, apple, pecans.
> lunch: zwieback, cherry sauce, eggnog.
> dinner: vegetable broth, beans, creamed potatoes, cottage cheese, graham puffs, apple juice, malt honey, celery, apples.[27]

Preoccupied with efficiency and purity, some progressive utopians ventured even further in pursuit of a radically simplified diet. Several anticipated what would later be called nutraceuticals—products streamlined to combine economy and taste with nutritional and medicinal benefits. The dream of scientifically reduced essences was not new. When Bellamy's Julian West awakes in 2000, he is revived by "some sort of broth"—a successor to the all-purpose bouillon that was the centerpiece of eighteenth-century French nouvelle cuisine, which had distinctly utopian roots and ultramodernist goals. "The new [eighteenth-century] cookery," Rebecca Spang writes in The Invention of the Restaurant, "would, in condensing foods to their component parts and hence, purifying them, effect a sort of chemical equation, a scientific advancement." Such "restorative" cuisine—served in pristine "restaurants"—would promote enlightenment by liberating diners from the "animal coarseness" associated with gross chewing and "laborious digestion." "Its partisans," Spang notes, "contrasted the old-fashioned eater, weighed down with extraneous and heavy, earthy foods, with a modern eater, released from corporeality by his subsistence on 'essences.'"[28] The search for such biochemical essences animated much of modernist science, which hoped to streamline the whole food chain, from sunlight to stomach, down to a few basic processes.

Here again, science fiction was almost indistinguishable from science "fact." In the views of both, less was more. In John Jacob Astor's 1894 visit to the New York of 2000, all the health properties of food are fully discovered, so people can cure diseases "simply by dieting." Thanks to "aseptic foods," Jules Verne predicted, the people of 2889 will live an average of sixty-eight years, and scientists will be on the verge of the next major breakthrough: "nutritious air which will enable us to take our nourishment . . . only by breathing." Along the same lines, patrons of pulp-science-fiction pioneer Hugo Gernsback's Scienticafe of 2660 first stop at a room simply marked "Appetizer," where they inhale "several harmless gases for the purpose of giving you an appetite." The subsequent main course combines a number of speculative fiction staples—tubes, buttons, automation, scrupulous sanitation, and the extreme simplification of food to a nutritionally correct, infantile mush:

> They then sat down at a table at which was mounted complicated silver boards with off buttons and pushes and slides. . . . From the top of the board a flexible tube hung down to which one fastened a silver mouthpiece, that one took out of a disinfecting solution, attached to the board. The bill of fare was engraved in the board and there was a pointer which one moved up and down the various items and stopped in front of the one selected. The silver mouthpiece was then placed in the mouth and one pressed upon a red button. If spices, salt and pepper were wanted, there was a button for each one which merely had to be pressed til the food was as palatable as wanted. Another button controlled the temperature of the food. Meats, vegetables and other eatables were all liquefied and were prepared with utmost skill to make them palatable. . . . They did not have to use knife and fork, as the custom in former centuries. Eating had become a pleasure.

Best of all, Gernsback's future diners enjoy the health benefits promised patrons of those eighteenth-century nouvelle-cuisine restaurants (as well as NASA's hapless early astronauts): "People soon found out that scientific foods prepared in a palatable manner in liquid form were not only far more digestible and better for the stomach, but they also did away almost entirely with indigestion, dyspepsia, and other ills, and people began to get stronger and more vigorous."[29]

Similarly, in another *Amazing Stories* piece, the people of 3024 consume "essences" of "roast beef, wheat, chicken, cheese, potatoes, oranges, coffee and wine" that allow them to "avoid taking waste matter into [their] stomachs," not to mention doing away with "servant trouble and expense." Jane Donawerth reports that the labor-saving, sanitary appeal of synthesized "liquid food"—along with broths, "foamy concoctions," "chemical nourishments," and other paplike emulsions—was a common motif for female science fiction writers in the 1920s.[30] All-in-one wonders like Metrecal, Ensure, and Super Smoothies were just around the corner.

Following the reigning reductionist paradigm—all foods are made of chemicals, and it does not matter where these chemicals came from—a few utopias synthesize foods directly from the elements. Mizora's diet of "pure synthetic foods" guarantees "long lives free of disease and the ravages of old age"—a fact apparently evidenced by the uniformly blonde, athletic, Aryan appearance of all Mizorans. But chemical origins aside, Mizoran food still takes familiar forms—bread, meat, chocolate. Prizing artistic creativity in cooking, Mizorans employ professional cooks (well trained in chemistry) who take great pride in catering to their clients' diverse tastes. Like all true Progressives, author Mary Lane abhorred waste, but she was relatively unusual in holding that culinary individualism was the most efficient system. "What was palatable to one would be disliked by another, and to prepare food for a large number of customers, without knowing or being able to know exactly what the demand would be, had always resulted in large waste, and as the people of Mizora were the most rigid and exacting economists, it was not to be wondered at that they had selected the most economical plan. Every private cook could determine accurately the amount of food required for the household she prepared it for, and knowing their tastes she could cater to all without waste." While *Mizora* did anticipate some of the outlines of the emerging home economics credo—private, home-cooked meals executed in the most scientific and efficient manner—its food was more complex than most utopian cuisines.[31]

The reductio ad absurdum of all simplification schemes was the meal-in-a-pill, a popular fantasy that combined many progressive requirements: efficiency, freedom from housework and farm drudgery, chemical expertise, economy, and comprehensiveness. The fact that meal pills might actually reduce food choices enhanced their efficiency value, for this was the era that would soon embrace Henry Ford's Model T, which came in "every color as long as it's black." Just as the Model T expressed the one-size-fits-all mentality of early mass production, the meal-in-a-pill best embodied the efficiency engineer's determination to reduce costs by concentrating and streamlining essential life processes. For example, in his 1899 novel *Looking Forward: A Dream of the United States of the Amer-*

icas in 1999, Arthur Bird predicted that scientific management will produce "Ready Digested Dinners." Fulfilling Frederick Winslow Taylor's emphasis on prudent time management, meal pills free busy modern workers from wasteful, lengthy lunches—and the naps that came after heavy lunches. "In order to save time, people [in 1999] often dined on a pill—a small pellet which contained highly nutritious food. They had little inclination to stretch their legs under a table for an hour at a time while masticating an eight-course dinner. The busy man of 1999 took a soup pill or a concentrated meat-pill for his noon day lunch. He dispatched these while working at his desk." As was sometimes the case with technological utopians, Bird combined far-out gadgetry with social conservatism. In line with inherently patriarchal assumptions, his "fair typewriter" of 1999 prefers feminine "ice-cream pills" and "fruit pellets" to the more masculine "bouillon or consomme pellets."

More often, however, the meal pill was depicted as another tool to liberate women. For example, in 1893, feminist/populist agitator Mary E. Lease predicted that by 1993, agricultural science would allow us "to take, in condensed form from the rich loam of the earth, the life force or germs now found in the heart of the corn, in the kernel of wheat, and in the luscious juice of the fruits. A small phial of this life from the fertile bosom of Mother Earth will furnish men with substance for days. And thus the problems of cooks and cooking will be solved." In Anna Dodd's 1887 satirical novel about New York in 2050, *The Republic of the Future,* pneumatic tubes deliver prescription bottles of food tablets directly to kitchenless apartments. "When the last pie was made into the first pellet," Dodd's narrator explains, "women's true freedom began." The notion lived on well past the heyday of Victorian utopianism. According to Jane Donawerth, by the 1920s even the apolitical women writers of pulp science fiction frequently allowed for "meat tablets" along with other synthesized "essences" that, "by doing away with eating, . . . revised women's domestic duties, doing away with shopping for food, gardening, cooking, canning, preserving, cleaning up, and managing servants." Perhaps sensing that true women's liberation required freedom from reproduction as well as housework, the 1930 futuristic musical comedy *Just Imagine* depicted a New York of 1980 in which young lovers popped pills for meals while automats dispensed infants.[32]

While Anna Dodd was a social conservative who deplored feminist aspirations, her spoof—subtitled *Socialism a Reality*—closely mimicks the sober tone of her period's utopian aspirations to revolutionize domestic work. It also rides the undercurrent of doubt expressed in the period's substantial dystopian literature. For Dodd, erasing all differences risks diminishing intimacy, individualism, and humanity. Thus her visitor to utopian New York laments that while the labor-saving machinery abolishes all degrading labor, it also means that she is often alone. "Meals are served in one's own room, by a system of ingenious sliding shelves, which open and shut, and disappear into the wall in the most wizard-like manner. . . . It is all well enough, I presume, from the laborer's point of view. But for a traveler, bent on a pleasure trip, machinery as a substitute for a garrulous landlord, and a score of servants, however bad, is found to be a poor and somewhat monotonous companion." Dodd also applies the word "monotony" to the utterly orderly, clean, parklike streets in "this city of Socialists," the unisex clothing ("baggy trowsers"), the "uninviting" shop windows displaying "only useful, necessary objects," and, of course, the pelletized "socialists' diet" prescribed by a State Officer of Hygiene to meet one's daily requirements of "phosphates."[33]

However crude her caricature of progressive aspirations, Dodd does suggest why some feared that the technological utopian project might override the divergent desires and tastes of ordinary citizens. Sometimes these fears were expressed comically, as in Dodd's satire, or in Frank Baum's Oz books. Baum was a subtle satirist of the Progressive Era's overrationalizing propensities, especially in his sketches of absurdly arch minor characters. In *The Magic of Oz* (1919), Professor H. M. Wogglebug delights college students by inventing "Tablets of Learning," which reduce a full course of education to a few pills—one for mathematics, another for geography, others for history, handwriting, and so on— thereby freeing students for more important pursuits like baseball and tennis. So far so good, but then the worthy professor—perhaps a sendup of the overreaching chemist Berthelot—cannot leave well enough alone and turns his attention to food: "But it so happened that Professor Wogglebug (who had invented so much that he had acquired the habit) carelessly invented a Square-Meal Tablet, which was no bigger than your little finger-nail but contained, in condensed form, the equal of a bowl of soup, a portion of fried fish, a roast, and a dessert, all of which gave the same nourishment as a square meal." His students object, however, because they want "food they could enjoy the taste of." When the Professor persists, members of the senior class throw him in the river, where he lies helpless on the river bottom for three days until a fisherman hauls him in.[34] Baum's humor reflected a recurrent reservation about technological utopianism—the fear that science marches on to its own beat, deaf or indifferent to human needs for variety, nature, and commensality. If the scientists want pills, we'll get pills. As the new century progressed—or regressed—the convergence between scientific and social goals no longer seemed like such a good idea.

FIVE

DYSTOPIAS

A vibrant forum for discussion of social and scientific hubris, the dystopian story dates at least as far back as Mary Shelley's *Frankenstein* (1818). Utopia's evil twin, the dystopian story starts with the same speculative question: Can we invent a better, indeed a perfect, world? But the answers are quite different, mainly because dystopian writers refuse to accept the big "if" that is the central utopian caveat: *what if* people were wise enough to use cornucopian technologies for democratic, egalitarian purposes? Dystopias distrust such convergences between mechanical and social engineering, for the law of unintended consequences dictates that gee-whiz technologies do not always produce happy social results.

Concerns about a modernist blowback began to mount in the twentieth century. While some Victorians had expressed their doubts about the direction modern civilization was taking, their works tended to be either hysterically apocalyptic (e.g., Richard Jeffries's *After London*) or utterly romantic (William Morris's *News from Nowhere*). More complex second thoughts began to be voiced at the turn of century, particularly from British author H. G. Wells, whose love of science and invention was restrained by a keen awareness of political and natural limits. A cornucopian with strongly socialistic as well as Malthusian tendencies, Wells produced works of remarkable subtlety and ambivalence—and in virtually every genre, from sober white papers to far-fetched fantasy fiction. No wonder he is considered one of the founders of professional futurism.[1] Four of his early novels in particular anticipated the darker mood to come: *The Time Machine* (1895), *The War of the Worlds* (1898), *When the Sleeper Awakes* (1899), and *The Food of the Gods* (1904).

In *The Time Machine,* an amateur inventor travels to the year 802,701, where he discovers what seems, literally on the surface, to be a peaceful, harmonic, happy, and egalitarian utopia, a lush garden of nonstop leisure. The Eloi are universally beautiful, gentle, and affectionate. "They spent all their time in playing gently, in bathing in the river, in making love in a half-playful fashion, in eating fruit and sleeping." Nature seems to have been fully domesticated. "The air was free from gnats, the earth from weeds or fungi; everywhere were fruits and sweet and delightful flowers; brilliant butterflies flew hither and thither. The ideal of preventive medicine was attained. Diseases had been stamped out." But the Time Traveler soon realizes that the Eloi's apparent paradise has been achieved at the cost of initiative and intelligence. Their immaturity is symbolized by their small stature, their "Dresden-china-like prettiness," and their baby-food-like foodstuffs, which, in a send-up of a common utopian theme, are primarily "frugivorous"—heaps of ultrasweet pulpy fruits. Like children, they have no idea where their food comes from. Ostensibly capping the utopian drive to rid food production of all hard work and "impurities," there is "no evidence of agriculture; the whole earth had become a garden." Then the Traveler uncovers the grim truth: rather than highly evolved utopians, the Eloi are "mere fatted cattle" tended and consumed by the hideous but industrious Morlocks, who live in "ant-like" tunnels below the ruins of previous civilizations. Marshaling Darwinian themes rooted in Malthus and Hobbes, Wells suggests that struggle makes for strength while the utopian search for stability, security, and order—the "great quiet," as Wells puts it—may be suicidal. Bred for placidity and beauty, the feeble Eloi risk cannibalistic predation by mutant descendants of the industrial working class who, through the struggle for existence, have proved themselves more fit. "Only those animals partake of intelligence that have to meet a huge variety of needs and dangers." In questioning the Victorian equation of evolution with refinement, *The Time Machine* warns us against getting what we wish for, especially if it is peace and quiet. "Very pleasant was their day, as pleasant as the day of the cattle in the field. Like the cattle they knew no enemies and provided against no needs. And their end was the same." Appropriately, after barely escaping back to his own time, the Traveler refuses to relate his adventures until he has some meat: "Where's my mutton? What a treat it is to stick a fork into meat again! . . . I won't say a word until I get some peptone into my arteries." The familiar British red meat dinner offers a sustaining middle ground between overcivilized vegetarianism (the Eloi) and savage cannibalism (the Morlocks).[2]

The Darwinian struggle between disparate societies continues in *The War of the Worlds* (1898), but here the bourgeois British comprise the inferior culture, subject to imperialistic predation. Playing out Malthus's predictions, the British have momentarily eased their overpopulation problem by expanding overseas, only to find themselves invaded by ecologically exhausted but technologically superior beings from Mars. Armed with heat rays and suffocating black gases, the Martians easily subjugate the outgunned Britains, who resemble ants scurrying about in panic. Near the end of the story, Wells's narrator has an opportunity to observe the invaders up close. Having evolved far beyond humankind, their bodies consist of giant-sized brains who direct eight pairs of tentacles to cobble together mechanical external skeletons for movement and fighting. In the most horrific moment, the narrator discovers that the Martians, who lack digestive organs, gain nourishment from human blood transfusions. Yet in an ironic turn, the Martians also represent the utopian search for efficiency and purity. Unlike humans, who are so easily made happy or miserable by the state of their "gastric glands," "the Martians were lifted above all these organic fluctuations of mood and emotion."[3] Also, as consummate colonialists, the Martians treat humans as suppliers of basic raw materials that are used for more "highly evolved" purposes by home industries on Mars. And like those subjected to British colonialism, a few brave resisters plan guerilla forays from underground sanctuaries. But, in a final twist, the Martians are felled by lowly bacteria to which they lack resistance—a prescient commentary on the biological vulnerabilities that come with conquest and (inter)global microbial exchanges.

When the Sleeper Wakes (1899) may be Wells's darkest commentary on progressive utopian aspirations, for rather than setting his parable in the pulpish context of a remote time or an interplanetary invasion, he focuses his anxieties close to home—on capitalist monopolization of everything from food to thought. Whereas the Bellamyites hoped that business consolidation would lead to a benevolent state socialism, Wells feared the personal and social costs of conglomeration. Following the popular Rip Van Winkle trope, Wells's neurasthenic protagonist, Graham, awakes in 2100 in a sophisticated corporate dystopia where people are well fed and comfortable but virtually enslaved by a business oligarchy that substitutes empty consumption for political freedom. An obvious forerunner to Aldous Huxley's *Brave New World,* Wells's *When the Sleeper Wakes* rebuts earlier utopian expectations. Like Bellamy's Julian West, Graham is initially restored after his long sleep by drinking "a colorless liquid . . . with a pleasing faint aroma and taste and a quality of immediate support and stimulus." But instead of a paradise he discovers a huge metropolis with many technological utopian accouterments, including skyscrapers joined by pedestrian skyways, glass-covered public plazas, personal airplanes, and television. As in other predictive writings, the countryside has merged with the city, but not in the pastoral, suburbanized way envisioned by technological agrarians. Instead, thanks to agricultural mechanization, one engineer has displaced thirty farmers, who now crowd London's "human Maelstrom" of 33 million. With a sense of "infinite loss," Graham recalls his own infatuation with the arcadian London of "Morris's quaint old *News from Nowhere* and the perfect land of Hudson's beautiful *Crystal Age.*"[4]

Socialized cooking and dining have clearly triumphed in Wells's London of 2100, but again not as utopians hoped. With the "disappearance of the household"—"that little brick cell containing kitchen and scullery"—London now resembles a "giant hotel." But socialism itself has clearly lost, for this hotel has a "thousand classes of accommodations," all catered by the British Food Trust. With their high-rise apartments and private flying machines, the rich live higher physically than the subterranean proletariat, but a visit to an elite restaurant reveals the comfortable but essentially soulless life of a cornucopian dystopia: the antiseptically metallic and orderly tables (none of the "confusion, the broadcast crumbs, the splashes of viand and condiment, the overturned drink and displaced ornaments, which would have marked the stormy progress of the Victorian meal"), the automated self-service of "tastefully arranged dishes" traveling "along silver rails" in front of each diner (thanks to "democratic sentiment," none of "that ugly pride of menial souls"), the individualized taps dispensing "chemical wine," and the ubiquitous advertising, which is embedded in tabletops, displayed in "dioramas that marched majestically along the upper walls and proclaimed the most remarkable commodities," broadcast on huge balloons and kites visible from every window in this "gigantic hive."[5] Outside, the General Intelligence Machine blasts news of the latest military triumph over communists in Paris and rebels in Africa—a reminder of the military muscle required to sustain such a parasitic system. In all, *When the Sleeper Wakes* sketches a totalitarian nightmare that would be reiterated and reworked in numerous contexts through the century to come—ranging from Harrison Brown's *Challenge of Man's Future* (1954) to Ridley Scott's *Blade Runner* (1982).

Food motifs are most explicit in *The Food of the Gods* (1904), a comparatively whimsical parable about modern agricultural and nutritional science, as well as the progressive faith in Growth. Seeking to improve food yields, two "distinguished scientists" develop a growth-accelerating wonder feed—dubbed Herakleophorbia after the Greek god of strength. To test it out, they buy an experimental farm and hire incompetent assistants to run it. Almost inevitably, employee negligence produces "leakages," and before long, wasps, rats, chickens, and other animals are growing to monstrous sizes, whereupon they run amok. Food manufacturers soon start marketing "Boomfood" as a human dietary supplement. Consuming this "Food of the Gods," the Children of the Food mature into forty-foot giants who demand their right to the pursuit of happiness, leading to further conflicts with the remaining "little people," who are led by activist groups such as the genteel Society for the Preservation of Ancient Statures and the more radical Society for the Total Suppression of Boomfood.[6]

Anticipating the Killer Tomato/Frankenfoods motif of later dystopian stories, Wells's novel is, above all, a satire on how humans adapt to the accidental side effects of their own hubris. Against a backdrop of their fellow citizens being assaulted by giant rodents, waterbugs, and pullets, some seek to make the best of a horrific situation. A few try to profit from the new food. Others find community in the organizations that fight it. Journalists build careers hawking sensationalistic stories about it. Politicians appoint commissions to study regulatory options, while their opponents rally class envy by complaining that the poor do not have equal access to the growth stimulant. Scientists rationalize their mistakes as the inevitable by-products of overall progress. "These accidents are nothing. Nothing," one advocate insists. "The discovery is everything." Making lemonade from lemons, unregenerate optimists applaud the "convenience" of having such giant workers to "level mountains, bridge seas, tunnel your earth to a honeycomb." In an uncanny harbinger of later contamination scares, no one is able to control this self-sustaining dynamic, for "all the best intentions in the world could not stop further leakages and still further leakages. The Food insisted on escaping with the pertinacity of a thing alive."[7]

A shrewd social ecologist, Wells shows how one "wild card" can have broad social, political, and economic implications: "To follow the Food of the Gods further is to trace the ramifications of a perpetually branching tree. . . . Always it worked slowly, by indirect courses and against resistance. It was bigness insurgent. In spite of prejudice, in spite of law and regulation, in spite of all that obstinate conservatism that lies at the base of the formal order of mankind, the Food of the Gods, once it had been set going, pursued its subtle and invincible progress." Wells also skillfully captures the inability of normal people to comprehend fully the changes they are living through: "Looking at it in a shortened perspective of time, those years of transition have the quality of a single consecutive occurrence; but indeed no one saw the coming of Bigness in the world, as no one in all of the world till centuries had passed saw, as one happening, the Decline and Fall of Rome."[8] As Wells insightfully points out, apocalypses do not happen all at once; rather, they evolve incrementally, punctuated by daily cups of tea and slabs of mutton.

Wells did embrace the latest techno-utopian wonders in some works—such as *A Modern Utopia* (1905)—but the darker side of his writing expanded as the new century matured—and with good reason. I. F. Clarke's axiom, "The more the world changes the more it grows worse,"[9] seemed especially apt after the Great War. A species of mass madness in which millions were killed in a pointless disaster fueled by crude patriotism and propaganda, the war refuted the utopian faith in reason and improvement. Major economic and social changes also fostered a significant backlash against progressivism, as big business and private greed, rather than the benign leadership of wise technocrats, reigned. As Wells had feared in *When the Sleeper Wakes*, consumer culture took a decidedly irrational direction not anticipated by the utopian celebrants of household gadgetry. As Fordist mass production resulted in a glut of consumer goods during the 1920s, economic vitality required an ever-increasing standard of living—so unlike the utopian hope that people would embrace a stable level of comfort and convenience. To spur consumption, advertising appealed not to utility and sufficiency—the utopian economic standard—but to envy and fear. Exploiting those same variables, personnel managers manipulated workers through subtle "human relations" techniques. With pop-Freudian psychology holding that sexual repression bred neurosis and dysfunction, mass entertainment offered a degree of sexual license far looser than anything advocated by most Victorian utopians. And thanks to improvements in sanitation, diet, disease control, and medicine, the world's population was increasing rapidly. As we have seen, Malthusians worried about imminent food shortages and resource depletion, racists worried about the West being overrun by people of color, and eugenicists worried that the so-called genetically inferior would out-breed those with "superior" genes.

All of these concerns and trends found their way into Aldous Huxley's *Brave New World* (1932), which rivaled *When the Sleeper Wakes* as another important bridge between the Victorian utopian novel and the heavily dystopian speculations after the Second World War. Whereas the Victorians hoped that modernization would solve the traditional problems of *insufficiency* (too little income, reason, control, stability, and order), later futurists were more worried about modernity's *excesses* (too much population, organization, production, and persuasion).[10]

Like Wells's Eloi, the privileged Alphas of Huxley's New World seem to be leading rich lives that fulfill all the cornucopian aspirations while defeating the Malthusians' worst fears. The world population six hundred years from now is fully stabilized at a sustainable 2 billion through a well-coordinated program of compulsory birth control (including contraceptive "Malthusian belts" worn by all women) and industrial reproduction (in central "hatcheries"). To insure an efficient division of labor, babies' mental and physical capacities are manipulated in the bottle, so that the relatively small elite group of blonde and beautiful Alphas can be fully supported by the dutifully "ant-like" lower castes.[11] Genetic "predestination" thus prevents an effete upper class from falling prey to a more brutal but smarter lower class—a fear widely voiced by the "race suicide" alarmists.

Accepting Malthus's belief that the "passion between the sexes" is fixed and unchangeable, Huxley's controllers encourage promiscuity with partners who are described as "pneumatic"—a play on that Victorian technological fixation. Like reproduction, agriculture is fully industrialized, with chemurgic farms supplying raw materials for a variety of uses, as exemplified by the Internal and External Secretion Trust, whose thousands of cattle "provided, with their hormones and milk, the raw material for the great [baby] factory at Farnham Royal." Food is abundant, highly processed, and "good for you." Following the New Nutrition's chemical paradigms, infants at the Nursery suck down "their pints of pasteurized external secretion," while an adult sips a "cup of caffeine solution." Vitamania rules, as the character Bernard Marx serves carotene sandwiches and vitamin A paté, washed down by "champagne surrogate" at a party, while another, John Savage, buys "pan-glandular biscuits" and "vitaminized beef-surrogate."[12]

Natural foods are rare. Children who are being conditioned not to fear death receive *real* chocolate éclairs if they can watch a patient die without emotion. Top-ranked Alphas might merit real coffee (laced with the ubiquitous pacifier "soma"). But on the uncivilized "reservation"—an unkempt colony of misfits and rejects located somewhere in the American West—residents eat real tortillas and sweet corn, and when John Savage decides to defy civilization, he scrounges up whole wheat flour, real seeds, and a bow and arrow to hunt rabbits. Such romanticism disgusts most utopians, who are taught the modernist purity fetish that "Civilization is Sterilization." Synthetics dominate virtually every area of life, from clothing to music. Still, Huxley's Controllers stop short of Berthelot's *totally* artificial arcadia, mainly for economic reasons—to keep farmers occupied and thus prevent the disastrous migration seen in *When the Sleeper Wakes*.[13] Efficiency—the primary focus of progressive reformers—is good only to a point, and after that it is counterproductive. This is Huxley's central insight: waste is essential for the operation of a modern economy, where consumption is psychologically conscripted through multifront "emotional engineering," as in: "The more stitches, the less riches" or "Ending is better than mending." And whereas the progressives assumed that scientific discoveries would automatically advance human happiness, Controller Mustapha Mond suggests there is a big difference between pure science dedicated to truth and applied science harnessed to happiness. The latter is acceptable to the state because it is essentially formalistic and conventional, while the former is potentially subversive—and thus banned.[14]

In all, Huxley develops themes sketched by Wells into a full-blown cornucopian dystopia—a place where *some* rationality is employed to increase human security, comfort, and happiness but at the cost of freedom, truth, and equality. The result is a taste of the bitter future to come later in the twentieth century. Unlike the progressive utopians, who believed that benevolent evolution was on their side and that they could have it all—technology, order, and democracy—subsequent futurists were more aware of the need to make hard choices.

Reflecting as well as anticipating the outpouring of critical white papers after the Second World War, the dystopian writers of what Harold Berger calls the "New Dark Age" were highly "suspicious of bright promises." They were "believers in the . . . eternal gods of limits."[15] Heirs of Wells and Huxley, writers like Frederick Pohl, Ward Moore, and John Brunner extended and polished the central themes of dissent: a radical critique of consumer capitalism, technocratic efficiency, and corporate globalization; fears of the unintended consequences of cornucopian science; a strongly Malthusian fear of overpopulation, congestion, and crowding; and a preoccupation with the details of devolution. And when their utopian counterparts attempted to set up positive alternatives, they were hardscrabble, quasi-anarchist sanctuaries that tended to be more vulnerable, tentative, and polarized than those of the Victorian progressives, who had been able to openly embrace socialism *and* technology, Fourier *and* Darwin, without embarrassment or ambivalence.

Even before national security uses of nuclear power derailed prewar hopes for its peaceful application, and well before chemical cure-alls like thalidomide and DDT proved themselves deadly, speculative fiction often beat the news cycle in questioning modern techno-enthusiasm. Elaborating upon Wells's warning against biotechnological panaceas, Moore's *Greener Than You Think* (1947) offers the Metamorphizer, a growth agent developed to boost grain yields to feed a growing population. "Sow a barren waste, a worthless slagheap with life-giving corn or wheat," the inventor explains, "inoculate the plants with the Metamorphizer—and you have a crop fatter than Iowa's or the Ukraine's best. The whole world will teem with abundance." But the new product finds its best market among suburban gardeners, not farmers—just as later critics would predict that genetic modification would benefit the affluent more than the needy. As one lawncare salesman reasons: "Southern California was dotted with lawns, wasn't it? Why rush around to the hinterland when there was a big territory next door? And undoubtedly a better one?" When applied to lawns, however, the grass grows uncontrollably, soon engulfing whole cities and then out-competing food-bearing grasses such as wheat, corn, and rice. As is often the case, disaster results not from the invention itself but from its incorrect use, which leads to Malthusian famines, mass migrations, food riots, cannibalism, and, after the U.S. government tries to stop the grass with atomic bombs, a new world war. Farmers do reap huge profits, but from shortages, not increased production. "For the first time in three quarters of a century the farmer was topdog."[16] The biggest winner is Consolidated Pemmican and Allied Concentrates, a firm established by the lawn care salesman who fomented the disasters in the first place. Capitalism thus profits from crises of its own making. And in the ultimate Carthaginian solution, salt is applied to stop the grass—but it also renders the soil unusable. So much for the cornucopian faith in human adaptation and ingenuity! By showing the domino effects of a single ecological change, stories like Moore's highlight modern humanity's acute vulnerability—the way we have proliferated based largely on the cornucopian gamble that modern agriculture can keep growing enough grass (cereals) to feed us a highly wasteful diet. Remove the grass, however, and the Malthusian dynamic reasserts itself.

Numerous postwar stories and films explored the devolutionary Hobbesian/Malthusian results of runaway monsters—whether natural or manmade. Many of these stories involve atomic-related disasters and do not explicitly address food issues, except perhaps to reiterate familiar survivalist themes: the Wasteland, human sterility, and stark rations. More relevant to the complex modern food system are the stories of bureaucratic steady-state dystopias that manage to feed most people, maintain order, and even provide some comfort, at least for the elites, but at a terrible cost to human freedom. Yes, mankind *might* devise ways to handle the population problem, they warn, but you might not like the results. And given the Red Scare hysterias of the early Cold War, speculative fiction of the immediate postwar years rarely dares to offer a positive socialist alternative, especially after the 1949 publication of George Orwell's *1984*.

In his determination to put the nail in the coffin of all Bellamyite welfare-state dreams, Orwell shuns the ironic ambivalence of Wells and Huxley. To enhance the book's unrelentingly oppressive mood appropriate to the Malthusian gloom of the late 1940s, he offers consistently distasteful sensory images, especially the "usual boiled-cabbage smell" coupled with the "sharper reek of sweat" pervading the dim hallways of overcrowded apartment blocks. Even white-collar operatives like Winston Smith live in peasantlike poverty, subsisting at home on just "a hunk of dark-colored bread" and synthetic "Victory gin," with its "sickly, oily smell, as of Chinese rice-spirit." The "regulation lunch" at Winston's Ministry of Truth consists "of pinkish-gray stew, a hunk of bread, a cube of cheese, a mug of milkless [and synthetic] Victory Coffee, and one saccharine tablet." The stew, Orwell adds—"probably a preparation of meat"—has "the appearance of vomit." Winston, a victim of his own ministry's destruction of inconvenient historical documents—disposed of through pneumatic tubes, of course—struggles to remember any alternative, political or culinary. "Had food always tasted like this?" Yet Winston still feels a residual longing. "Always in your stomach and in your skin there was a sort of protest, a feeling that you had been cheated of something that you had the right to. . . . " Unlike Huxley's Freudian dictatorship, which encourages bountiful (if artificial) sex and food as useful diversions, Orwell's dystopia represses all sensual pleasure as subversive deviance. Sure enough, when Winston starts an illicit affair with

Julia, the sexual rebel, she also serves real sugar, "proper white bread, not our bloody stuff"—and "a little pot of jam," as well as real coffee, tea, and milk—all luxuries reserved for the ruling Inner Party. As the affair deepens, Winston fattens up and also shuns the Victory gin. Prompted by the madeleines of real food, Winston begins to remember and research the buried past—and it is this recovery of memory that does him in. Scanning banned documents, Winston reads Emmanuel Goldstein's "Theory and Practice of Oligarchical Collectivism," which exposes the basic economic premise of Orwell's dystopia. Like much speculative fiction, *1984* relies heavily on didactic memos and conversations to explain itself. And like the oligarchs of *When the Sleeper Wakes* and *Brave New World*, the rulers of *1984* seek total stability. But to attain order they must deal with the irksome surpluses that have long destabilized capitalist economies. While Wells's and Huxley's softer dystopias dispose of such surpluses through wasteful consumption, Orwell's harder, Hobbesian future relies on wasteful warfare. Inverting the usual Malthusian axiom that war is a check on excessive demand, Orwell asserts that it curbs oversupply. And in a jab at agrarians like William Morris, the Goldstein article observes: "To return to the agricultural past, as some thinkers about the beginning of the twentieth century dreamed of doing, was not a practicable solution," mainly because a deindustrialized, pacified society would be militarily vulnerable to more "advanced rivals." In the cruel final scene, after Winston's memory has been erased, he contentedly sips his Victory gin, spiced with clove-flavored saccharine, and cheers Big Brother's latest victory over "the hordes of Asia." As if to illustrate the irrelevance of all pastoral dreams, he does so at the Chestnut Tree, which, rather than a protective, "spreading" benefactor of romantic poetry, has become a desolate haunt for doomed artists and betrayed Party outcasts.[17]

1984 may have been the most widely known speculative novel of its time, and it was also the most humorless. More commonly, postwar dystopian writers relied on lighter satire. Speculative fiction aired critical perspectives, but resistance came covertly, through stylistic irony, and generally without the egalitarian or cornucopian alternatives posed by Victorian utopians. In the 1993 of Shepherd Mead's *The Big Ball of Wax* (1954), Con Chem runs everything, its products including a Mix-o-Mat, "from whose nozzle squirts (to a Tschaikowski theme) Ham-N-Egg Mix, containing every nutriment, a deodorant, and an antibiotic." The old feminist dream of liberated housework receives satirical treatment in Isaac Asimov's 1957 story "Satisfaction Guaranteed," in which a lonely housewife falls in love with her robot cook, who is more attentive and sensitive than her executive husband. In "The Last Trump"—published in the same Asimov collection—the brazen manufacturer of Bitsies, a breakfast cereal "teeming with energy in every golden, crispy flake," pleads with God to delay Judgment Day because there would be no need for food (especially Bitsies) in God's Kingdom. A few stories questioned the tendencies and assumptions of industrial agriculture. In Thomas Disch's *The Genocides* (1965), unseen aliens convert the earth into a farm for raising skyscraper-sized plants, with humans relegated to the role of garden pests. And in "To Serve Man," the 1950 story by Damon Knight that would become a memorable *Twilight Zone* episode in 1962, ostensibly well-meaning aliens offer a definitive culinary solution to overpopulation and famine—much in line with Jonathan Swift's "modest proposal" (1729) to turn surplus Irish children into tasty roasts for British carnivores.[18]

Dramatizing the case for birth control—still controversial in this period—sardonic stories about overpopulation extrapolated unchecked, exponential growth, with the dread consequences of synthetic foods, teeming cities, rampant crime, and the other Malthusian "vices." In Asimov's "Living Space" (1957), one trillion inhabitants crowd the planet in 2300. Recapitulating the migration solution to Malthusian conditions, those able to afford it purchase planets of their own, complete with self-sufficient glass-domed farms. To accentuate the distasteful effects of unhindered population growth, most Malthusian stories included at least some artificial foods. In Henry Slesar's "Ersatz" (1967), scientists develop "chemical beef made of wood bark" and smoke cigarettes made of "treated wool fibers." In Robert Sheckley's "The People Trap" (1968), people subsist on "processed algae between slices of fish-meal bread."[19] Suggesting that old association of overpopulation with Asiatic "coolie rations," the predominant flavor principle of dystopian cuisine is "fishy."

Following the migration imperative, overpopulated societies must expand somewhere—out, up, or down. In Richard Wilson's 1966 story "The Eight Billion," the 8 billion residents of New York, tiring of a diet based on "essence of plankton," dig downward to make room, only to be met halfway by Asians digging up. Many other stories head upward into huge skyscrapers and, beyond that, to the last frontier. In Robert Silverberg's *The World Inside* (1971), a twenty-fourth-century world of 75 billion live in thousand-floor urbmons (urban monads) as well as in outer space. The Malthusian nightmare touched even the ordinarily supercornucopian world of primetime television: in the popular series *Lost in Space* (1965–68), the Robinson family is selected from 2 million applicants to leave an overcrowded earth as humanity's last hope. Over-population also played a small role in two episodes of the original *Star Trek* series (1967–69).[20]

Though television just barely mentioned the overpopulation rationale in the 1960s, Malthusian novels grew more strident in depicting invasions of the earth not from outer space but, as Harold Berger puts it, "by her own kind." These stories clearly helped build a youthful audience for the think tank Malthusians of the period, especially the Paddock brothers, Georg Borgstrom, and Paul Ehrlich. In James Blish and Norman Knight's *A Torrent of Faces* (1967), continued opposition to birth control leads to a world population of over one trillion by 2794. The planet is covered by planned cities ruled by a technocratic elite. In this "frightful termitary," citizens "vegetate" in cubicles, eating synthetic food, enjoying sex, and watching three-dimensional television. Some humans have evolved gills to live in the seas, while pro-propagation leaders promote space settlements as the fulfillment of the human destiny to "seed the universe." In an ironic reversal, however, their plans are spoiled by an asteroid slamming into the earth—rather than man going into space, space comes to man.[21]

In many of these dark comedies, cornucopian improvisation represents, according to Berger, a "triumph of ingenuity over common sense." In Kobo Abe's *Inter Ice Age 4* (1970) scientists react to the melting of the polar ice caps not by reducing greenhouse gases but by eugenics experiments designed to create a new race of aquatic humans. In Robert Bloch's *This Crowded Earth* (1968), the scientific solution to the "moiling megalopolitanism" of cities like Chicago (with 38 million people) is to bioengineer genetic mutations that would keep humans under three feet tall (called "yardsticks"). Such pragmatic adaptations to man-made crises were no more far-fetched than the real-life fallout shelter craze, which seemed to fulfill H. G. Wells's fear that dire conditions would eventually force all humans underground. Similarly, later on, real-life biotechnologists would design plants able to withstand salinization, urban smog, global warming, and other disastrous consequences of human misengineering.[22]

Occasionally a story offered more active resistance to techno-corporate tyranny. Huxley's most immediate successor after the war was Frederick Pohl, whose absurdist parable, *The Space Merchants* (1952), coauthored with C. M. Kornbluth, sketches a hypercapitalist society ruled by ad men. Politicians are elected by corporations—for instance, the senator from DuPont Chemicals. Pohl and Kornbluth devote considerable

space, even more than Huxley did, to detailing the food system of a society facing extreme overcrowding, resource depletion, and conservationist unrest. "There's an old saying, men," one ad man intones. "'The
world is our oyster.' We've made it come true. But we've eaten that oyster." The fortunate white-collar worker might live in a tiny apartment
alcove, drive a bicycle (called a car), subscribe for police protection, and,
by playing along, show that he "knows which side his bread is oiled on."
Almost all food is artificial and foul: fabricated soyaburgers, regenerated
steaks, and recycled cheese sandwiches are washed down with cheap
"Coffiest," which "smelled of the yeast it was made from" and, with its
three milligrams of "simple alkaloid," is so addictive that it takes $5,000
worth of treatment to shake it off. A similarly self-sustaining cycle of
profitable addiction is engineered into canteen snacks; to ward off with-
drawal after a taste of Crunchies, workers drink Popsies, whose with-
drawal pains prompt a Starr cigarette, to be followed by more
Crunchies, and so on. The whole consumption process is reinforced by
ads with "compulsive subsonics" reminiscent of *Brave New World*'s sub-
liminal hypnopaedia. Mitch Courtenay, rising ad "copysmith, star class,"
grumbles about dinner at an expensive restaurant, where he pays "new-
protein prices and gets regenerated protein merchandise." In the familiar dystopian motif, natural foods are derided by experts: "If 'Nature'
had intended us to eat fresh vegetables, it wouldn't have given us niacin
or ascorbic acid." Exaggerating the postwar cornucopian fascination with
microbial food sources, most of the meat substitutes are fabricated from
Long Island kelp nourished by New York City sludge, plankton harvested
near Tierra del Fuego, and chlorella imported, according to hype written by Courtenay himself, "from the sun-drenched plantations of Costa
Rica, tended by the deft hands of independent farmers with pride in their
work."

Forced to visit the source of "the juicy goodness of Costa Rican proteins," Courtenay discovers an eighty-six-story "plantation," where
slave laborers skim algae from massive tanks to produce glucose, which
is then piped to feed the ultimate in biotechnological efficiency, Chicken
Little, a headless, legless, wingless mass of ever-regenerating white meat
"who would be sliced and packed to feed people from Baffinland to Little America."[23] (The idea was not quite new, as Winston Churchill had
heralded almost this exact wonder back in 1932.) But even with the elaborate synthetics and surrogates, there is not enough land and food, so a
giant cartel aims to colonize Venus next. Such moves are fiercely opposed,
however, by underground terrorists—"consies"—who, merging Malthu-

sian and egalitarian agendas, advocate soil conservation, population planning, reforestation, small farms and villages, radical redistribution of income, and the end of wasteful gadgets and "proprietary foods for which
there is no natural demand." The corporate establishment describes them
as "those wild-eyed zealots who pretended modern civilization was in
some way 'plundering' our planet. Preposterous stuff! Science is always
a step ahead of the failure of natural resources. After all, when real meat
got scarce, we had soyaburgers ready." As in Edward Abbey's *Monkey
Wrench Gang* (1975), the consies mount an opportunistic resistance—
in the form of blowing up a DuPont mining machine when it begins to
tunnel under a corn field. Radicalized by his own experience with Chicken
Little, Courtenay goes underground too, and in a sequel, *The Merchants
War* (1984), the consies are awarded an ecologically virtuous, ad-free
colony on Venus.[24]

By 1984, however, Pohl and Kornbluth's formula of synthetic/
corporate adaptations being attacked by nature-loving eco-saboteurs
seemed somewhat stale, for it had been repeated quite a few times in the
decades since their first book. For example, in Asimov's *Caves of Steel*
(1953), most of the world's 8 billion people are crammed into enclosed
cities (thus the title) living on fortified yeast derivatives such as "zy-
moveal" and "protoveg," prepared by centralized Section Kitchens that
fashion such glop into edible analogs. Like the globalized fast food chains
still to come, the Section Kitchens are the same all over the world. Still,
people have come to individualize and customize their massification—
much the way individual McDonald's franchisees would learn to "lo-
calize" their menus to suit native cuisines. "Be it ever so humble, the old
saying went, there's no place like home-kitchen. Even the food tastes better, no matter how many chemists are ready to swear it to be no different from the food in Johannesburg." Soil, air, and water outside the cities
are all polluted beyond use, and there are few wild animals left. Belying
the chemists' argument that synthetics would liberate labor, producing
enough yeast to feed the world takes an enormous amount of labor. To
make staples palatable—and profitable—the New York Yeast Company
sponsors genetic research to develop a strain of yeast that resembles strawberries. Indeed, just about the only city creatures to eat natural foods
regularly are zoo animals. But there is another group of people living
outside the cities—Spacers—who have reestablished agriculture and a
natural foods diet, and these are idolized by the rebellious Medievalists,
who subversively nibble bits of real food—such as sandwiches and juice—
while discussing plans to leave the cities and start dirt farming again. In

the post-Bellamy utopia, reformers not only look backward, they try to move there, too.[25]

Such scenarios appeared more regularly in the 1960s, reflecting and reinforcing that decade's apocalyptic mood. The most overtly Malthusian work of science fiction was Harry Harrison's *Make Room! Make Room!* (1966), which predated Paul Ehrlich's *Population Bomb* by two years. In a clear example of the interaction between speculative fiction and nonfiction, Ehrlich penned the introduction to the 1967 paperback edition of the novel, thanking Harrison for creating an imaginative extrapolation of the possible consequences of current "collective behavior." In Harrison's scenario, governments refuse to pursue population planning policies, and world population booms to 7 billion by 1999, with the United States at 340 million. While not all that far off from the realities of 1999, these numbers seemed huge in the 1960s, and to accentuate that sense of horror Harrison describes New York City as populated by 35 million people, who squat in hallways, sidewalk boxes, and, if they are fortunate, closet-sized apartments where they can run stationary bicycles to generate their electricity. As in J. G. Ballard's "Billenium," "the whole country is one big farm and one big appetite." With water either polluted, depleted, or diverted to agricultural use, residents use outdoor privies, line up at central fountains, and wash rarely, so the typical residential building is "a stifling miasma compounded of decay, dirt, and unwashed humanity." The rich elite live in air-conditioned condominiums behind turreted walls and moats—"feudal style"—where they might occasionally dine on scraps of scrawny red meat and wilted vegetables bought at extortionate prices through the underground black market or served at illegal (and also underground) "meateasies." The ordinary people shop at street "crumb stands" selling "beanwiches" and "weedcrackers," which are thinly spread with margarine made from reprocessed motor oil, whale blubber, and that dystopian staple, chlorella, with its "fishy" taste. Plankton, yeast, and algae are indeed the primary commodities, the last figuring in some intrigue to market a new and improved version, Soylent Green. The 1973 film adaptation of Harrison's book suggests that Soylent Green consists of recycled humans—a conflation of the utopian dreams of efficiency and the dystopian dread of cannibalism. But in the novel, it is horrible enough to ponder an algae-based diet, especially as even this invention cannot feed everyone. Fertilizer and water shortages reduce grain harvests, pesticides poison soybeans, and the greenhouse effect increases flooding, violent storms, and drought.[26]

Against a background of food riots and mounting malnutrition ("the kiwash"), some hopeful resistance is offered through the two main characters, the hard-boiled detective Andy and his aged roommate, Sol, who raises herbs in a window box, makes his own vermouth for old-fashioned martinis, and voices—rather didactically to be sure—Harrison's plea for birth control and conservation. And because the "naturist" Sol was a student in the 1960s, he remembers how to cook "real food." He serves as a bridge to the audience: shape up now or else! But Sol is killed in a riot, and Andy, after being displaced by a family with seven children, wanders Times Square alone and homeless amidst the celebration of the new millennium.

John Brunner's *Stand on Zanzibar* (1968) and its sequel, *The Sheep Look Up* (1972), present the most detailed—and certainly the longest—exposition of the Huxley-Pohl-Harrison theme: a hypercapitalist civilization confronting environmental degradation, class warfare, and underground resistance. In the first, a densely populated planet attempts to control reproduction through eugenics, forced sterilizations, and subsidized homosexuality, while replenishing depleted resources from space and the seas. The richest nations import sugar, fishmeal, cotton, and some "gourmet" specialties from the poorest, whose people barely get by on "mealie flour, sago and other starches."[27]

The sequel tells the story of eco-terrorist Austin Train, whose "Trainites" sabotage factories, automobiles, and power plants while raging against pesticides, veterinary antibiotics, and fast food. The dominant food conglomerate is The Trust, whose dome-covered hydroponics factory—which has a "vaguely yeasty smell"—turns cassava into Nutripon, a fungi-fortified base for a variety of analogs ranging from spaghetti to cheese substitutes. In a close approximation of what in fact did happen beginning in the late 1970s, the only people to enjoy "real" organic foods are the rich. At an insurance company luncheon, top executives discuss the "growth industries of the 80s"—scrap reclamation, sewage plant construction, and rehabilitating congenital defects—while feasting on "freerange, rich in carotene" hard-boiled eggs (in their shells!) along with "lettuces whose outer leaves had been raped by slugs; apples and pears wearing their maggot-marks like dueling scars; in this case it had been known for fruit growers to fake them with red-hot wires in areas where insects were no longer found; whole hams, very lean, proud of their immunity from antibiotics and copper sulphate; scrawny chickens as coarse as sandstone, dark as mud, and rubbed with wheat grains." Washed down with bottled mineral water, this meal is supplied by the Puritan Health

Supermarket chain, where one can also buy organic Okinawan spinach, penguin eggs (certified low in DDT), unwashed Pacific potatoes, New Zealand butter, and other trophies of the globalized health foods trade.[28]

Such fare is the co-opted version of the real countercuisine concocted by Train, whose Colorado commune attempts, William Morris–style, to subsist on organic gardening, handicrafts, and the customary freak bricolage of "glutinous African sauces of fine-chopped okra, tasteless cakes of anonymous grain." After an especially dismal summer of "dead plants, dead animals, dead rivers," the movement gains popular momentum— and cooking skills—and opens a natural foods restaurant serving "savory soups, home-baked bread, vegetables, and salads grown under glass." Scientists developing new synthetic foods deride the Trainites as "chlorophyl addicts" whose program would mean mass starvation. Yet even with Nutripon, millions starve, and the rebels themselves doubt that their resistance will add up to much. "What kind of future do we have?" one asks, in a clear link to themes well explored by Shelley, Wells, and other Last Man story writers. "A few thousand of us living underground in air-conditioned caves, fed from hydroponic plants? While the rest of our descendants grub around on the poisoned surface, their kids sickly and crippled, worse off than Bushmen after centuries of proud civilization." At the end, with Denver burning and the captured Train condemned to crucifixion (on television), the reader is left to ponder the meaning of the book's title, which refers to a corrupt church's unresponsiveness to hungry parishioners and comes from Milton's "Lycidas":

> The hungry sheep look up and are not fed
> But swoln with wind, and the rank mist they draw,
> Rot inwardly, and foul contagion spread.[29]

In the era of Johnson's and Nixon's presidencies, such tales seemed no more feverish than the news headlines, which featured burning cities, campuses, rice paddies, and rivers. Reflecting the mounting pessimism, the Sierra Club's chief editor quipped in 1970, "Some people are beginning to suspect that, due to a lack of interest, tomorrow has been cancelled." The Last Man genre of speculative fiction showed exactly how that cancellation might happen. Yet even amid the malaise, utopian stories thrived—as part of a youth-driven experimentation with communes, co-ops, natural-food restaurants, and other countercultural institutions. "If we choose to be plagued by big nightmares," an Earth Day 1970 handbook reasoned, "we are entitled to offset them with equally big daydreams." But unlike the Progressive Era reformers, hip utopians rejected modernist culture, labor-saving technology, and big government. Instead, as Harold Berger observes, the new rebels were primitivists who celebrated the survival value of "wild strains" as a protection against a stagnant monoculture. Hoping that cultural diversity, not progressive simplification, would save humanity, utopians looked to undomesticated cultural variants as a source for "hybrid vigor."[30]

If Harrison's *Make Room! Make Room!* was the most Malthusian dystopia, Ernest Callenbach's *Ecotopia* (1975) proposed the most didactic version of a sustainable and equitable future. Callenbach relocates William Morris's Nowhere to Northern California, which secedes, along with Washington and Oregon, from the United States in 1980. Playing out the familiar two-worlds pattern, a skeptical American journalist, William Weston, visits the rebel country, Ecotopia, in 1999 and writes diary notes for those of us left behind in the land of bad air, bad water, and bad food. Ecotopia spices a sober post–Earth Day think tank menu with zesty tastes of Aquarian popular culture. Crossing the border from Nevada at Tahoe, Weston boards a train packed with hanging ferns, beanbags, recycling bins, and marijuana-smoking cars. En route, he spies small farms, with well-tended tiny plots and ramshackle houses built of unpainted, well-weathered local wood. San Francisco is a "bucolic," neomedieval fair, with traffic-free narrow lanes full of denim-clad pedestrians, kiosks, ancient bikes, chestnut vendors, magicians, jugglers, and "absurd little gardens surrounded by benches." His first impression is of a return to the Stone Age, as even city residents hunt the now-abundant local game, which is prized for its "spiritual" qualities. A chapter titled "Food, Sewage and 'Stable States'" outlines organic farming basics, such as composted sludge, manure, nitrogen-fixing plants, beneficial insects. In "regressive" disdain for synthetics, packaging, and planned obsolescence, food co-ops feature core staples, few precooked or processed goods, and considerable education in "study groups" that compile "bad practice lists" of unhealthful foods. Similarly, restaurant patrons volunteer "cooperative criticism" of poorly cooked meals, along with constructive suggestions and affirmative hugs. Moving up the food chain, food scientists are "objective," with no ties to agribusiness and chemical companies. Pesticides are of course forbidden. As part of the stable-state ideal, all products must decompose, and 99 percent of wastes are recycled: "Better living through biology." With autos severely restricted, people move back to the central cities, and the suburbs revert to farmland serving regional markets. Avid ecological cost accountants, the Ecotopians "spout statistics . . . with reckless abandon. They have a way of introducing 'social costs' into their calculations which inevitably involves a certain amount of optimistic guesswork." They also devour histories detailing the prerevolutionary abuses of American food manufacturers—a focus on corporate responsibility that Weston finds "humorless," "moralistic," and "depressing"—the same disapproving adjectives employed in the 1970s by mainstream journalists accustomed to a much lighter, proindustrial approach to food issues.[31]

Habituated to highly processed synthetic meats, Weston dislikes the sugarless natural cuisine, although the local wines consumed at leisurely, talkative lunches are "excellent." Much of the culture seems openly Mediterranean, including the propensity of Ecotopians to gesticulate wildly while talking, although at other times they seem more like Native Americans with their "tree-worshiping" religion, tribalistic communities, and ethic of walking "lightly on the land." Like the Indians, hunters use only bows and arrows, study wild herbs and berries, and send very young children on survivalist wilderness hikes. With all their walking, noontime volleyball games, dancing, jogging, and skiing, they are much fitter than the "flabby" Americans. Most relevant to the think tank debate, Ecotopia's feminist social structure has actually prompted a reduction in the population—an egalitarian alternative to the coercive eugenics favored in Weston's own United States of 1999. Weston comments that by rejecting genetic engineering the "Ecotopians have blinded themselves to the exciting possibilities offered by modern scientific advances." Still, after much talk, many lengthy communal meals, and some good sex with accommodating natives, he concludes that Ecotopia does work, despite his doubts about its "fetishistic decentralism." Even the food, while not quite tasty enough, "is plentiful, wholesome, and recognizable." At the end, having discovered the California version of the womb—the hot tub—he decides to stay.[32]

A year after the publication of *Ecotopia,* Marge Piercy elaborated on Callenbach's themes in *Woman on the Edge of Time* (1976), though this time the two juxtaposed worlds are a disintegrating New York City in the 1970s and an eco-feminist countercultural utopia in 2137. Culinary details enhance the stark contrasts. At the very start, oppressive food imagery suggests the dreary life of the Mexican-American protagonist, Connie Ramos, who is beaten up and then sent to a mental hospital after fighting to protect her niece from an abusive boyfriend: "Lunch was a gray stew and an institutional salad of celery and raisins in orange Jell-O"—in other words, a mix of progressive New Nutrition and formalistic 1950s decorative cookery, with a dash of the baby-food mush predicted by some science fiction writers. Connie's inability to find affordable Mexican food conveys the homogenized, rootless quality of modern life. "Ridiculous to live in a place where the taste of your own soul food was priced beyond you." Like many poor people facing tough choices, Connie sometimes sells her tranquilizer pills to buy some pork or chicken to supplement her staple beans and eggs. Her normal breakfast consists of a scrap of stale bread dunked in diluted sweet coffee; to stifle snacktime hunger pains she drinks two cups of hot water. And more than once the only meat she can afford is canned dog food, which she spices heavily with chili powder and herbs. While Connie gratefully cooks any food, regardless of source or safety, her hip-gourmet contact from the environmentally purified future, Luciente, is terrified by the foods of 1976. "It's not true, is it, the horror stories of our histories? That your food was full of poisonous chemicals, nitrites, hormone residues, DDT, hydrocarbons, sodium benzoate—that you ate food saturated with some preservatives?" Even a bountiful Thanksgiving feast shared with Connie's rich suburban relatives is overprocessed and lifeless: canned sweet potatoes, stuffing from a bag, a boiled turkey (thanks to the aluminum foil wrapper) carved by a noisy electric knife.[33]

Transported to 2137, Connie first sees the arcadian anarchy of Mattapoisett, Massachusetts, through the filters of modernist pulp fiction. Expecting "rocket ships, skyscrapers into the stratosphere, an underground mole world miles deep, glass domes over everything," Connie is disappointed to encounter a "podunk future" of "little no account buildings" made of "scavenged old wood, old bricks and stones and cement blocks . . . wildly decorated and overgrown with vines." Clothing flaps on washlines in the breeze, cows graze ordinary grass, and a dark-skinned old man reminiscent of some uncle in her peasant past putters around the spinach plants. "Goats! Jesus y Maria, this place is like my Tio Manuel's in Texas. A bunch of wetback refugees! Goats, chickens running around, a lot of huts scavenged out of real houses and the white folks' garbage. All that lacks is a couple of old cars up on blocks in the yard! What happened—that big war with atomic bombs they were always predicting?" As a poor person, Connie is not sure she wants to wind up "stuck back home on the farm. Peons again! Back on the same old dungheap with ten chickens and a goat." Familiar with twentieth-century science fiction formulas, Connie asks herself, "Well, what did I expect from the future? Pink skies? Robots on the march? I guess we blew ourselves up and now we're back to the dark ages to start it all over again." What has happened to the technological utopian project? "She stood a moment, weakened by sadness she could name. A better world for the children—that had always been the fantasy. . . . But how different was [Mattapoisett] really from rural Mexico with its dusty villages rubbing their behinds into the dust?"[34]

Gradually, through Luciente's patient orientation, Connie comes to realize that this is not the Hobbesian wasteland of post-apocalyptic fiction, but rather a carefully planned attempt to construct a sustainable, egalitarian alternative. Over the course of several trips back and forth, Connie learns about the elaborate network of fishponds, greenhouses, double-dug beds, composting systems, windmills, cooperative farms, and vibrant local markets that make Mattapoisett "ownfed" *and* well fed. "We put a lot of work into feeding everybody without destroying the soil, keeping up its health and fertility," Luciente explains. Locally raised chickens, goats, rabbits, and turtles contribute animal protein, while most mammal meat is avoided because, following the classic argument, it requires too much land and resources—at least in the Northeast. In northern Mexico, on the other hand, an abundance of grazing land and a shortage of good soil make a beef diet more appropriate and sustainable. While Victorian idealists envisioned strong nations or global states with centralized warehouses and department-store-style commissaries, these postmodern utopians think locally. Sounding like neo-agrarians Wendell Berry and Wes Jackson, one of them asserts, "Place matters to us. A strong sense of land, of village and base and family. We're strongly rooted." And contrary to Connie's first impressions, there *is* a complex economy here. Located near the sea, Mattapoisett skillfully exploits its considerable seashore resources. When Connie notes the laid-back "mañana attitude" of Mattapoisett's workers, Luciente indignantly replies, in one of the more lyrical expositions of anarchist economics: "We have high production! Mouth-of-Mattapoisett exports protein in flounder, herring, alewives, turtles, geese, ducks, our own blue cheese. We manufacture goose-down jackets, comforters and pillows. . . . We build jizers [low-tech hovercraft], diving equipment, and the best nets this side of Orleans, on the Cape. On top we export beautiful poems, artwork, holies, rituals, and a new style of cooking turtle soups and stews!"[35]

As Piercy was more enamored of cool gadgets than most utopian writers of the time, *some* science is deemed appropriate to this goal: mild genetic engineering of plants to eliminate the need for pesticides or to increase the protein content of grains, personal computers ("kenners") that bolster memory, and, in probably the most striking revival of Victorian feminist science fiction, "brooders" that grow embryos. Uncoupling gender from reproduction frees men to be "co-mothers." To be sure, there is some debate about extending the uses of genetics; the "shapers" want to breed humans more deliberately for selected traits, while the more cautious "mixers" fear the "power surge" of intentional eugenics. But both sides distinguish such targeted interventions from the disastrous, large-scale engineering projects of the twenty-first century, such as weather control experiments that almost brought on a new Ice Age to northern areas and plagues of insects to the drought-stricken south. "We're cautious about gross experiments," Luciente explains, invoking the law of unintended consequences. "In biosystems, all factors are not knowable." So genetic engineering is mainly used to increase biodiversity and counter homogenizing modernism.[36]

While the gimmicks are almost too good to be believed, the book offers a credible blueprint for workable anarchism through reconciliation of individual and community needs. The most important institution is the "fooder"—a communal kitchen and dining room where, amidst animated discussions, people share large platters of the earthy, Moosewood-style fare that might also have sustained Morris's romantic rebels:

> a cornbread of coarse-grained meal with a custard layer and a crusty, wheaty top; butter not in a bar but a mound, pale, sweet, and creamy; honey in an open pitcher, dark with a heady flavor. The soup was thick with marrow beans, carrots, pale greens she could not identify, rich in the mouth with a touch of curry. In the salad were greens only and scallions and herbs, yet it was piquant, of many leaves blended with an oil tasting of nuts and a vinegar with a taste of . . . sage? Good food, good in the mouth and stomach. Pleasant food.

At first wary of the village's rich organic foods, Connie confronts her guide, Luciente: "You're trying to tell me you come from the future? Listen, in fifty years they'll take their food in pellets and nobody will shit at all!" Another meal—a lunch of cold leftovers—veers toward the nouvelle California cuisine of Berkeley's Chez Panisse (five years old in 1976): "A cold cucumber soup flavored with mint. Slices of a rich dark meat [local game] not familiar to her in a sauce tasting of port, dollops of a root vegetable like yams, but less sweet and more nutty—maybe squash? . . . A salad of greens with egg-garlic dressing. Something rubbery, pickled, hot as chili with a strange musky taste. Young chewy red wine." Mattapoisett's hip cookery resembles what Mike Davis calls the "gourmet survivalism" of many apocalyptic California novels, such as *Ecotopia*, Starhawk's *Fifth*

Sacred Thing (1993), and Carolyn See's *Golden Days* (1987), where the eco-feminist survivors of a nuclear catastrophe scrounge luscious weeds and berries in their "lushly Edenic" Topanga Canyon refuge.[37]

Like the didactic Ecotopians, Piercy's utopians avidly teach about the irresponsible corporate food system of the twentieth century; for example, one instructor illustrates a talk about "agribusiness, cash crops, and hunger" with holographic images of Sweetee Pyes (a children's breakfast cereal from Connie's time) and of braceros picking lettuce. As in Oxfam's Hunger Banquets of the 1990s, residents reenact historical inequities through week-long role playing, in which the community is divided into two groups, "rich and poor, owners and colonized. For two days," Luciente recalls, "all of us who got poor by lot fasted and had only half rations two other days. The rich ate till they were stuffed and threw the rest in the compost."[38]

As it turns out, Connie discovers that these class battles are not over. Rather, just as Callenbach's Ecotopians must fend off the rest of the United States, Piercy's utopians wage a guerilla war against a techno-fascistic alternative dominated by "multis" which "own everybody" and are controlled by "the Rockemellons, the Morganfords, the Duke-Ponts." Tapping corporate dystopian conventions, Piercy sketches a highly stratified world of "richies" living in fortified skyscraper-cities protected by genetically designed "cybos" (soldiers) from proletarian "duds" and "woolies" whose main legal income source is selling their own organs. Connie is transported into the tacky, gadget-filled (but kitchen-less) apartment of Gildina, a surgically enhanced "chica"—contract sex worker—who cheerfully fills her in on this violent, porn-crazed, terminally toxic extrapolation of pre-Disneyfied Times Square. Ultraprocessed food sharpens the differences with Mattapoisett. Lacking a stove or refrigerator, Gildina pushes a button that dispenses "a heavily spiced but ultimately tasteless and gummy" plate of "Vito-goodies ham dinner," made from the dystopian staples "coal and algae and wood by-products" on huge factory farms. Only the "richies" can afford real vegetables and meats and are thus spared the "chronic malachosis" and "ulceric tumors" of those who can't afford the "live stuff." Realizing that much of this world is a totalitarian outcome of the synthetic science of the late twentieth century, Connie returns to her own world determined to shape the future, and she does so, appropriately enough, by pouring a poisonous pesticide into the coffee of her psychiatrists, who are pioneers in surgical mind control. Declaring her revolution against an age that unthinkingly equates Chemistry with Progress, Connie moves us toward a future whose approach to nature, food, and society is best expressed in the pastoral scene of "older people, children, young people working here and there, weeding and feeding, picking off beetles, setting out new plants, arguing earnestly with scowls and gestures, hurrying by carrying a load of something shiny balanced in a basket on the head or on hip or back." Morris would have loved it—as did generations of young people interested in building a sustainable food system. Piercy's Mattapoisett was perhaps the 1970s' most extensive, affirmative, and overtly delicious utopian vision. In the literary equivalent of therapeutic forced feeding, it was quite possible to gain weight just by reading Marge Piercy.[39]

Such was not the case with another popular feminist utopian novel, Dorothy Bryant's *The Kin of Ata Are Waiting* (1971). A famous (male) author crash-lands in a self-sustaining Polynesian-style island community of ascetic, androgynous vegetarians who work their communal organic gardens and then feed one another at extended feasts that include— following the infantile regression theme—sweet pulpy fruits and a surprisingly tasty warm gruel. While seemingly inefficient, the mutual feeding has important ecological and social functions. The ritual stretches the island's limited food supply, for it is so time-consuming that natives cannot overeat. And the lengthy meals give community members time to tell each other stories, particularly the previous night's dreams. Unlike in the Callenbach and Piercy novels, however, the visitor never quite adapts, in part because he is always hungry, and perhaps also because he never couples with a nubile utopian.[40] Bryant's pristine utopia is almost a throwback to the more sterile, indeed puritanical, visions of *Mizora* and *Herland*. Most countercultural utopias attempted a more inclusively sensual approach to diet and sexuality.

More in tune with New Age sensibilities was Starhawk's *The Fifth Sacred Thing* (1993), which crosses Piercy's gourmet survivalism with Callenbach's eco-righteous Northwest secession from the rest of the country, particularly from Los Angeles, the perennial locale of disappointed dreams and apocalyptic disintegration. (According to Mike Davis's count, Los Angeles has been destroyed in art an average of three times a year since 1952.) Here, too, food signals contrasting ecological and political scenarios. Toxic Southern California is ruled by the corporate Stewards. While the rich elite can buy just about anything they want— including cloned "Angels" bred as sexual toys—the poor masses subsist on rationed beans, white bread, corn, thin soups, and polluted water. Southern culture is as oppressive as the food: fundamentalist, intolerant, patriarchal, and militaristic, with territorial designs on its opposite up north. With the Central Valley parched by the greenhouse effect, San Francisco feeds itself through community gardens, backyard chickens, and aquaculture. Precious rain water collects in small reservoirs and is pumped by wind generators into tiny streams that tumble down sculpted waterfalls into neighborhood plots and fish ponds. These natural streambeds attract geese, salmon, and playing children.[41]

Unlike the more static Victorian utopias, which reside placidly at the end of history, *this* pastoral future must be won and constantly defended. As in Callenbach's and Piercy's stories, the utopians in Starhawk's account confront not just an immediate military threat from outside (the Stewards), but also the "toxic stew" left by the corporate cornucopians of the twentieth century. In many ways, the latter battle is more difficult to win. In detailing the mess that our successors may need to clean up, Starhawk warns us to consider the inheritance we are leaving. And like Piercy, Starhawk whets our appetite for revolution with a gastro-erotic menu of open, mutually satisfying sex (which contrasts with the more exploitative variety down south) and "real," natural foods—garlicky multicultural stews, pupusas, dark brown breads, ripe local fruits, tangy wild salads, and so on. Even more of a mystic than Piercy, Starhawk details religious rituals, myths, and feasts that reinforce the north's sustainable ethic. For example, during a harvest festival, a story is told of the Four Old Women, who sparked a major rebellion in 2028 against the Stewards when they broke up pavement with pickaxes and their bare hands to plant trees and seeds (much as the People's Park rebellion of 1969 had animated the environmentalist movement of the 1970s). "Remember this story. Remember that one act can change the world. When you turn the moist earth over, and return your wastes to the cycles of decay, and place the seed in the furrow, remember that you are planting your freedom with your own hands. May we never hunger."[42] It is hard to imagine a more vivid embodiment of the activist priorities of Frances Moore Lappé's Food First, the Bay Area think tank.

The idea that planting a seed can found a new civilization is as old as civilization itself, and it is the central motif of Octavia Butler's *Parable of the Sower* (1993). Set in a Hobbesian world of 2024, *Parable* offers familiar California dichotomies, except that here we see things through the eyes of a *Southern* Californian attempting to head north. In Starhawk's version the south has attempted to establish order through heavy-handed Orwellian repression—a scenario also suggested in Ridley Scott's *Blade Runner* (1982). In Butler's L.A., there is hardly any order at all, even of the corporate fascistic variety. More disturbing than Piercy's or Starhawk's vision, *Parable* comes closer in mood to the most pessimistic dystopias. Its Wasteland is far more violent—with vivid suggestions of cannibalism, torture, gang rape, dogs eating people, and people eating dogs—while the glimmers of salvation are much dimmer. There are no full-fledged counter-cultural colonies presided over by aging hippy matriarchs, no animating visions of earthy banquets or fulfilling sexuality.

Instead, Butler invests just one grain of hope in one biracial teenage mystic, Lauren. Lauren's father attempts a Mattapoisett-type organic refuge, surrounded by walls and armed guards, in the L.A. suburbs, but it falls to pillaging gangs. Lacking money or connections, she cannot find shelter in the upper-middle-class fortress of Olivar, a coastal town that, in return for social and environmental security, has surrendered full control to a private corporation that profits from scarcity and chaos, much like Piercy's Multis and Starhawk's Stewards. But civilization is deteriorating so quickly that even Olivar's high walls may not withstand the drug-crazed barbarian hordes, not to mention the rising sea. Fleeing the doomed metropolis with just a small backpack of first-aid supplies, extra clothes, and a few vegetable seeds, Lauren leads a ragtag band of refugees toward a marginally safer rural retreat up north. While Callenbach, Piercy, and Starhawk all allow for some use of science to achieve sustainability, Butler's refugees must resort to scavenging clothing, wallets, and weapons from dead bodies just to survive. Still, the group does finally make it to Mendocino, where they hope to establish a multicultural, eco-spiritual community, Acorn. Though the reader is denied the usual utopian banquets, he or she is still left feeling hopeful as, near the book's end, Lauren inventories her seeds and plans her civilization-regenerating garden: "Most of it is summer stuff—corn, peppers, sunflowers, eggplant, melons, tomatoes, beans, squash, winter squash, onions, asparagus, herbs, several kinds of greens. . . . We can buy more, and we've got the stuff left in the garden plus what we can harvest from the local oak, pine, and citrus trees. I brought tree seeds too: more oak, citrus, peach, pear, nectarine, almond, walnut, a few others. They won't do us any good for a few years, but they're a hell of an investment in the future." The book's final lines—from Luke 8:5–8—reveal the archetypal roots of this against-the-odds horticultural future: "A sower went out to sow his seed: and as he sowed, some fell by the way side; and it was trodden down, and the fowls of the air devoured it. And some fell upon a rock; and as soon as it was sprung up, it withered away because it lacked moisture. And some fell among the thorns; and the thorns sprang up with it, and choked it. And others fell on good ground, and sprang up, and bore fruit an hundredfold."[43]

Butler's Last Man scenario is at least grudgingly hopeful—not like that offered by one of the twenty-first century's very first speculative novels, T. C. Boyle's *A Friend of the Earth* (2000), set in the ecologically degraded Southern California of a Malthusian 2025—with the world population at 11.5 billion. Normally one of the more original stylists, Boyle does not stray much beyond the corporate-dystopian recipes of Wells, Huxley, and Pohl, spiced with a dash of *Blade Runner* and *Soylent Green* and leavened with what Mike Davis calls "the gleeful destruction of Los Angeles."[44] Amorally opportunistic corporations serve up cheap sushi and fishy synthetics, while the super-rich hoard ancient frozen steaks in underground vaults. Homeless marauders threaten cocooned suburbanites, and cancer and dengue fever spread amidst a dying biosphere of clear-cut forests and rising oceans. Intensely hot summers buckle roads, seal cars shut, and foster pineapples in Sonoma and grapes in Norway. True to convention, Edward Abbey–type eco-radicals seek to avert catastrophe through creative monkey-wrenching and well-sexed communal living, but *these* "friends of the earth" fail: a young vegetarian tree-sitter—Boyle's equivalent of Butler's Lauren—falls out of the ancient redwood she is attempting to save, her father is arrested attempting to topple a power line, and a last-ditch, Noah's Ark–like attempt to protect a few surviving species of wildlife is overwhelmed by a massive El Niño storm—no Biblical reenactments here. As the book closes, the main character is left to proclaim, "I am a human being," but given the wreckage around him, it is not clear that this is a good thing.[45]

Welcome to the twenty-first century, when the devolutionary scenarios of speculative fiction would soon be overtaken by the real destruction of New York's World Trade Center by antimodernist terrorists, when deadly letters containing anthrax would recall the Anthrax Wars that had paved the way for Huxley's *Brave New World,* and when the U.S. government's response to global crises would be to invade the Middle East, curb domestic civil liberties, cut population planning, run up a huge debt, and walk away from international climate change treaties. Would H. G. Wells be surprised? Probably not, for he had predicted such things. But one suspects that Wells would also be more than a bit disappointed, for dystopian fiction apparently had failed in its primary purpose—to invent a better future by imagining a worse one.

PART III

THINGS TO COME

Three Cornucopian Futures

SIX

THE CLASSICAL FUTURE

If we were to focus solely on recent policy debates (part I) or on the more vivid, predominantly dystopian fantasies of the past half century (part II), we could quite possibly become terminally depressed, for according to most of these visions tomorrow's dinner prospects look precarious indeed. Even many cornucopian think tankers stipulate that the world will be able to feed itself adequately *only if* we behave in altruistic ways that can seem hopelessly unattainable in light of real world politics. As we have seen, this utopian caveat—that miracles can happen *if* humans act well toward each other—seemed quite plausible in the Progressive Era but became increasingly strained later in the twentieth century.

Yet even though we may dine on a daily diet of depressing news and apocalyptic entertainment, in America, at least, a hopeful culture endures—albeit somewhat privatized. Recent surveys reveal an "optimism gap"—a growing disparity between Americans' social and personal expectations. As social pessimists, we predict that life is getting worse for *other* people, but as personal optimists, we still expect our own lives to improve. Similarly, in what might be called the grass-isn't-greener syndrome, we may think *our neighbors* are in trouble while we are fine ourselves. Thus a 1993 poll showed that people in many Western countries believed the environment to be in much worse shape in *other* countries—a disconnect that statistician Bjorn Lomborg attributes to the "lopsided reality" of news reporting. By franchise, the press tends to focus on the bad things that happen to others, but many people still expect good news for themselves—

and rightly so, Lomborg asserts in his brash critique of environmental alarmism.[1] Likewise, scary stories about future food supplies do not seem to have lessened the high personal expectations for food, which has long represented the American Dream of abundance.

The news media probably do foster this divergence between social and personal anticipations, as front pages headline disaster while inside ads and feature sections spotlight the new and improved. A scan of "future food" articles of the 1990s reveals that food policy analysts and food marketers were inhabiting disparate universes. While dour, production-oriented farm and science reporters relayed the latest warnings and misgivings from reputable think tanks, the upbeat consumption trend-spotters in the "style" section forecast a healthier, tastier, and of course quicker culinary future. Similarly schizoid tendencies surfaced earlier, too, as when underground newspapers in the late 1960s and early 1970s proclaimed the end of the world up front and offered tasty recipes and hip restaurant reviews in the back pages. For example, page 1 of the July 3, 1968, edition of the *San Francisco Express Times* announced "War Declared" as national guardsmen gassed Berkeley protesters, while page 14 served up Alice Waters's recipes for marinated tomatoes.[2] Private life does go on, even in the worst of public conditions. And given the symbiotic dialectic by which pessimistic projections have inspired cornucopian inventiveness, utopian hopes can coexist with dystopian fears. Consider, for instance, the glittering world's fairs of the 1890s and 1930s, which were held during two exceptionally deep economic depressions.

Since the late nineteenth century, such fairs—and their Disney theme park successors—have offered a powerful education in the cornucopian future, a schooling reinforced by all those upbeat section 2 feature stories. Turning abstract scenarios into tangible experiences, fair displays offered tantalizing visions of bountiful meals to come. And their impact extended far beyond the fairgrounds, for the cornucopian ethos of world's fairs was matched by the daily retail environment of stores and restaurants, with their seemingly unlimited options. No wonder that infinite affluence is the default assumption of modern American culture.

Not all cornucopian visions have been alike, however. In this third section of the book I discuss three versions of the plentiful future: classical, modernist, and recombinant. The classical future is a continuation and elaboration of past progress—a future of ever bigger and better things made available largely through materialistic, quantitative, and often imperialist expansion. In the classical vision, the new evolves seamlessly out of the old. The modernist future, on the other hand, breaks sharply with the past to posit a radically new vision based on the very latest technologies and scientific breakthroughs, often producing a simpler, more consolidated result. For the modernist, the new requires a rejection of the old. The recombinant future is a self-conscious, self-referential blending of old and new, a reflection of ambivalence about the future.[3] Each of these schools of thought has had a heyday of sorts—the classical before 1920, the modernist between 1920 and 1965, and the recombinant since 1965—but with considerable overlap and blurring among them. At any one time or site—dining room, restaurant, or fair—one might simultaneously experience several futures, although one version is likely to prevail. Furthermore, while each version of the future can support a dominant, corporate-capitalist ideology, a more subversive, egalitarian-sustainable reading is also available. With such contested, porous categories, there are considerable political and economic stakes in the classification.

The classical future, which was the dominant cornucopian vision before 1920 or so, extends an idealized past, particularly the past of Western civilization, into the future. It is the future that looks the most like ancient Egypt, Greece, or Rome, only with bigger columns and better plumbing. It is a prosperous future achieved through imperialist appropriation of other lands, peoples, and resources. As we have seen, such colonial encroachments have been criticized by Malthusians and egalitarians as "the Big Grab," the "Bandit Plan," a parasitic "swarming." For its proponents, however, expansion into new frontiers signifies overall progress from savagery to civilization. According to the classical view, there are still many new places to find and grow food, and the conquest and colonization of these places stands to improve the lives of just about everyone, including the displaced and annexed.

A good, albeit somewhat late, example of the classical creed was geographer J. Russell Smith's compendium of untapped food potential in *The World's Food Resources* (1919). Addressing the resurgence of neo-Malthusian worries during the First World War, Smith exulted: "The earth is still a potential Eden with room . . . for many, many more of the children of men." The key, Smith argued, was a continued expansion of "sea trade"—the widening network of seaborne commerce that had created earlier empires—Phoenician, Greek, Roman, Venetian, Spanish, and British—and now, hopefully in service to more democratic forces, would enrich everyone. Conversely, the countries most in danger of starvation in 1919—Russia, China, Japan—were the most cut off from world trade.[4]

Smith went on to catalog the riches yet to be distributed by international commerce. Opening with cereals, the world's primary food source, Smith saw great potential for growing more wheat through the opening up of new lands (especially through irrigation, that most ancient of civilization-creating technologies) and the expanded use of minor cereals such as corn (still used in the West mainly for animal feed), quinoa ("a cultivated pigweed"), buckwheat, barley, and rice ("the cereal of the swamp"). Sounding an Edenic theme, Smith had high hopes for perennial tree crops, particularly acorns and nuts, as well as the "starchy foods of the tropics" (cassava, yams, bananas, palm). As for the largely unexploited tropics, "the great land resource of the future," Smith argued that it would take only a few whites to run plantations there. Expressing confidence in a benign white hegemony, Smith dismissed the Malthusian fear of being overrun by starving nonwhite hordes: "The white races of America and Europe would have nothing to fear from three or five or ten billions of black, brown, or yellow people in the torrid zone. They would be non-militant agriculturalists, carrying out, *as now,* the instructions of white men." Smith also extolled horticultural imperialism, the discovery of new plants by heroic botanical explorers whose dangerous expeditions to the "darkest" regions were well-known. (A good example of such successful acquisitions was the soybean, which was imported from China in the early nineteenth century as an obscure specialty crop and would revolutionize industrial meat production after World War II.) Like the British, Smith enthusiastically advocated suburban kitchen gardening—a species of domestic "improvement" revived during wartime food shortages. With world trade making foreign varieties available to gardeners, "the future supply of vegetables . . . is capable of indefinite increase." And since the seas were so important in Smith's cornucopia, he devoted an entire chapter to fish—"the great untapped reservoir." In all, Smith voiced considerable faith in the classical futurist package: expansion into the deserts, the tropics, and the oceans. And like many cornucopians, Smith also sounded the utopian caveat: all of this will be available for our use *if* we are wise enough to cooperate in a "world organization with a free sea permitting a great world trade."[5] Yet even though his rhetoric seemingly called for a new world, his explicit racism made the new order sound remarkably like the old.

The nineteenth century was the heyday of classical futurism, which repeatedly rationalized the imperialist "swarming" of the era as a triumph of the civilized over the primitive. To show off its gains and aspirations, Victorian material culture invented world's expositions, which

President William McKinley termed "timekeepers of progress." Starting with London's Crystal Palace Exhibition of 1851, the great Victorian fairs put on display huge quantities of the world's acquired bounty. Fair visitors could also appreciate how far civilization had progressed as they viewed the exhibits of displaced or conquered "primitives." Robert Rydell argues that such "ethnographic" exhibits dramatically charted the trajectory of the future by identifying resources awaiting further appropriation by "civilized" interests. "Depicted as resource-rich and lacking the material goods that anthropologists equated with civilization, 'primitive' cultures on display at the fairs had the effect of underwriting the predictions of a bountiful future for the culture of imperial abundance." And by displaying the numerous goodies to be enjoyed from this extension, fairs became—in Walter Benjamin's words—"sites of pilgrimage to the commodity fetish."[6]

Millions made the trip. According to Rydell, 100 million people attended the international expositions staged between 1876 and 1916, with another 100 million visiting the modernist fairs of the 1930s. In *The Making of Modern England,* Asa Briggs argues that the 1851 Palace of Industry, with its thirteen thousand exhibitors and 6 million visitors, testified to Britain's power in international trade and signaled that the "cult of progress" was displacing the Malthusian mood of earlier nineteenth-century British politics. The "classically imperialist" fair also dramatized economic evolution, Curtis Hinsley writes, by treating colonial products as raw materials to be refined in the more civilized mother country. Americans, too, soon learned the value of imperialism. At the 1876 Centennial Exhibition in Philadelphia, visitors to the palatial Horticultural Hall sampled bananas, chocolate, figs, and pineapples acquired, thanks to expanding capitalist supply lines, from distant tropical lands. They also admired a huge statue of Iolanthe sculpted from butter, and ogled Native Americans defeated in the ongoing Indian wars, which were transforming Indian hunting grounds into subsidized homesteads producing butter, grain, and meat for urban markets.[7]

The most influential of the classical fairs was Chicago's 1893 World's Columbian Exposition, which commemorated the four hundredth anniversary of Europe's invasion of the Americas, as well as the ensuing Columbian Exchange, which shuffled the world's food resources, enriched the West, and sparked a major population explosion wherever people got American maize and potatoes—especially in Europe, China, and Africa. Held amid mounting farmer and worker protests during a major depression, Chicago's White City celebrated riches already accumulated and reminded visitors that future progress required still further expansion. And as numerous historians have shown, the fair effectively *invented* that future by inspiring several generations to pursue it in the twentieth century. This lesson was repeated at the 1904 fair in St. Louis—held to commemorate another imperialist milestone, Jefferson's Louisiana Purchase—as well as at later expansionist celebrations such as Portland's 1905 Lewis and Clark Centennial, and the 1915 San Diego and San Francisco fairs marking the completion of the Panama Canal. Joining classical themes identified by historians David Potter and William Appelman Williams, Rydell argues that these world's fairs taught that being a "people of plenty" required "empire as a way of life."[8]

Since the 1893 fair at Chicago was the most famous of these fairs, it merits closer scrutiny. Befitting the assumption of continuity, the massive Agricultural Building resembled a Renaissance palace—an apt monument to its sponsoring merchant princes, whose ranks included meat packers Gustavus Swift and Philip Armour, agricultural implement manufacturer Cyrus McCormick, dry goods retailer Potter Palmer, and numerous railroad barons who had prospered by building routes that opened up new farm lands and transported farm products. This same neoclassical thinking guided the design of the USDA's Washington headquarters, countless newly founded agricultural colleges, department stores, museums, banks, and other monuments dedicated to cornucopian ideals. Appropriate to a palace of agriculture, as one guidebook noted, decorative motifs featured ancient gods of "abundance" and "fertility"— including a statue of Diana under the central dome—along with Edenic vine-olive-fig designs.[9]

Inside the Agricultural Building, both states of the union and manufacturers wowed visitors with piles of oversized commodities, such as "giant pumpkins, immense cereals, and phenomenal growths that attested careful and intelligent cultivation." As at earlier agricultural fairs, such displays of super-sized foods and animals celebrated the genetic selection process by which farmers had long improved their stock. That evolutionary progress would gradually increase the size of everything was a staple of classic futurism—as in John Elfreth Watkins's 1900 predictions that by the year 2000 people would be two inches taller, live fifteen years longer, and consume "strawberries as large as apples," "peas as large as beets," "cranberries, gooseberries, and currants as large as oranges," and cantaloupes large enough to "supply an entire family."[10] The Chicago fair simply provided an advance peek at inevitable, incremental growth. (Later, more cynical times would see such giantism as a cliché—as in

Woody Allen's 1973 spoof, *Sleeper*, in which a time traveler is chased by an elephantine chicken and is nearly injured as he lifts a celery stalk the size of a telephone pole.)

Especially popular in 1893 were an eleven-ton cheese from Ontario that took ten thousand milkings to create, pyramids of canned goods, obelisks of olive oil bottles, towers of oranges, and a very large map of the United States made of pickles, with vinegar rivers and lakes, dotted with spices marking the larger cities. The sheer enormity of these exhibits reinforced the sense of wealth, while the archetypal statues, monuments, and tableaux into which many foods were shaped suggested a comforting familiarity. One state offered its capitol building, "complete with noble porticos and columns," constructed entirely of grains and seed. Florida's exhibit included butter sculptures of Lady Godiva and Sleeping Iolanthe—mythic figures matched by New York's 1,500-pound chocolate Venus de Milo. A favorite construction material, chocolate was the building block of a 1,700-pound French statue of Columbus, whose third voyage to the New World had resulted in the first European encounter with cacao. Chocolate manufacturer Stollweick Brothers built a thirty-eight-foot-high temple made of 30,000 pounds of chocolate and cocoa butter; inside stood a ten-foot statue of Germania made of 220 pounds of solid chocolate, surrounded by six columns topped by flying eagles—all chocolate. Pennsylvania hung a copy of the Liberty Bell—built of wheat, oats, and rye—in "a beautiful temple of native products, surmounted by a cap of multi-colored beans." California plum growers shaped prunes into a medieval knight and horse, "complete with coat of mail, helmet and sword."[11]

The only basic foodstuff not to receive such architectural treatment was the "homely potato"—perhaps because of its association with the Irish famine, a Malthusian disaster that most Anglo-Americans still preferred to ignore. But on the whole these displays encouraged genuine delight in the diverse agricultural products now available to consumers. "All exhibits are so arranged as to give an idea of the variety and perfection of the farming products of the world," one visitor observed, "and art has so lent its aid that the homeliest products of farm and garden are wrought into pleasing forms." Such artistic arrangements bespoke progress from barbarism to civilization, as one commentator observed: "Oklahoma, though just emerged from the rule of Indian chiefs, made a grain exhibit which placed her in the front rank of great producing sections."[12]

In a sublime conjunction of two forms of "cultivation"—agricultural and aesthetic—farmers created displays pleasing to *all* the senses. Noting the seductive sensuality of the agricultural exhibits, one journalist marveled how "the perfume of fruits mingles with the fragrance of the harvest field and the odor of spices, and there is a freshness and sweetness pervading the atmosphere that one finds nowhere else." No classical futurist could imagine that diversity might actually decrease in a modern food system, or that basic grains like corn might someday be reduced to powdery raw materials for chemurgic transformation. Rather, just as the classical cornucopia—the horn of plenty—promised a never-ending, colorful melange of foods, the classical future envisioned an ever more diverse array of seeds. One catalog noted that Iowa's exhibit boasted of 130 varieties of corn ("worked into a Pompeiian palace"), Ohio's, 130 types of wheat, and California's, over 300 varieties of grain. Next to Los Angeles County's thirty-two-foot Tower of Oranges citrus growers spread "the finest specimens of Malta Bloods, Mediterranean Sweets, Wilson Seedlings, Joppas, St. Michaels, Konahs, Australian and Washington Navels," along with "Lisbon, Sicily, Villa Franca, Bonnie Brae and Eureka lemons, shaddocks, pomelos . . . China lemons, citrons, Mexican limes and apples." Modernist monoculture—a general contraction rather than expansion—had not quite taken hold yet, nor had consumers yet become indifferent or oblivious to nature's astounding variegation. At a time when Pillsbury was beginning to consolidate its hold on the flour milling business, its home state of Minnesota showcased 153 different brands of flour. While no longer "the granary of the Western world," New York State took pride in offering "an exhibit of the most highly developed and diversified agriculture of any state." And Massachusetts, too, "dispelled the error" of assuming that "husbandry was a neglected or forgotten art in the East." Even the fair's quasi-modernist foods—meat biscuits, saccharine, margarine—were presented as elaborations, not simplifications. It is a telling indicator of the effects of world trade, however, that foreign agricultural exhibits were more specialized—Costa Rican bananas, Mexican peppers, Brazilian coffee, Ceylon tea, Jamaican rum, Cuban sugar—an accurate reflection of the way commerce was annexing colonial economies to metropolitan markets. The metropole boasted of diversified farms, while the periphery congealed into monocultural plantations.[13]

As a tribute to horticultural imperialism, horticulture merited its own domed hall, which housed separate divisions for pomology, floriculture, and viticulture. Such plant palaces were a vital and familiar part of Victorian material culture, which prized the discovery and appropriation of exotic flora. The Crystal Palaces of the 1850s were in effect giant greenhouses—a technology long used to extend the growing season and to accommodate alien plant species. As a way of inventing the future, such displays had inspired the establishment of grand plant conservatories in numerous imperial capitals. Following the formula set by the Crystal Palaces at earlier expositions, Chicago's version offered lush palms, orchids, fountains, lily ponds, and live pineapples that created a fragrant tropical atmosphere. The result, according to one account, was a "perfumed palace." Capitalizing on the Edenic mood, individual states, particularly in the west, sought to attract new immigrants to establish commercial vineyards and orchards, which were depicted as virtually effort-free. Given the importance of the seas in the classical future, the Fish and Fisheries Building amassed large collections of fishing tackle, boats, and other "conveniences for fishermen." To sharpen the sense of evolutionary progress, one U.S. government exhibit contrasted a "lazy Negro" sleeping by a stream, with nary a fish in sight, with a "scientific angler" in a rubber suit using all the "latest methods" to land a very large (wax) bass.[14]

Such contrasts reinforced the pedagogy of the fair. A visiting Latin teacher from Minneapolis had little trouble detecting the point of the "ethnological" exhibits scattered throughout the grounds: "Beginning with the cliff dwellers and other primitive races, one can trace the progress of mankind in all stages of civilization and barbarism through the ages until he reaches the wonderful works of the nineteenth century." Most dramatic were the *real* "natives" inhabiting the "living villages" of the Midway, the fair's entertainment zone, where Otherness highlighted how far civilization had progressed. Observes one character in a novel set at the fair: "That Midway is just a representation of matter, and this great White City is an emblem of mind." Delineating the evolutionary triumph of mind over matter had in fact been a practice common to all imperialist fairs starting with the Paris exposition of 1867. "As a collective phenomenon," Curtis Hinsley writes, "the industrial exposition celebrated the ascension of civilized power over nature and primitives." Like white explorers, visitors to the fair discovered exotic views, tastes, and smells in reconstructed ruins, plazas, and bazaars. For example, along the popular "Streets of Cairo"—a "jumble" of orientalist stereotypes—Arabs skewered garlicky meats over smoky fires and, in brazen ignorance of Victorian dining etiquette, ate with their hands while seated on the ground. Dancing girls purportedly imported from Cairo and Algiers reinforced the exotic carnality. The encounters could be quite vivid and visceral; the same visitor who rapturously described the Hall of Agriculture's ethereal perfume complained of discomforting bodily odors at the Esquimaux Village.[15]

Descending "the spiral of evolution" down to humanity's "animalistic origins," visitors encountered the alleged cannibals of Dahomey, whose apparent depravity reinforced Victorian culinary cognitive maps that located Anglo-American beefsteak as the "moderate" ideal between savage cannibalism and vegetarian "coolie rations." In J. W. Buel's *The Magic City,* a photographic portfolio of the exposition, one caption asserts that two rather placid-looking black men practiced the "savage" and "cruel" practice of eating captives and (only during times of Malthusian scarcity) even their own kin. A caption under a photo of the Samoan village exhibit also hinted at cannibalistic practices, but the photo itself shows two young girls with arms around each other, staring sweetly at the camera. That these people never ate human flesh *in Chicago* seemed proof of the fair's "civilizing" influence. An editorial for *World's Columbian Exposition Illustrated* extolled the "boundless and unrivaled education" offered savages transported to Chicago's "object lesson" in "civilization and enlightenment": "If the cannibal loves to dine on human flesh will he not, by observing the evident advantages common to civilized methods of eating, learn to mend his barbarous ways?" Written in the midst of a deep economic depression, such bromides may well have been intended less for the African and Samoan performers than for unscrupulous American capitalists whose unchecked economic appetites were "devouring" their own society. For whites, Rydell suggests, sensationalized depictions of "darkness" also supported the spread of Jim Crow segregation during a period of escalating racial violence. Indeed, civil rights activists Frederick Douglass and Ida B. Wells critiqued the fair's racist underpinnings in a pamphlet titled *The Reason Why the Colored American Is Not in the World's Columbian Exposition.*[16]

Jim Crow ideology was made digestible at the fair's theme restaurants, such as the Louisiana Building's Creole Kitchen, a nostalgic vision of "snowily turbaned and aproned colored cooks and waiters, and superintended by young ladies of Caucasian blood, representing the beauty and hospitality of that Grand Commonwealth." And to take home, visitors could purchase Cream of Wheat and Aunt Jemima pancake mix, both of which debuted at the fair using minstrel show "uncle" and "mammy" stereotypes—an example of how, in Doris Witt's words, new processed products were "marketed in an expanding consumer system via the appropriation of the iconography of slavery." In another illustration of the fair's using real people to represent subordinated "primitives," Aunt

Jemima's makers, the Davis Milling Company hired Chicago cook Nancy Green to stand outside a gigantic flour barrel—yet another over-sized cornucopia—dressed as the legendary cook, flipping pancakes and telling nostalgic tales about the Old South. The act was so popular that Davis Milling issued a pseudobiography of Aunt Jemima right after the fair and hired Green to tour the country promoting the product, which she did until her death in 1923. Since many marketers followed this pattern of sending world's fair exhibits on the road, such images reached audiences throughout the country.[17]

The moral hierarchy of food, and of meat in particular, was elaborated even more fully at the St. Louis fair of 1904, which featured not only head-hunting cannibals but also the "dog-eating" Igorots of the Philippines. Here again, public policy coincided with exposition pedagogy, as the display graphically highlighted the stakes in the recent U.S. campaign against Philippine guerillas resisting the 1898 U.S. acquisition of those islands—a future source of many foodstuffs for Western markets. That Asians supposedly ate dogs was already a staple of Yellow Peril propaganda. Here, however, the threat to "man's best friend"—and to civilized norms in general—made a long-lasting, visceral impression. In a memoir of the 1904 fair written in 1970, Dorothy Daniels Birk still remembered the "dog-eaters," whose savage tastes contrasted with those of white visitors who preferred hot dogs, which were just then becoming an American pop cultural icon. "Up until several years ago," Birk recalled, "I did not know whether these tribes ever got real dogs to eat or whether they had to be satisfied with hot dogs. . . . I have since learned that they were given dogs, furnished by the city dog pound. Either the quality or the quantity didn't satisfy the dog-eaters, because dogs from homes around the perimeter of the fairgrounds were soon disappearing; when your pet didn't come back quickly, you could be pretty sure that it had landed in the soup kettle." This apocryphal story may have persisted in part because the popular Filipinos went on the road after 1904 and appeared in assorted fairs, carnivals, and sideshows. At Seattle's 1909 Alaska-Yukon-Pacific Exposition—another celebration of American territorial expansion—a local reporter joked about an Igorot's love of "The Simple Life. All he requires is his Pipe and his Pup. He smokes his Pipe and boils his Pup, and he is not particular about the Pedigree of the Pup." That the Igorots seemed content to eat *any* canine was further evidence of their distance from civilized "tastes."[18]

In addition to showing mock envy for the Igorot's "simple life," the same correspondent noted that the nearly nude Igorot was "visible to the Naked Eye. The Igorot is a very happy Individual. He ought to be Happy. He does not have to pay Two Bits every four days to get his Pants creased." While the humorist treated nudity as a matter of economics, what he was really talking about was sex, especially the highly erotic nature of these "primitives." Links between food and sex were well-established at these fairs. Repressive principles applied to both Victorian sexual and dining practices. Both had to be kept under control for the sake of civilized progress; otherwise a reversion to savagery might ensue. "An important element in [late-nineteenth-century] table manners," John Kasson writes, "was a recognition that the process of eating might reduce all involved to an animal level of appetite and competition, a Hobbesian 'war of all against all.' In a period of American history when economic competition was at its fiercest, rituals of refined dining guarded against the spread of such struggles into the private realm of friendship and family."[19] Confined to tight strictures within their own domestic circles, these people were intensely interested in what the "animalistic" Other might look like—hence the fascination with eroticized "cannibals" and "dog-eaters" who seemingly lacked genteel self-control.

Having established, through stark contrast, the outer limits of civilized etiquette, the fairs then afforded visitors opportunities to dine graciously at a cornucopia of restaurants, lunch counters, and exhibits. The 1893 Chicago fair had thirty-five different restaurants, a remarkably high number for an institution that was just coming into its democratic own. Restaurants were, in fact, still seen in futurist terms—part of the same evolutionary dynamic that inspired utopian writers to predict kitchen-less apartments, cooperative community dining rooms, and home delivery services. According to Rebecca Spang, although restaurants of the late eighteenth century had ultramodernist aspirations—to simplify the diet through the sale of "restorative bouillons"—in the nineteenth century they took on a more expansive, neoclassical role as "privileged locations for the experience of global variety." Victorian restaurants thus celebrated Roman-style overindulgence, not just in the multicourse menus but in the imperial decor and opulent windows displays of fresh fruits, flowers, and fish. Just as the fair presented "everything under one roof"—much like the department store, another late nineteenth-century marketing innovation with considerable utopian baggage—so the restaurant "promised the universe on a platter." At Chicago, the options ranged from Louisiana's Creole Kitchen and San Antonio's Chili Stand, to the "severely English" White Horse Inn and a Vienna café serving creamy desserts. Unlike the laissez-faire world outside the gates, however, prices were controlled by central management.[20]

Abundant "walking foods" further expanded the cornucopian choices a fair visitor could sample. Handheld hamburgers may have debuted at the 1904 St. Louis fair. Also at the 1904 fair, a Middle Eastern immigrant vendor stuffed ice cream into bent waffles, which he called, quite appropriately, cornucopias. Chicago fair visitors could also assemble "a good square meal" from all the free samples, journalist Marian Shaw wrote: "Here a dish of breakfast food with cream, here one of Aunt Dinah's pancakes, hot from the griddle, a little further on a delicious muffin, shortened with cottolene [lard substitute made of beef suet and cottonseed oil], your fill of soup, bovril, and bouillon, a nice cup of cocoa." As we shall see in the next chapter, there were also opportunities to try more modernist meals at the Electricity Building's automated dining room or at Ellen Richard's Rumford Kitchen, but on the whole the fair's food simply expanded on foods and tastes already well known. Thus Cracker Jacks, which debuted at the 1893 fair, incorporated two native American foods—corn and peanuts. Just as agricultural exhibits constructed myriad architectural variations on the theme of grass, the Illinois Corn Kitchen of 1893 hired noted cookbook writer Sarah Tyson Rorer to demonstrate innumerable ways to incorporate corn into breads, pastries, soups, and so on. Reflecting Rorer's cornucopian ebullience, a *New York Times* writer extolled the three hundred dishes Rorer had enhanced with this underappreciated grain, including "cream of cornstarch pudding, strawberry shortcake, strawberry meringue plunkets, strawberry float, hominy fluorandine, pilau, Brunswick stew, mush croquettes, cream pie, Boston bread, Victorian corngems, corn dodgers." As corn may be the Americas' greatest culinary gift to the post-1492 world, its promotion by a noted home economist reinforced the Columbian Exposition's theme of seamless progress through expansion.[21]

Although the fairs of 1876–1916 were the primary sites for celebration of the classical future, remnants persisted in later fairs and formats. For example, exhibits in the New York fairs of 1939 and 1964, and in Disney's EPCOT (1982), reiterated expansionist dreams of exploiting deserts, oceans, and tropics for future resources. At the 1939 fair, the Beech-Nut Packing Company Building featured an animated diorama depicting "a jungle scene in Central America where chicle, the basic ingredient of chewing gum, is collected from the Sapota trees and prepared for shipment to the United States." The 1939 Food Building likened the groaning modern table to a "veritable magic carpet upon which may be set at any season (and all at one time, if we will) food from any part of the world"—transported, perhaps, in the "treasure ship" constructed of Libby's cans. At the high-class end of the food displays, the 1939 fair also debuted the prototype of restaurateur Henri Soule's "citadel of civilization," Le Pavilion, which for the next two decades would be considered the "paradigm of haute cuisine in America"—and a major neoclassical imperialist beachhead.[22]

Later fairs sometimes dressed classical futurism in high-tech, modernist garb. In what Michael Smith calls the technocolonialist vision, General Motors' 1964 Futurama exhibit depicted enormous "jungle harvesters" converting tropical forests into "modern highways, towns, and industrial plants . . . in one continuous operation," while in desert wastelands "massive nuclear-powered irrigation projects fed large-scale, remote-control 'electronic farms,' which produced bumper crops from 'land too long sterile.'" Visitors to Futurama also journeyed to a submerged "Hotel Atlantis," where they could view aquacopters searching for "the riches of the deep." These visions carried over to Disney's institutionalized world's fair, EPCOT (Experimental Prototype Community of Tomorrow), where General Electric's Carousel of Progress depicted automated desert farms and floating sea colonies. Also at EPCOT, Kraft's The Land exhibit highlighted Sea Base Alpha, a corporate ocean settlement; Tropics House, a greenhouse demonstrating ways to convert rain forests into food factories; Desert House, yet another proposal for massive water projects that would make "the deserts bloom"; and Creative House, which showed how "aeroponics" and "lunar soil simulants" might enable us to farm on the moon. These "cosmic colonies" may have been more technologically complex than those of the 1893 fair, but the overall paradigm of feeding the future through continued colonization was as old as civilization—and indeed, as Roland Marchand and Michael Smith suggest, the goal of these corporate-sponsored exhibits was to rationalize their own expansionist agendas within that "timeless" context.[23]

Classical cornucopian themes also persisted in more vernacular sites. The spectacular, potlatchlike giantism of world's fair exhibits found echoes in mundane food retailing, as when grocers piled canned goods into pyramids and columns or seduced shoppers with pastoral streetscapes fashioned from seasonal vegetables. "Turn around and go into Mulberry Street, where both sides are lined with fruit-stand push-carts," Konrad Bercovici marveled in *Around the World in New York* (1924). "What strikes one first is the beauty and the variety of the vegetables and fruits sold there in what is supposed to be one of the poorest quarters." As Hasia Diner documents in *Hungering for America*, the very abundance of food stores and pushcarts in immigrant neighborhoods convinced new-comers that America was a classless utopia—at least in terms of food: "Immigrants never believed that the streets of America were paved with gold. Instead, they expected that its tables were covered with food." Even William Dean Howells's critical 1893 traveler from utopian-socialist Altruria was uncharacteristically charmed by the great "variety and harmony" of grocery store windows enhancing the "crazy gayety" of "plutocratic" New York's bustling avenues. One German "provisioner" began his display

> with a basal line of pumpkins well out on the sidewalk. Then it was built
> up with the soft white and cool green of cauliflowers, and open boxes of
> red and white grapes, to the window that flourished in banks of celery
> and rosy apples. On the other side, gray-green squashes formed the founda-
> tion, and the wall was sloped upward with the delicious salads you can find
> here, the dark red of beets, the yellow of carrots, and the blue of cabbages.
> The association of colors was very artistic and even the line of mutton car-
> casses overhead, with each a brace of grouse, or half a dozen quail in its
> embrace, and flanked with long sides of beef at the four ends of the line,
> was picturesque.[24]

The practice of such displays continued into the twentieth century, when roadside vendors attempted to snare speeding motorists with stands shaped as larger-than-life hot dogs, chickens, corncobs, root beer bar-rels, milk cans, and picnic baskets, all suggesting the great abundance available through expanding transportation and production. Design his-torian Chester Liebs observes that such "mimetic architecture" has roots that "reach at least as far back as the sculptured fountains and grottoes of ancient Rome, extend into the Middle Ages . . . , and are linked as well with the Renaissance art of topiary, eighteenth-century garden fol-lies, and the iconic work of French visionary architects." By the end of the nineteenth century, Liebs writes, "the public had become conditioned to associate this kind of representational giantism with both recreating and spending money"—two key elements of the cornucopian ethos. Early-twentieth-century chain restaurants also knew that security-conscious consumers valued architectural references to castles, churches, and colo-nial houses—the last perhaps the most popular as an enduring reminder that American prosperity required successful conquest, settlement, and growth. It was fitting, then, that the suburban roads lined with such eye-catching icons led to homes designed along the same expansionist principles. Take, for example, the 1950s ranch-style house, with its Spanish-cattle-kingdom name, its low-lying, land-consuming spread, its large picture window overlooking an expanse of well-grazed meadow, and its backyard barbecue designed to burn up large amounts of America's growing meat surplus.[25]

While providing the template for new strips and subdivisions, revivalist styles also pointed to major limitations of classical futurism. For one thing, assuming a smooth evolutionary path from the distant past to a glorious future ignores the bumps, wrong turns, breakdowns, surprises, and wild cards of actual history, which sometimes charges ahead in quantum leaps rather than small steps. As the automobile itself showed, change can be quicker and more drastic than anyone envisions. Early car manufacturers tried to ease the transition to the automotive age by calling their inventions horseless carriages, but these powerful machines turned out to have their own innovative capabilities and dangers. Similarly, there were new ways of making, selling, and even consuming foods that could not easily be tied to ancient Mediterranean models and metaphors. Moreover, it was by no means clear that classical archetypes could adequately address the increasing Malthusian concerns of the twentieth century. According to most analyses of future food needs, there would be very little new land available for farming—and the automobile-based urban growth of the twentieth century would actually encroach on land already being cultivated. So the old model of moving on to new lands when the old places have worn out would no longer suffice. At a time when the world population was increasing at an unprecedented rate, classical precedents were simply too conservative, blinding classical futurists from seeing the drastic changes already underway. J. Russell Smith, like many classical cornucopians, was so confident that the future would be a smooth extension of the past that he even dismissed the potentially revolutionary power of the tractor, which was just beginning to make inroads in 1919. "It is true that the farm tractor is on the way, but it has less prospect of displacing the work animal in food production than the automobile has of driving the work horse off the road." In fact, both unlikely changes did happen, almost overnight. Similarly, Smith's blindness to the just-emerging systems of intensified animal management led him to predict that meat consumption would likely drop—or return to more traditional levels.[26] While the classical vision promised security, it could also be stagnant, unimaginative, and complacent. And as the First World War belied the Victorian era's confidence in steady progress the whole classical vision began to seem archaic, even ridiculous.

The classical future also invited criticism. Where cornucopians saw a steady expansion of civilization, Malthusians saw an ill-fated attempt to escape ecological limits, and egalitarians saw exploitation, domination, and robbery. As we have seen, such alternative readings of the colonial/imperial dynamic gained considerable voice in the twentieth century, not just in policy debates but also in popular arts, thereby reinforcing growing resistance to imperialist agendas. Indeed, in the battle of archetypes it was possible to find classical precedents for arcadian futures that were very anti-imperialist. Thus some patrons of tea rooms in the early twentieth century welcomed the neocolonial style as a distinct return to the seemingly more "honest," informal, and democratic values that had been displaced by Victorian imperial grandeur.[27]

With the past an insufficient and highly contested ideological resource, some futurists turned to modernist images and paradigms to express their sense of radical *dis*continuity. And these, too, became firmly embedded and commodified in the culinary landscape of fairs, restaurants, stores, and kitchens.

SEVEN

THE MODERNIST FUTURE

The modernist future is one of radical discontinuities, of unprecedented needs, drives, and breakthroughs. It celebrates purity, shortcuts, simplification, automation, and mass production while dismissing soil, sweat, labor, craftsmanship, and ornament. Its favorite forms are tubes, beakers, buttons, domes, dials, and tunnels—the tools of engineering. It fosters consolidation, condensation, and reduction over expansion, extension, and elaboration. If the classical future exploits the visible riches of geographic frontiers, modernism finds wealth in the invisible— nitrogen from air, protein from microbes, energy from atoms. In culinary terms, it values nutrients over taste, fortification over wholeness, digestion over dining, health over habit, eating-to-live over living-to-eat. Seeking standardization, it defies season, geography, and time. While classical futurists are missionaries for an established, self-confident civilization, modernists are more like lone visionaries scaling a high mountain to take in the uncharted land on the other side. Preferring new to old, modernism exhibits a youthful impatience with history. And yet, while forward-looking, modernism also values the primitive and savage, not because it loves the prehistoric past but because, like the barbarians sacking Rome, it hates the classical. In this respect, modernism's disdain for excesses of the past echoes the Malthusian call for ascetic self-discipline and also the egalitarian cry for revolutionary change. Indeed, the modernist declaration of independence from tradition is quite volatile, as it unleashes forces that both support and subvert the growth of consumer capitalism.[1]

THE TRANSITION TO MODERNISM

While the Victorian fairs were largely classical in orientation, visitors could also find early hints of modernism there. Even as they popularized neoclassical architecture, these fairs also offered suggestions of the tightly controlled, totally artificial environments that were to become a staple of technological utopian fantasies. Thus the Crystal Palaces of London (1851) and New York (1852) were, in effect, domed, weatherstabilized cities—glass-and-iron forerunners of the modernist bubbles of H. G. Wells's *Things to Come* and Arizona's Biosphere 2, as well as shopping galleries and countless science fiction space colonies. Fairs also debuted the magic of electricity, whose invisibility and mystifying physics fostered belief in what Rosalind Williams calls "artificial infinities"—the aspiration to synthesize riches from unseen (in this case, subatomic) sources. According to David Nye, the electric lighting at late nineteenth-century world's fairs fostered a general receptiveness to "dramatic artificiality," while electrified moving sidewalks, railways, and boats unleashed new possibilities of movement. "Unmoored from daily habit and immersed in a fantastic environment, the visitor was prepared to receive new ideas about the larger direction of American culture."[2]

Primed by such artificial environments, fair goers then ogled displays of agricultural technologies that would revolutionize food production. While British visitors to London's Crystal Palace were disappointed in America's lack of aesthetic achievement, they were quite impressed by U.S. mechanical inventions—especially McCormick's reaper and Prouty and Mears's draft plow. While "artistic" European food exhibitors promoted elitist gastronomy and *terroir,* the "practical" American Gail Borden won a prize for his meat biscuit—an all-in-one functional food designed for efficiency rather than taste or elegance. The American propensity for radical convenience over neoclassical elegance was again the lesson of the 1867 and 1889 Paris fairs, which hailed American agricultural machines and advanced livestock as harbingers of a more productive industrial agriculture.[3]

While the neoclassical architecture of Chicago's 1893 White City emphasized America's imperial pretensions, some farm and food exhibits suggested that America's future might in fact be more modernist. The same Agricultural Building that featured monumental pyramids of produce and temples of commodities also gave space to USDA experimental stations and laboratories promoting a more "scientific" production of those commodities. Meat packers Swift and Armour showcased innovations in refrigeration, recycling, and mass disassembly that were making America an unmatched purveyor of cheap, if not always safe, animal products. Supplementing the colonial search for more cane sugar, domestic growers lobbied for beet and sorghum alternatives, and chemists offered tastes of "a wonderful chemical product called saccharine, derived from coal tar, 500 times sweeter than sugar." Processed food manufacturers promoted canned meats, desiccated soups, evaporated milk, packaged gelatins, meat extracts, and Butterine, a new oleomargarine, as well as the synthetic lard substitutes Vegetole, Cotosuet, and Cottolene. In the Electricity Building, visitors could marvel at the new "fireless cookers"—electric broilers, stoves, griddles, flatirons, tea pots, and stewpans powered by a resource said to be more sanitary, efficient, and economical. Public enthusiasm for these inventions led *Scribner's* to complain that while Europeans were excelling in the arts, Americans seemed more excited by "the application of electricity to filling teeth or converting sawdust into table butter."[4]

The 1893 fair also showcased the New Nutrition, which aspired to put American foodways on a more "scientific" foundation. The Rumford Kitchen served cheap, nutritionally balanced broths slow-cooked in Edward Atkinson's Aladdin Oven, a kerosene-heated box. True to her training and orientation as MIT's first female graduate and faculty member, Ellen Richards posted a chemical analysis of her largely vegetarian Rumford Soup—named in honor of the American-born Bavarian count who had crusaded for the "science of nutrition" in the early nineteenth century. Accompanying lectures and pamphlets spelled out the progressive paradigm, which, Laura Shapiro writes, prized quantitative recipes over qualitative results, efficient digestion over fine dining, economy over taste. According to Dolores Hayden, over ten thousand people tasted the Rumford Kitchen's thirty-cent meals, comprised mainly of stews, baked beans, and brown breads. But Richards failed to excite the working classes, who detected the prudish, even Malthusian belief that the poor should not be indulging in luxury chops and roasts. Still, the Chicago fair display inspired a generation or two of middle-class home economists, nutritionists, settlement house workers, and feminist utopians. As the public kitchen became part of the platform for social reform, Hayden writes, "a new approach to collective domestic life seemed to be emerging under the leadership of a small group of highly educated women trained to use the latest technological inventions." Indeed, Harvey Levenstein shows that the fair's New Nutrition publicity helped to propel middle-class Americans toward lighter, more health-conscious eating.[5]

Anxious to win the respect of her male colleagues, Richards kept her Rumford Kitchen out of the feminist Woman's Building, which celebrated the emerging New Woman but which Richards feared would be a marginalized "white elephant." Instead she had her kitchen built near the Anthropological Building—a fitting modernist coda, perhaps, to that building's chronicle of human evolution from savagery to civilization. Next door to the Rumford Kitchen—and nicely reinforcing its progressive premise—stood a kitchen run by Juliet Corson, head of the New York Cooking School. Corson was well known for her advocacy of the white sauce, whose bland consistency, Shapiro shows, suggested an obsession with purity, smoothness, and control. But those who ventured into the Woman's Building found improvements perhaps more useful than Richards's unpalatable scientific soup or Corson's blanketing white sauce. Unlike those top-down reforms, the labor- and space-saving devices on display in the Woman's Building came from ordinary working people and were much appreciated, according to one fair manager, by "crowds of despairing housekeepers." Reflecting a vernacular modernism, these pragmatic inventions included a sleek cooking cabinet, bread kneader, beef mangler, assorted cake beaters, a kitchen table with built-in containers for utensils and dishes, a "convertible chair" that combined an ironing table, clothes rack, and laundry basket, a frying pan with its own integrated ventilation hood, and a *gas* stove that worked better—and was more immediately usable in unwired homes—than the electrical prototypes hyped elsewhere. An automatic dishwasher was put to the test cleaning plates in some of the fair's restaurants. Reflecting the demand for public dining opportunities congenial to women, a "model lunch room" in the Woman's Building served healthy food that, according to one partisan, tasted better than most of the food at the fair.[6]

Some of the food exhibits at the Woman's Building aimed to raise housekeeping to a more educated level—like the popular Corn Kitchen demonstrations by home economist Sarah Tyson Rorer, who preached that "the inventor of a new wholesome dish is of greater value to his fellow creatures than the discoverer of a new planet." And to emphasize the sweat-free virtues of modern cooking, Rorer prepared her various corn dishes in a spotless silk dress—a dramatic touch employed in many ensuing "kitchen of tomorrow" demonstrations. But other presenters—there were over six hundred lectures—addressed a wider range of social and political issues of interest to modern women. And some exhibits openly explored feminist utopian possibilities, as in Mrs. Coleman Stuckert's model of a community designed for cooperative housekeeping—a block of forty-four attached homes surrounding a large common kitchen and dining room. Another spelled out plans for a cooperative child-care center and kindergarten. Pursuing and popularizing the utopian suggestions of Edward Bellamy and others, such proposals directly influenced proponents of socialized cooking, such as Henrietta Rodman, Lewis Mumford, and Charlotte Perkins Gilman, who joined a branch of the National Household Economics Association formed at the fair. For visiting school teacher Marian Shaw, the Woman's Building signaled "the emancipation of woman, who from her ancient condition of disgraceful servitude, has risen to be the equal and co-laborer of her former master."[7] Things to come indeed!

While the 1893 fair certainly contained the seeds of modernist culture and cuisine, these hints may be more apparent to historians than they were to contemporary visitors, for whom the White City's overarching theme was classical grandeur rather than radical discontinuity. Subsequent fairs continued to mix classical and modern motifs—as at the 1900 Paris world's fair, which may have been the best attended of all time, with over 50 million visitors. Food exhibits included a German coin-operated restaurant—perhaps the first automat—along with familiar mimetic touches such as cheese cows, chocolate ships, and a three-story champagne bottle. With its proliferation of exhibits modified by that favorite progressive adjective, "model," the fair at St. Louis (1904) clearly boosted the overall ratio of modernism. Along with the customary pyramids of commodities and Beaux Arts decor, the twenty-acre Palace of Agriculture featured a "model creamery," which produced five thousands pounds of milk daily "with all the latest butter and cheese-making apparatus of today," and an adjoining "model dairy lunch counter," which propagandized on behalf of pasteurization, a still-controversial reformist cause of the time. Showcasing the crusade to regulate American food production were a six-day International Pure Food Congress, a Pure Food Day sponsored by state governments, and, most dramatic, a Federated Women's Clubs test of well-known processed foods that found two thousand "adulterated" samples, including jars of candy with poisonous dyes and "orange phosphate that never saw an orange." Such events reinforced momentum toward the Pure Food and Drug Act of 1906, which, as both Levenstein and Susan Strasser have shown, actually helped to legitimize corporate consolidation of the food industry. The marked growth in branded convenience foods since 1893 was clear from a long list of displays that, according to one chronicler, "reflected the variety, enterprise, energy and color of a truly modern age." Perhaps the most "modern" were the packaged breakfast cereals, termed "pre-digested" in the unsentimental parlance of scientific nutrition.[8]

Although these late Victorian fairs had glimpses of modernity, their dominant mood emphasized imperial continuity. A more jarring break with the past came at the "century of progress" exhibitions—especially Chicago in 1933 and New York in 1939–40 and 1964–65. Modernist enthusiasm continued well through the mid 1960s, making the period between the two New York World's Fairs the heyday of the push-button style Thomas Hine calls Populuxe. But the route to these modernist worlds of tomorrow was actually paved in the 1920s, a period of wholesale questioning of the classical notions of Progress.

THE PLASTIC AGE

If there was a single event that undermined the Victorian faith in Civilization, it was the First World War, which killed millions in the heartland of the West. As we have seen, for Malthusians the war seemed evidence that Europe might have nowhere to relieve its "population pressure" and find additional resources. Rising anti-imperialist agitation in colonies reinforced a sense of disappearing frontiers. Even the generally cornucopian USDA agreed that because the American agricultural empire had now reached its geographical limits, increased food production would entail modernization of existing farms rather than the traditional expansion into new lands.

A convergence of dramatic technological innovations licensed modernist fantasies in the 1920s. The Model T's spectacular triumph fostered feverish extrapolations of Fordist paradigms to every facet of production and consumption. If transportation could be automated, then why not everything else, including agriculture, housing, housework, and eating itself? Rapid electrification also encouraged dreams of sweat-free all-electric farms, factories, and kitchens. Extending the romance and mystery of electricity, scientists focused increasingly on other invisible forces—X-rays, the ether (radio), dust, germs, genes, bacteria, cells, vitamins, and micronutrients. Early success with synthetics in dyes, plastics, fertilizers, and some foods (saccharine, margarine, yeast) also encouraged hyperbolic expectations. At the same time, advertising sought to unleash consumers from tradition, while highly sexualized popular entertainment further weakened the hold of classical civilization. And the rising prestige of engineering and scientific management lent considerable corporate support to the progressive crusade for efficiency and waste reduction.[9]

Food consumers encountered the modernist ethos everywhere. As Shapiro and Levenstein have shown, "scientific eating" may have failed to impress the poor, but its tenets filtered into much of middle-class culture during the early decades of the twentieth century. Everyone who faithfully followed a cooking school recipe's precise measurements or attempted "gastric stimulation" by floating raw vegetables in a gelatinous "perfection salad" or replaced butter with Crisco—"An Absolutely New Product" billed as "A Scientific Discovery Which Will Affect Every Kitchen in America"—or sat through a "domestic science" class or counted calories "on a diet" or tried to eat hospital food was, in effect, helping to establish a new cuisine that reduced cooking to chemistry. Similarly, any shopper who bought Grape-Nuts, Sun Maid raisins, or Fleischmann's yeast for the vitamins and minerals was buying into an industrialized food paradigm that treated eating as resource extraction.[10]

As Levenstein notes, New Nutrition also flourished at new restaurants that served quick, lighter meals, especially sandwiches and salads. Automats, cafeterias, luncheonettes, and lunch wagons institutionalized the cheap, convenient, self-service, tipless, solitary dining once confined to speculative fantasy (and to working-class precincts). By 1910, middle-class customers were gobbling a quick meal all alone perched on a stool or in a "sanitary lunch chair" in a "one-arm" lunch place. And by the 1920s, some visionary restaurateurs were experimenting with conveyor belts, dials, push buttons, and pneumatic tubes. In 1921, Lazarus Muntean, from Highland Park, Michigan—the birthplace of Ford's assembly line—proposed an "eat-as-you-go" lunchroom in which, Philip Langdon writes, "tables and chairs were set on a platform that slowly moved around the room, past serving counters from which the customers took whatever portions they wanted. In the center was to be a spigot dispensing ice-cold drinking water. Each table was also to be fitted with a lamp and with an electric motor which, at the push of a button, would turn on a fan." While it is unclear whether Muntean ever put his design into practice, a West Coast chain called Merry-Go-Round Cafes devised a more workable alternative in which a counter loaded with platters moved continuously in front of customers who stayed put. This resembled the mechanized public restaurants described in H. G. Wells's 1898 novella, *When the Sleeper Wakes*—only the date was considerably pushed forward from Wells's 2100 A.D.[11]

Science-fiction dining aside, many more restaurants adopted white porcelain, stainless steel, and plate glass to suggest what Langdon calls the "crisp-and-clean esthetic." Restaurants were among the first public places to use flashing electric signs to convey modern excitement and theatricality. Better ventilation, particularly air-conditioning, also helped to create a more comfortable, refreshingly artificial, techno-utopian atmosphere. At the same time, restaurant chains replaced the tired, dark vestiges of Victorian civilization—especially the natural wood floors, neoclassical marble, heavy drapes, overflowing window displays, and plush leather chairs—with bright, unabashedly synthetic materials like Sanionyx table tops, "better than marble" Vitrolite counters, linoleum floors, and molded metal stools. Impressed by this rejection of Beaux Arts decadence, Lewis Mumford, in 1921, praised the cheap lunchroom as one of the "main sources of the modern style at present."[12]

Modernists expected that electrification would create a more professionalized, push-button world. Embracing the no-sweat dream, but without the socialist aspects of utopian fiction, Thomas Edison predicted that automated machinery would turn manual laborers into "superintendents watching the machinery to see that it works right." Thanks to "electric cooking," "the housewife of the future will be neither a slave to servants nor herself a drudge," but "rather a domestic engineer . . . with the greatest of all handmaidens, electricity, at her service." Freed from debilitating drudgery, women would now "be able to think straight" and join the ranks of businessmen, scientists, and other "brain workers." While only 10 percent of farm homes had electricity by 1930 (compared with 85 percent of nonfarm dwellings), the prospect of electric farming inspired science popularizer Edwin Slosson to wonder: "What will be the effect on the farmer and his family? Will he continue his commendable habit of early rising if he can milk a dozen cows at a time by simply turning on the juice? Will not the farmer's wife lose the well-rounded arms that she developed by long hours at the churn and the rosy complexion that she acquired over the cook stove? Will the tennis racket adequately take the place of the buck-saw in the development of the muscles and the sense of duty?" Rhapsodizing upon the leisure-creating possibilities, Slosson missed a few unintended consequences, such as the high electricity bills that would require farmers to take on more cows, or the extra jobs in town so farm women could help to pay for new equipment, or the many small farmers displaced altogether by costly electrification. His reductio ad absurdum was intended to be funny, but it was not all that far removed from the utopian, but myopic, expectations for electricity. The push-button mystique offered what seemed a desirable consolidation of all labor into one small (and probably plastic) button or switch. Not so obvious was the consolidation of power by bigger farmers and manufacturers, particularly Edison's conglomerate, General Electric, which promoted the "all-electric farm" boasting one hundred appliances.[13]

Modernist consolidation also transformed the corner grocery. Mass marketers equated their branded, labeled, packaged, chemically preserved products with progressive ideas of purity, predictability, and transparency. Grocery chains, too, marshaled reformist rhetoric. One move at the turn of the century was to append "sanitary" in front of "grocery store." During the war, Piggly-Wiggly's self-service "combination stores" embodied Taylorized "consumer engineering," as shoppers entered through a one-way turnstile and then passed through a maze of aisles designed to maximize impulse purchases before reaching the checkout counter. Unlike service-oriented mom-and-pop groceries, chains delivered cheaper goods with a minimum of interpersonal contact or negotiation— the modern urban experience. Being less likely to discriminate among different ethnic groups or against women shoppers, chains did seem somewhat more egalitarian than the independents.[14]

At the giant self-service "cafeteria store"—the supermarket—of the early 1930s, bargain-hungry shoppers enjoyed the "price-wrecking" advantages of modern economies of scale as they wheeled steel carts to automobiles parked in large paved lots. One step further was a drive-through "automarket" in Louisville, Kentucky, where motorists navigated the store's grocery-lined interior streets. But even the auto-free pedestrian version would have seemed very remote in 1900, and in the 1930s it still seemed "futuristic." "To a public dispirited by the depression," Chester Liebs writes, "the ability to shop at a place called 'supermarket' rather than just a plain old grocery or food store was to participate in the future, now. The very use of the word was enough to give the illusion that profound advances had taken place." And it had, according to the trade journal *Progressive Grocer*, which viewed the supermarket as a "scientific food store," a "machine" for efficient distribution. The layout was carefully calculated to "engineer" sales: produce aisles came first to suggest freshness; overflowing "gondola" shelves and bins of sale items encouraged impulse buying; shoppers had to go through aisles of processed goods to reach the meats along the back wall; sweets, for dessert, came last, just before the toll-gate-style checkout. The toll road analogy was intentional, for limited-access expressways were still rare and exciting in the 1930s. In another avant garde move, supermarkets of the late 1930s introduced packaged, chilled meats and "frosted foods," even though most Americans lacked sufficient electric refrigeration. The fact that the stores had them ahead of consumer demand reinforced their futuristic aura. Supermarkets were also among the earliest and heaviest users of the "streamline moderne" style—the up-to-date, slightly aerodynamic look of curved corners trimmed with stainless steel, black structural glass, enameled Art Deco letters, and neon signs.[15]

STREAMLINING

Historians have paid considerable attention to streamlining, which affected virtually every design in the period between the world wars, from cars, trains, and toasters to refrigerators, roadside restaurants, and grocery stores. "Streamlined architecture," Jeffrey Meikle writes, "provided a wish-fulfilling set for a secure, effortless future whose complexity would run no deeper than a polished surface."[16] In Meikle's view, all those superficial, ornamental curves, teardrops, and egg shapes were aimed to boost Depression sales by pretending to be revolutionary improvements. Yet, in another sense, streamlining also reflected the modernist upheavals underway in agricultural science and food production—and not just in the "dynamic obsolescence" sought by corporate "consumer engineers." As a metaphor for radical efficiency, waste reduction, functional consolidation, and simplification, streamlining aptly suggested a blueprint for the future of food production.

In the opinion of many modernizers, the struggling, horse-powered, diversified small agricultural production units needed to be consolidated into highly mechanized corporate farms specializing in one or two commercial crops. Fordism worked, farm journalist Wheeler McMillen insisted in *Too Many Farmers: The Story of What Is Here and Ahead in Agriculture* (1929): "Here is an opportunity by which farming may be put on a parity with industry, and by which farm incomes may be made more comparable to urban incomes." Division of labor would supposedly assure higher productivity:

> The management will not have its mental abilities dulled by long hours of physical labor. The farmer whose preference and skill is for handling hogs will be able to devote his time to the swine herds. The man who likes to work with cows will not have to divide his affections with chickens and tractors. The power and machinery will be in the hands of men with mechanical inclinations and ability. Each man should be happier doing the

kind of work he likes, and when engaged in the kind of work for which he is best suited, should be able to produce more efficiently.

If, as some agrarian critics complained, this consolidation into "corporate latifundia" resembled the enclosures that had delivered masses of English peasants into urban factories centuries earlier, then so be it. In the modernist future, most people would work in cities, not on farms. Welcoming the likely industrialization of food production, British scientist J. B. S. Haldane wrote, "Personally I do not regret the probable disappearance of the agricultural labourer in favour of the factory worker, who seems to me a higher type of person from most points of view."[17] Doubting the intellectual ability of the average farmer to master the technologies needed to grow more food, many Malthusians (and Stalinists) agreed. And modern industry did need the displaced peasants. Whereas the classical future would colonize *other* people, the modernist future would colonize its *own* people. This was the industrial development package that some international aid agencies would attempt to transfer to the Third World after the Second World War.

The system had its glitches, however, particularly the gluts that followed when farmers stepped onto the technological treadmill. Advocates of "chemurgy" then suggested ways to channel farm waste and surpluses into nonfood uses such as plastics, industrial solvents, paints, and clothing. There was another element of Fordism here, as Henry Ford publicly vowed to someday build a car entirely from soybeans—and squandered quite a bit of his company's research funds in that chemurgic quest. Outlining his vision of farm-to-factory integration, Ford sounded the distinctly modernist theme that, classical claims to the contrary, "our times are primitive. True progress is yet to come. The industrial age has scarcely dawned as yet; we see only its first crude beginnings." Adopting the same visionary tone, McMillen noted with pride that a typical car's paint job consumed three pecks of corn in the form of butyl alcohol, a raw material used in car lacquers.[18] While today's automotive paints no longer come from plants, another farm-to-car project did eventually become a highly subsidized agricultural staple of agricultural policy—gasohol distilled from the country's perennial corn surpluses.

Some futurists, emboldened by advances in synthetic chemistry and genetics, went beyond Fordist industrial models and dreamed of streamlining natural evolution itself. Equating speed with electricity, some turn-of-the-century futurists pinned their hopes on the direct electrification of plants, as in John Elfreth Watkins's prediction that "electric currents applied to the soil will make valuable plants grow larger and faster." After the 1900 publication of Gregor Mendel's laws of genetics, however, applied genetics seemed a more likely way to accelerate the time-consuming and inexact processes of seed selection. As noted earlier, the primary success story was hybrid corn, which revolutionized American corn and livestock production. In 1985 American farmers would raise 400 percent more corn than they did in 1912—and on half the acreage. Ironically, much of the credit for hybrid corn belonged to the pioneering work of Edward M. East, the preeminent Malthusian of the 1920s. But more than irony was involved. In a classic example of the synergy between Malthusians and cornucopians, East's gloomy predictions of overpopulation inspired farm editor Henry Wallace to found in 1926 the first seed company devoted to developing and distributing commercially viable hybrid seeds—the Hi-Bred Corn Company, which eventually became the industry leader, Pioneer Hi-Bred. While the greatest gains in corn productivity came after World War II, Wallace's crusade for "hybrid power" gave him the status of a public prophet and laid the groundwork for his political rise during the New Deal, first to USDA secretary, then to U.S. vice president, and eventually to Progressive Party presidential candidate in 1948. Hybridization also smoothed the way for the corporate consolidation of agriculture. Whereas farmers using older, open-pollinated corn varieties could save their own seed, they might have to buy each year's hybrid seeds from the company that held the patent. With this shift in the control of seed stock—and all the accessory inputs—power moved from farmers to agribusiness suppliers like Pioneer Hi-Bred, which eventually became a subsidiary of DuPont.[19]

The explosion in corn production would fuel an unprecedented expansion of the fast food industry, for cheap feed meant cheap hamburgers and fried chicken. Indeed, hybridization seemed to solve *two* basic Malthusian worries: the fear of running out of meat and the fear of being overrun by the "wrong" people. The two came together in the eugenics movement, which proposed to apply genetics lessons learned from animal production to the improvement of human "stock." Here again, East and Wallace played a major role, East as an outspoken advocate of eugenic solutions to overpopulation, and Wallace as a funder of the basic animal and plant research that eugenicists hoped to apply to human reproduction.[20] It was appropriate, then, that local and international fairs alike during the interwar period often featured exhibits of both animal breeding and "race betterment." Marking a shift from a classical to a modernist futurism, such displays of "Burbankism" gradually displaced those of newly colonized "savages," for evolutionary Progress would now come in the laboratory rather than on the imperial battlefield.

In *World of Fairs,* Robert Rydell shows how the "fitter families" exhibits of the 1920s and 1930s explicitly connected the selective breeding of animals and humans. When a proponent of eugenics argued that "I think it is about time people had a little of the attention that is given to animals," her enthusiastic rural audience at the Kansas Free Fair of 1920 knew exactly what she was saying, for breeders were anticipating major advances in the redesign of livestock to meet the growing demand for animal products. Mindful of the Malthusian warnings, animal science researchers had been busy working on ways to reduce those well-known wasteful feed-to-meat conversion ratios. In 1900, John Elfreth Watkins predicted that by the year 2000, "food animals will be bred to expend practically all their life energy in producing meat, milk, wool, and other by-products. Horns, bones, muscles, and lungs will have been neglected." William Bateson, who has been called the founder of modern genetics, conducted his most important work on poultry inheritance.[21]

The very modest gains actually achieved in animal breeding by the 1920s did not deter the enthusiasm of the press. For optimists, it was the *potential* that mattered. Reflecting the magical powers accorded chemists in these years, influential science journalist Edwin Slosson suggested that the recent work on genetics "may put it in the power of the chemist to control the size and shape of plants, to fix the number and location of their branches and leaves, or legs and eyes, to modify color or complexion, and to determine or alter sex." Since chemistry could do just about anything, as Slosson's Science News Service audience already knew, complete genetic control seemed inevitable. Extrapolating such hopes in his 1932 *Popular Mechanics* piece, "Fifty Years Hence," Winston Churchill envisioned a headless, wingless chicken genetically engineered to maximize meat production and reduce waste—a poultry version of the streamlined cars, trains, and airships that illustrated Churchill's techno-utopian article. And, in a clear illustration of how these meat projects cross-fertilized with human eugenics, Churchill went on to predict the superefficient "breeding of human beings and the shaping of human nature" in a way to "produce beings specialized to thought or toil." Applying "the principle of mass production . . . to biology," Aldous Huxley's *Brave New World* also made the link between animal and human reproduction—at the central "hatcheries" human embryos were "budded" and then raised in bottles lined with "fresh sow's peritoneum." However, the Holocaust severely discouraged popular fantasies of applying genetics to "race betterment," at least for a while.[22]

As outlandish as such ideas sounded, applied hybridization did not constitute the outer limits of scientific streamlining. While geneticists hoped to accelerate what was still a natural, evolutionary process, some chemists hoped to avoid it altogether, much as "highways of the future" would bypass congested towns. Hence the enthusiastic discussion of synthesizing nitrogen fertilizers directly from the air. Soon after William Crookes's famous warning that depleted nitrate supplies threatened the world's wheat production, popular science journals were talking up the Haber process, which used electricity to synthesize ammonia—a building block of fertilizers—from atmospheric nitrogen.[23] Although this actually required a lot of energy, science had seemingly found a "free" vital resource—or *almost* free, according to enthusiasts, who assumed the imminent perfecting of new electric power sources, whether hydroelectric, solar, radio waves, or nuclear.

When two apparently unlimited resources—air and electricity—are joined, the result is a euphoric leap of infinite expectation. "With boundless atmospheric nitrogen and with water power [to provide the electricity needed to 'fix' it] . . . man need never fear an insufficient nitrogeneous food supply," one Iowa State researcher exulted in 1911. If humanity could at last be liberated from the need for fertile soil, an era of universal peace beckoned. After all, a 1903 *Harper's* discussion of research into nitrogen observed, "the effort to supply this one-hundredth of the plant's food has caused most of the wars and conflicts of the world." And when wartime German weapons research improved the ammonia synthesizing process, its archetypal "swords into ploughshares" appeal soared. McMillen wrote that Haber's discovery "is one of the most momentous of the modern era. It sets forward for centuries the fulfillment of the Malthusian prediction." To be sure, a 1924 survey written up in an article titled "Our Nitrogen Problem" found that, all the puffery notwithstanding, atmospheric nitrogen was actually made in just "two little plants" in Seattle and Syracuse that were "so small as to have no effects" on the market, which still relied primarily on imports of Peruvian guano and Chilean nitrates. And in 1932 Joseph Davis concluded that global markets were awash in wheat *not* because of artificial ammonia fixation, which remained a *potential* nitrogen source, but because world wheat production had expanded the old-fashioned, imperialistic way—by plowing up new land, much of it unsuitable to long-term intensive cultivation. But even during the ensuing dust storms of the "dirty thirties," cornucopians continued to tout the happy "lesson" of atmospheric nitrogen as the key to the future.[24]

Moreover, as is often the case with hopeful speculation, one success story inspired expectations of many more. If fertilizer could be synthesized directly from nitrogen in air, could harvesting *food* directly from the elements be far behind? Citing what seemed obvious precedents, the *Washington Post* disputed the Malthusian gloom of the 1920s: "Why should the production of synthetic food remain a dream? Science has produced other synthetic matter of equally complex structure as soon as there was genuine need of it." Proponents of synthetic foods did have several precedents to draw from, particularly the success of margarine, saccharin, and artificial dyes—all displayed at the 1893 Chicago fair. Echoing Berthelot's boasts from the 1890s, some chemists claimed that they would soon be able synthesize basic food elements from coal—an obvious source of carbon—or, again, from the air, which had great quantities of protein-building nitrogen. Noting the recent successes with nitrogen fixation, a 1907 *Everybody's* magazine article on the "miracle of synthetic chemistry" predicted that scientists would soon want to make "a loaf of bread or . . . a beefsteak" from "a lump of coal, a glass of water, and a whiff of atmosphere."[25]

In 1913, Belgian chemist Jean Effront suggested that "human nutriment" might be recycled from "the refuse of breweries and distilleries"; the resultant paste was "said to be three times as nourishing and to possess a strongly 'meaty flavor,'" yet "near meats" made from this substance would be more economical because they would not need to go through "the intermediary of the animal that transforms them into meat." Given this obvious efficiency, "the chemist may take the place of the aforesaid ox or sheep." Effront's idea of turning waste into pseudosteaks did not seem so inconceivable after the wartime transformation of wood wastes into "cellulose silk" (later dubbed rayon). Citing the work on synthetic clothing in his 1919 encomium, *Creative Chemistry*, Slosson asserted that it was quite possible to use the same cellulose as a medium for yeast-producing sugars and starches, and perhaps for proteins and fats as well. By 1929, synthetic foods were a fait accompli in the mind of business guru Roger Babson—one of "twenty ways to make a million": "Chemists can now make milk, cream, butter, and cheese out of kerosene oil; and steaks, chops, and sausages out of yeast." The vitamania of the 1920s reinforced this belief that nutrition could be reduced to specific chemicals, which could easily be synthesized in the test tube—the streamlined modernist cauldron.[26]

Progress in plastics technology—particularly Bakelite, "the material of a thousand uses"—bolstered confidence that chemists could outdo Mother Nature. In *American Plastic,* Meikle observes that the "abstract Chemist assumed heroic proportions" in the 1920s—a veritable "master of 'the science of the transformation of matter.'" Edwin Slosson was sure that the chemist could synthesize edible oils from "the oil shales with which our country is so abundantly supplied." (The automobile industry also had high hopes for such sources, as many worried about limited gasoline supplies in the mid-20s.) Indeed, Slosson argued that fats could be made from "any kind of carbonaceous material," including "wood tar, sawdust, and other unappetizing stuff." "How such a synthetic food would taste I don't know, but doubtless the chemist could fix up the flavor to suit." In allowing that food required some flavoring Slosson was relatively old-fashioned compared to the Belgian scientist Jean Effront, who argued, in line with the New Nutrition: "It would be a hundred times better if foods were without odor or savor. For then we should eat exactly what we needed and would feel a good deal better." That scientific standards of healthfulness trumped gastronomic considerations seemed self-evident to Babson: "Synthetic vegetables are said to be not only tasty but more healthful than natural vegetables, because they contain more vitamines. 'Beef' broths are being manufactured from products that have never been near a cow, while eggs can be made direct from grasses and cereals without calling in the aid of a hen."[27] Such incongruities were the staple of modernist rhetoric, which prized boundary-crossing disjunctions.

Effront did at least derive his synthetic foods from plants, just as Babson's henless eggs did originate, somehow, in grasses. But in what became a litany of biotechnological utopianism, other visionaries bemoaned the scandalous "inefficiency" of normal photosynthesis, which, according to conventional computations, converted only around 1 percent of sunlight into calories available as food energy. For example, in 1925, Carnegie Institution plant physiologist H. A. Spoehr reckoned that the amount of solar energy received by an acre of Carmel, California, farmland during a ninety-day growing season was the equivalent of 1476 tons of coal. Almost all of this was "lost," however, for even if the acre produced an unheard-of fifty bushels of wheat, the calories in that grain amounted to the energy stored in just two-thirds of a ton of coal. And Carmel is a particularly sunny place, assuming exceptional yields; thirty years later, the national average was barely twenty bushels of wheat per acre, forty-two in 2000. A 1926 audit found that an Illinois cornfield turned just 1.2 percent of the total solar energy into actual corn and silage—a slightly better showing than Carmel's wheat field, but still disappointing returns in a land whose "business," its plainspoken president, Calvin Coolidge, pronounced, "is business."[28]

In *The Economy of Nature* (1977), Donald Worster argues that the New Ecology of the early twentieth century sought professional respectability by replacing the romantic naturalism of nineteenth-century conservationists with a more managerial rhetoric of productivity, efficiency, and energy accounting. The emerging "bio-economic paradigm" turned nature into "a modernized economic system, . . . a chain of factories, an assembly line."[29] Forsaking the more holistic, subjective approach of earlier ecologists, the technocratic auditors of "energy budgets" reduced all food-related social, economic, and cultural practices to a simple equation: food = solar energy. If the plant (so also the animal that ate the plant) was merely a conduit for this energy transfer—and a very wasteful one at that—why not redesign the whole process to eliminate the middle stage (agriculture) and thus maximize the solar profit? Such proposals became even simpler if all food needs could be reduced to a single factor—calories—which in turn could be derived from a single source, usually yeast grown from cellulose. If streamliners hoped to trim bothersome clutter and complexity, then this was certainly the analytical equivalent when it came to food.

A good example of such rhetorical streamlining was a 1924 article by Carl Alsberg, head of Stanford University's prestigious Food Research Institute. Titled "Progress in Chemistry and the Theory of Population," it appeared, appropriately enough, in *Industrial and Engineering Chemistry*, although it might just as well have appeared in *Automotive Age*. Noting the ongoing speculations about whether population growth would outstrip the food supply—this was the year of Edward East's well-publicized Malthusian wake-up call, *Mankind at the Crossroads*—Alsberg asked, "Can the chemist so manipulate the elements as to enhance the food supply indefinitely?" Alsberg's response had two parts, both reductionist. First, in discussing human nutrition, he likened the "adult animal" to an automobile in need of fuel (carbohydrates), repairs (protein), and "accessories" (vitamins, fats). Fortunately, while "accessory" needs were important, they were very small. Human protein ("repair") requirements were also much smaller than customarily thought, and not in short supply, especially if humans skipped that inefficient process of converting vegetable protein into livestock. (For hard-core streamliners, the animal had to go—not just as transportation, but as food as well.) Besides, protein was composed of amino acids, which "have already been synthesized." The main challenge of the future, Alsberg argued in his second reduction, was finding enough fuel (carbohydrates), which he argued was the primary focus of agriculture, which "is just as much a fuel-producing industry as coal mining or oil well drilling." If, after leaving out the minor incidentals, "one can speak of foods as fuel," what were the prospects for the human fuel supply of the future? Citing a seminal 1899 British paper titled "Revenue and Expenditure Account for a Leaf," Alsberg estimated that a single leaf stored only 0.0033 calories, which represented just 1.2 percent of "the total solar radiation incident per minute upon a square centimeter of leaf," and these "revenue" figures became even worse when one considered that, as a rather laggard employee, "the plant works only a part of the year." Like other auditors, Alsberg concluded that plants were miserably poor providers.[30]

So where could we turn for more efficient production? Differing with Berthelot, Slosson, and other chemistry enthusiasts, Alsberg was not particularly sanguine about synthesizing human fuel from other energy sources—say, coal or oil or carbon dioxide—because such conversions would themselves require a considerable expenditure of energy. And since fossil fuel supplies were finite while industrial needs for them were growing along with the population, it seemed best not to count on that energy source indefinitely. The trick, then, was to devise some *nonbiological* way to store solar energy *directly*. If such a process were developed—a mighty vague "if" whose particulars would presumably be worked out later—agriculture might then be relieved of its "primary burden of producing all the world's food calories, perhaps leaving to it the task of producing the foods that give color and flavor and tickle our fancy and our palates." In automotive terms, agriculture would be relegated to optional status, serving the aftermarket with pleasant "accessories" and frills, while the core engine would be thoroughly rationalized. While Alsberg doubted that there was an imminent "economic necessity" to bypass land-borne agriculture, he had little doubt that "the work in pure science is likely to be completed before this necessity arises." In short, if a Malthusian breakdown did materialize sometime down the road, basic bench science would be ready with an alternative route.[31]

Ignoring, or perhaps unaware of, Alsberg's caveats and hedges, however, modernists of the 1930s routinely included the streamlining of photosynthesis among their menu of things to come. After repeating the mantra that "ninety-nine parts of the solar energy are wasted for every part used" by field agriculture, Winston Churchill predicted that "microbes" would be enlisted to convert nitrogen directly into protein "under controlled conditions." While such conversions did require solar energy, perhaps even sunlight might be bypassed someday. "If the gigantic sources of power become available"—Churchill had high hopes for nuclear power—then vast underground cellars "may replace the cornfields and potato patches of the world," leaving vacant farmland available for the spread of parks and cities. In this forecast Churchill was simply trying to keep up with his political colleague Frederick Edward Smith, First Earl of Birkenhead, whose well-publicized book, *The World in 2030 AD*, also suggested that the vast stores of energy "locked up in atoms" might somehow enable scientists to convert cellulose directly into digestible sugars, thereby circumventing the "wasteful and round-about method" of deriving solar energy through plants.[32]

The fact that both Churchill and Birkenhead took time to make such similar predictions is interesting for two reasons. First, as politicians directly responsible for the administration of British imperial interests—in the 1920s Churchill served as colonial secretary, Birkenhead as a secretary for India—both seemed to be confirming the shift from classical to modernist ways of conceiving the future. That is, in looking ahead fifty or a hundred years, both saw additional food coming *not* from expanding colonies but through consolidated synthetic production. Second, both popularized ultramodernist visions that, while somewhat irrelevant to the depressed food prices and slowing population growth of the 1930s, would receive far more serious, scholarly attention during the post–World War II Malthusian scare. In the meantime, while no one quite knew how to boost the efficiency of photosynthesis, the very idea that there was an enormous reserve of unexploited calories gave heart to cornucopians, and perhaps to the public in general. The calculations seemed to show that there were ample reserves of untapped food energy which could feed everyone once the economic and scientific details were worked out. That such details of supply *would* be worked out, given sufficient demand, was an article of cornucopian faith dating at least as far back as Condorcet, who in 1793 was confident that, under the pressure of increasing population, scientists would explore the "feasibility of manufacturing animal and vegetable substances artificially, the utilization of substances which were wasted, [and] the possibilities of diminishing consumption without a concomitant loss of enjoyment"—in all, the basics of the modernist diet.[33]

THE MODERNIST FAIRS

In a textbook intended to accompany the 1939 New York World's Fair, the fair's science director, Gerald Wendt, addressed head-on the question of whether citizens of the World of Tomorrow would have synthetic foods. Yes, Wendt stated, and at first these would mimic foods derived from plants and animals, much as the original automobiles had resembled horse-drawn carriages. But within two or three generations our "basic energy-producing foods may be produced in chemical plants operating with direct sunshine as a source of energy," thereby "liberating" us from conventional agriculture. Foods will "abandon all pretense of imitating nature." The older, stick-in-the-mud generation will probably not like such artificial wonders, Wendt allowed, "but our children will shrug their shoulders, call us old-fashioned, and go on to new and better ways of living." That Wendt, a serious public scientist, could be so glib about the streamlining of photosynthesis was testimony to the modernist underpinnings of the Flushing Meadow exposition—and of the 1930s fairs in general. Attracting over 100 million visitors, the expositions in Chicago (1933–34), San Diego (1935–36), Dallas (1936), Cleveland (1937), and New York (1939–40) set the futurist agenda for the second half of the twentieth century.[34]

Streamlining certainly dominated the most popular exhibit of the 1939 fair, General Motors' Futurama, which previewed the "very near future" of 1960 as a time when, in the words of historians Joseph Corn and Brian Horrigan, "all of life could be like the swift, controlled superhighway—frictionless, free from accident and brought to you by enlightened scientists, technologists, and businessmen." This megatheme suffused all the fairs of the 1930s. For anyone remotely acquainted with "scientific eating" and the cult of the chemist, the slogan of Chicago's 1933 Century of Progress Exposition made perfect sense: "Science Finds—Industry Applies—Man Conforms." The sign overhanging the USDA's 1939 nutrition exhibits was similar: "Man = Chemicals = Food." Similarly, they would not have found the 1939 Food Building's mural "depicting food as a source of energy and health" exceptionally reductionist, nor would they have found much dystopian danger, or irony, in the fair's official song (despite its allusions to Huxley's 1932 publication):

We're the rising tide coming from far and wide
Marching side by side on our way,
For a brave new world,
Tomorrow's world,
That we shall build today.[35]

Much had changed since the classical Victorian fairs, which were organized by self-made industrialists and which grouped exhibits by function—agriculture, machinery, women, electricity, and so on—in Renaissance-style pavilions. At the 1930s fairs, large corporations constructed separate, branded buildings planned by youngish, college-educated managers, engineers, and public relations experts. Whereas the classical fairs equated progress with gross production (hence all those piles of commodities), the modernist fairs emphasized consumer-oriented applied research. Anthropological exhibits traced the familiar evolution from "savage" to modern. But while the Victorian fairs proudly drew links to the country's founders, the modernist fairs repeatedly drew severe distinctions; for instance, dioramas in New York's Community Interest Building presented the living conditions of 1789 as primitive compared with the "personal independence and leisure" supposedly enjoyed by the average consumer citizen of 1939. Even George Washington "had no way of enjoying fresh vegetables and fruits out of season," USDA Secretary Henry Wallace observed in a *New York Times* article heralding the opening of the fair. "The contrast between 1789 and 1939 is overwhelming."[36] The architecture of the 1930s fairs accentuated this sense of a radically new era. Beaux Arts had given way to a utilitarian, Machine-Age aesthetic of air-conditioned, windowless artificiality and well curved and ramped frictionless movement.

Gone were separate halls dedicated to agriculture and horticulture—the largest buildings in 1893—and agriculture was now demoted to a sub-field of The Chemist's research. Reflecting the breakthroughs in irrigation, pesticides, mechanization, and hybridization, the 1933 USDA exhibit confidently asserted that "science has conquered the fear of famine and has created abundance, and now we must learn to live with abundance." With surplus, not scarcity, as the primary challenge of modern times, Ford's 1933 Industrialized American Barn highlighted chemurgic research on nonfood applications for the soybean, including soy-based plastics, shock absorber fluid, meat substitutes, textiles, and even soy coffee. At its Wonder World of Chemistry exhibit at the 1936 Texas Centennial Exposition, DuPont detailed products made from agricultural raw materials, including plastics, artificial rubber, antifreeze solutions, refrigerants, dyes, and paints. Meikle observes that such shows were part of DuPont's campaign to remake its image from a disreputable munitions maker to a utopian promoter of "Better Things for Better Living through Chemistry." Similarly, the ultramodernist (and fascist) Italian

Pavilion at the 1939 fair trumpeted Italian scientists' efforts to turn surplus milk into synthetic wool fibers.[37]

Even the Electrified Farm at the 1939 fair, with its radio-controlled tractor, was less an industrial "food factory" than a showroom for promoting light bulbs and appliances—selling, not teaching, was the real goal. If there was a primary agricultural lesson to be learned, it was that in the World of Tomorrow, food production would be so automated that no one would get dirty. The Heinz Dome featured a robotic Aristocrat Tomato Man dancing near a hydroponic Garden of the Future, complete with ten-foot-high tomato vines "deriving nourishment from a chemical solution." Hydroponics ("soil-less gardening") was—and remains—a perennial of agricultural futurism, but also a very expensive technological system, requiring enormous investments in glass, tanks, chemicals, and skilled supervision. Heinz's goal, however, was less to lay out a workable blueprint for the future than to dramatize the sanitary purity of its ketchup and pickles. Along the same lines, over 7 million visitors to Borden's Dairy World of Tomorrow witnessed 150 friendly, "shower-bathed" cows being mechanically milked on a revolving Rotolactor—a stainless-steel bovine merry-go-round—"demonstrating the modern hygienic methods of milking that may be used universally in the future for the benefit of the mankind." Nearby (during the 1940 season only) stood a whimsical "boudoir" for Elsie the Cow and Her Milky Way—"20 calves, replaced every three weeks to insure their being of a cute age."[38] An adjoining milk bar gave visitors the chance to sample the pasteurized, irradiated, and bottled milk that had come off the Rotolactor. The exhibit's comic irrelevance to real dairying—which in the twenty-first century still entails drudgery for operators and misery for nonproductive calves and aging Elsies—suited modernist aspirations to make food production disappear, if not from the land at least from consumer consciousness.

Since modernism meant simplification and reduction, farming exhibits at the 1939 fair were often miniaturized. Behind the giant Continental Baking Company's building—dotted in red, blue, and yellow balloons just like a Wonder Bread wrapper—visitors could find an eleven-thousand-square-foot plot of real wheat—the first wheat grown in New York City since 1871; the rear location and small size relative to the full-scale bakery in front aptly suited agriculture's subordinate, diminutive status. Beech-Nut Packing Company's building offered small dioramas of coffee, chicle, and peanut plantations. At General Motors' Futurama, visitors surveying the 1960 countryside could barely make out tiny streamlined barns and silos of the "modern experimental farm and dairy," with its thimble-sized trees under glass, a teacup-scaled aeration plant to purify water from a tub-sized lake, and terraced fields the size of bacon strips. Futurama's finale accentuated consumer priorities, as visitors emerged in a full-scale "modern intersection" crowded with the latest GM models. On the modernist mental map, farms might be microscopic but not automobiles. Diminishing the role of agriculture even further was the focal exhibit, captioned "Will the Chemical Flask Do the Work of a Thousand Farms?" A large chemist's flask at the center of the exhibit contained—and thus controlled—"a rolling agricultural landscape." On either side, moving bands illustrated "advances in the science of agriculture and researches into synthetic vitamins"—the twin hopes of reductionist science.[39]

As Roland Marchand, Peter Kuznick, and Eve Jochnowitz have argued, most of the Depression-era business exhibits aimed less to enlighten fairgoers about the intricacies of the scientific process or industrial production than to cultivate good public relations at a time when large corporations were targets of significant public resentment. For all the modernism, the fairs also functioned much like medieval cathedrals, which, assuming a largely illiterate public, resorted to allegorical representations to teach their lessons of faith and submission. Jochnowitz detects an "earnest yet wacky didacticism" in the 1939 fair's Modern Food Production show that represented the "miracles of futuristic technology" with winged lobsters flying over mountains (caption: "modern transportation makes it possible to have fresh fish in landlocked mountains"), a clock running backward in a tin can ("canning has perpetuated harvest times"), a trans-Atlantic aqueduct spilling roses into a desert ("irrigation has flowered wastelands"), a cauliflower knocking out a centipede with boxing gloves (pesticides), an eye blinking mysteriously from a cave ("man's victory over night-blindness through Vitamin A foods"), and an avocado with five jeweled eyes (representing "the five precious nutritional elements found in food—carbohydrates, proteins, fats, minerals, and vitamins.") "Miracle" was an often-used term in the fair lexicon, as when the guidebook to the 1939 fair argued that the "miracle of loaves and fishes" was now not so incredible, given the "food miracles of today": "Picture, for example, the amazement of great-great grandma could she but return to earth to find our tables veritable magic carpets upon which may be set at any season (and all at one time, if we will) food from any part of the world. She would be astounded, too, to learn that like witches' potions certain diets may affect our love life, our sex, may make us grow, can actually make us live longer."[40]

To accentuate modernist discontinuity, swooping parabolas and color-ful lightning bolts adorned the architecture; no more gargoyles and stained glass. Exhibits asserted Machine-Age efficiency with mechanical manikins, moving dioramas, abstract animation, revolving stages (such as the Rotolactor), and anthropomorphic robots (such as Heinz's robotic Aristocrat Tomato Man and Westinghouse's Elektro, the hunky butler). The 1939 Swedish Pavilion was a box designed in the International Style, and its architect went on to help design the United Nations headquar-ters. Inside, the Three Crowns restaurant echoed earlier automated cafés in offering an electrically powered revolving smorgasbord, with unseen servers refilling dishes from behind a partition. The motorized displays were mainly intended to generate a gee-whiz response. Typical, for in-stance, was the 1933 General Foods exhibit with its revolving stage boast-ing bright aluminum doors that opened to reveal products bathed in "a splendor of changing colored lights." None of this had anything to do with the way, say, Post Toasties were really produced; rather, the intent was to show that this growing conglomerate was "appropriately attuned to the modern spirit." Roland Marchand argues that even the working model factories constructed in 1933 by Coca-Cola, National Biscuit, and Kraft were popular not because they showed how products were made but because visitors were mesmerized by the "perpetual motion" of the assembly line. And, determined to show the public what John Burnham calls "the results, rather than the ideas, of science," these food compa-nies often offered samples at the end of the line for visitors to nibble. These edible rewards did win a restless public's attention better than the wax models of the "fruits of tomorrow" sponsored by 1939's New York State Agricultural Experiment Station. Few took time to study the nearby poster explaining "how giant plants are produced by using colchicine to stimulate the chromosomes" or the display emphasizing "the importance of bacteria in food processing."[41] No attendance figures are available for the New York State exhibit, but we do know that it did not reappear in the fair's second season.

The most popular displays employed humorous Disney or radio char-acters to distract from the sponsors' rather oppressive message—that the public would have to accept whatever science and industry dictated. Whimsy also deflected attention from that fact that the audience (*and the scientists*, for that matter) did not know exactly how the fully auto-mated, frictionless future would be achieved. Despite the appearance of total control and purity, no one really knew how to take the dirt and sweat out of food production, whether on the farm, in the factory, or even in the private kitchen. Even today these are zones of considerable toil and danger. The light touch of the exhibits seemed to free the future from any gravitational moorings to physics, biology, politics, or economics. In the unseen reality offstage, bonafide scientists, engineers, and line workers were plodding along toward a somewhat less magical future at somewhat less than lightning speed. But out in front it was all zippy graphics, lightning bolts, conveyor belts, giant gears, and spotless lab coats.

The modernist future was thus more ethereal than the future presented at the Victorian fairs, whose heavy temples, obelisks, and pyramids of corn, chocolate, and oranges signaled weighty achievements and aspirations. By the 1930s, less was more. Jochnowitz observes that when the USDA's 1939 exhibit dramatically stacked the "ton of food" supposedly consumed by the average American alongside scale models of New York skyscrapers, "the sight . . . turned out not to be as appealing to the public as they might have wished." Who wanted to be reminded of our age-old corporeal nature? Purporting to break with nature, the modernist future required a more abstracted theatricality. As *Business Week* noted in its review of the exhibits that "pulled," visitors to General Electric's always-packed House of Magic did not understand the "pure science," but the dazzling tricks left them "thrilled, mystified, and soundly sold on the company."[42]

In the iconography of modernism, the laboratory was a particularly potent symbol, representing the commitment to research, purity, and professional vigilance of a food system whose scale, power, and remoteness often frightened modern consumers. Tended by white-coated female technicians, Swift's streamlined, stainless steel Premium Kitchen at the 1939 fair manufactured frankfurters so antiseptically as to offer clear proof that Upton Sinclair's dark and dirty age of immigrant sausage-making was over. Sealtest's Dairy Goods for a Brave New World exhibit showed "how the Sealtest System of Laboratory Protection insures the production and distribution of high quality milk and dairy products." After viewing "how Sealtest dietitians translate the great nutritive value of milk into nourishing recipes for everyday household uses," visitors could then sample Sealtest products at a "modernistic dairy-bar." Even the Distilled Spirits Building (designed by Morris Lapidus of later Miami Beach fame) included "a laboratory with qualified attendants present to answer your questions"—presumably about the whiskeys displayed nearby on a "revolving spiral stage." Also at the 1939 fair, Standard Brands' pavilion included "A Corner of the Million Dollar Fleischmann Laboratory" to demonstrate how yeast and coffee "are tested daily." Tested for what?

The actual target mattered less than the notion that Standard Brands cared enough to keep looking. Marchand and Smith suggest that the corporate laboratory bolstered a vision of "progress-without-enervation": while consumers could indulge themselves fully in the labor-saving conveniences of mass consumption, a few serious scientists—"dreaming boys"—would work hard behind the scenes to make sure that the rest of us are safe and secure. The message was "trust us and we'll do it all for you."[43]

The "home of tomorrow" exhibits of the 1930s domesticated these dominant themes. While socialistic architects like Buckminster Fuller, Frank Lloyd Wright, and Le Corbusier hoped to mass-produce sleek, ultrafunctional houses for everyone, the corporate-sponsored versions narrowed the focus to providing electric appliances for the middle class. Still, despite the commercial self-interest, their gadget-filled model kitchens seemed vaguely utopian as they elevated women from "drudges" to household managers—or perhaps to household "engineers" presiding over all-white, built-in "laboratories" designed by streamliners. General Electric's 1933 model kitchen aspired to be "as comfortable, efficient, and time-saving as the modern office." The exhibit's booklet, titled *Freedom*, even suggested that the revolutionary electric appliances would delay the process of aging: "Yesterday! The kitchen clock tolls away a woman's life. Toil worn hands, scarred by labor, monotonously dip into a greasy dishpan. . . . Today! A youthful hand that defies the years, touches a switch and a brilliant room is flooded with light. Clean, beautiful, efficient . . . every inch of this kitchen is arranged to save woman's steps. Magic electric servants work for her . . . she *directs* and they *do*. Her days are her own . . . her hours are free."[44]

Since such liberation would truly be miraculous—especially if fostered by streamlined toasters, refrigerators, and ovens—GE's fully automated "talking kitchen" of 1933 did seem to have supernatural qualities. "As if by magic," one reporter related, "the door of the electric refrigerator opens and the voice, coming apparently from the refrigerator, relates how it saves money for the owner. Then a spotlight falls on the electric range, the oven door lowers." Pursuing the same theme in 1939, Westinghouse's House of Wonders featured a dishwashing contest between a slovenly "Mrs. Drudge" and a more composed and youthful "Mrs. Modern," whose automatic dishwasher "won" each time, after which "the disgusted Mrs. Drudge literally threw in the towel." Similarly, the Electric Light and Power Company's tableaux vivant titled "When Washday Was Slosh-day" contrasted women in rags scrubbing clothes on washboards with modern beauties who simply pushed buttons. And back at GE's House of Magic, four young women in bathing suits effortlessly fried an egg in a bowl levitated by magnets—yet another demonstration that modernity defied all constraints, even gravity. Westinghouse's "Elektro," the studly household servant, further eroticized automation by representing the idealized househusband: an ever-attentive domesticated man unafraid to water plants, dust furniture, or, of course, cook. Within this radical liberationist context, Jochnowitz observes, the housewife was "no longer a servant, more an artist."[45]

The numerous cooking demonstrations, tips, and pamphlets complementing these gadget displays linked factory-made foods to women's supposed emancipation. Jochnowitz describes an exhibit entitled "Factory Preparation Frees Mrs. 1939," that showed "a well-dressed woman surrounded by tiny icons representing sports equipment, playing cards, programs from concerts and a charity bazaar, a psychoanalysis text and a ballot"—all symbols of an independent life dedicated to recreation and civic involvement. No other fair presented more opportunities to buy freedom. While some manufacturers were still giving away free samples of the latest convenience foods in 1939, others just sold them. Over twenty thousand visitors a day bought samples of General Foods' new "quick-frozen foods" and Kate Smith Bake-a-Cake Kits. To emphasize that convenience was compatible with elegance, the "Live Dinner Party"—presented twice daily on a turntable stage at the America at Home pavilion—featured two formally dressed couples consuming a meal that started with Campbell's soup and ended with Jell-O.[46]

The lively conversation and impeccable manners of the diners seemed to prove what utopian modernist Charlotte Perkins Gilman had insisted upon at the turn of the century: "In any home, even more important than the food which is on the dinner table is the conversation that goes around the dinner table." In the essentially conservative corporate modernism of the World of Tomorrow, however, women might push buttons to heat processed foods, but contrary to the more radical predictions of Bellamy, Wells, and, yes, Gilman, they would still be housewives serving others from their own kitchens. No kitchenless apartments, cooperative housekeeping, or communal dining rooms in *this* future. In Westinghouse's promotional film about an Indiana family's experiences at the 1939 fair, daughter Babs Middleton is temporarily infatuated with slick Marxist intellectual Nicholas Makaroff, who loves modern art, denounces mechanization, and espouses "simple" working-class tastes, yet loves expensive fair food. But she inevitably returns to her square hometown boyfriend Jim Treadway, who defends Westinghouse appliances and automation as a way to increase jobs and improve the general quality of life. In a way, Babs's homecoming after a fleeting flirtation with the deceptive leftist was meant to represent a larger cultural trend. Yes, during the Depression Americans might toy with socialism, but in the end they would return to traditional values. In mainstream modernism the nuclear family, the separate spheres for the sexes, and the private home were all considered to be timeless. In a *New York Times* overview of the woman's role as presented at the 1939 fair, Barnard College's dean, Virginia Gildersleeve, opined that women in the future would enjoy "the modern home, mechanically perfected, equipped with the gadgets so dear to our American hearts," but they were "bound to" marry, to have children, and to be "deeply concerned with the home," which would remain a private sanctuary, for "efforts to substitute a more communal existence have generally proved unsuccessful." This conservative vision carried over into the postwar period as well.[47]

THE AGE OF POPULUXE

During the early 1940s, much of the World of Tomorrow remained a distant fantasy—except perhaps for the ultramodernist military rations designed according to reductionist principles of nutritional adequacy and unpalatability. But the ensuing economic boom did embed much more of the modernist vision into the real landscape, albeit in an eclectic, superficial, and sometimes frivolous way. In the age of "Populuxe," Thomas Hine writes, "progress was not merely an abstraction, but an array of goods that could be touched, switched on, photographed, improved, and fantasized about." Befitting the heavy dose of amnesia that accompanies modernism, "never before," Hine observes, was the operative slogan for the apparently unprecedented wonders of cornucopian capitalism.[48]

Trumpeted loudly in the popular media, this upbeat message did offset—or at least contradict—the gloomy neo-Malthusianism of postwar think tank and dystopian discourse. Needless to say, the more disruptive utopian socialist aspects of modernism were almost completely buried beneath a heavy layer of Cold War conformism and complacency. "With all its faults and perils, this is a marvelous era," *Life*'s editor concluded in "Sunny Side of the Street," a review of the American Chemical Society's 1951 convention. Who could think otherwise, given the predictions made in the Society's *Chemical Engineering News?* In seventy-five years:

Starvation, another ancient enemy, will be a curiosity in the history books. Mankind will be producing synthetic foods from sunlight, water, ammonia, and the carbon dioxide in the air. Fertilizer substitutes will be sprayed right on the leaves of plants, producing yields beyond anything ever seen before. We will feed cattle on treated sawdust, to a sleek and tender fatness unknown today, and will even farm today's wasted salt marshes by using chemical plant foods and vegetables that thrive in a briny medium. Drought will be licked by water from the ocean. The jungle and the polar regions will be the new frontiers, made comfortable to live in by air conditioning. We will have rain or dry weather at our will. Our houses will be powered by atomic energy, and the telephone will have given way to two-way radio communication with any other house in the world.

Reviewing the same gathering, *Business Week* found a "future that seemed to be straight out of Buck Rogers"—the embodiment of apolitical, adolescent techno-enthusiasm.[49]

If there was a unifying cornucopian icon, it was the steel shopping cart—a piece of technology from the 1930s that reached full usage in the 1950s. The cover of *Life*'s 1955 "Special Food Issue" combined two symbols of American fertility—a young child sitting in an overflowing shopping cart—with the subhead: "Mass Luxury: A $73 Billion Market Basket." That Americans were feeding so many babies so well seemed to refute the doomsayers. And the landscape of highways, subdivisions, and parking lots was increasingly resembling the decentralized future predicted by GM in 1939. Thanks to motorization, supermarkets mushroomed from ten thousand in 1946 to seventeen thousand in 1953—and that was just the beginning. These stores had so much food to sell because American agriculture was indeed moving toward McMillen's industrialized, corporate future. In 1950, farmers grew 20 percent more wheat and 75 percent more potatoes per acre than in 1925. Similarly, thanks to advanced genetic selection, Holsteins produced 20 percent more butterfat in 1949 than in 1918. A 1949 *Popular Mechanics* article titled "Engineering Better Meat" invoked automotive streamlining to describe the genetic redesign of the nation's food supply: "The animal engineers now are copying the revolutionary process that transformed yesterday's tall, top-heavy automobile into a long, low car with built-in running boards and smoothly streamlined body. . . . Tomorrow's farmer would no more want to turn out a runty, rawboned pig or scrawny, thin-wooled sheep than a Detroit motor manufacturer would let an automobile leave his production line minus radiator grille or steering wheel."[50]

Ironically perhaps, this cornucopian bounty was achieved largely through a drastic reduction in biodiversity. Homogenization fit the needs of mass marketers, as evidenced by A&P's "Chicken of Tomorrow" contests, which encouraged poultry scientists to produce a large-breasted broiler that would sell as prepackaged cuts in supermarket refrigerator cases. By the early '50s, William Boyd writes, more than two-thirds of all commercial chickens carried the winning breed's genes. While not quite as simplified as the headless, wingless bird envisioned in 1932 by Winston Churchill (and parodied in 1952 as Chicken Little in Pohl and Kornbluh's *The Space Merchants*), this was clearly a "designer chicken" attuned to industrial "performance" standards. Vulnerable to numerous maladies and very expensive to feed, house, and maintain, these hybrids required a lot of chemicals, drugs, and machinery. These higher input costs favored further concentration of production, which in turn increased biological and economic vulnerability—a feedback loop resulting, almost literally, from putting too many eggs in too few baskets.[51] Such negative consequences had not quite been expected by futurists who, conditioned perhaps by the 1939 fair's Rotolactor and Elsie's Boudoir, had assumed that the new, modern chicken would live a life of spoiled ease. For example, a 1955 *Science Digest* article on "Streamlining the Henhouse" depicted a happy hen fanning herself while lounging in front of a television, cold drink nearby. Because confined hens supposedly fed and drank "at will" from conveyor belts carrying feed and water, they did not have to scrounge in dirty barnyards. "In some hen factories soft music plays to keep the birds in a contented egg-laying mood."[52] The realities in egg and broiler production were not so nice. But lower prices did move chicken from Sunday specialty to daily staple. In a major cornucopian triumph, the per capita consumption of chicken almost tripled (from 15 pounds to 43.3 pounds a year per person) between 1938 and 1976.[53]

The same intensification dynamic—a reduction in genetic diversity and in the number of producers, at the cost of increased biological and social fragility—was widely duplicated. As chain supermarkets and restaurants extended their reach across the land they standardized cuisine— and fostered a greater incidence of diet-related "diseases of affluence." Aspiring to feed the exploding world population through advanced genetics, the Green Revolution reduced the world's food problems to daily calorie deficits and then offered Third World countries shorter plants that would yield more grain—more calories—without "lodging," or falling over. However, such specialized plants required more water, fertilizer, pesticides, and tractors—in short, the same technological treadmill that was displacing small farmers while producing such gluts in the First World. That these displaced peasants would then serve as industrial laborers was another welcomed ingredient in the whole "development" equation—a model that took on special urgency as the United States and the Soviet Union competed for Third World allies.[54] While the Cold War context was new, the elements of the basic modernization package would not have surprised the cornucopian visionaries of thirty years earlier.

Likewise, earlier advocates of scientific eating, household engineering, and streamlining would not have been amazed by the proliferation of value-added convenience products and appliances that promised to liberate women and simplify family life. In 1953, food writer Poppy Cannon dubbed the can opener an "open sesame" to "the four freedoms from tedium, space, work, and your own inexperience." Extending the prewar fascination with automated cooking, the dream kitchen's myriad push buttons promised to reduce all human effort to "the tiniest flick of a finger." The push-button utopia coupled new refrigeration, microwave, and cybernetic technologies with Ford-era images of continuous, conveyor-belt mass production. In 1957, Campbell Soup's president observed that packaged foods were turning the kitchen into "the point for assembling the menu." Victor Cohn's 1956 version of the typical kitchen of 1999 spared housewives from having to expend a single calorie stooping, mixing, stretching, or even thinking: the push of a button would eject precrushed ice cubes from a wall dispenser, raise an electronic oven to waist height, or fry foods without burning. The housewife of 1999 would not even need to know how to read, as she could simply choose meals from computerized photo cards, which could then be popped into the slot to do the rest. Such images of instantaneous, effortless command also accompanied predictions of "push-button farming" aided by "push-button weather" (automated irrigation) and other domesticated versions of push-button rocketry. After all, if politicians could destroy the world in a few minutes by simply pressing "the button," then certainly housewives should be able to prepare a full dinner in even less time. It was perhaps no coincidence that the same manufacturers of push-button dishwashers, television sets, vacuum cleaners, and ovens—Westinghouse, General Electric, Chrysler, and so on—were also heavily involved in building America's "push-button defense."[55]

As the Space Race straddled agendas that were both military and civilian, international and domestic, aerospace symbols abounded. Extending the streamlining conceits of Gaudi, Le Corbusier, and the Bauhaus style, parabolas soared everywhere—from the arches of Ray Kroc's McDonald's and Eero Saarinen's St. Louis gateway to the "butterfly chairs" and rounded coffee tables of suburban split-level homes. According to architectural historian Philip Langdon, the parabolas suggested "a feeling of skyward momentum, symbolic of an aerospace age in which man could hurtle himself into the heavens." Thomas Hine even detects such symbolism in the popular California dip of the 1950s, especially when scooped with the parabolic potato chip—"a thoroughly modern food" that suggested an informal spontaneity somewhat akin to the gravity-defying rocket-shaped tailfins also popular in the 1950s. The period's "buoyant spirit" also dressed up postwar diners, motels, drive-ins, and supermarkets with boomerangs, wings, fins, handlebars, kites, A-frames, soaring folded-plate roofs, and starbursts. According to Langdon, many of these touches came together in the "Googie" style of Southern California's coffee shops, whose well-padded bucket seats, pastel Formica counters, and rocketing rooflines suggested "an architecture of superabundance. From its extravagant gestures and its lack of inhibition sprang a sense of exhilaration." The same gleaming artificiality, Fordist automation, and rapid turnover likewise underlay the emerging fast food system. To spread his Golden Arches across the land, Ray Kroc perfected the ultra-Taylorist principles of KISS (Keep It Simple, Stupid), which also guided the convenience food cuisine that would supposedly free women from effort and stress.[56]

While we may question whether many women in fact felt liberated by their canned goods and appliances, the processed meal certainly came of age in the 1950s and early 1960s. Culinary historians differ on whether the most iconic representative of quick-and-easy cuisine was Miracle Whip, Crisp Vegetable Salad made with Jell-O, Cherry Coke Salad (also with Jell-O), California dip (made with dried onion soup mix), the TV dinner, or Eight-Can Casserole (don't ask). Underlying all such dishes was impatience with traditional, labor-intensive cooking. Yet forecasts fell short if they overdid the hype. Few supermarket products were quite as revolutionary as claimed. People still ate meats, starches, and vegetables that looked more or less like those of the 1920s, the 1880s, and even the 1820s—and, automated-synthetic fantasies notwithstanding, they still do. Inspired by modernism, futurists expected even more artificial wonders to come, but they also assumed that underlying social and economic parameters would endure. In this, their predictions fell prey to two of the basic fallacies highlighted by historian of the future Joseph Corn: total revolution and social continuity.[57] Much as earlier predictions had assumed that hot technological innovations like pneumatic tubes, "air nitrogen," electricity, radio, and airplanes would eventually "change everything," postwar cornucopians expected the latest breakthroughs to invade and transform virtually every material sphere, from farming down to the most mundane domestic activities. If we had nuclear bombs and reactors, then why not nuclear wristwatches, tractors, and stoves, too? At the same time, even as they extrapolated a complete technological revolution, they wrongly assumed the unchallenged *social continuity* of patriarchy, the nuclear family, capitalism, and white hegemony. And they also wrongly assumed that people would love modernism *forever*.

Total revolution presupposes "mission creep" and infinite linear improvement. Take, for example, the popular image of the fully automated farm. If, as *The Wall Street Journal* reported in 1945, the number of machines on farms had increased 50 percent during the war, why not extrapolate *total* mechanization in a few more years? With surplus military planes being used to spray crops with new pesticides, it seemed logical that "aerial farming" might soon expand to include seeding, plowing, and, why not, weather control too? With air-conditioning, helicopters, combines, electronic controls, and airborne crop dusting already well-established technologies, it made sense to speculate that all these might come together in the "push-button farm" of the future as described in a 1954 ad for National Oil and Grease Seals: "Some day soon, in the air-conditioned comfort of his helicopter 'control tower,' the farmer will flip a switch and send teams of ingenious machines out to till his fields. In a single integrated operation, the robot gangs will pulverize, condition, and furrow the soil, drill seed and fertilize, perhaps implant soluble water capsules and transmit a pest-killing electronic bath."[58] Interestingly, despite the "superb achievement in engineering," this ultracomplex machine would still need old-fashioned grease and O-rings—an assumption of continuity that obviously benefited the sponsoring company. And the operator would still be a white male operating his own personal farm. Modernization was good to a point—as long as it did not threaten established industries, social patterns, and yeoman farmer myths. Similarly, in the 2000 foreseen in the 1950s, personal helicopters would still transport breadwinning fathers home to private suburban homes where housekeeping wives would employ push-button automation to cook traditional meat-and-potato family meals.

Given the priority accorded animal foods, it was inevitable that new "wonder drugs" (total revolution) would be enlisted in the service of conservative meat preferences (social continuity). Soon after penicillin was first used to fight human infections (in the 1940s), scientists found that antibiotics accelerated the weight gain of farm animals subjected to factory-farm crowding and stresses. Here, then, in apparent repudiation of those inefficient feed-to-meat conversion ratios, was a way to grow more meat on less grain. *Science News Letter* enthused that pigs raised on "synthetic milk" laced with terramycin "were happier (if getting fat faster is an index of pig happiness) than piglets who were fed by Mamma Sow in the old-fashioned suckling way." If animals grew better dosed with antibiotics, why not humans? Taking that leap, *Science News Letter* extrapolated: "A pinch of penicillin or aureomycin added [as a growth stimulant] to the rice bowl in China, India, and other rice-eating regions might solve a large part of the world's food problem and through this contribute to world peace." Defeating Malthus was still the goal, but the "fix" was to be technological, not social or political—an example of Corn's third basic fallacy of prediction. Better to spike poor people's rice with questionable drugs than address the underlying causes of malnutrition.[59]

Moreover, following the "better living through chemistry" dicta of DuPont's traveling exhibits, it seemed logical to extend one "wonder drug" application to other cornucopian uses. If antibiotics could defeat microbes in living animals, why not add them to refrigerated meats and canned goods as a preservative? Likewise, wartime successes with organochlorine pesticides like DDT encouraged fantasies of *total* eradication of bugs and weeds. Noting that the common house fly was "an insult to the human race," *Science News Letter* asked whether DDT would allow a future historian to look back at the United States of 1950–2000 and call it the "Fly-Free Half Century." Since some pesticides were by-products of chemical warfare research, the story seemed a particularly satisfying example of the "swords into ploughshares" archetype. *Science News Letter,* for instance, reported that "chemicals now being investigated at the Army's wartime biological warfare laboratories hold the possibility of increasing the food production of the world so that a population suicide of civilization can be averted."[60] In the transgressive, category-defying rhetoric of modernism, war was indeed peace, Orwell notwithstanding.

No technology invited more extravagant "swords into plowshares" hyperbole than irradiation, the application of a deadly force to now save lives by staving off microbial contamination. In a clear example of what historian Paul Boyer calls the "search for a silver lining" inside the mushroom cloud, the Arthur D. Little consulting firm reported in 1949 that "The power of the atom may give the final knockout to the tiny agents that spoil the flavor and goodness of processed foods." *The Wall Street Journal* enthused that "three-week-old hamburger, four-month-old bread and two-year-old potatoes may be typical fare at tomorrow's table." Marshaling the same iconoclastic bravado, journalist Victor Cohn extolled the University of Michigan scientist walking around with a year-old hamburger in his pocket, "its bacteria killed by atomic waste-material radiation." By 1975, Cohn predicted in 1956, "we may have replaced the refrigerator and freezer . . . with an ordinary storage cabinet filled with atomic-ray-preserved food."[61]

While fewer than half of American households actually had mechanical refrigerators as late as 1941, and deep freezers were not even available commercially until the early 1950s, boosters of irradiation found hopeful precedents in such recent progress. If frozen foods could come of age in just twenty years, they reasoned, irradiated foods could easily become commonplace in the next twenty. And by 1985 nuclear-generated electricity would no doubt operate many household gadgets, including a garbage disposal, dishwasher, air-conditioner, kitchen mixer, phonograph, and, perhaps most remarkable, "an automatic coffee maker" that will brew your first cup while you shower (with water heated, to be sure, by atomic power). In the modernist future, less was more; a uranium pellet the size of a vitamin pill might fuel a house for a year. Streamlining agriculture, uranium would run tractors, irrigation pumps, and combines. Similarly, cheap atomic energy would desalinize oceans, irrigate deserts, cool tropical plantations, warm arctic soils, and power the "artificial suns" of indoor cornfields.[62]

To boost yields indefinitely, some speculated, radiation might displace or supplement the newly introduced petrochemical fertilizers. Citing evidence of "increased plant growth at Nagasaki as a result of the atomic-bomb explosion," Progressive presidential candidate Henry Wallace hoped that the "by-products" of the nuclear research at Oak Ridge would provide "material sufficient to fertilize all the crops of the US," and he applauded Russian research on the direct application of radioactive "rays" to increase plant growth. In a sensationalistic article about how agricultural research's "brave new world" was, yes, beating "swords into plowshares," two USDA engineers extended Wallace's idea to include a whole array of "barnyard death rays" that would simultaneously boost plant yields; kill insects, rodents, and bacteria; sterilize milk; and, as if that were not enough, accelerate beneficial mutations "that would enable science to get new varieties much more quickly than heretofore." One particularly sublime mutation would be "beef cattle the size of dogs" that could graze "in the average man's backyard, eating especially thick grass and producing especially tender steaks." With suburban ranch lawns thus converted to mini-ranges for mini-steers, how could there ever be a meat shortage? Conversely, another article pondered the promotion of genetic mutations that would make humans smaller while increasing the size of animals. "Half-size humans would then be able to dine on double-size animals!"[63]

While this desire to streamline evolution had predated the nuclear age, the goal now seemed more achievable. For example, radioactive isotopes might make it easier to improve photosynthesis. *The New York Times'* William Laurence observed that after using "tagged elements" to learn how plants build food from sunlight, carbon dioxide, and water, "we would no longer be dependent exclusively on the soil to give us our daily bread. Man at least may be able to produce enough food to provide abundantly for the world's population." According to a *Scientific American* article, the application of nuclear power to cell research promised "to emancipate us all some day from our bondage to chlorophyll."[64] Such liberationist rhetoric echoed prewar dissatisfaction with natural photosynthesis, which, as we have seen, was deemed inefficient by many modernizers. And unlike the more far-fetched fantasies of atomic cars, toasters, and lawnmowers, work on photosynthesis was already underway. Particularly exciting was new research concerning *Chlorella pyrenoidosa*, a high-protein algae that grew rapidly using two inexhaustible resources: sunlight and carbon dioxide. In many ways, the enthusiasm about chlorella cuisine represented the peak of modernism—and also exposed its underlying flaws and limitations.

CHLORELLA CUISINE

Looking back from an age when "natural" and "traditional" are far more appetizing food adjectives than "synthetic" and "artificial," it may be hard to understand how anyone could ever have been intrigued by a future of air-conditioned, fully automated "skyscraper farms" that would raise algae on raw sewage in enclosed ponds and then pipeline the protein-rich green "scum" to factories synthesizing cheap hamburgers, pasta, animal feed, and fuel.[65] Barely imaginable today, such a prospect seemed quite plausible in the ultramodernist 1950s—and not just in *Popular Mechanics* and the science fiction pulps. In fact, for about a decade after World War II, many cornucopian think tankers were quite taken with algae. As we have seen, with the world population likely to double, and with half the postwar world already defined as hungry, many serious analysts voiced significant concerns about the limits of conventional agriculture. So to feed a much more crowded world, it seemed plausible, indeed mandatory, that scientists develop radically unorthodox food sources.

Algae emerged as a possible antidote to Malthusian catastrophe in the late 1940s, and through the 1950s it made the short list of potential high-tech solutions to the world food crisis. Ambitious pilot projects were sponsored by major research institutions such as the Carnegie Institution, Rockefeller Foundation, National Institutes of Health, University of California at Berkeley, Atomic Energy Commission, and Stanford University. Reputable periodicals like *Scientific American, Scientific Monthly,* and *Science* reported preliminary results, while Nobel laureates and highly regarded heads of MIT, Harvard University, the University of Wisconsin, the Food and Agriculture Organization, the American Chemical Society, and the American Association for the Advancement of Science cheered the researchers from the sidelines and urged Manhattan Project–scale funding.[66]

For almost a hundred years science fiction and utopian writers had been forecasting a future with synthetic foods, but now even Nobel laureate John Boyd-Orr was urging a closer look at nonagricultural food production. Some proposals stemmed from the previous Malthusian scares of the 1890s and 1920s, particularly the claims of chemists that they could grow high-protein yeasts on a substrate derived from sawdust and agricultural waste. (Looking ahead from 1956 to 1999, Victor Cohn wrote, "For lunch the Futures ate wood steak, planked, and loved it.") Even more daring, of course, was the hope—going back to Berthelot— that carbohydrates, fats, and protein might be synthesized directly from coal, petroleum, or just air. Pursuing the consolidating trajectory of synthetic science, one biochemist even devised a "Universal Diet No. 1," which consisted of casein, corn oil, cornstarch, cellulose, sucrose, and assorted vitamins and minerals.[67] Measured against such bravado, the new algae research of the 1940s actually seemed moderate, even natural, for it came not from the Brave New World of synthetic chemistry but from the more familiar world of marine biology.

For years naturalists had been urging a closer look at unexploited sea resources as another way out of the Malthusian trap. Why bother concocting artificial meals from coal when there was so much *real* food from the sea just out there for the taking? While discussion of marine resources focused mainly on aquaculture (fish farming) and on unappreciated "trash fish," mollusks, and mammals, more ambitious proposals targeted highly nutritious kelp (macroalgae) and plankton, the floating stew of microalgae and tiny animals that constitute the base of the food chain.

("By 1999," Cohn wrote, "deep-sea harvesters with flexible hoses sucked plankton and deep-sea creatures into their holds, and the Future teens enthusiastically landed their auto-copters at Joe's Fly-in for late-night plankton burgers.") Harvesting wild kelp and plankton was difficult, however. Given the diversity of life contained in the typical batch, nutritional quality could be quite variable, some even toxic. And since plankton tend to move around unpredictably, gathering it in large quantities was not an easy task, Cohn's vision of electromagnetic herding nets notwithstanding.[68] But in 1948, amid all the publicity accorded William Vogt's ultrapessimistic *Road to Survival* and Fairfield Osborn's almost equally alarmist *Our Plundered Planet,* researchers announced that they were able to grow a particularly nutritious algae using inexpensive materials under controlled laboratory conditions.

The alluring news came from pilot projects sponsored by the Carnegie Institution and conducted by the Stanford Research Institute in Menlo Park and by Arthur D. Little, Inc. in Cambridge. Initial results suggested that chlorella algae was an astounding photosynthetic superstar. When grown in optimal conditions—sunny, warm, shallow ponds fed by simple carbon dioxide—chlorella converted upwards of 20 percent of solar energy (compare this with the conventional 1 percent) into a plant containing over 50 percent protein when dried. Unlike most plants, chlorella's protein was "complete," for it had the ten amino acids then considered essential, and it was also packed with calories, fat, and vitamins.[69]

Since these results were very preliminary, researchers hedged the early scholarly reports with caveats about the need for a lot more work. Yet even the most responsible investigators were unable to resist heady expectation. Dean Burk, a National Institutes of Health scientist actively involved in the Stanford pilot, speculated that scientists would soon be able to quadruple chlorella's already impressive photosynthetic efficiency. Based on a mere 100 pounds of chlorella produced at the Cambridge pilot plant, Carnegie's scientists projected possible yields of 17 to 40 tons (dry weight) per acre. This meant 17,000 to 40,000 pounds of protein per acre—compared to 250 to 800 pounds of protein from soybeans, the most efficient conventional plant—and all at a reasonable cost of 25 cents a pound. Taking the lower yield, a plantation the size of Rhode Island would be able to supply half of the world's daily protein requirement of 65 grams per capita. And these yields were low compared to other estimates. One scientist predicted possible yields of 55,000 pounds of protein per acre, with virtually insignificant harvesting costs. Another estimated that one thousand-acre chlorella farm, staffed by just twenty workers, could produce 10,000 tons of protein a year—all at a cost of just $10 a ton. Devoting 50 million tropical acres to algae production would *double* the world's food supply.[70]

If scientists could be so fast and free with the figures, popular journalists felt licensed to draw up full scenarios. In "Food Pumped from Pipelines," *Collier's* sketched the "farm of the future" (just twenty-five years ahead), to be located somewhere on the shoreline of the Texas Gulf, or in Southern California, Galilee, or some other sunny place: "For miles— as far as the eye can see—twist fat coils of glass pipe, two and three feet thick. Greenish-yellow fluid courses sluggishly through the transparent mains. . . . Great pumping stations dot the shore. The coils lead inland and terminate in a huddle of other plants from which a mile-long train of tank cars—the only sign of human life—is just gliding away." In the sun-drenched tubes billions of algae, "microscopic factories," multiplied "to produce edible foods—butter, tissue-building proteins, starches, fodder for cattle." Hardly a human hand would be involved, as "automatically operated devices, requiring only switchboard control, swirl the harvest through batteries of centrifuges," separating "crop" from water before pipelining it to "solvent extraction tanks for processing into food for man and beast." Although the scene had "the appearance of a Dali surrealist landscape," the implications were anything but absurd: "In the farm of the future . . . man has learned how to grow food in water in such abundance that, for the first time in history, there is enough for everybody, and hunger is banished from the earth"—a biotechnological utopia.[71]

The algae story fit nicely into the basic conventions of popular journalism. For one thing, its very baseness—lowly "pond scum"—created dramatic incongruity, an essential ingredient in modernist rhetoric. Headlines like "Vast Energy from Tiny Plants" immediately invited quizzical attention. That something so small, so low, so foul might save mankind suggested an intriguing dissonance somewhere between "The Little Engine That Could" and "Ripley's Believe It or Not." Algae offered a heroic role reversal ("single-cell organism saves civilization") that evoked surprise and awe ("gee whiz!"). Some hard-boiled reporters of the steak-and-bourbon variety may also have found sardonic pleasure in contemplating the depths to which modern humanity was being driven by insatiable appetites for food and sex. After reluctantly allowing that the population explosion made synthetic foods inevitable, a dyspeptic *Fortune* article titled "Let Them Eat Kelp" ended with a petulant "Will somebody pass the ketchup?"[72]

But on the whole, most coverage was not cynical, or even skeptical. This was a story validated by impeccably credentialed sources. In line with the declarative overstatement so common in speculative discourse, elite certification hardened possibilities into certainties. For example, when the Carnegie Institution issued its optimistic but preliminary report on work then in progress, *Science News Letter* titled its summary with the more definite-sounding "Algae to Feed Starving." While the Carnegie report suggested that "algal culture *may* fill a very real need," *Science News Letter* asserted that "future populations of the world *will* be kept from starving by production of improved or 'educated' algae." As if to speed the transition from pilot to commercial plant, the newsletter's cover photograph of Arthur D. Little's Cambridge laboratory—the site of the very small rooftop pilot project—implied that the entire building was a "future food factory." A few years later, in an article titled "Tomorrow's Dinner," *Science News Letter* pronounced: "There is no question in the minds of scientists" that future farms would be "factories" producing carbohydrates and protein from microorganisms. According to "reliable sources," *Science Digest* reported, "common pond scum" would soon become "the world's most important agricultural crop," especially if the U.S. government funded a "scum-producing program on a scale comparable to the original Manhattan project for the atomic bomb."[73] If the Manhattan Project—a common reference point—could "tame the atom," why not chlorella?

While it is tempting to attribute the hyperbole mainly to press sensationalism, it would be wrong to focus solely on the pitfalls of popular science reporting. Reporters were picking up on the enthusiasm of the scientists themselves. And these scientists jumped to conclusions because they shared the same modernist faith in technologies that appeared to transcend known boundaries. For a generation that had experienced the once-unimaginable breakthroughs wrought by electricity, radio, automobiles, airplanes, and X-rays, streamlining photosynthetic efficiency did not seem such a stretch.

Hopes ran a bit ahead of the data because the story already had legs. Algae was the very base of the food chain, the essential building block of all life, and may also have been the primary ingredient in the formation of petroleum, the lifeblood of industrial civilization. Modernism enlisted classical elements to describe algae's benefits, for mythical allusions abounded and helped to make algae seem less bizarre, more central to life, more continuous. According to the microbiological interpretation of Genesis, primordial algae were responsible for converting a carbon-dioxide-choked wasteland into a fertile green Eden. The "manna from heaven" that had saved Moses's people wandering in Sinai was nothing other than blue-green algae, *Scientific American* asserted; ancient Africans and Aztecs were also thought to have flourished on algae as a protein source. Scientists seeking to augment photosynthesis were modern shamans tapping the "vital force," as well as Prometheans who would "harness the sun" for the benefit of starving mankind; they also were alchemists turning scum to gold.[74]

Two can play the game of archetypes, of course, and critics of chlorella had their own myths to draw upon. Fairfield Osborn dismissed the dangerous "hubris of the chemist" who thought he had discovered the "secret of life." Conservationist Samuel Ordway doubted that consumers in the overcrowded future would relish "wooden meatballs" downed with "cornucopian wine made from fermented sludge." Malthusian demographer Robert Cook ridiculed "scientists who tilt at windmills" in their quixotic quest for synthetic food solutions to feed a "runaway population." And as we have seen, in the socially critical science fiction of the period, food from algae symbolized a technologically ingenious but ultimately inhumane, desensitized world where people were no longer able to recognize the ersatz. In all, the battle of the metaphors added to the story's dramatic value.[75]

But proponents of algae did not have to rely on myths and archetypes alone, for they also had the best ally in modernist culture—the rhetoric of efficiency. As prewar progressives had already insisted, conventional agricultural, with its dependence on the vagaries of nature and human labor, seemed shamefully hidebound and inherently wasteful. The twentieth century had witnessed the radical modernization of housing, transportation, and war-making, but not farming, with its bondage to highly variable factors: plants, weather, soil, and peasants. Not only did the so-called higher plants (corn, wheat, rice) "waste" virtually all of the sunlight that fell on them, they converted most of the remaining solar energy to inedible stems, leaves, and roots. Algae, on the other hand, was almost completely usable. In fact, according to some proposals algae would actually *consume* waste—animal, human, and even industrial sewage. To further the chemurgic loop, algae could also serve as a source of industrial raw materials, particularly fuel, pigments, glycols, and sterols. This remarkably versatile plant would thus not only supply industry but feed its workers and recycle its more obnoxious by-products.[76]

Algae also wasted less time. On traditional, temperate-climate grain or produce farms, only a few weeks were actually devoted to harvesting.

The rest of the year was essentially unproductive, and costly equipment sat idle. On an algae farm, however, the crop could be harvested as a continuous flow, with no unproductive downtime. Moreover, unlike conventional farms, whose location depended largely on accidents of geography and history, an algae factory could be located in any sunny place, even the desert. Other inputs could be carefully controlled—especially human labor. Whereas conventional agriculture depended on conservative farmers who were often resistant to modern management techniques, algae would be grown by highly trained technicians whose air-conditioned, push-button "skyscraper farms" represented a desirable evolutionary leap forward. Released from primeval peasant drudgery, farmers could find better-paying jobs more suitable to modern, urban-industrial civilization. And, following this "demographic transition," by working in factories and living in cities they would no longer need to have so many children. In all, University of Chicago sociologist Richard Meier concluded, chlorella's "industrialization of photosynthesis" was inherently progressive. As McMillen and his chemurgic allies had long insisted, it was time for agriculture to enter the twentieth century, a world of rational and consolidated exploitation of a wider range of available resources. Conversely, it was time for people to transcend their irrational prejudices for "higher" plants and family farms.[77]

Whether people would overcome their prejudice for traditional *food* and *taste* was another matter, for even algae's enthusiasts admitted that chlorella was a "nauseating slime" when wet, an unappetizing green powder when dried. Some advocates were not fazed by the palatability issue. "Raw algae paste does not taste too good," Victor Cohn observed, "but neither does flour." Since "plankton soup" derived from a sewage treatment plant had been successfully served to malnourished Venezuelan lepers, the boldest spirits asserted that good chemical and human engineering might induce the public to eat almost anything, even green algae burgers. After all, in the 1950s processors churned out all sorts of synthetic convenience foods, and with remarkable market success. Fabricated algae burgers might be more of a stretch, but Meier hoped that food chemists and psychologists would work together in smoothing public acceptance of "microbial" foods "with a flavor and texture that is a delight to the connoisseur." The discovery in the West of an old "Oriental" flavoring secret, monosodium glutamate, encouraged confidence that chemists could devise even better ways to "perk up" processed foods. Noting these breakthroughs, Cal Tech biologist James Bonner expected that the "craft of food technology" would soon be able to create "wholly satisfactory" steaks made entirely from vegetable protein flavored with "tasty synthetics" and "made chewy by addition of a suitable plastic matrix." While such foods might *not* delight the connoisseur, Bonner predicted that in the more rational future, "human beings will place less emotional importance on the gourmet aspects of food and will eat more to support their body chemistry." As ascetic missionaries of the New Nutrition had been preaching for years, in a truly efficient world one would eat just to live, and what one ate would be determined by chemical analysis, not superficial aesthetics. Some enthusiasts also invoked vegetarian virtue in defending synthetic proteins. Chemist Jacob Rosin sounded almost like Percy Shelley and George Bernard Shaw in predicting that "our grandchildren will hardly believe that we were so primitive and barbaric that we had to eat cadavers of dead animals to stay alive." Algae burgers would thus represent a great advance in human evolution.[78]

Pondering the limits of popular modernism, other algae researchers were more cautious about overcoming conservative food habits. Instead of displacing traditional dishes altogether, they hoped to add a neutralized chlorella powder to conventional foods, much as processors were already fortifying bread, noodles, and snacks with vitamins and minerals. One Japanese experiment found that consumers would accept green algae powder if it was hidden in already-green foods like spinach noodles and mint ice cream. Similarly, a flavor panel at Arthur D. Little's Cambridge lab found that when chlorella was diluted in chicken soup, "the stronger, less pleasant 'notes' were much reduced and the 'gag factor' was not noticeable."[79]

Mindful of the "gag factor"—and the longstanding association of kelp with "coolie rations"—most algae backers doubted that humans would *ever* eat algae directly; instead, if added to animal feed, it might increase the protein supply indirectly. It was this last possibility that intrigued mainstream researchers and the futurists least prone to science fiction scenarios. Because it allowed people to have their animal protein without wasting feed grains, feeding algae to animals seemed more realistic, less radical than using it to create totally artificial foods. Algae farming would be modern, yes, but nothing to get really scared about. Food production would be more streamlined, but the raw materials would still be green plants grown with real sunlight, there would still be barns with cattle and chickens, and consumers would still be eating eggs, beef, and ice cream. Here was chlorella not as some distasteful, Martian-green meal-in-a-pill but as a sensibly efficient, middle ground solution to a pressing global problem.[80] In some ways, this vision was less far-fetched than the Rotolactor version of dairying—with a hint of the recombinant model of the future, the topic of the next chapter.

Capping the case for chlorella production were reassurances that, with the technical feasibility almost proved, economic viability was just a matter of time. The basic ingredients—sun, water, carbon dioxide, and algae—were essentially free. If an algae farm was coupled with a sewage treatment plant, algae could be "produced for nothing or less than nothing" as a serendipitous by-product. A new algae farm dedicated solely to food production might have significant start-up costs, but year-round operation would amortize the investment. Furthermore, economies of scale would eventually reduce algae prices. Even if the bottom-line price of algae initially came out higher than conventional protein, population pressure and diminishing agricultural returns would *eventually* increase grain prices. Even supporters of conventional agriculture assumed that food prices were destined to rise as population grew, so it was easy for algae's advocates to downplay the cost question as "only" a matter of economics that would surely be resolved down the road.[81] As usual, cornucopians covered their utopian hopes with a major caveat—that supply required demand—and then proceeded to forget that rather significant "if."

But economics cannot be dismissed so lightly. History is littered with the debris of projects that were theoretically possible but economically impractical. Algae's economics did not work out for two basic reasons: the production of grains and soybeans (algae's closest high-protein competitor) skyrocketed, and algae cultivation turned out to be far more complicated and expensive than originally thought. Between 1950 and 1990, the world population doubled faster than predicted (from 2.6 billion to 5.3), yet food production increased even faster. Overall world grain yields jumped 150 percent per acre, and in the United States grain yields almost tripled. Gross soy production increased sixfold. Much of this increase in soy was due to the successful application of Asian soybean varieties acquired in the 1920s by American plant explorers. Thus the classical future (horticultural imperialism) trumped the modernist (biochemistry). Ironically enough, as cheap soy—the *other* staple of the despised "coolie diet"—became an essential component in feed grain, it enabled a major expansion of the Western, meat-centered diet. Since the world had almost 40 percent more grain per capita and 300 percent more soy in 1990 than it had during the Malthusian gloom of 1950, food prices did not rise. In the absence of food price inflation, industry had no incentive to develop alternative sources.[82] And while conventional "higher plants" turned out to be more efficient than their detractors had alleged, algae production proved to be far less so; in 1990 algae still cost over $1,000 a ton, one hundred times the costs projected forty years earlier.

Algae's economic problems became clear in the late 1950s, after a decade's worth of experimentation. For example, researchers determined that chlorella's photosynthetic efficiency peaked at about 25 percent, not the 50 to 70 percent previously projected by some enthusiasts. While this was still impressive, achieving it required considerable capital investment. In a thorough review of the research literature for the Charles Pfizer & Co. laboratories, engineers Dean Thacker and Harold Babcock found that chlorella converted 25 percent of light into carbohydrates only under artificial laboratory conditions. When exposed to uncontrolled sunlight, chlorella captured just 2.5 percent—not much better than conventional crops. To achieve higher rates, light had to be held to twilight levels, which required either complex shading arrangements or artificial illumination. Moreover, in natural conditions chlorella's photosynthesis automatically shut itself off when the plants became crowded. To increase yields, the cells needed to be stirred with energy-consuming rotors or paddles.[83]

Chlorella's nutritional needs and inherent delicacy increased equipment and energy costs. While wild algae subsisted well on atmospheric carbon dioxide, to be superproductive chlorella had to be grown in carbonated water; this meant pumps, pipes, and storage tanks for the carbon dioxide. Moreover, like conventional grains, it grew best with artificial fertilizers, which necessitated more electricity, materials, and storage. And whereas natural ponds hosted a diverse assortment of toxic bacteria, molds, and competing algae, a facility dedicated just to chlorella would have to take complex and expensive steps to exclude unwanted microorganisms. Even worse contamination problems bedeviled those hoping to grow chlorella on sewage. Chlorella also proved to be very temperature sensitive. It reproduced best within a very narrow range of daytime temperatures—25 degrees Celsius was optimum—and it also tended to burn up valuable calories if nighttime temperatures dropped too low. So for maximum productivity chlorella might need air-conditioning by day, heating at night.[84]

Then there were the difficulties of converting raw chlorella into food fit for animals and humans. Since chlorella cells were too small to be collected with simple filters, they needed to be harvested with centrifuges and coagulants. Drying the cells was tricky. Exposure to sunlight invited bacterial contamination, but excessive artificial heat destroyed nutrients. Perhaps most daunting, chlorella's hard cell wall rendered it virtually indigestible in its natural state. Cooking improved digestibility, but heat reduced its nutritional benefits, so breaking down the wall necessitated still further mechanical processing. And then, after all this fussy cultivation and processing, one was left with what one otherwise sympathetic analyst called "a nasty little green vegetable." While food technologists were excited about using chlorella powder to enrich breads and noodles, removing the objectionable green color and seaweed taste destroyed valuable vitamins and protein. Worse, the green powder turned rancid on the shelf and could not be preserved without, once again, losing nutritional quality.[85]

After citing the challenges, Pfizer's Thacker and Babcock totaled the energy and equipment costs of chlorella production and came up with an estimate of 48 cents a pound when everything went right, and $1.00 a pound under "realistic" conditions. Either price could be considered astronomical, since soy meal was then selling for 6 cents a pound. As solar energy engineers, Thacker and Babcock sympathized with the hopes of algae's proponents, but they concluded that for algae to become viable as a food source, either the earth's population would have to increase so much as to require new sources of food "regardless of cost," or researchers would have to discover a new algae species that grew better "under less stringent conditions."[86] As it turned out, a somewhat less demanding type of algae was discovered in the 1960s—spirulina—but by that time algae research had turned away from its original goal of feeding a starving world.

Chlorella may have been too problematic to feed ordinary people, but it was not considered too expensive or bizarre to feed Soviet and American astronauts. As both countries launched crash programs to put humans in space, algae technology became a possible way to feed astronauts on long-duration space flights. Concerned that it would be impossible to stock a moon base or journey to the outer planets with enough food, water, and oxygen to sustain a mission of several months or years, space researchers investigated algae's recycling potential. In what has been called the "algae race," Soviet and American projects competed to develop a self-contained "aerospace life support system" that would use algae to convert astronaut wastes into clean air, water, and perhaps food as well. As a spin-off, NASA and aerospace contractors such as Boeing and Martin Marietta funded basic research on a wide variety of chlorella problems—from waste treatment to bleaching out the troublesome green color to determining the precise nutritional value of chlorella protein. In the 1970s, however, NASA deemphasized its chlorella research, partly because of persistent problems with contamination, partly because new nutritional research showed that it was not quite the complete food needed for long flights. And then loss of public support forced the termination of most research on long-duration space travel, although, as the next chapter discusses, some work on microbial foods continued, largely below the public radar.[87]

Meanwhile, work on algae's food potential persevered, albeit at a much lower level of funding, in another quarter: the health food industry. At $1,000 a ton, chlorella was far too expensive to be used for animal feed or even as a protein additive in enriched mass-produced breads and pasta, but as a nutritional supplement selling for $30 to $50 a pound in health food stores, it proved quite profitable. Most of the work in improving chlorella production was conducted in Japan, whose cuisine was more receptive to algae's taste and color. By 1980, forty-six small Asian factories were manufacturing two thousand tons of chlorella a month, primarily for the 100-million-dollar Japanese market—but also for export to Western health food stores. Ironically, the same natural-foods consciousness that steered Americans away from algae as a synthetic food in the 1960s brought some of them to seek it out in health food stores in the 1970s and 1980s. Since Americans did not generally lack for protein, algae marketers asserted algae's other nutritional benefits more appropriate for affluent consumers, especially weight control, cancer prevention, and immune system support. The discovery in the 1960s of the blue-green algae spirulina in the Saharan Lake Chad and in Mexico's Lake Texcoco gave another boost to the health food uses of algae. Spirulina has a high-nutrient profile similar to chlorella's but without two crucial production problems: being a much larger microalgae than chlorella, spirulina can be harvested with simple screens, not centrifuges; and because it does not have a hard cell wall, it does not need expensive mechanical processing to be rendered digestible.[88]

Reflecting their liberal clientele's environmental and political consciousness, the chlorella and spirulina promoters of the 1980s were not content just to sell health food supplements to the well-fed. In pamphlets and books published by New Age presses, they showed genuine concern about feeding the hungry. Echoing the small-is-beautiful paradigm of countercultural utopian fiction, they proposed village-scale algae farms that would convert animal and human wastes into clean water and high-protein livestock feed, thereby enhancing local hygiene and agricultural sustainability. While they were sincere, the New Age algae marketers were remarkably naive. Even small-scale village industries required large-scale

support to make much of an impact worldwide. But aside from a few pilot projects scattered throughout the Third World, there was little government funding. Algae's health food sales increased in the 1980s and
1990s, but few outside the health food industry saw it as a future food
for the masses, despite mounting concerns that conventional agriculture
might finally be running out of steam. Perhaps the most promising algae
project of the 1980s entailed feeding blue-green algae to crabs and snails
destined for European gourmets—hardly a solution to world hunger.[89]

Notwithstanding all the hopes for algae, its actual fate as a food source
shows how, in the absence of an explicit, well-funded public commitment specifically to feeding the poor, new foods research may drift toward high-end markets—a dynamic that would also undercut the philanthropic potential of genetic engineering. Industrial sponsors may use
altruistic language to rationalize their pursuits, but the bottom line is that
the poor cannot afford expensively produced food. High production costs
may not matter when selling to affluent specialty markets (such as astronauts and health faddists), but to serve the masses, food needs to be
literally dirt cheap. And it needs to be compatible with mainstream food
habits. Given the widespread resistance to its seaweed taste, the best hope
for algae was as animal feed. But in economies of scale, algae could not
even begin to compete with the building blocks of a meat-centered mass
cuisine: corn and soy. Spurred by the same Malthusian worries as algae
research but much better funded, conventional agriculture outdid the expectations of even its most optimistic defenders. As a modernist cure-all,
algae was irrelevant. But as a natural foods accessory that blended ancient and modernistic elements, it suited another cornucopian vision—
the recombinant future.

THE LIMITS OF MODERNISM

The rise and fall of chlorella cuisine illustrate modernism's strengths and
weaknesses. On the positive side, modernism accommodated an almost
revolutionary zeal to do something really big about major food problems that seemed likely to increase exponentially as the population
boomed. Determined to start over by seeking fresh solutions, modernists
sometimes embraced changes that could potentially disrupt established
interests. Some were even willing to question home cooking, farming,
and the whole devotion to meat. Yet, as exemplified in International Style
architecture and abstract expressionist art, modernism could seem extreme, hubristic, and scary if taken straight—a fear reinforced by tech-

nological dystopians since the time of Mary Shelley. While many people were willing to jump ahead to a brighter tomorrow, they were not quite willing to reject the past. Clearly, a line was drawn somewhere between empowering convenience and enfeebling automation.

The limits of modernism were apparent even at the ultramodernistic 1939–40 New York World's Fair. Jochnowitz observes that the revolving "Live Dinner Party" at the America at Home pavilion offered visitors traditional commensality, etiquette, and formal dress alongside the liberationist ethos of convenience foods and kitchen gadgets. A *Business Week* recap in the article "What Shows Pulled at the Fair" found that the "human element" represented by a "pretty girl" was worth more than a robot. Likewise, was it the high-tech steel turntable or the cute, well-brushed cows that attracted crowds to Borden's Rotolactor? Understanding the public's resistance to modernism's impersonal abstractions, exhibitors promised more "showmanship," less "symbolism" for the 1940 season. The pedantic food exhibits sponsored by nutrition educators and agricultural researchers gave way to Coca-Cola's expanded "Garden of Refreshment." Noting the "refreshing" atmosphere of Coke's Edenic waterfall and "rustic" garden, the trade magazine *Food Industries* predicted that the company would likely "net" far more goodwill "than buildings full of focal exhibits whose value is in a symbolism beyond the grasp of all but an insignificant few." Clearly some businessmen were tiring of a technocratic arrogance that seemed to ignore common sense. And after the second season, *Food Industries* concluded that "the most popular success" of the entire fair was not GM's Futurama or Borden's Rotolactor but "the unpretentious Childs' frankfurter stands." That modernism could be too ascetic and elitist was also evident in the failure of "scientific eating" to capture much mass appeal. Yes, people would count calories and pop vitamins, but they resisted the totalizing mission creep of those who wanted to modernize *everything,* especially when such dietary reform reduced the fun of eating. Blasting the "brave new world of totalitarian technics," Lewis Mumford ridiculed promoters of algae who sought to reduce eating to its bare essentials and thus ignored food's role in enhancing conversation, pleasure, and the landscape.[90]

Along the same lines, Hine argues that most people wanted "enrichment," not simplification—Danish modern, not Bauhaus modern. Similarly, Brian Horrigan concludes that consumers welcomed the interior gadgetry displayed in numerous "home of tomorrow" exhibits but not the austere exteriors of Le Corbusier. "Americans did not want machines to live in," Horrigan notes, "they wanted machines to live with." There is, indeed, a long history of popular selectivity when it comes to modernism. Despite the "electrical millenarianism" of appliance manufacturers, David Nye suggests, it was lower prices, not streamlining, that sold refrigerators in the 1930s. Moreover, Nye observes, while utopians saw electrification as a way to consolidate, integrate, collectivize, and otherwise streamline society, Americans *used* electricity in regressive ways—to decentralize and privatize their lives. The same went for automobiles, which fostered neotraditional suburban ranch houses and antimodernist wilderness camping. While people valued Ford vehicles, they did not want Fordist lives. Farmers liked mass-produced tractors, but many still fought the corporate rationalization of agriculture.[91]

Such contradictions abounded even during the height of modernism— the 1950s. The same popular magazines that enthused about the latest chemical breakthroughs also ran articles pondering the dangers of pesticides, growth hormones, and animal antibiotics. One month after trumpeting the synthetic wonders predicted at the American Chemical Society's seventy-fifth anniversary convention (September 1951), *Science Digest* reprinted "Peril on Your Food Shelf," a sober warning by U.S. Representative James J. Delaney about thioura (a frozen food additive), silbestrol (a synthetic hormone used in chicken feed), agene (a bread softener), and chlordane and selenium (insecticides). Delaney also worried that DDT, which stored itself in body fat, might have long-term cumulative effects on the liver. Two months later, the Food Protection Committee of the National Research Council issued a statement denying that DDT, parathion, or any other insecticide in use posed a threat to human health. Voicing a familiar corollary, the *American Journal of Pharmacy* asserted that "the use of chemical aids in foods is no new phenomenon" and that "Grandma's pantry" was full of them. Still, the very appearance of such statements revealed lingering anxieties about modernization. These worries were reinforced by many other warnings issued over the next two decades—especially when the publicity led to bans on substances previously deemed harmless. When Rachel Carson made headlines in 1962 with *Silent Spring,* she was simply citing articles that had circulated in the 1950s. For example, in a 1956 article "Food and Cancer: The Suspicious Chemicals in Your Marketbasket," the *Saturday Review* reported that, after a five-day symposium in Rome in August of that year, "cancer specialists from all over the world" had voted unanimously "to recommend precautionary action" when it came to testing and regulating food additives, growth hormones, pesticides, and preservatives.[92]

The symposium attendees also expressed concerns about the safety of food irradiation. While some experts professed full confidence in nuclear-preserved foods, *Science Digest* did note lingering difficulties with the "scorched taste" resulting from irradiation. Or, as one researcher—the same scientist who walked around with a year-old hamburger in his pocket—told *The Wall Street Journal,* "sterilized meat smells like a dog when it comes in after a rain." Using somewhat unfortunate syntax, the *Journal* reassured its readers that "scientists are striving to lick this problem." The same challenges bedeviled engineers of frozen and microwavable meats. But the "taste problem" associated with modern technologies was more than an issue for the laboratory. Using it as an arguing point, Malthusians pointed out that in a less crowded world no one would have to put up with distasteful synthetic solutions.[93]

Ambivalence even tempered the modernist enthusiasm for automated appliances. Despite the apparent compulsion to devise a push button for everything, housewives resisted a totally automated future. Just as motorists rejected the push-button gearshift and steering because they liked to be more physically engaged in driving, cooks wanted to be involved in preparing meals. Interviewed for a *U.S. News and World Report* article (1957) on the "Revolution in the Kitchen," a General Electric executive doubted that cooks would be happy just pushing buttons to get their meals: "We have made some mistakes in the past as an industry"—including the "shortsighted" 1930s vogue for a "clinical, sterile, white" kitchen, which proved "a little deadly." "I think probably one of the worst ones we made was trying to visualize a so-called fully-automatic kitchen. . . . For if you ever get that, all the meals in Mrs. Smith's house and in Mrs. Jones's house and all the others would taste the same, and I don't think people want that. Also, cooking ought to be a creative thing." Similarly, cake-mix marketers discovered that cooks wanted *some* creative participation in baking cakes—hence what futurist Alvin Toffler called the "psychic cake mix," which required the addition of an egg as well as water.[94] Such recombinant examples became the staple of post-Fordist marketing texts, yet the forecasters still had trouble calculating exactly *how much* modernism customers wanted. The same GE executive who sagely questioned the fully automated kitchen also believed that, within ten to fifteen years, consumers would welcome a push-button plastic molding press that created a dish on demand and then ground it up when dirty—clearly a case of conflating and overextrapolating the dishwasher and the garbage disposal. Yes, people would happily push buttons to clean their plates and also to grind their garbage, but not with the same machine. And notwithstanding the popularity of plastic plates, they would still want *some* old-fashioned china.

Gauging the extent of the push-button future involved a degree of political and psychological foresight probably unattainable by mere mortals in the 1950s. For one thing, significant Cold War uncertainties clouded the horizon. In light of the famed "kitchen debate" in which Vice President Nixon, in an exchange with Soviet leader Nikita Khruschev, cited American washing machines as evidence of U.S. superiority, editorial writers wondered whether a push-button society would be too soft, too passive. And then there was the anxiety that an inadvertent press of a button could trigger World War III—the theme of numerous apocalyptic novels and movies. "Just pushing the button brings with it the implication of power, but also lack of control," Hine writes. "Housewives said they wanted to be able at least to point their appliances toward the task, and there was a general worry about the amount of faith the country was placing in push-button warfare." Scientists and politicians did try to steady the public's nuclear jitters. One nutritionist even argued that the increasing fat in the meat-based American diet offered good protection against radiation damage, while starving Eastern Europeans and vegetarian Asians were deemed more vulnerable. "A svelte figure in the atomic age is out," *Science News Letter* quipped. On the same page, a scientist at Argonne National Laboratories foresaw a pill that would offer mass protection against atomic bomb radiation. Still, there was no avoiding the fact that no one could "be sure" about the finger on the button, even if it was, as the ad slogan went, Westinghouse.[95]

Issues of faith and control underlay much of the popular ambivalence about modernism. If, as the slogan at the 1933 Chicago fair proclaimed, "Science Finds—Industry Applies—Man Conforms," there is not a lot that Man can do except sit back and try to enjoy the ride. The belief that modernization is both unstoppable and indifferent to individual desires probably explains the persistent popular belief in the inevitability of the meal-in-a-pill, that scary New Nutrition extrapolation. While most people vow and hope that *they* will never rely on pills for food, they presume future generations will conform to whatever "science finds"—pills, algae, or other dystopian horrors proposed by the "brave new world of totalitarian technics."[96]

While this attitude suggests a rather dreary popular perception of the gap between the lab and real life, it also offers some hope, because that same gap offers space for resistance to the high-tech wonders being concocted in the lab. People may feel that the lab will ultimately win out, but they won't let it happen on *their* watch. On their watch they adopt the parts of modernism that best suit their needs and fantasies while rejecting those that seem too alien or repressive. This is no small thing. Indeed, the struggle over the latest cornucopian technology—genetic engineering—is likewise a battle over how to categorize this new set of tools. Will advocates of bioengineering repeat the mistakes of the proponents of chlorella cuisine or the mythical meal pill by urging us to accept an ultramodernist break with the past, or will they attempt to soften the strangeness by putting it in the somewhat more ambiguous frame of a recombinant future?

EIGHT

THE RECOMBINANT FUTURE

As reductio ad absurdum expressions of modernism, both algae and the meal pill broke too sharply with traditional food practices and values. Foods of the recombinant future are by comparison less threatening because they blend the radicalness of the modern with the familiarity of the classic. Recombination reflects the fact that people will accept only a certain amount of newness; they don't want to entirely sacrifice their traditions. With their arrogant, take-it-or-leave-it homogeneity, both the classical and the modernist futures are served table d'hôte; reflecting uncertainty and ambivalence, recombinant futures come à la carte in the choice-maximizing menu of late consumer capitalism.

While the term "recombinant" derives from a basic process of genetic engineering by which DNA is mixed and matched, my use of it here borrows from sociologist Todd Gitlin's pioneering book on the late-twentieth-century television industry, *Inside Prime Time* (1983). Gitlin examines how television programmers seek to satisfy viewer demand for entertainment that is both new *and* nostalgic:

> The genius of consumer society is its ability to convert the desire for change into a change for novel goods. Circulation and employment depend on it. Popular culture above all is transitory. . . . But curiously, the inseparable economic and cultural pressures for novelty must coexist with a pressure toward constancy. Nostalgia for "classics'"—old movies, "oldie" songs, antiques—is consumer society's tribute to our hunger for a stable world. Consumers want novelty but take only so many chances; manufacturers,

especially oligopolists, want to deploy their repertory of the tried-and-true in such a way as to generate novelty without risk. The fusion of these pressures is what produces the recombinant style, which collects the old in new packages and hopes for a magical synthesis.[1]

In television, the recombinant style produced shows like *Hill Street Blues,* which spliced together elements of past hits with more avant-garde techniques of editing and sound to produce a hit show that seemed both revolutionary and comfortably familiar. In food futurism, the recombinant style is best exemplified in Walt Disney's EPCOT, the post-Apollo space program, "smart" farms and kitchens, and "functional" foods.

Predicting an elusive future that incorporates novelty without risk requires more self-conscious cultural processing than do either of the other two cornucopian futures. In the classical version of what is to come, the future evolves smoothly and inevitably—risk-free—out of the past. In pure modernism, the novelty is jarringly disruptive. In recombination, however, references to the past and the future are more scattered, selective, sometimes ironic, and never quite serious. Classical futurists are sober missionaries of empire, and modernists are earnest visionaries, even revolutionaries, but recombinant futurists are more mercenary and improvisational—willing to tap whatever images will benefit the immediate bottom line. At times, recombination substitutes murky bet-hedging for genuine vision, and the hubbub of upscale marketing may obscure more substantial global issues.

Recombinant culture also has a briefer shelf life. In search of precedent and perspective, classicism has millennia to draw upon; hence it draws on the seemingly eternal appeal of Mediterranean imperial archetypes. The verities of modernism—efficiency, consolidation, reduction, streamlining—are also relatively long-lasting; radical new ideas like artificial photosynthesis, meal pills, push-buttons, and synthetics persist along with the chemical paradigms that make them possible. But recombinant culture, with its greater sensitivity to contradictory needs, whimsies, and styles, is transient and volatile—perhaps more suited to the fluff of television (as Gitlin shows) than to the more weighty issues of global carrying capacity.

ANTICIPATIONS

Despite its trendiness, recombination as an approach to the future is almost as old as professional futurism. Arguing that the future and the past interact in unpredictable ways, novelist J. B. Priestly cautioned in 1927 against the linear assumptions of most projections: "Nearly everyone who writes about the future assumes that the most marked tendencies of our time will go on asserting themselves without ever being checked by any opposing tendencies." According to this reasoning, "if our food today is largely artificial, our food tomorrow will be completely so, probably consisting of a few chemical tabloids." Yet though he professed to have "not the slightest idea what the future will bring," Priestly did an excellent job of anticipating the late 1960s, especially when he warned that the "swing of the pendulum" could very well bring about a complete contradiction of the modernism of the 1920s. "It would not surprise me if our great-granddaughters are wearing vast voluminous skirts and hair as long as they can possibly grow it. . . . Possibly they may even live entirely on fruit and nuts and know nothing whatever about those chemical foods that we are always promising them." But more likely than a complete reversal or extension of present trends, Priestly reasoned, was a complex combination of two or three leading ideas to produce "the most curious offspring." Since such combinations are more varied and thus harder to pinpoint than straight-line extrapolations, Priestly hoped that futurists "will remember that history will go on twisting and turning and that there is a variety without end in the experiments and adventures that we call this life of ours."[2]

For an example of simplistic modernism Priestly pointed to H. G. Wells's fascination with "convenient little mechanical devices." Yet Priestly was unfair to Wells, whose turn-of-the-century sketches were quite sophisticated. In *Anticipations* (1902), Wells left ample allowance for residual nostalgia amid his resolutely modernistic predictions. For example, he speculated that the electrically heated home of 2000 A.D. might be "tinted, . . . even be saturated, with the second-hand archaic," such as sham chimneys with artificial smoke, and its automatic window-cleaning mechanisms would still be hidden by old-fashioned mullions. Women of the "leisure class" will "ransack the ages for becoming and alluring anachronisms, the men will appear in the elaborate uniforms of 'games,' in modifications of 'court' dress, in picturesque revivals of national costumes." Cooking would be shifted for the most part to scientific central kitchens serving working men and women living in kitchenless apartments, "but with a neat little range, with absolutely controllable temperatures and proper heat screens, cooking might very easily be made a pleasant amusement for intelligent invalid ladies." Unlike Aldous Huxley and George Orwell, whose modernist dystopias firmly prohibited all references to history, Wells shrewdly anticipated that modern rational-ization might require some "old-fashioned corners" for relief. While the growth of great urban centers would entail the organization of agri-culture "upon the ampler and more economical lines mechanism per-mits," there would still be touristic districts where "a handful of opu-lent shareholders will be pleasantly preserving the old traditions of a landed aristocracy." Wells's English countryside of 2000 would accom-modate both "big laboratories" with "men and women reasoning and studying" and picturesque, windmill-powered model cottages housing "home industries . . . in a quite old English and exemplary manner," sur-rounded by "ripe gardens" and laughing children "going to and fro midst the trees and flowers." Disciples of William Morris and Henry David Thoreau would live on as "ramshackle Bohemians" providing meaning, diversity, and perhaps even legitimacy for a modern urban-industrial civilization. (Just a few years later, some would in fact be fulfilling ex-actly this role as proprietors of cozy tea rooms and nostalgic inns serv-ing motorists.)[3]

Similarly, looking one hundred years ahead from 1930, Lord Birken-head envisioned both industrialized photosynthesis and the persistence of old-fashioned farming as "a rich man's hobby" for those wanting to grow their own wheat. "Ploughing may even become a fashionable ac-complishment, and pig-keeping a charming old-world fancy." On the whole, however, Birkenhead predicted that the people of 2030 would so prefer tastier, more digestible synthetic foods "that agriculture will sur-vive only in historical romances." Wells was more prescient in allowing room for an array of anachronistic subcultures. What Wells called "seg-regations" (voluntary groupings according to particular "moral ideas and pursuits and ideals") postmodern sociologists and marketers a century later would call "taste cultures," "segments," and "niches"—the social building blocks of a dispersed, discordant, pluralistic future character-ized by Wells as "a great drifting and unrest of people, a shifting and re-grouping and breaking up again of groups, great multitudes seeking to find themselves."[4]

For his predictions Wells drew on a recombinant tendency already visible in Victorian culture, which was less confident about the future than either the official classicism or the emerging modernism suggested. Did the great Corinthian-columned hotels that Daniel Boorstin dubs "Palaces of the Public" reflect a brash American claim to empire, or did they serve as modernist depots for the latest improvements (e.g., electricity, eleva-tors, indoor plumbing)? Or did they reveal, in their garishness, a latent insecurity about the rootlessness of a "transient and upstart" society?[5] Perhaps all of these applied.

Keen analysts have detected a similar ambivalence in the great Victorian world's fairs, where pedantic futurism competed with "jumbled" entertainment. Although 1893's White City presented itself as the orderly culmination of classical civilization, many visitors seemed overwhelmed by the element of spectacle, the crowds, and the plethora of options. Henry Adams complained quite notoriously about the fair's "incoherence": "Since Noah's ark, no such Babel of loose and ill-joined, such vague and ill-defined and unrelated thoughts and half-thoughts and experimental outcries as the Exposition, had ever ruffled the surface of the lakes." Later historians agree that Chicago was a "great costume party," a "deliberately constructed chaos," a site of "confusion, competition, diversity, bewilderment, and cosmopolitanism"—in short, a preview of the recombinant stew to come. It is telling that like the Disney parks of the future, all of the exotic food concessions—including a Swedish Restaurant, Japanese Tea House, and a Polish Café—were operated by a single company.[6] Recombinant theme marketing would skillfully reconcile the contradictory pulls of consolidation and segmentation, as when fast-food pioneer Howard Johnson draped a neocolonial facade over his Fordist food service. This eclectic design strategy came into full bloom in the Vietnam War era, when hamburger drive-ins sported mansard roofs, but its parameters were already quite clear in the 1920s, when William Childs tired of the "sanitary" modernism of his chain of 101 coffee shops and adopted a more ornate Old World style.[7]

Kitschy delights also invaded the bastion of modernism, the 1939 New York World's Fair, with its Heineken's on the Zuider Zee, Casino of Nations, Cuban Village, Winter Wonderland, Midget Village, Merrie England, and Old Prague Restaurant. A fair seemingly dedicated to a streamlined World of Tomorrow certainly offered a plethora of tastes. The tensions between purist and hedonist themes surfaced in an overview of future food trends by the Waldorf-Astoria's legendary maître d'hôtel Oscar Tschirky, who soundly denounced "those who predict a fantastic diet of pills and compressed victuals" and instead pointed to the 1939 fair's "wonderful variety of national dishes." Yes, agricultural modernization would result in cheaper, more abundant food, but contrary to the dietary modernizers, he predicted, "it is going to be a good world for the epicure as well as for the man who is just plain hungry." As "epicure" still had unattractively elitist overtones dating from Tschirky's own classic banquets at Delmonico's and the Waldorf, Oscar's prediction smacked of wishful thinking. But the food exhibits at the even more recombinant New York World's Fair of 1964–65 seemed to confirm Oscar's forecast of a turn away from the modernist "eating to live."[8]

For historian Thomas Hine, the year 1964 signaled the end of the Populuxe era, as the future represented by the fair's Unisphere, General Electric, and General Motors pavilions—with their underwater cities, robotic farms, and jungle-clearing lasers—looked "a bit tired"; "by 1964 even monorails were starting to look old-hat." Neil Harris agrees that the "post-modernist" fairs of the 1960s and 1970s lacked "any totally confident vision of the future" and were, instead, "committed to the triumph of mass marketing, popular entertainment, and electronic gadgetry." Harris is correct that 1964 was less modernistic than 1939. But the fair certainly did present a "confident vision" of a more complex future. Opportunities for "international dining" abounded at a variety of price levels. Upscale national pavilions introduced Americans to paella, Belgian waffles, Swiss fondue, Mexican turkey mole, and Thai coconut chicken curry. A somewhat more affordable "round the world eating" experience was available at the 7-Up Pavilion's International Sandwich Garden, which served, buffet style, "the food specialties of 16 countries in elaborate sandwiches, plus [the cornucopian clincher] all the 7-Up the customer can drink."[9]

For the most ambitious preview of the recombinant future, gourmets especially liked "Festival '64, America's Restaurant," operated by Restaurant Associates, a savvy New York firm known for its repertoire of sumptuous theme restaurants, including the Four Seasons, the Forum of the Twelve Caesars (neo-imperialist), and Fonda del Sol (Spanish), with others soon to come, including Zum Zum (German beer garden), Charley O's (Irish pub), the Hawaiian Room, the Trattoria, and Paul Revere's Tavern and Chop House ("colonial American"). Restaurant Associates was guided by Joe Baum, who fondly merged modernist design with regional American fare. The Four Seasons, his 1959 creation, was America's most expensive restaurant and also one of its more "avant-garde" in the sense that it spanned several categories. Located in Mies van der Rohe's ultramodern Seagram Building—the consummate glass box—it served only the freshest, most seasonal foods (very unmodernist), inspired by both American regionalism (Amish ham steak, Vermont Cheddar cheese soup) and pan-ethnic improvisation (moussaka orientale). According to the 1964 fair guidebook, Baum's fair eatery paid "tribute to the native gourmet cooking of the United States with such dishes as St. Augustine Shrimp Ramekin, Plantation Wedding Cake, Shaker Herb

Soup, Green Corn Pie with Shrimp, West Coast Lime-Broiled Chicken, Crackling Bread and California Broiled Fig on Ham." All of this was served up in the American Gas Association's Festival of Gas pavilion, designed by streamliner extraordinaire Dorwin Teague, with hanging glass walls, molded swivel chairs, a "superbly-equipped gas kitchen," and gas air-conditioning "for all-weather comfort." The overall tone was quite relaxed, even light-hearted, befitting Baum's belief that upscale dining needed to become less "serious," more playful than the formal tone set by classical restauranteurs and Bauhaus architects; thus the serving staff introduced themselves by first name. That such diverse cookery would be sponsored by kitchen stove marketers revealed how far the "kitchen of tomorrow" had evolved from the antiseptic laboratory look of the 1930s.[10]

THE DISNEY VERSION

Especially visible at the 1964 fair was the influence of Walt Disney, who had animated many 1939 fair exhibits and was well-known for the 1955 debut of Disneyland, which heralded a new era of marketing "synergy"— the canny cross-promotion of film, television, toys, fashion, tourism, and food. Many scholars have analyzed the recombinant aspects of Disney's parks, where visitors traverse a variety of "zones" from "pretemporal" Adventureland through nostalgic Frontierland and Main Street to futuristic Tomorrowland.[11] Florida's Walt Disney World (1971) repeated this formula on a vaster scale. And in 1982, the Disney Company allocated more acres to one futuristic zone—the Experimental Prototype Community of Tomorrow—than to the entire Anaheim original. Kraft's The Land offered EPCOT's most comprehensive peek at a cornucopian agricultural future. Its gee-whiz tone closely matched recently inaugurated Ronald Reagan's repudiation of dystopian "malaise"—and it was certainly more upbeat than Ridley Scott's Dark Age masterpiece *Blade Runner*, which appeared the same year. According to a Kraft spokesman, The Land's examples of "intelligent and constructive agriculture" would "help to dispel current doomsday prophesies that the availability of food will be limited in future decades."[12]

The Land mostly followed the familiar modernist script, albeit with a bow to environmentalist critiques of "areas almost destroyed" by "poor farming techniques." The need for a scientific approach to feeding a growing population was emphasized in the "Listen to the Land" boat ride, which carried visitors smoothly through the human evolution "from hunter to farmer," then lingered briefly at a "picturesque" family farm. Faintly scented with real hay and sanitized manure, "the old red barn" on the farm evoked considerable nostalgia. But the ride went on to visit scenes of "large-scale agriculture," which offered "better machines, better seed, better fertilizer, and better pest management." And then the recorded guide asked, "What about tomorrow?" Emerging from a darkened tunnel, the boat entered the future of "controlled environment agriculture" (CEA), whose "experimental growing systems" recycled earlier hydroponic and greenhouse schemes—with the same dubious relevance to real land, farms, and markets. Like the system exhibited by Heinz at the 1939 fair, CEA was extremely capital intensive—think of the power needed to run all the conveyors and pumps. Despite the disclaimer that "we don't think CEA will ever replace traditional agriculture," the exhibit's enthusiastic tone could certainly lead tourists to think otherwise. Similarly, visitors to the Tropic Farm could marvel at the "miracle plants" that held "significant potential for feeding much of the world population"—amaranth, winged beans, peach palms, triticale—but they were never shown how the tropical poor would be able to afford the "advanced" techniques needed to grow these crops. Even the demonstration plot of intercropping—inspired by the intense, diversified practices of traditional small farmers—was grounded not in home compost or real soil but in sterile white sand fertilized by chemicals from drip tubing. In fact, as Joan Dye Gussow noted, the disconnect between The Land and real dirt farming reflected the real distance between consumers and producers: "The epitome of Disney World is sitting and being conveyed through a world in which you have no involvement, you don't touch anything, you don't feel anything, you don't handle anything, and you don't have to work. And that's the future . . . the whole message is concentrated power, concentrated control"[13]—in other words, the future as envisioned by Wheeler McMillen over fifty years earlier.

But EPCOT was offering another future as well. Despite The Land's irrelevance to the real needs of hungry people, its ultraintensive indoor systems *did* preview how, in a few more years, some savvy "boutique" farmers would grow high-quality vegetables (and marijuana) for urbane "niche" markets. Similarly, its Aquacell heralded the capital-intensive farming of premium seafood—trout, oysters, shrimp, tilapia—again for affluent consumers. In *Mickey Mouse History*, Mike Wallace observes that EPCOT addressed not the mass audience of the earlier world's fairs or even of the original Disneyland, but a "dramatically narrow" demographic of upscale professionals and managers. In offering CEA as an alternative to the soil-destroying, highly polluting effects of conventional agribusiness, Kraft was acknowledging the environmental concerns of this "green" segment of the food market. And to enhance the suggestion of sustainability, crops and fish harvested from The Land were used in such EPCOT eateries as the Garden Grill, a revolving restaurant hosted by "Farmer Mickey."[14]

While the scientific and economic assumptions of The Land were not new, Disney World's recombinant smorgasbord of tastes, images, and price ranges signaled a more heterogeneous approach to marketing. Over 150 restaurants served up dining options ranging from the $20 entrees at Levy's Italian Portobello to burgers and meat loaf at the "1950s-style" Sci-Fi Dine-in Theater, the most popular restaurant at the Disney-MGM theme park that opened next door in 1989. At the Sci-Fi, Populuxe boomerangs, pastels, and parabolas spoofed the wide-eyed exuberance of postwar modernism, and customers dined in booths resembling "vintage" tail-finned cars. In typical recombinant fashion, "authentic carhop service" was offered by a three-person wait "team"—who relayed orders on a handheld computer to a kitchen printer. The menu featured "1950s-style food with a 1990s twist"—the beef patties were lean, the frying done in canola oil. Another "1950s" concept, the Prime Time Café, featured formica-topped kitchenette tables, curvilinear Philco television sets, and—in a bow to those days when synthetic was better—plastic bowls of waxed fruit. Unlike the 1950s, however, Prime Time's meat loaf was topped with shiitake mushrooms, and meats were "roasted on screens to keep the fat off."[15]

Real modernism now seemed too innocent—or too toxic—to be taken straight; rather, it had transmuted into a '50s nostalgia theme. Wallace notes that Disney World favored ironic, self-referential "time travels" showing progress in a light-hearted, nonserious way—very different from the in-your-face brashness of pure modernism. Thus EPCOT's General Motors exhibit treated history as half-vaudeville, half-sitcom, a mother lode of "wacky" and "zany" bits to be mined for laughs. When "GM's robot Leonardo turns from culture to engineering," Wallace writes, "he is shown tinkering with a flying machine while a scowling robot Mona Lisa model taps her feet." While The Land's ride through history was more serious—especially its fleeting acknowledgment of industrial agriculture's environmental impact—much of that tone was undercut by the Kitchen Kabaret exhibit awaiting visitors once they left their boats. In a twelve-minute "nutrition show," animatronic Kraft products portrayed familiar show-business types spelling out key "lessons" of scientific eating and home economics. After a Dixieland number blasted by the Kitchen Krackpots (Salsa Jar, Mustard Squeeze Bottle, Parmesan Cheese Can, and Bar-B-Que Sauce Bottle), the 1950s-housewife host, Bonnie Appetit, led "the Stars of the Milky Way"—Miss Cheese (Mae West), Miss Yogurt (French accent because she was so "cultured"), and Miss Ice Cream—in a cabaret act about the Basic Fours/Three Squares. Timeworn sight gags were performed by the wise-cracking Hamm 'N' Eggz and the singing Cereal Sisters (Maizy Oats, Rennie Rice, and Connie Corn), who were accompanied by a loaf of bread, Boogie Woogie Bak'ry Boy. Since many of these swing-era references may have escaped those under the age of sixty, a later "Food Rocks" update featured Fud Wrapper, the Peach Boys, Pita Gabriel, Chubby Cheddar, Neil Moussaka, and the Get the Point Sisters. Kraft's promotional literature did intone the sober "educational" goal of "helping these young people achieve good nutrition and balanced meals along with the proper shopping skills now and for the future." But those taking this mission seriously could come away disappointed—as did one early Memphis visitor who demanded and received a refund: "EPCOT was misrepresented in that it was just a glorified shopping center. . . . From all that I had read and all that I had heard about it, I thought I was going to go and see a city of tomorrow, and there's no such thing." Had he still been alive, Walt Disney himself might have been equally disappointed, for he had hoped to establish a full-scale utopian community, "a living blueprint of the future, where people will live a life they can't find anywhere else in the world today."[16] But Disney's Bellamyite ambitions threatened to bankrupt his company, and after his death in 1966, the firm's "imagineers" pursued a somewhat less reverent approach to the future. Visitors to Orlando could rationalize their expensive stay by saying they had been educated about the future at EPCOT before having fun at the rest of the park. Like a world's fair, Disney World juggled solemn education and carnivalesque amusement, only with a lot more Midway than White City.

The Disney Company abandoned straight modernism altogether in 1997 when it refashioned Tomorrowland into a retro-ironic send up of Jules Verne/Buck Rogers/1950s B-movie fantasies. Walt's favorite zone, the original Anaheim Tomorrowland had seriously promoted the corporate and bureaucratic futures envisioned by its industrial and government partners. Monsanto's Hall of Chemistry recruited acolytes to, as it were, the Order of the Chemist. Faithfully carrying the torch for Bauhaus architecture and synthetic utopianism, Monsanto's all-fiberglass House of the Future (1957) was well-equipped with self-dialing telephones and an "Atoms for Living Kitchen" that boasted an ultrasonic dishwasher and a "revolutionary microwave oven." At the General Electric Carousel of Progress exhibit, an animatronic mother and father testified to how electric appliances had vanquished household drudgery and dreamed of the day when televisions would have built-in tape recorders and downtown would be enclosed by a "climate-controlled" dome—powered, of course, by a GE nuclear plant. Supplemented by Disney's television documentaries featuring rocket engineer Wernher von Braun, Tomorrowland's Rocket to the Moon ride strongly supported the American space program.[17] As the century matured (or soured), however, such wonders seemed less wonderful.

These changes were quite obvious to Disney's most creative people. Quoted in 1997, head imagineer Bran Ferren contrasted the sensibilities of the 1950s and 1990s:

> Tomorrowland's ethic is synthetic is better than real, plastic is better than nonplastic, press a button and your food is delivered by robots. In the last decade, that has been replaced by the middle-class-American sensibility— the house with a lawn, real plants, a white picket fence, a recycling plant down the road, a house with cool moldings. Events like the explosion at Chernobyl and Three Mile Island diffused the sense of an ideal vision of the future as clockwork. We used to think that Tang was wonderful, but then there came the sense that Tang was all we got out of a multitrillion-dollar space program.

The retooled Tomorrowland of the late 1990s blended warm nostalgia for a time when the modernist future could be taken seriously with cool disbelief that anyone could ever have believed such promises. At Redd Rocket's Pizza Port, "a way station for hungry space explorers," one could find salads made to order served in the same retro mood as Florida's Sci-Fi Dine-In Theater. Mixed in with the Buck Rogers kitsch were many markers of America's "browning"—paving stones, planters of edible organic fruits, more Garden of Eden than Mission to Mars. "The future is Pottery Barn," quipped the *Washington Post*. Disney imagineer Ted Baxter observed, "We could all be dressing in silver lame jumpsuits and riding monorails, but the thing is we don't want to. What we want is a comfortable pair of Levis." Or as the *Post* reporter added: "The future is a relaxed fit." And essential to the "relaxed fit" was the ability to recombine your fantasies.[18]

While the rebuilt Tomorrowland was really just a spoof—a five-year holding action—it was not quite true that Disney lacked a serious futurist vision. According to the same *Washington Post* article, Disney

chairman Michael Eisner's "Montana Future" envisioned "a Ralph Lau-
renized mega-cabin in the Bitterroot Mountains, wired with fiber op-
tics and a fast modem. We want to go back to the land, as long as the
land is devoid of the kind of hardscrabble mongrels who used to live
in the West. We want to be cable-ready. We want good takeout. We want
aromatherapeutic herb gardens and a nearby trout stream where nothing ever dies." And like Walt himself, Eisner wanted to see his utopian
visions put into practice in Florida, which rivaled California as the
American Dream's last chance. Hence the Disney corporation's development of Celebration, Florida, an upper-upscale synthesis of neo-
Victorian landscape with interesting food and "the technology of the
new millennium"—an almost too-perfect fulfillment of H. G. Wells's
"second-hand archaic."[19]

Interestingly, observations concerning the decline of modernism have
often used food as the touchstone, especially the food most often (and
wrongly) associated with the space program, Tang. "In the future," the
Washington Post observed, ". . . we don't want to wear polyester, vaca-
tion on the moon and drink Tang, the drink of astronauts. Instead we
want copper pots and fresh pastas with virgin olive oil and really good
reproduction Shaker furniture."[20] With Disney's original Tomorrowland
so closely harnessed to the heady days of the space program, it was inevitable that the two futuristic sites—Disney and NASA—would evolve
in tandem. And by the 1990s it was clear that astronauts did not want
Tang either.

SPACE FOOD

While the rest of the country went "brown" in the 1970s, NASA did
linger for a while as an outpost of culinary modernism—the last best hope
for tubes, algae, wood pulp, yeast, synthetics, irradiation, and meal pills.
But even NASA could not hold out indefinitely, for as Howard McCurdy
has shown in depth, the space program has always followed American
cultural trends.

Space has longed loomed as an emblem of the future. Indeed, because
space is *the* future for so many people, popular futurism almost invariably invokes Buck Rogers, the Jetsons, flying saucers, *Star Wars,* Stanley
Kubrick's *2001,* and other pulp fiction icons. To some extent, serious futurism has always had to fight these frames, for such discourse tends to
be seen as "light," indeed "spacey." Given their escapist function, very
few space stories addressed mundane details such as how people might

actually eat once they left the earth. Or if science-fiction space travelers did cook, they did so much as affluent suburbanites of the late twentieth and early twenty-first centuries might—pop a frozen meal in the magnetron (microwave). Such vagueness about domestic matters enhanced space exploration's larger-than-life aura. As McCurdy suggests, the fewer the mundane details—especially those related to private bodily functions—the greater the opportunity to project extravagant expectations.[21]

While romantic daydreaming was a necessary prerequisite to actually venturing into space, leveraging taxpayer support for a multibillion dollar space program in the 1950s took concerted lobbying by committed space evangelists like Walt Disney and Wernher von Braun, whose relatively realistic space documentaries and exhibits made space travel seem almost viable. The Soviet Union's early success with satellites and manned flight was the "precipitating event" that crystallized the U.S. political commitment to a lavish Space Race. Although von Braun and Disney's description of rocket specifications was quite detailed, their discussion of how and what people would eat in space was remarkably imprecise—in part because no one really knew how to feed them. Until John Glenn sucked some applesauce from an aluminum toothpaste-type tube as he circled the globe in 1962, scientists were not even sure if humans could swallow food under weightless conditions.[22] So even as humanity was reaching toward the heavens, it had to start from scratch when it came to meeting basic metabolic needs. How fitting, therefore, that much of the fare for the early space program resembled baby food. In line with the modernist credo to "make it new," space scientists had to reinvent the spoon, along with the knife, fork, and bowl.

At first the space program adhered to modernist principles of sanitation, reduction, extreme calculation, and efficiency that would have made Ellen Richards or Marcelin Berthelot proud. Racing to reach the moon by the end of the 1960s, NASA attempted to project what McCurdy calls an "aura of competence"—a can-do, no-nonsense dedication to getting the job done. In line with this Progressive ethos, NASA's exemplary "scientific eaters" would maximize their intake of required nutrients using the most advanced processing technologies—especially dehydration, compression, and irradiation. For these "single combat warriors," taste and pleasure were irrelevant, even feminine, considerations. (Tom Wolfe hardly mentions their food in his otherwise detailed chronicle *The Right Stuff*.) As the space agency's own food history puts it, "The food that NASA's early astronauts had to eat in space is a testament to their fortitude." If NASA could have found a meal pill large enough to get the job done, they might have used it, for a food pellet represented the ultimate in portability and stability. Seeking to minimize weight and maximize sanitation, they did compact meals into freeze-dried chunks coated with edible gelatin to keep crumbs from floating around the cabin and ruining delicate equipment. A spaceship's "kitchen of tomorrow" *was* truly a laboratory. The early Mercury astronauts hydrated these food chunks with their own saliva. Later, "rehydratables" were injected with sterile water and then kneaded into a puree which was squeezed through a tube into the astronaut's mouth.[23]

None of these features—the tubes, the distillation of food into essences, and so on—would have surprised the technological utopians and radical dietary reformers of the late nineteenth century, and millions of moviegoers had their first full view of such cuisine when Stanley Kubrick's *2001* opened in 1968. But whereas Kubrick's crew contentedly sucked their strained peas through straws, real astronauts were considerably less sanguine. Given the dismal track record of scientific eating, NASA's dieticians should not have been surprised that most astronauts preferred to starve than ingest their "edible biomass." By the Gemini missions (1965–66), menus were somewhat more varied (including shrimp cocktail, chicken and vegetables, cinnamon toasted bread cubes, and butterscotch pudding). The Apollo missions added *warm* water for rehydration, and a few foods that could be eaten with a spoon first made it into space in 1968. Further recapitulating the evolution of human dining, Skylab (1973–74) added forks and knives and refrigeration and even provided a dining table to which weightless astronauts could moor themselves and thus "sit down" to a common meal. Still, eating in space remained a strictly functional, backpacking-type experience through the 1980s. While NASA's daily food ration of precisely 0.58 kilograms a day provided 2,800 calories, most astronauts consumed less than 1,000 calories, and they often came home famished, underweight, and dehydrated.[24]

Fortunately, astronauts were not subjected to the microbial foods being developed for NASA's proposed long-distance flights, which would require that almost all food, water, and oxygen be manufactured through "bio-regenerative" systems. Thus did chlorella research—once proposed as the final solution to earthly overpopulation—find a niche in spaceships, where Malthusian conditions would indeed apply. Also rejuvenated was Berthelot's idea of synthesizing food from coal. "If we can make the material for our shorts," one NASA contractor reasoned in 1984, "we should be able to make the stuff of our lunches." Sobered by the likely doubling of world population by 2015, this University of Maryland chemist stood true to his discipline by predicting: "Agriculture might be something of the past. Agriculture is a very energy-consuming, time-consuming—I hate to say it—wasteful process." Similarly, in his 1975 sketches of life in space titled "The High Frontier," Princeton physicist Gerard K. O'Neill looked to giant, wheel-shaped space colonies to house earth's surplus population. Reiterating the streamliners' contempt for earth-based agriculture, O'Neill suggested that space farming, with its longer days, controllable seasons, and freedom from pests, would be "efficient and predictable, free of the extremes of crop failures and the glut which the terrestrial environment forces on our farmers. Only 111 acres would be needed to feed all 10,000 residents."[25] In short, what scientific management had failed to achieve on earth—with its diverse ecosystems, complex traditions, and messy politics—seemed quite feasible in weightless, sanitized outer space.

Such unadulterated modernism suited the early years of the space program. As long as NASA framed space travel as something truly special and extraordinary, it did not really matter if astronauts ate really weird synthetic foods. But as political support for the program waned—with critics citing synthetic icons such as Tang and Teflon as questionable legacies of a very expensive program—NASA sought to reposition space travel as something more ordinary, even normal. In keeping with this domestication, NASA acknowledged that humans derived significant "psychological rewards" from eating good food. "We are looking to deliver to astronauts not just nutrition, but eating pleasure," NASA contractor Jean Hunter declared in 1998. Even more so, NASA recognized that eating together enhanced camaraderie and morale, especially on long journeys in isolated, total environments. "When people are living in a closed system for a long time," Hunter noted, "food becomes larger than life"—a fact well known to submariners, who have long enjoyed relatively good food.[26]

NASA's "astonishing array" of new food choices now vaguely resembled the natural, ethnic, and regional cuisines consumed back on earth. Shuttle astronauts packed granola and nuts along with irradiated beef, thermostabilized chicken teriyaki, and rehydrated rice pilaf. International missions furthered culinary multiculturalism, as when a French astronaut brought foie gras and duck breast to share, and a Japanese crew member brought curry and rice. To accommodate an Israeli passenger on the shuttle, NASA contracted for nouvelle kosher meals, which, following the pan-ethnic trend found even among Orthodox Jews, included Florentine lasagna, chicken Mediterranean, and an Old World stew consisting of beef with brown rice, pinto beans, and assorted "flavors of the Middle East." Shelf-stabilized flour tortillas made crumb-free wrappers for chicken strips with salsa. "Looking both to the past and the future for food-processing approaches," researchers investigated the possible uses of tofu, tempeh, basil pesto, seitan, amazake, vegetable fajitas, pad Thai noodles, spring rolls, lentils, and sweet potatoes on multiyear flights to Mars that would be vegan by necessity. With Cornell University doing this research, some interplanetary menus seemed to be lifted from Ithaca's countercultural haven, Moosewood Restaurant. A skeptical *Washington Post* food reporter praised the "surprisingly good . . . quiche-like thing filled with spinach and tofu and onion and basil worthy of any highbrow vegetarian restaurant." Jane Brody was impressed by a cream of red pepper soup (creamed with soy milk) and the gluten-based fajitas topped with tofu sour cream and served on whole wheat tortillas. And one of the most popular recipes on the "hedonics" scale was a sandwich of oven-roasted vegetables with shiitake mushrooms and sprouts on whole-wheat bread. It is telling, however, that NASA's public relations campaign to normalize its space cuisine said little about the concurrent work on algae-based pasta or the "fish chunks" cultured from myoblasts. Perhaps the tissue engineers had not quite worked out the gag factor.[27]

Befitting the recombinant culture of the 1990s, irony prevailed in journalistic reports on space—a clear shift from earlier days when "space age" could be applied without embarrassment to toasters, pig farms, and station wagons. Take for example the spate of NASA-generated publicity about Cornell's vegan space-food research: "Moonstruck: Cosmic Cuisine," "Far-Out Dining," "The Restaurant at the Edge of the Universe," "'Houston, We Have a Recipe': What's Cooking in Outer Space," and "Recipes for Beyond a Small Planet." Such self-referential treatment humanized the program but also depicted "gastronauts" as spoiled yuppies (a frame also applied to military cuisine, which underwent a parallel evolution from modernist rations to multi-ethnic ready-to-eat meals). "It hasn't always been that way," Space.com quipped. "Along with the hazards of space travel, early astronauts proved their bravery again during meal times. Eating like the shuttle astronauts is as easy as going to the grocery store or neighborhood market." Deprecating tone aside, the market analogy was apt, for the research behind this culinary diversification linked major universities (Cornell, Purdue, Rutgers, Iowa State) with major economic interests (including Kraft, Pioneer Hi-Bred, and the National Food Processors Association). And much as marketers were finding ever more ingenious ways of crosspromoting their products in places once considered exempt from commercialism—museums, schools, parks, public restrooms—Pizza Hut hoped to "break the final frontier," as the headline put it, by blazoning its logo across a Russian rocket headed for the International Space Station. To emphasize this sardonic turn away from *Star Trek*'s more idealistic modernism, the press release began: "Advertising for a pizza company is to go where no fast food chain has gone before." Noting that the "next advertising frontier" might be to project an image on the moon, one advertising executive observed that "technologically the sky's the limit."[28] Well, not exactly, as the goal was to go *beyond* the sky, but the pun served its purpose anyway.

SMART MARKETING FOR THE MILLENNIUM

Puns, inside jokes, clichés, and cute alliterations were not confined to space news. In the decade leading up to the new millennium, wary reporters on the futurism beat expressed the same ambivalence that flavored Disney's nostalgic retooling of Tomorrowland. Just as recombinant television recycled fragments of earlier programming formulas, situations, and characters, recombinant futurism drew its analogies from familiar sitcoms, movies, and speculative fiction. Inevitably, classic dystopian stories about scientific hubris were used to frame critiques of genetic engineering, as in "Brave New Farm" and "Frankenfoods." But self-referential irony hedged even the more positive reports, as in "Fields of Genes," "Strange Fruit," "Friendly Farming: How Green Is My Acre," "Food Technology's Excellent Adventure," "Brave New Trends," and "What Are Jane and George (Jetson) Having for Dinner?" Much as end-of-the-century assessments of family decline treated *Father Knows Best, Leave It to Beaver,* and *Ozzie and Harriet* as touchstones of a lost Golden Age, so *The Jetsons, Star Trek,* and *Buck Rogers* represented a lost age of modernist innocence when people had seriously believed in Tang, meal pills, robotic butlers, and push-button everything. Noting that "it won't be hard to swallow" tomorrow's meals, one "look ahead" opened with the familiar icons: "Jane Jetson will not be setting the dinner table for the future. Vitamin pills, space sticks, and Tang will not dominate the menus of the new millennium." Sometimes these Golden Age reference points themselves were recombined, as in a 1990 forecast for the twenty-first century: "June and Ward Cleaver don't live here anymore, but neither do the Jetsons. All the Buck Rogers soothsayers who predicted we'd be popping pills instead of eating real food at the turn of the 21st Century can now start munching on their words."[29]

To report the predictions, projections, and speculations straight meant letting down your guard, but the unguarded, open-armed embrace of the future had begun to fade around the time of Walt Disney's death in 1966, and even the Disneyesque Ronald Reagan was unable to sustain a wide-eyed cornucopianism in the 1980s. In fact, stories about the future of food during the Reagan-Bush years were comparatively drab. Challenged by the backward-looking nutrition of the counterculture, the food industry spent most of that decade addressing the demand for natural, organic, quasi-ethnic, "lite" foods. With chemicals, processing, and machines falling into disfavor, it was hard to muster enthusiasm for new gadgets and synthetic foods. "What's Old Is New," *Washington Post* food critic Phyllis Richman reported after attending a 1989 convention of cooking professionals. "Everyone seemed to be catching up with the past." The most popular convention sessions were master classes on antique cooking, and a panel on the future predicted "nothing newer than white chocolate and flavored pastas." At the same meeting, professional futurist Martin Friedman—editor of *New Product News*—observed that people "don't want to go too far into unexplored territories." Friedman did detect a minor pan-ethnic trend—exemplified in Chinese egg rolls with pizza fillings and pizzas topped with Chinese vegetables—but these innocuous novelties were downright avant-garde compared to *Grocery Marketing*'s "Dawn of the Non-Traditionalists" (1989), which predicted (somewhat correctly) that the "'next wave' of movers and shakers" in the food industry would be lead by Sam Walton, founder of Wal-Mart. A more accurate title would have been "Yawn of the Traditionalists."[30]

Similarly unexciting was the USDA's prediction that "tomorrow's foods will consist largely of the same, basically wholesome foodstuffs we have today—but with a few modifications": no freeze-dried pastas or vacuum-packed hamburgers (those all-too-familiar space foods), but just sweeter grapefruit, golden potatoes, and high-fiber barley cereals. In the same conservative mood, the *New York Times* forecasted that most changes by the year 2000 would be "low profile" ways to reduce negatives (fat, calories, chemicals) without sacrificing taste. Even "the changes due to biotechnology will be invisible to the consumer," a food scientist predicted—a little behind-the-scenes tinkering to improve freshness, delay ripening, reduce processing. While some old-school food scientists still relished plans for soygurt, fish hot dogs, reconstituted beef, surimi, and high-fiber barley bars (the stuff of "scientific eating"), reporters often dismissed such fabrications as too "good for you"—a clear turnoff for those who held health and taste to be irreconcilable.[31]

Only the microwave seemed remotely revolutionary in the 1980s, and even that excitement settled down as it became clear that while this handy appliance could heat frozen foods, it was inferior to the conventional toaster oven when it came to baking, broiling, and browning. Generally disappointed with the "wizards of futurology," a 1989 *Newsweek* article ridiculed earlier predictions of flying cars, colonies on Mars, and voice-activated typewriters, and reserved its greatest enthusiasm for a far more prosaic "marvel of the future": a genetically engineered tomato that might actually taste good. Similarly, in "Future Schlock," a half-hearted 1990 review of modernist "food flops" such as soy analogs, algae burgers, and "test tube lamb chops," *In Health* reporter Edward Dolnick lamented, "What kind of a puny future is this? In a culture almost unable to resist the magical words 'new and improved,' the foods we eat seem hardly to be changing at all." True, there were a few "promising stars"—"active" packaging that emitted gases to prevent mold, corn on the cob that sweetened in the refrigerator, and low-cholesterol eggs—but unless such innovations were hidden in familiar forms, they met strong consumer resistance. "Modern food researchers may be the only scientists obliged to strive toward innovation in a field where 'old-fashioned' is a gush of high praise. Americans may cherish convenience (think of nondairy creamer and cheese spread), but they want their food to keep looking and tasting the way it always has." Even the Institute of Food Technologists—bastion of technological utopianism and the master navigator of "the wave of the future"—had downsized its expectations to "tailoring within tradition." "What a let down," Dolnick sighed. How would we ever progress this way? If the Wright Brothers had "tailored within tradition they'd have built the world's first pinstriped glider." It was tough being a reporter on such a stagnant beat, especially when, with the approach of that mystical year 2000, more exciting changes beckoned in *other* industries, on *other* beats—3-D televisions with holograms, automatically steering cars, credit-card-sized computers. "But at dinnertime, we'll all sit down to meals that could comfort Thomas Jefferson. It's a measly tomorrow, all right. Apple pie again?"[32]

That tomorrow's meals would be *exactly* like those of Thomas Jefferson was a gross oversimplification, however, for marketers knew that consumers also wanted convenience. True, they wanted their meals to take familiar forms, rather than the pills, pulps, sticks, and tubes of modernist fantasy, but they also wanted everything faster and easier. While families wanted to "nest" or "cocoon" in restored Victorian houses, they were not about to go back to Victorian social and labor relations (and even if they wanted to, few families could afford it). Rather, to support a middle-class lifestyle, both partners had to work outside the home, and the retreat homeward after work was more likely to lead to the couch than to the stove. Although the working poor were probably more stressed than the upscale professionals who could best afford time-saving goods and services, such class distinctions rarely worked their way into mass-mediated trend-spotting.[33] Rather, conventional wisdom held that *all* Americans were time-poor and, in effect, working class. The overused notion of the busy American turned "convenience"—once a perk of the leisured gentry—into a self-flattering token of superindustriousness.

The idea that consumers are too busy to cook dates back at least as far as the late Victorians, who bought the first generation of ready-made breads and canned soups. Selling convenience to an expanding urban market was the basis for almost every food marketing innovation that followed, from the lunch counters and processed cereals of the early twentieth century through the drive-ins and boxed pizza kits of the 1950s and on to the microwave popcorn and take-out "home meal replacements" of the 1990s. Equally constant throughout the century was consumer demand for foods that seemed safe and wholesome, authentic and natural. Hence the recurrence of health claims and historical allusions from companies like Quaker Oats, Kellogg, and Nabisco at the start of the century and down through its end. In other words, the demand for meals that were convenient, healthy, and "traditional" was nothing new.[34]

But "nothing new" was anathema to a consumer economy energized by obsolescence, and also to a media culture dependent on celebrating it. Even if continuity reigned (as in "tailoring within tradition" and "what's old is new"), growth required differentiation and freshness—whether in the proliferation of new products or in the proliferation of stories about new products. As the new millennium loomed, marketers and journalists alike rushed to develop stories about radical changes to come soon after 2000—the perennial target date of futurist fantasy. Whereas forecasts in the 1980s seemed preoccupied with "catching up with the past," those of the 1990s could not avoid looking ahead to the big party waiting at the end of the decade. And while the 1980s seemed starved for really new technologies, the trend watchers of the 1990s speculated wildly over the far-reaching applications of computers, cell phones, remote-sensing satellites, lasers, biotechnology, and nanotechology. To accentuate the impression of newness, much was made of the rising Generation X—the baby busters.[35] Unlike the World War II generation, who still had trouble programming their VCRs, and unlike the baby boomers, who were well beyond college when they shifted from manual typewriters to rudimentary word processors, the Gen Xers seemed, according to The Food Channel (a breezy trend site), "more comfortable with technology when it comes to shopping for food. Brought up in the age of scanners, few probably remember life without UPC symbols." Unlike the boomers "raised in the cozy kitchen of June Cleaver," these busters were said to be the latch-key children of dual-income families, well-versed in microwavable cuisine and other push-button wonders. "For most in Generation X, the word nuclear is associated with medicine, not bomb. They do not fear technology, they expect it to work for them. They will not be as suspicious of irradiated products, additives, hormones, antibiotics or other technologically enhanced foods as their parents." At the same time, they also seemed the most nostalgic for the idealized family dinners of the ersatz sitcom past—witness the frequent June Cleaver allusions, or this cutting sketch in *Newsday:* "Future generations, who as children were raised without set meal times with the family gathered around the table, may even try to create what they never had, spurred by watching reruns of 'Father Knows Best' and 'Leave It to Beaver.' These future folks may not cook all the food themselves. Maybe their microwaves, fridge and counters will do it for them. But they will serve it with a dose of nostalgia for the good old days they never experienced"[36]—shades again of H. G. Wells's "second-hand archaic."

The adjective often used to describe these new processes and products, as well as their youthful denizens, was "smart." Implying an extra sharpness—the word itself derives from a Middle English verb meaning to cause sharp, stinging pain—smartness suggests a pointed, piercing precision, an extraordinary "accuracy of definition," as *Webster's* puts it, that targets needs, desires, and trends more sensitively than ever before. Just as "smart bombs" supposedly hit targets without the high collateral damage wrought by "dumb" carpet bombs, smart technology would maximize efficiency without committing the totalitarian hubris feared by dystopian fiction. In a future of smart farms, stores, kitchens, and foods, consumers would experience the best time-saving features of modernism while retaining old-fashioned individuality, control, heritage, and diversity.

There was another term for this highly individualized, piecemeal approach to the future of food: "compartmentalization," a word particularly applicable when it came to understanding the global food chain. Maintaining a fragmented, compartmentalized perspective enabled savvy consumers to keep up on the latest restaurant dishes without having the slightest idea where their food came from. It also produced the remark-ably schizoid nature of futurism in the 1990s—rapturous stories about "smart" technologies sharing news space with the despair and outrage discussed in parts I and II of this book. While classical and modernist paradigms aspired toward a single, homogenized future (symbolized by the uniform dress, speech, and architecture in those scenarios), the re-combinant mind had little trouble envisioning a future where the North would enjoy unprecedented abundance and convenience while much of the South devolved into unprecedented poverty and despair.[37] While clas-sicism and modernism projected One World, an integrated empire of rea-son, the "smart" mind of the 1990s accommodated at least three or four worlds.

Of course, no one could be sure that all of the "smart" innovations would fulfill the hype. Just as the famous sitcom spy of the 1960s Maxwell Smart was actually a complete idiot whose gadgets never worked right, there was some reason to believe that the smart technologies of the im-pending millennium might make us much dumber, or that they might make corporations "smarter" than their customers. Such misgivings, along with an enduring reluctance to commit wholeheartedly to a tech-nological utopian future, further encouraged that dichotomous, sardonic tone that has characterized so much of the multifaceted, recombinant fu-ture.[38] Aldous Huxley's story about a *brave* new world that in fact catered to cowardice and insecurity had suggested a similar irony, and that Hux-leyan ambivalence sometimes flavored the news stories that recycled his title. As Huxley knew well, there was a clear difference between smart *things,* which commanded premium prices for the services they suppos-edly rendered, and smart *people,* who, according to Enlightenment hopes, would take charge of their own lives. It was not always easy to detect the dividing line between the truly smart and the "smart-ass" (or the Vic-torian "smart alec," defined by *Webster's Unabridged* as "a person who is offensively conceited and self-assertive, a cocky, bumptious person"). This uncertainty became even more disturbing after 2000, when "tech" stocks tanked, taking with them many smart operators on Wall Street and in the Silicon Valley. In its various meanings, "smart" ably encom-passed the recombinant future—moderately optimistic yet chastened, confused, and contradictory.

Such ambiguity may have become more obvious post-2000, when it was hard to muster *any* hope, however tempered. But in the 1990s, smart-ness did purport to benefit the whole food chain: from farm and store to kitchen and fork. For each stage, enthusiasts forecast a modernism tamed, restrained, and redirected to serve human needs, an automated yet responsive future.

For example, according to "O Brave New Farm" (1997)—one of *Newsweek*'s weekly "Millennium Notebook" previews—the smart "techno-farmer" of the future would live in a "Jetson-style techno-utopia . . . long on gadgets and short on hard work and skinned knuckles." But unlike the modernist farmer with his "laser-guided robots" growing "supersize crops," the "precision farmer" of the future would resemble a small-time organic grower paying close attention to biodiversity, variability, and micro-ecology. Much the way liberal culture encouraged people to acknowledge and even prize differences, "precision farming is based on the idea that no two clumps of dirt are alike." Employing Global Positioning Satellites (GPS), a "Star-Trek-like crop monitor that uses beams of light to get a reading of 'plant health,'" along with infrared sensors, computer mapping, and an affordable laptop, tomorrow's farmer would be much more "sensitive" to the varying topography, soil composition, and nutrient needs of his farm. ("Sensitive" was also the adjective applied to the new French agricultural robots that would soon be "lending a hand" in fields by "gently" transplanting seedlings and uprooting weeds.) Unlike the industrial farm of the twentieth century, which "has tended to treat whole tracts of land, from back porch to fence post, as great, homogeneous plots of potting soil," and which requires a heavy-handed "carpet-bombing" of agrichemicals on huge, monocultural fields, precision farming would entail micromanagement of small plots according to each one's unique characteristics. "Smart zappers" on his cybertractor would direct minute amounts of chemicals exactly where needed, thereby saving money, improving yields, and reducing environmental damage. Similarly, genetically engineered seeds would be designed to match plants to local soil and climatic conditions—such as salt-resistant tomato seedlings for oversalinized fields, frost-tolerant strawberry runners for northern areas, and ultrashort wheat for especially windy plains. In all, "prescription farming"—a USDA variant on the same idea—would further the utopian cause of low-input, sustainable agriculture. Or so its proponents hoped. Noting that few farmers were in fact investing in this "futuristic whimsy," *Newsweek* concluded that "the jury—prospective techno-farmers—is still out, but don't be surprised to see John Deere pocket protectors soon."[39]

Pocket protectors suggested geeky engineers glued to calculator and monitor. "Most farming today is indoor work," went one scenario for 2025. "The farmer can sit with a computer and view fields for moisture content, groundwater levels, key soil nutrients, plant health, growth progress, and in some cases, fruit ripeness. He or she can take action to fill a need or correct a problem without leaving the console." The idea that farmers would become button-pushing desk jockeys harkened back to the "electric farming" scenarios of the twentieth century in which rough hinterlands were transformed into genteel utopias managed by white-collared professionals. Even older were cornucopian claims that super-productive, smart farming would "keep food abundant" while furthering environmental conservation. Conversely, blaming food shortages, environmental degradation, and farm bankruptcies on ostensibly "dumb" farmers, rather than on global politics and market inequalities, was an enduring trope of the food security debate. But actual examples of cyberfarms were rare—belonging usually to the largest, most highly capitalized producers. Most farmers were slow to adopt such innovations, not because they were "dumb" but because, as one USDA researcher put it, "prescription-farming techniques require farmers to spend substantial extra time and effort to achieve results."[40] Since farming was already a 24–7 occupation, it was hard to find more time to invest.

Moreover, these technologies did little to address the present-day realities of global competition, overproduction, dropping prices, and mounting debts incurred from *previous* adoptions of components of the technological treadmill. Such problems rarely made their way into the feature pages. Recombinant culture, with its piecemeal, à la carte approach, reinforced and widened the distance between producers and consumers. Ideally, journalism should bridge this gap, but few mainstream reporters knew much about agriculture, which was not a highly prized news beat, and even the smart version of agriculture received little attention. The closer to the consumer, however, the more the coverage. Hence there were far more stories written about smart stores, kitchens, and foods.

While few consumers of the '90s had visited a farm recently, everyone went grocery shopping regularly, and according to market research, many of them hated the experience. "People think of shopping for groceries as slightly more pleasant than a root canal," *Progressive Grocer*'s editor in chief Ryan Matthews told *Wired,* the glossy chronicle of cyberhype, in 1997. To liberate consumers from the time-consuming inconvenience of acquiring time-saving convenience foods, smart stores would step up the use of scanners and universal product codes. One small development was the self-checkout lane that bypassed slothful human cashiers. Citing the success of ATMs, some hoped that the inefficient grocery checker might someday go the way of the supercilious bank clerk. The next step would be the *home* scanner—literally a wand—which would allow consumers to scan a near-empty package at home and then transmit that reorder via the Internet to a store, who would home deliver. Newspaper ads would also contain bar codes, further facilitating home scanning. Microchips in smart packages would indicate freshness and communicate with smart refrigerators and pantries, whose sensors would note which items were running low and then reorder automatically, paying the bill with smart cards embedded with credit, medical, and personal information. Some packaging might also be edible or recyclable, thereby reducing waste, while other varieties would automatically heat or chill their contents when you pulled a built-in cord (much the way athletic trainers can activate self-cooling ice packs on the field).[41]

In many projections into the future, smart kitchens were themselves integrated into a larger smart-house information system coordinating security, maintenance, energy use, the home office, Internet access, and entertainment. But mindful of the neotraditionalist consumer mood, visionaries emphasized that these technologies would not in any way resemble those obnoxiously autonomous cyborgs of modernist science fiction who intimidated the neighbors (Roll-O at the 1939 fair), expressed their own opinions (Robbie of *Forbidden Planet*), or disobeyed orders (HAL of *2001*). *Newsday*'s Kitchen of the Future forecast hoped that the smart refrigerator would not turn out to be a "sassy" gourmet snob criticizing one's wine choice or nagging you to finish up the leftover spaghetti forgotten at the back of the second shelf. According to the director of MIT's Laboratory for Computer Science—one of the more creative zones for smart technologies—fears of enslavement to an anthropomorphic monster or machine were outmoded. "If we think of a robot that looks like us and does what we do in the kitchen, we are thinking in the wrong direction." Instead of "those clunky metal contraptions with arms and legs, predicted earlier this century," we were more likely to get "a collection of dedicated and far simpler robots that are part of the microwave, stove, and sink and have bearings and levers that can manipulate foods, pans, and utensils." Similarly, the sensors required for the fully integrated smart house would be embedded (and thus hidden) in materials that still resembled wood and brick.[42]

Truly subservient (or "dedicated"), such unobtrusive technologies would finally free us from insubordinate servants, whether human or mechanical. People wanted help, but they also needed to feel in charge. Or, as one kitchen designer put it, they "want intelligent appliances that use technology which does not shout at you." And part of this recombinant version of "intelligence" was a sense of involvement. Reviving Alvin Toffler's "psychic cake mix" theory, Food Channel publisher Christopher Wolf extolled "speed scratch"—kits, bags, and boxes for stir-fries, fajitas, or soups in which cooks "are rediscovering their skillets in an attempt to create family meal without a lot of time or effort," in other words, without the inconvenience of *really* cooking from scratch.[43] Similarly, the fully computerized smart kitchen might have an oak-surfaced dinette for those Cleaveresque family meals and generous shelving (also oak) for the ethnic cookbooks, artisanal tools, and Old World wines, olive oils, and condiments essential for the fusion cuisine of the future.

While a few older futurists of the 1990s updated the modernist dream of fully automated ovens that assembled an entire meal at the push of a button (in the '90s version, the click of a mouse), more practical visionaries seemed content with the prospect of a toaster that actually turned itself off before burning the toast, or a microwave that could brown. Such chastened expectations also guided hopes that even if biotechnology didn't end hunger—the utopian dream—it might at least produce an edible tomato. While radical Victorians had hoped to remake the world, the smart futurist resembled those conservative Victorians who hoped to remake the home into a "haven in a heartless world." In "Oh, Give Me a Home Where the Monitors Roam," *Newsweek* suggested in 1997 that the "casual, fun house" of the future might not "look like the kind of place George Jetson would hang his space helmet." No "domes or pyramids." Instead, behind its neotraditionalist bricks and pediments, hidden sensors, monitors, interfaces, and smart materials would "allow us to personalize nearly every facet of our environments, and, as time goes on, do it in ever more personal ways." Here again, "smart" suggested individualization, involvement, and sensitivity. In the smart future, the autonomous consumer used the latest gadgets to made "personal" choices and "customize" an idiosyncratic menu of nostalgic values and tastes. Fulfilling H. G. Wells's astute anticipation of a lucrative market for "alluring anachronisms," perhaps the most successful '90s pioneer of this recombinant future was ultrasmart (and rich) Martha Stewart, who employed a full array of modern media—television, books, magazines, catalogs, internet, kiosks in K-Mart—to mass market what appeared to be Victorian skills and frills. As Amy Bentley observes, Stewart addressed a powerful longing for seemingly timeless crafts and courtly manners. The same values had blocked the kitchenless apartment and cooperative housekeeping of Progressive utopias; likewise, hardly any forecasts in the 1990s envisioned a future of socialized cooking and dining. Private kitchens and dining rooms would remain, even if, by most estimates, people would be too busy to use them except perhaps on weekends.[44] But forecasters seemed quite enthusiastic about another essential feature of the Bellamy/Gilman commissariat: home delivery, now enabled by fiberoptics cable rather than pneumatic tube.

With much of routine shopping transferred to dial-up delivery services, grocery stores of the future would evolve into "supermarkets selling solutions rather than ingredients," according to the director of Chicago's Smart Store 2000. "With the boring parts of grocery shopping taken care of almost automatically, consumers could then focus on the part of shopping that is fun," such as planning dinner parties. Instead of trying to assemble a full meal from ingredients found in aisles scattered throughout the store, shoppers might find prematched products in sections labeled "dinner," "kids' lunch," "tight budget," "bridge club," and "new and exciting." Glimpses of this vision were already available in supermarkets' themed kiosks selling a particular manufacturer's cluster of goods and accoutrements—a Campbell's Soup kiosk that included breads, crackers, and plastic spoons; a Starbuck's kiosk with a variety of coffees and pastries; a Borden's Italian Corner topping its ready-to-go Novita pastas with Classico Sauce and Borden's Parmesan. Encouraging impulse buying, kiosks seemed a promising venue for "home meal replacements"—chilled (but not frozen), premium-priced, ready-to-go meals. While these preassembled "turnkey" operations required little labor on the part of the retailer (who simply "turned the key" to set it going), they did vaguely recall the old pushcarts that had also inspired nostalgic, "marketplace" concepts such as Boston Market, Eatzi's, and Whole Foods Market. Similarly, the new home delivery services like Peapod and ShopLink reminded some of the days when most mom-and-pop stores delivered. Such memories made the thought of Internet shopping less threatening or far-fetched. "Online shopping is a cyber-twist on an old idea—home-delivered groceries," Newsday observed. "The first supermarkets didn't arrive until the 1930s; before that, and even afterward, vendors often came to city neighborhoods with pushcarts and many small merchants delivered." Such "back to the future" appeal was of course an essential aspect of the recombinant vision. What was the shopping mall but a suburban reworking of the mythical village commons?[45]

Coating all such forecasts was the rhetoric of consumer sovereignty: service, diversity, choice, and options. In tomorrow's made-to-order food market "the consumer will be more regal than ever," The Grocer enthused. Similarly, in scenarios for 2025 developed by the highly respected futurist consulting firm Coates and Jarrett, privileged World 1 (but not Worlds 2 or 3) enjoys "unprecedented choice." True, few people actually cook, as the "tunable microwave," "automated pantry," and "robot chef" do most kitchen drudgery, but menus vary enormously. "In the past five years [2020–25], we have seen the popularity of rainforest fruits, vegetable stews, Hausa shakes (milk and papaya or mango), and for the adventurous, spit-grilled iguana imported from Costa Rica and Mexico." Popular "walkaway foods" include tropical fruit sticks, hydroponic banana pears, and "Andean spiced dumplings." In a "typical food day" for a U.S. family in 2025, Mom, age thirty-seven, enjoys a "well-cooked and tasty" microwaved "California-style lunch" on her supersonic flight to London and that evening dines on a ploughman's platter from the pub down the street from her hotel. Dad, thirty-nine, a surgeon, grabs a multivitamin fruitshake from a machine for breakfast, lunches on a McDonald's chicken sandwich (from a full-automated Model H-13 unit), and dines with his children at a Taste of America theme restaurant, where his Polynesian-style meal consists of parrotfish (fed Milwaukee brewery wastes in underground tanks), roasted taro, and coconut milk. His son, eleven, has Fruit Rockets cereal and pizza sticks earlier in the day and at dinner opts for "rainforest food," including tapir cutlet with cassava. His daughter, eight, selects waffles with passion fruit syrup for breakfast and Austrian food for dinner. Grandma, age seventy, prepares a blueberry muffin in her Cuisintech for breakfast, lunches on angelfish over salad greens at the senior center, and chooses open-ocean tuna, Inuit-style, with tundra greens for dinner. The Taste of America unit uses "robotic assistance and frozen and vacuum-packaged prepared entrees" and just six employees to serve over 312 different entrees. But not all cooking is fully automated. Ashton, another typical American, is a certified gourmet cook who employs assorted smart technologies to prepare "a small Angolan feast" for his friends: using a kitchen video console he consults directly with a chef *in* Angola, then searches for exotic produce from local retailers catering to "consumer interest in hand-made, non-automated fancy cuisine." No Luddite, Ashton also "updates his standing order at Meijer's Megamarket" and then "orders breakfast from the robotic chef in the kitchen." His Angolan feast is a great hit with his friends, who "are used to either automated cooking, prepared foods ordered in, or relying on an electronic coach to talk them through preparing a dish." After dinner he piles the dishes into a machine "which washes, sorts, and stacks the dishes for easy unloading."[46]

Such scenarios suggested that the smartest aspect of the recombinant future was its ability to disengage seemingly eclectic products from fully modernized processes. The automobile industry had pioneered this strategy many years earlier, combining Fordist factory techniques behind the scenes with Sloanist segmentation in the showroom, and many major industries—including food—had followed. But perhaps the processes only *seemed* fully modernized. Just as the ostensibly streamlined automobile assembly line involved considerable old-fashioned sweat and danger, virtual shopping would still need entry-level staffers—most of them unskilled, poorly paid, and unprotected by unions—to pull goods off shelves in warehouses. And someone would still be needed to lug groceries from warehouse to doorstep.

The same inequities applied to culinary fusion—spit-grilled iguana from Costa Rica, "rainforest" fruits from tropical lands, "authentic" recipes from Africa. The imperialist food supply system of 2025 sounded much like that of 1925: "Commodity foods [for the 1.3 billion residents of affluent World 1] are often supplied by middle tier countries" of World 2, whose 5.1 billion people "are getting along," still cooking and dining along "largely traditional" lines with little convenience or variety. Such limits are modest, however, compared to the "hard line" of famine experienced by the 2 billion people of World 3, including Angola, which apparently has nothing edible left to export except video recipes. While smart technologies allow easy communications between Worlds 1 and 3, the underlying economics have become even more inequitable by 2025. True, Ashton's Angolan advisor might be tipped for his culinary contribution, but the larger situation remains decidedly Malthusian. And like Malthus himself, the authors of *2025* conclude that since "the world cannot feed everyone," famine and starvation should be allowed to work their course without any self-defeating aid programs "creating soup kitchens on the million-person scale."[47]

Moreover, the exotic trends in eating described in *2025* only appeared to be diverse, for in the 1990s they were actually beginning to coalesce into what Christopher Wolf called "universal forms," which he defined as "food carriers not necessarily limited to a specific ethnicity," such as burgers, chicken, noodles, wraps, sausages, and grains. Because these "carriers" could accommodate various flavorings and ingredients, they were ready-made for franchising and mass production. For example, a single global pasta kiosk or store might offer an array of stereotyped toppings—Santa Fe, Thai-style, and spicy Mexican. Wolf also predicted growth for "global hummous" and "global couscous"—as in Hormel's

Marrakesh Express couscous mixes, meant to be topped with one's choice of mango salsa, sesame ginger, Greek olive, or roasted garlic flavoring. A similar versatility attracted restaurant chains to the "Global Meal" trend—a world-spanning, easily convertible menu in an all-purpose crossroads atmosphere. At Chicago's Taza, a Saudi Arabian–based "fastcasual" chain, diners could find "fresh Amish chicken in a variety of guises," including Tuscan, Chinese, and Southwestern.[48] So 2025's seemingly multicultural menu of Angolan, Andean, Hausa, and Inuit cuisines suited both corporate modernism and classic colonialism, for while the ingredients, tastes, and decor might come from the exotic periphery, ownership and clientele were almost always metropolitan.

A similar separation between product and process applied to smart shopping, whose resemblance to the mom-and-pop grocery system was only superficial. While mom-and-pops had relied on intensely personal, neighborhood, and ethnic relationships to track local tastes, extend credit, and promote sales, smart stores fostered an unprecedented centralization of intelligence gathering. Such consolidation was often disguised in progressive rhetoric. After all, who could be against more precise "information"—the essence of enlightenment? Coates and his coauthors lauded the retail "information centers" of 2025 that would serve customers better with personalized news about "nutrition, recipes, new products, and preparation tips." Who could object to "a pharmacy console at which the shopper can . . . consult computers about foods available that meet the shopper's nutrition needs"?[49] Such consultations did suggest heightened "sensitivity," "dedication," and "responsiveness."

But one could reasonably wonder what information was being served to whom. Generally, only processed, branded items had universal product codes (unlike the bag-your-own commodities and produce of farmers' markets and co-ops.) Moreover, the scanner and the UPC collected and consolidated private data solely for corporate gain. The frequentshopper's card of the 1990s, with its built-in data-gathering and sales incentives, was only the start of a campaign to steer consumers more efficiently toward particular products. A Dutch semiconductor company was developing a "smart label" that would automatically read a passing shopper's smart card, which might contain not just a record of recent grocery purchases but also full credit, employment, and medical histories, and assorted security data. Should this shopper fit a desirable profile, a screen on his smart shopping cart might immediately alert him to a good deal on a particular product.[50] And by 2054, according to Steven Spielberg's 2002 film *Minority Report,* such information would be automatically scanned from the eyes, facilitating both security monitoring and "personalized" shopping promotions—when Jon Anderton (Tom Cruise) walks through a shopping mall, every signboard vocally reminds him of past purchases and alerts him to new products. Similarly, cross-promotional arrangements might guide smart fridges to reorder a corporate partner's juices, and smart microwaves might be keyed to cooking instructions embedded in particular brands of frozen dinners. The "turnkey" kiosk system also favored mutual back-scratching—a Campbell's soup cart could feature Nabisco crackers. And just as processed food manufacturers had long provided recipes to increase sales of their products, these kiosks offered much useful "information" about how to use their particular goods.

The "free" web pages of the Internet were already full of such inside deals. But a flaw in these services was that they still required some human intervention. Personal computers were complicated (and expensive) tools, requiring significant patience and tinkering. One early trial of Internet grocery shopping found that it took more time to scroll through all the options than to drive to the store and pick the items off the shelf manually. And this did not include the time lost waiting to dial up (and then redial if you were cut off)—an increasing problem with overburdened servers and phone lines. In the "intelligent" kitchen of the future, however, appliances might communicate with each other (and with stores) without any human involvement. Sun Microsystems' Jini technology promised "the Jetson-like fantasy of the self-operating kitchen or restaurant." The main advantage of Jini's "seamless and invisible" interface was that in bypassing the problematic PC, it also bypassed the problematic PC operator. The technology may have been smart, but the user was assumed to be incompetent. Observed one tech analyst for an investment house: "If it's remotely harder than programming a VCR, people won't [use it]." One detects some corporate self-interest in these presumptions of ignorance. Food marketers were no doubt thrilled by the prospect of microwaves that could automatically prepare and then reorder *their* particular products "without the need for human guesswork or error."[51] However, avoiding human guesswork or error may have had more to do with reducing consumer discretion than coping with consumer incompetence.

But would such complex tools actually work? And did consumers actually want them? Perhaps not, according to an Whirlpool executive who noted that people were saying, "That's just more to break down," "We don't need all those bells and whistles," and, dismissing a talking microwave, "My god, I have to listen to my kids all day and then I have to listen to this?" If survey research was to be believed, *Newsday* suggested, consumers were interested in more "practical gizmos," such as a place to store and organize "the lids for pots and refrigerator boxes, the ones that never match the pots or containers. Duh. Just ask any homeowner." Perhaps people were not quite so dumb after all. While it was certainly in marketers' interest to have sales-enhancing technologies that bypassed "human guesswork," were consumers *really* too dumb to order their own paper goods, organize their own dinner parties, pay their own bills, follow a recipe, boil their own pasta—or even push their own microwave buttons? And there was still the problem of "getting people to give up picking over oranges, which may be easier said than done."[52]

Still, the futurist news of the '90s conveyed a feeling of inevitability about the smart future, much as people still believed in a future of meal pills, even if they didn't like it for themselves. Fully 75 percent of respondents to a 1999 *Newsday* poll felt that by 2050 we will be doing most of our grocery shopping on computers, even though fewer than 1 percent actually did so in 1999. And according to some studies, some people did not find shopping so repugnant or inconvenient. For one thing, store shopping offered immediate gratification; it was a lot quicker to pick something up at the store than to wait for it to be delivered. And there was also the pleasure of the hunt. The same *Progressive Grocer* editor who likened shopping to having a root canal admitted that going to the market was still an intimate, "tribal" experience for those who preferred to select their groceries personally, just as most people did at least *some* cooking from scratch. Still, some experts insisted otherwise. While only 200,000 households bought food through the Internet in 1999, Andersen Consulting "expected" that number to "skyrocket" to 20 million— 15 percent of all households—by 2007. Such estimates merited skepticism, however. As was often the case with speculative hype, Andersen's research was financed by companies that may have had an interest in making that future happen. The more objective market research of the 1990s admitted that consumers were, in fact, schizophrenic, contradictory, and unpredictable, torn between the desire for convenience and the hunger for more traditional experiences, intrigued by the "seamless interface" of automated shopping but still not quite ready to give up squeezing the tomatoes. Indeed, the future was still up for grabs. Just as many prophecies attempt to be self-fulfilling, forecasts of smart stores and kitchens may have hoped to assure that outcome by *encouraging* consumer ineptitude. The more people relied on the convenience-based commissary system, the dumber they *would* become—at least when it came to finding and preparing food. In light of the increased "cooking illiteracy," market consultants envisioned growing demands for "idiot-proof food."[53]

FUNCTIONAL FOODS

Dependent on consumer ignorance and incompetence, processors simply adored functional foods—tomatoes with extra doses of cancer-fighting lycopene, lutein-enhanced eggs for stronger eyes, vitamin-enriched "brain snacks" for increased learning ability, echinacea-laced fruit drinks to fight colds, chicken soups with St. John's wort to combat depression, cholesterol-reducing margarines and noodles, and so on. *Ginkgo biloba* was the hottest smart food of the 1990s, perhaps because it supposedly increased alertness, the simulacrum of intelligence. Dubbed the "dietary supplement du jour" by Christopher Wolf, ginkgo found its way into raspberry lemonade, apple crepes, canned soups, breakfast cereals, puffed snacks, and frozen waffles. A close second in the recombinant sweepstakes was ginseng, whose "extra energy" appealed to those complaining of never having enough of that resource. Because the nutritional benefits of these smart foods were built right in—like those self-activating smart refrigerators and microwaves—they bypassed the human guesswork involved in trying to eat right. Termed "magic bullets" by enthusiasts (and human "kibble" by critics), functional foods aspired to integrate the ostensibly incompatible opposites: "tastes good" and "good for you." Addressing the common belief that eating your vegetables could not be fun, functional foods such as Broccoli Power Puffs (greenish low-fat snacks fortified with vegetable concentrates) did suggest a wondrous reconciliation of contradictions. Even more miraculous was the prospect that fast food might some day be good for you, too, as in: "It may not be too long before you stop at the fast-food restaurant for a healthful serving of french fries or fried chicken." Such prospects certainly merited the "gee whiz" reserved for boundary-crossing marvels.[54]

True, as nutritionists knew, many ordinary foods already spanned this gap, especially if they were fresh, well cooked, and eaten in moderation. Even fried chicken could be both tasty and healthful if prepared and consumed with care. And when it came to increasing alertness, few drinks could rival an old-fashioned cup of caffeinated coffee. But no one called coffee a functional food. What made *these* particular products seem so novel, indeed progressive in a high-tech sort of way, was that they would supersize nutrition by injecting *extra* healthy doses *more* efficiently in combinations that Mother Nature had never considered: bananas and potatoes with built-in vaccines, orange and prune juices with extra calcium, golden rice with added vitamin A, eggs with fish oil. Such supernutrification bore only a superficial resemblance to earlier cornucopian solutions to hunger. While biotech firms pitched genetically engineered edible vaccines and fortified rice as a charitable boon to the debt-ridden Third World, for the most part their functional food entrées were designed for the cash-paying First World—that same high-profit matrix of "delectable demographics" that, according to Wolf, motivated most smart marketing.[55]

Functional foods intrigued both marketers and technologists—an impressive conjunction of interests given the frequent squabbling between those two departments. While marketers almost always won those intracorporate feuds, one detects here a spot of revenge for the engineers, whose modernist dreams of totally synthetic foods had been undercut by appeasement of the back-to-nature countercuisine. The "natural" rollouts of the 1980s usually came at the instigation of sales departments and were often strongly protested by the engineers, who deplored such craven catering to popular superstitions. By the 1990s, the food industry's own research showed that most people strongly preferred to get their nutrients in their natural state—in, say, a carrot rather than a pill or an artificially fortified Twinkie.[56] But while food marketers generally accepted such beliefs, many food engineers still firmly retained the techno-cornucopian faith, dating back to Bacon, Condorcet, and Berthelot, that ingenious humans could outsmart nature—and perhaps even live forever. Now functional foods seemed to confirm that faith. Take the super carrot genetically bred for extra beta-carotene. Here was something *almost* as ingenious as synthetic foods, for it involved considerable value-adding engineering, yet because it *looked* natural, it eluded popular suspicions of the artificial (and thus reassured the nervous marketing department).

On the surface, functional foods did purport to co-opt countercultural food practices and politics. For example, some drink vendors almost outdid the fruit-and-nuts health food entrepreneurs in ransacking the plant kingdom for unusual fruits, herbs, and spices, which they then blended into "smart drinks" like Pepsi's Josta (made with the allegedly "energizing Brazilian guarana berry"), Nantucket Nectars' Red Guarana and Gingko Mango teas, and Jamba Juice's ultrafortified Smoothies. Tapping the rising envy of high-achieving (i.e., "smart") Asians, South Beach

Beverages took an orientalist tack with its Zen Blend (ginseng, ginger, and schizandra) and Wisdom (St. John's wort, gingko, and gotu kola). With their quirky names and exotic ingredients, these potions suggested potable diversity. They definitely were global. To meet the surging interest in smart drinks, American imports of mangoes, guavas, and papayas soared in the mid-1990s. Plant scientists also canvassed the world for unusual species to be crossbred into a nutritionally enhanced "rainbow of foods"—purple carrots, golden potatoes, orange cauliflower, red grapefruits. While modernist science had equated whiteness with purity and health, recombinant science valued orange, antioxidant-rich beta-carotene (carrots, sweet potatoes, cantaloupes), bluish anti-inflammatory anthocyanins (blueberries, plums, cherries), yellowish zeaxanthin (corn, egg yolks), and so on. "Think variety and color," the American Dietetic Association advised. Some of these amalgamations, elixirs, and concoctions would be produced through conventional fortification, genetic selection, and synthesis, others through genetic engineering. From a public relations standpoint, functional foods were the consumer-friendly facade of biotechnology, whose alleged precision would advance the same qualities of sensitivity, diversity, and choice associated with other smart technologies. With each food designed to cater to specific needs, the customer would truly "call the shots," as The Grocer exclaimed in a 1999 article, "A Taste of Tomorrow"[57]—no Frankenfoods here.

Such foods also seemed smart because they were conflated with doing the "right thing" for your body, and by the 1990s few denied that most Americans were out of shape—the opposite of svelte smartness. Yet because they were billed as enhancements of existing products, they seemed less negative, less puritanical than previous generations of dietetic foods—and potentially far more profitable. As Marion Nestle argues in Food Politics, the best (and cheapest) way to stay healthy is to eat less and move more, but the food industry profits mainly when people eat more. The functional food diet, with its carefully targeted and segmented benefits—calcium-fortified juice for your bones, enhanced tomato sauce for your prostate, rice for your eyes, and so on—certainly did imply a lot of consumption.[58]

Clearly, the name "functional" had more to do with sales than science. Strictly speaking, all foods have a function, however marginal. Nestle writes: "Because all foods and drinks include ingredients (calories, nutrients, or water) that are essential for life, any one of them has the potential to be marketed for its health benefits." Add the social, psychological, and cultural dimensions of eating, and the functions seem almost infinite. This very inclusiveness enhanced the concept's business appeal but also made it a bit hard to pin down. A number of names were offered up, but few had the marketing function, so to speak, of "functional." "Nutraceuticals," "pharmafoods," and "foodaceuticals" rightly conveyed the druglike claims of what *Newsweek* called "the prescriptive palate" but also veered too close to meal pills in the suggestion of mixing medicine with food. From a legal standpoint it was also dangerous to tread too near the highly regulated medical sector, as when the FDA warned Hain's about its herbally enhanced "Kitchen Prescription" soups. "Designer foods" rightly reflected the human manipulation involved in these unnatural recombinations, but the label also smacked of 1980s fashion industry elitism. Those who understood Huxley's *Brave New World* also worried about issues of designer control, especially when framed in the inevitable media puns, such as "designer genes." "Mood foods" rightly described the herb-laced juices, soups, smoothies, and potions designed to boost mental functions, but they also sounded a bit effete, neurasthenic, and wimpy. A much more masculine early label, "power foods," aptly suggested extra strength and vitality but also seemed ridiculous (Starbucks' Power Frappuccino, a smoothie-like total meal) or childlike (Power Rangers and the Power Puff girls). Curiously enough, despite their name's overt link to smartness, Campbell Soup's nutritionally enhanced mail-order meals, called Intelligent Quisine, were a failure. One suspects that such overt intellectualism was doomed to fail in the American market.[59]

In all, while "functional" was not exactly the most dynamic rubric— the *Washington Post* quipped that the term "has all the zip and clarity of a government abbreviation (think HOV)"—its very dryness suggested a no-nonsense, businesslike approach. Just as convenience was seen as a perquisite not of the idle rich but of the busy worker, functional foods worked for you, saving time and enhancing productivity. Befitting this labor-oriented slant, the "typical food day" in Coates's 2025 featured nutribagels, multivitamin fruitshakes, and Fruit Rockets ("a cereal for prepubescent boys") in the weekday breakfast slot, long considered by Americans as the time to fulfill one's nutritional obligations with fortified cereals, citrus, and vitamin pills. Lunch—the quick pit stop in the rat race of work or school—could include a fruit juice laced with drugs to combat jet lag (for Mom on her trip to London), a quick-energy gum (for Dad between surgical operations), or fortified milk and cookies (for the kids at school). Functional foods' quick fix of energy and nutrients reflected the growth in what Christopher Wolf called "cruise chews"—handheld snacks eaten on the run. But dinner, both Coates and Wolf shrewdly predicted, might be reserved for more diverse neotraditional meals—whether "speed scratch," home meal replacements, or franchised fusion.[60]

"Functional" thus accorded well with Condorcet's axiom that the pursuit of utility—"the law of least action"—was the primary driver of progress. Whether these foods would actually perform as envisioned remained unclear. But their business utility was obvious. In addition to diverting attention away from the unprofitable "eat less" paradigm of the "food police," many functional foods seemed to escape the regulatory harassment of government agencies, especially when they were offered as dietary supplements—a category accorded significant leeway by an act of Congress. This legal loophole was enhanced by its lack of clear definition. According to a 1994 attempt at clarification by the National Institute of Medicine's Food and Nutrition Board, a functional food was "any food or food ingredient that may provide a health benefit beyond the traditional nutrients it contains." Since there were about fifty "traditional nutrients"—vitamins, minerals, and amino acids, for instance—known to be essential to life but over one thousand phytochemicals that *might* provide a benefit, the product-proliferating, line-extending possibilities in functional foods were vast. "Phytochemicals may well become the soul of the new life-science machine," *Fortune* predicted in 1999. Anticipating substantial growth in the "unprecedented melding of edibles and pharmaceuticals," chemical, food, seed, and drug companies merged to form life-science conglomerates united in "selling molecules [the consumer] can use."[61]

The functional foods portfolio was risky, however. A 1999 report from the Grocery Manufacturers of America warned that nutritional science was quite uncertain about micronutrients: "Today's research confirming the benefits of an ingredient or product may be invalidated or even reversed tomorrow." No one quite knew how much of a particular phytochemical was necessary, or how to assure proper doses or prevent harmful interactions. If monitoring doses from conventional pills was hard enough, imagine trying to control the intake of dietary substances laced with drugs! The potential for toxic overdoses—not to mention legal difficulties—was enormous. No wonder, then, that most of the early rollouts incorporated relatively noncontroversial or innocuous ingredients—fiber, gingko, calcium—in familiar categories with a high rate of obsolescence, especially snacks, drinks, and cereals. The more utopian "magic bullets," such as edible vaccines, were relegated to gee-whiz journalism and nonprofit research. A sensible businessmen could very well think it more cost effective to develop cheaper needles and syringes.[62]

The future of functional foods was further clouded by customer uncertainty. Accustomed to the quick rise and fall of the latest trends in what's good for you, customers were quite skeptical of health news. Such wariness was reflected and reinforced by the slightly disbelieving tone of reports afraid to commit fully to these wonder foods (sample headlines: "Candy and Coffee Are the New Health Foods? We Wish" and "Magic Bullets: Pumped-Up Foods Promise to Make Us Happier and Healthier. We'll See"). There were also fundamental flaws in the concept of functional foods. "If people become accustomed to viewing foods as medicines," Marion Nestle writes, "the functional-foods approach could backfire. People might stop eating such foods if they do *not* feel better when they eat them (because the products do not work) or if they *do* feel better (because the products are no longer needed)." Much of the marketers' enthusiasm was based on heady extrapolations from the surge in the sale of food supplements, which tripled from $4 billion in 1990 to $12 billion in 1999. But was this the right analogy? Didn't people draw strong lines between food and medicine? Yes, they took vitamins, but no, they did not appreciate meal pills. Despite breezy references to Hippocrates—"let food be thy medicine"—for the most part people preferred to keep the two separate.[63] Food categories, prejudices, and notions were malleable but not easily transgressed. Would consumers really want their lettuce enriched with beef protein? Would Asians really eat yellow rice? Would Americans really eat soy?

With so many products "ranging from the truly useful to the truly hokey," there was also the danger of having too many options, especially when the benefits were so narrowly targeted. Even if marketers could figure out how to cater to bio-individuality, the resultant diversity could lead to confusion and a backlash. Christopher Wolf detected "regression nostalgia" in sugared-cereal ads that seemed to give adults "permission" to indulge their childlike, atavistic hunger for Frosted Flakes and Cap'n Crunch. A similar reaction had already occurred in the 1980s, when the rise of hip natural foods had spawned a reactionary yearning for modernist "comfort foods" such as multican casseroles, Jell-O molds, and, yes, Tang. At some point, addled consumers might seek solace in modernist simplicity or neoclassical opulence. The same surveys announcing the boom in functional foods, exercise, tropical fruits, and overall health consciousness also found a surge in "self-indulgent" martinis, cigars, and oversized steaks. Indeed, these trends coexisted, and often among the same affluent demographics.[64] Rather than a trend in itself, recombination was more of a safe fallback, a confession that it was almost impossible to predict eating patterns.

THE DAY AFTER Y2K

Forecasting is precarious largely because the future is an invention of the present, and the present is always contentious and changing. To a certain extent, the smart future envisioned in the 1990s was a reflection of the need for marketers and journalists to generate some premillennial buzz as January 1, 2000, approached. With so much invested in finding great meaning in what amounted to just a numerical detail, it was almost mandatory that great advances be identified and promoted. But almost as soon as the millennial parties were over, futurism was old news, and the techno-hype tapered off sharply. Thus, barely three weeks into the third millennium, one ultrasober analysis of why Americans were not flocking to Peapod, Webvan, HomeRuns or other online shopping services observed: "If there is a Murphy's Law of Internet commerce, it might be this: Just because people hate doing something offline, that doesn't mean they'll love doing it online." In the postmillennial hangover, it seemed that food shopping and consumption were just as conservative as its denigrators had noted back in the drab 1980s, before the uptick of the 1990s. "The grocery business is light years behind in Internet time," a Nabisco executive lamented at a conference held to explore why consumers had not yet taken to all the much-anticipated modes of smart shopping. Appropriately, one moderately successful postmillennial supermarket innovation was self-checkout, which required a simple scanner—a technology, *Newsweek* observed, "that debuted during the Reagan era, not the Internet Age." Sometimes the future was shaped not by "the latest gizmos" but rather by "the lagging edge of technology."[65]

As the world struggled with the same old problems of poverty, greed, inequality, ecological limits, political corruption, and terrorism, it was not so clear that much had changed at all. Techno-futurism's "been there, done that" quality was evidenced by the collapse of "tech" stocks, including the much-vaunted smart shopping services. Like so many dot.coms, Webvan and HomeRuns hemorrhaged cash and went bankrupt, while Peapod—motto: "Smart Shopping for Busy People"—survived only because it was acquired, "at a bargain-basement price," by the Dutch conglomerate Royal Ahold, owner of Stop and Shop, Giant Foods, and over nine thousand traditional brick-and-mortar supermarkets in twenty-five countries. By 2002, food industry analysts "roundly panned" online food shopping "as the biggest of the dot-com follies" and "a debacle," and expressed surprise when one actually prospered—a small Wisconsin supermarket chain that simply added a dial-up option to a well-established phone order service.[66] From the chastened perspective of the early 2000s, online food shopping might succeed best as an auxiliary service of a regular store, much the way the local mom-and-pop might have dispatched cousin Billy on his one-speed bike a few decades earlier. But few analysts now thought that web shopping would ever rival, much less replace, the standard supermarket. As was so often the case with technological innovation, the established industry had managed to absorb and co-opt a "revolutionary" upstart.

What had seemed refreshing and sharp in the '90s now looked dead on arrival, much like earlier "kitchen of tomorrow" fantasies. Despite the recent spate of "nifty ideas," Forbes.com lamented in 2001, "our toasters don't talk, our refrigerators don't think, alarm clocks blare just as they always did, and the oven mitt is just an unfeeling piece of cloth." Reviewing some smart kitchen ideas on display at the 2000 National Restaurant Association convention, a trade reporter wondered which was more useful to the average chef, an Internet-ready convection microwave oven or an old-fashioned pop-up toaster. Conservative skepticism seemed prudent. As of 2002, smart cards had not evolved much beyond the old credit cards. Home meal replacements were not so different from TV dinners and takeout deli. Fusion cuisine was the same old imperialist appropriation. Smart bars were not all that different in boosting mental capacity from Hershey's or Almond Joy (a point made clear in the revival of conventional candy bar ads after 2000). How different were Power-Bars from "space sticks" or granola bars? How much of a paradigm shift were the herb- and fiber-enhanced cereals that purported to do much the same thing as Kellogg's original corn flakes—put consumers on "the road to wellness"? Were the microflora in a BasicsPlus smart drink any more effective in "maintaining gastrointestinal health" than those in plain old Dannon's yogurt? Functional recycled fortified and nutrified, with a dash of Grandma's herbal remedies, chicken soup, Mom's meat loaf and mashed potatoes, and other comfort foods that often healed better than drugs. If the best advice experts could offer was to eat a moderate, varied, balanced diet, how far was this from the days of the Basic Four? *Food Technology*'s top three food trends of the new century closely resembled those of the previous one: "do-for-me foods" (convenience), "super savory and sophisticated" (tasty, healthier), and "overall balance and moderation." Detecting the same continuities, *Food Processing* predicted that healthy, ethnic, and convenience foods would still be the main focus of research and development, and, as in the past, only about 22 percent of new products would be really new, with the rest either extensions (48 percent) or reformulations (31 percent) of existing products. Similarly, in *Foodservice 2010: America's Appetite Matures* (2002), the consulting firm McKinsey and Co. predicted that the "big winners" of 2010 would be "full-service restaurants" of the type that would have been quite familiar in 1910.[67]

Adding to the sense of déjà vu was the resurgence—complete with banners, blue jeans, and tear gas—of a competing, countercultural version of a smart future: a neoagrarian world of small farms, local markets, intimate producer-consumer relations, "slow" foods, and genuine biological and cultural diversity. Protests against a World Trade Organization meeting in Seattle in November 1999 melded socialist outrage at neo-imperialist injustice with sober, neo-Malthusian assessments of technological hubris and ecological overload. Hoping to invent an equitable and sustainable future worthy of Ernest Callenbach's Ecotopia and Marge Piercy's Mattapoissett, the antiglobalization movement pushed a different sort of smartness—attention to the processes behind the products, especially the speedy convenience foods that drove the food business. In the alternative view, the demand for convenience was an expression of moral bankruptcy and exhaustion—of dumbness and numbness—rather than, as the cornucopians had long contended, the engine of progress. Skeptical of myopic, aggressive accounting practices that inflated short-term profits while hiding long-term costs, this version of smartness reasserted the conservationist view of the future as a mortgage to be paid by our children, with high interest. Defining an "honest" food system, environmental educator David Orr invoked Thoreau's axiom: "The cost of a thing is the amount of what I will call life which is required to be exchanged for it, immediately or in the long run." Decrying our "insensate high-tech barbarism," Orr lamented the loss of the "sort of intelligence about the land that once resulted from the close contact with soils, animals, wildlife, forests, and the seasons fostered by farming and rural living." To insure honesty, the food system would best be regulated not by conglomerates forging self-serving synergies but by democratically elected officials capable of taking an arm's-length view of complex issues. Here smartness was being characterized not by sharpness and cleverness but by humility and prudence. Central to this populist version of smartness was "transparency"—the conscientious, responsible citizen consumer's right to know more about every step of the global food chain, even if gaining such knowledge proved challenging and time-consuming, that is, inconvenient.[68]

While much of the insurgency seemed too radical for mainstream tastes, the crusade for the consumer's "right to know" did have considerable political support beyond the antiglobalization barricades. "More and more consumers are now considering the source and production method used in the food they buy," Christopher Wolf wrote in 1994, "asking whether the packaging is recyclable or composed of recycled material, whether the manufacturer tests on animals or exploits its workers, and whether the food is organically produced." Ever alliterative, Wolf noted that some food marketers catered to this "cause cuisine" by advertising their use of recycled paper and by donating a small share of profits to feeding the hungry and homeless. By the end of the decade, however, it was not so clear that private philanthropy—the oligarchs' traditional palliative—could buy off public demand for corporate integrity. Take, for example, the growing interest in more extensive food labeling. Pitched as a way to inform and thereby improve consumer choice, labeling had been a popular Progressive Era legacy—and it was as potentially subversive in the 1990s as it had been in the 1890s. While the food industry usually dismissed every labeling proposal as confusing to consumers and burdensome to manufacturers, polls always indicated wide public support for such freedom of information. Of one thousand adults surveyed in 1998 by the National Cattlemen's Association, 80 percent wanted to know where their meat came from, especially the national origins. Such information could prove highly inconvenient to a globalized economy, however. Noting that Congress had approved a cost/benefits study of labels that indicated a meat product's country of origin, Wolf extrapolated the alarming implications for the food industry in general: "The initiation of the study hints at what other food manufacturers may face in the near future if safety-conscious consumers continue to become more interested in the growing conditions and specific processing techniques of all foods. The study may also signal a potential political landmine to manufacturers who buy and sell food products in international markets"—which would include just about every major food company. And sure enough, soon after this 1998 report, major political battles broke out worldwide over the labeling of genetically modified foods—the very same products billed as the food industry's smart future.[69] While the daily news tended to treat the fight as a revival of the '60s, it was of course a much older story, as debaters struggled, as had Malthus, Godwin, and Condorcet before them, to imagine a future that fed more people more equitably and within ecological limits.

POSTSCRIPT

So where are we headed? How do we decide which trends, inventions, and ideologies will transform the future and which ones will be remembered as laughable nonstarters? It is all too easy for a history of the future to dwell on "famous last words," those confident predictions that prove to be dead wrong. Take, for example, Victor Cohn's scenario from the mid-'50s: "For lunch the Futures [of 1999] ate wood steak, planked, and loved it—all except Billy, who bawled, 'I want an oil-cream cone.'" Or T. Baron Russell's 1905 declaration in *A Hundred Years Hence:* "Such a wasteful food as animal flesh can not survive." Or *Science Digest*'s 1955 speculation that, thanks to radiation, by 1985 "beef cattle the size of dogs will be grazed in the average man's backyard, eating especially-thick grass and producing specially-tender steaks."[1]

Although amusing, humbling, and sometimes instructive, reading too many of these anecdotes can foster a sense of helplessness when it comes to facing the future. If all predictions are so silly, then we might as well forget about foresight and just live for the moment. However, while therapeutically valid, dwelling in the here and now may seem too fatalistic for Americans; after all, the expectation of progress is enshrined in our cultural constitution. The opposite extreme—and more attuned to our Las Vegas/Old West tendencies—might be called the "high roller" strategy: since it seems impossible to tell which predictions are more credible, we might just as well bet the farm on the wildest possibilities. After all, if geniuses like Microsoft's Bill Gates and IBM's Thomas Watson couldn't gauge the future market for their computers, then who can say that some other smart improbability—say, a genetically enhanced tomato that can be grown organically, lasts forever on the shelf, and tastes great, or a fortified rice that "could save a million kids a year"—won't be equally successful?[2]

But clearly some predictions are better than others—and they are not always the safest ones. As part I of this book suggests, for much of the past two hundred years a safe prediction—shared by Malthusians, egalitarians, and cornucopians alike—was that as population grew, food prices would rise and meat consumption would decline. While analysts differed sharply over whether such basic trends would spark famine, revolution, or technological innovation (those irradiated dog-sized cows), they did tend to agree on the basic trend. We know that things have turned out quite differently—so far—for world markets are glutted with grain and meat, and even the Asian Harbingers have shifted from "coolie rations" to Big Macs. Before 1980 or so, such a scenario would not likely have emerged from a Delphi survey of expert opinion.[3] But history is full of cases where the unimaginable becomes the unremarkable—human flight, antibiotics, McDonald's in Beijing, an ethnic food revival in St. Paul—so we are right to laugh at definitive pronouncements from the experts, such as Lord Kelvin's infamous fin de siècle declaration "Radio has no future" and Paul Ehrlich's more recent "The battle to feed humanity is over. In the 1970s the world will undergo famines—hundreds of millions of people are going to starve to death in spite of any crash programs embarked upon now."[4] Some people may actually feel quite comforted, even liberated, by this debunking of the intelligentsia.

But if we agree that there is nevertheless some merit in thinking ahead, how do we keep a grip on reality while still allowing ourselves to dream of a better future? This is a complicated question, and I'm not sure I have a single answer. One possible solution is to remember that being correct is only one of many reasons to study the future. Some reasons are realistic, some romantic. As far as realism goes, studying past predictions should build a healthy skepticism. We may not be able to "know" the future, but at the very minimum we can question the agenda of those who claim they do. As should be clear from this book, self-interests invariably shape forecasts, which are employed both to undergird the status quo and to resist it. Predictions are used to win political support, to generate funding for particular research projects, to rationalize imperi-

alist ventures, to critique the present, to displace anxiety, to energize activists, and, not the least, to sell things.

To demystify these forecasts we need to be more savvy about the
rhetorical conventions, false dichotomies, inappropriate analogies, questionable assumptions, and dubious calculations that keep cropping up
whenever the future is discussed. Especially suspicious are the transgressive, gee-whiz conceits of the feature pages—the lowly pond scum
that will save mankind from starvation, the push-button factory farms
that will eliminate sweat and return the countryside to parkland, the genetically modified french fries that will lower your cholesterol. But we
also need to be wary of the more serious think tank discourse that occasionally reaches the front pages—especially the tendency to pose forced
choices, such as: it's either biotechnology or starvation, capitalism or socialism, imperialism or revolution, primitivism or modernism, Malthus
or Condorcet or Godwin. And we need to be careful about using the collective "we"—especially the tendency to think in terms of one future for
all of us. Just as no two people experienced the year 2000 in exactly the
same way, there are many futures available for each of us.[5]

One advantage of the recombinant version of the future is that it does
accommodate a diversity of references, interests, and experiences. And
it does seem especially appropriate for a complex food culture that as-
pires to convenience *and* authenticity, efficiency *and* artisanship, mass
distribution *and* class distinction. As chapter 8 argues, recombination is
the basic approach of marketers attempting to profit from the consumer's
need for the quick and easy yet comforting and traditional. It is also the
preferred path of the biotech companies attempting to avoid accusations
of imperialism (the classical future) and Frankenfoods (the modernist future); hence the category-straddling allusions to a "doubly green revolution," "sustainable" agribusiness, and "the nature of what's to come."[6]
And recombination may also work for the new breed of environmentalists, who employ the latest electronic media, especially the Internet as
well as an ever more sophisticated distribution apparatus (think Whole
Foods) on behalf of a relocalized, "slow food" system.

Recognizing the incremental, uneven, and often contradictory means
by which complex futures are invented is very pragmatic—but can realism alone solve the huge challenges facing us, especially such large-scale
issues as climate change, water and energy shortages, environmental
degradation, and the world's widening income gap? I doubt very much
that such problems can be overcome through pragmatism alone. Where
are the outrage, the urgency, the sense of mission? And where are the will-

power, the shared altruism, the international Marshall Plans—all key elements of the utopian caveat? Realism favors small steps, while the problems we face may require quantum leaps. For these we may need much more romance than our ironic postmillennial era has been able to muster so far—more utopians proposing "dreams to live by," more public intellectuals issuing impassioned wake-up calls, and more public citizens hungry to foresee and act.

NOTES

PREFACE

1. Paul Rozin, "Food Is Fundamental, Fun, Frightening, and Far-Reaching," *Social Research* 66 (winter 1998): 9–30.

2. Homer, *Odyssey,* and *Ecclesiasticus* 18:25, both quoted in *Since Eve Ate Apples: Quotations on Feating, Fasting & Food from the Beginning,* ed. March Egerton (Portland, OR: Tsunami Press, 1994), 179–80.

3. Joel E. Cohen, *How Many People Can the Earth Support?* (New York: W. W. Norton, 1995), 370.

4. A sampling: Joseph J. Corn and Brian Horrigan, *Yesterday's Tomorrows: Past Visions of the American Future* (Baltimore: Johns Hopkins University Press, 1984); Joseph J. Corn, ed., *Imagining Tomorrow: History, Technology and the American Future* (Cambridge, MA: MIT Press, 1986); Christophe Canto and Odile Faliu, *The History of the Future: Images of the 21st Century* (Paris: Flammarion, 1993); W. H. G. Armytage, *Yesterday's Tomorrows: A Historical Survey of Future Societies* (London: Routledge, 1968); I. F. Clarke, *The Pattern of Expectation, 1644–2001* (New York: Basic Books, 1979); and W. Warren Wagar, *The Next Three Futures: Paradigms of Things to Come* (New York: Praeger Publishers, 1991).

5. Tolstoy's *Anna Karenina* opens: "All happy families are like one another; each unhappy family is unhappy in its own way."

ONE. THE STAKES IN OUR STEAKS

1. For a highly speculative analysis of why earlier scholars may have been hesitant to discuss food, see Warren Belasco, "Food Matters: Perspectives on an

Emerging Field," in *Food Nations: Selling Taste in Consumer Societies*, ed. Warren Belasco and Philip Scranton, 1–11 (New York: Routledge, 2002).

2. Warren Belasco, *Appetite for Change: How the Counterculture Took on the Food Industry* (Ithaca: Cornell University Press, 1993), 6–9.

3. Frances Moore Lappé, *Diet for a Small Planet* (New York: Ballantine Books, 1971), 1–29 (italics added).

4. Frances Moore Lappé, *Diet for a Small Planet: 10th Anniversary Edition*. (New York: Ballantine Books, 1982); Frances Moore Lappé and Anna Lappé, *Hope's Edge: The Next Diet for a Small Planet* (New York: Jeremy P. Tarcher/Putnam: 2002).

5. According to a 2003 report from the Worldwatch Institute, "Producing 1 calorie of flesh (beef, pork, or chicken) requires 11–17 calories of feed. So a meat eater's diet requires two to four times more land than a vegetarian's diet. Soybeans, wheat, rice, and corn also produce three to eight times as much protein as meat." Danielle Nierenberg, "Meat Production and Consumption Grow," in *Vital Signs 2003* (New York: W. W. Norton, 2003), 30.

6. Carol J. Adams, *The Sexual Politics of Meat: A Feminist-Vegetarian Critical Theory* (New York: Continuum, 1990), 115; Michael Allen Fox, *Deep Vegetarianism* (Philadelphia: Temple University Press, 1999), 7; Jared Diamond, *Guns, Germs, and Steel: The Fates of Human Societies* (New York: W. W. Norton, 1999), 157–75; Massimo Montanari, "Food Systems and Models of Civilization," in *Food: A Culinary History from Antiquity to the Present*, ed. Jean-Louis Flandrin and Massimo Montanari (New York: Columbia University Press, 1999), 77–78; William Cronon, *Changes in the Land: Indians, Colonists, and the Ecology of New England* (New York: Hill and Wang, 1983), 128–29; Kirkpatrick Sale, *The Conquest of Paradise: Christopher Columbus and the Columbian Legacy* (New York: Plume, 1991), 163–64; Jeremy Rifkin, *Beyond Beef: The Rise and Fall of the Cattle Culture* (New York: Plume, 1992), 50; Jeffrey M. Pilcher, *Que Vivan los Tamales! Food and the Making of Mexican Identity* (Albuquerque: University of New Mexico Press, 1998), 30.

7. Paley and Phillips quoted in Adams, *Sexual Politics of Meat*, 115–16; Percy Bysshe Shelley, "A Vindication of a Natural Diet," in *Ethical Vegetarianism: From Pythagoras to Peter Singer*, ed. Kerry S. Walters and Lisa Portmess (Albany: State University of New York Press, 1999), 73.

8. Adams, *Sexual Politics of Meat*, 111; Thomas Malthus, *An Essay on the Principle of Population* (1798; London: Penguin, 1985), 187–88; Fernand Braudel, *The Structures of Everyday Life* (Berkeley: University of California Press, 1992), 105.

9. William A. Alcott, "The World Is a Mighty Slaughterhouse and Flesh-Eating and Human Decimation," in *Ethical Vegetarianism: From Pythagoras to Peter Singer*, ed. Kerry S. Walters and Lisa Portmess (Albany: State University of New York Press, 1999), 87; William Godwin, *Of Population* (London: Longman, Hurst, Rees, and Brown, 1820), accessed May 21, 2003, available from http://dwardmac.pitzer.edu/Anarchist_Archives/godwin/population/chapter3.htm.

10. Malthus, *Population*, 188; Rifkin, *Beyond Beef*, 60–64.

11. Malthus, *Population*, 138; Garrett Hardin, *Living within Limits: Ecol-*

ogy, Economics, and Population Taboos (New York: Oxford University Press, 1993), 213.

12. Alcott, "The World Is a Mighty Slaughterhouse," 87, 82.

13. Marquis de Condorcet, "The Future Progress of the Human Mind," in *Esquisse d'un Tableau Historique des Progres de L'Esprit Humain* (1794); accessed May 21, 2003; available at http://ishi.lib.berkeley.edu/~hist280/research/condorcet/pages/progress_main.html; Frank E. Manuel, *The Prophets of Paris: Turgot, Condorcet, Saint-Simon, Fourier, and Comte* (New York: Harper Torchbooks, 1965), 98; Malthus, *Population*, 125–31, 168–73; William Godwin, "Of Body and Mind," in *Thoughts on Man, His Nature, Productions, Discoveries, Interspersed with Some Particulars Respecting the Author* (London: Effingham Wilson, 1831), 28, accessed May 21, 2003, available at http://dwardmac.pitzer.edu/Anarchist_Archives/godwin/thoughts/TMNPDfrontpiece.html.

14. "All human history attests / That happiness for man—/ the hungry sinner—/ Since Eve ate apples / Much depends on dinner!" Lord Byron, *Don Juan* (1823), quoted in *Since Eve Ate Apples*, ed. March Egerton (Portland, OR: Tsunami Press, 1994), 101.

15. Isaac Bashevis Singer, *The Penitent* (New York: Fawcett Crest, 1983), 27.

16. Vaclav Smil, *Feeding the World: A Challenge for the Twenty-First Century* (Cambridge, MA: MIT Press, 2000), 262, 144; Danielle Nierenberg, "Factory Farming in the Developing World," *World Watch* (May/June 2003): 13–14. For an overview of the extent and dietary consequences of the nutrition transition, see Gary Gardner and Brian Halweil, *Underfed and Overfed: The Global Epidemic of Malnutrition*, Worldwatch Paper 150 (Washington, DC: Worldwatch Institute, March 2000).

17. Beard quoted in Adams, *Sexual Politics of Meat*, 30–31 (italics added); Claude Rawson, "Unspeakable Rites: Cultural Reticence and the Cannibal Question," *Social Research* 66 (spring 1999): 167–93; Nicholas Mirzoeff, "Transculture: From Kongo to the Congo," in *An Introduction to Visual Culture* (London: Routledge, 1999), 129–61; Nick Fiddes, *Meat: A Natural Symbol* (London: Routledge, 1991), 121–31.

18. Williams quoted in Laurel Thatcher Ulrich, *The Age of Homespun: Objects and Stories in the Creation of an American Myth* (New York: Vintage Books, 2001), 67; Woods Hutchinson, *Instinct and Health* (1909), quoted in Harvey Green, *Fit for America: Health, Fitness, Sport, and American Society* (New York: Pantheon, 1986), 303; Robert B. Hinman and Robert B. Harris, *The Story of Meat* (1939), quoted in Adams, *Sexual Politics of Meat*, 31; J. Gordon Cook, *The Fight for Food* (New York: Dial Press, 1957), 107; Sombart quoted in Hasia Diner, *Hungering for America: Italian, Irish, and Jewish Foodways in the Age of Migration* (Cambridge, MA: Harvard University Press, 2001), 11, 84–145; Harvey Levenstein, *Revolution at the Table: The Transformation of the American Diet* (New York: Oxford University Press, 1988) 98–108. E. Melanie DuPuis, in *Nature's Perfect Food: How Milk Became America's Drink* (New York: New York University Press, 2002), notes a similar Americanization/assimilation dynamic in the turn-of-the-century transformation of milk from "white poison" to "perfect food."

19. Shaw quoted in Deidre Wicks, "Humans, Food, and Other Animals: The Vegetarian Option," in *A Sociology of Food and Nutrition: The Social Appetite,* ed. John Germov and Lauren Williams (Victoria, Australia: Oxford University Press, 1999), 108; Fiddes, *Meat,* 129; Willard quoted in Adams, *Sexual Politics of Meat,* 144.

20. James Whorton, *Crusaders for Fitness: The History of American Health Reformers* (Princeton: Princeton University Press, 1982), 89; Beecher quoted in Green, *Fit for America,* 47.

21. Graham quoted in Stephen Nissenbaum, *Sex, Diet, and Debility in Jacksonian America: Sylvester Graham and Health Reform* (Chicago: Dorsey Press, 1988), 126, 46–47; Shelley, "Vindication," 72; Adams, *Sexual Politics of Meat,* 108–19.

22. Levenstein, *Revolution at the Table,* 72–160; Susan Strasser, *Never Done: A History of American Housework* (New York: Pantheon, 1982), 202–62; Marion Nestle, *Food Politics: How the Food Industry Influences Nutrition and Health* (Berkeley: University of California Press, 2002), 31–50; DuPuis, *Nature's Perfect Food,* 90–121.

23. 1943 OPA pamphlet quoted in Amy Bentley, *Eating for Victory: Food Rationing and the Politics of Domesticity* (Urbana: University of Illinois Press, 1998), 96.

24. Jeffery Sobal, "Food System Globalization, Eating Transformations, and Nutrition Transitions," in *Food in Global History,* ed. Raymond Grew (Boulder: Westview Press, 1999), 178. See also *Feeding a World Population of More than Eight Billion People,* ed. J. C. Waterlow et al. (New York: Oxford University Press, 1998); Gardner and Halweil, *Underfed and Overfed;* Nierenberg, "Factory Farming." See also chapters 2 and 3.

25. Adam Drewnowski, "Fat and Sugar in the Global Diet: Dietary Diversity in the Nutrition Transition," in *Food in Global History,* ed. Raymond Grew (Boulder: Westview Press, 1999), 203; Lester R. Brown, *Who Will Feed China? Wake-Up Call for a Small Planet* (New York: W. W. Norton, 1995). Almost seventy years earlier Sir George Handley Knibbs anticipated Brown's worries about a rising Asian demand for meat in *The Shadow of the World's Future* (London: Ernest Benn, 1928), 32.

26. Robert Shapiro's speech at the October 1998 State of the World Forum is quoted in Ryan Matthews, "Biotechnology: The Future of Food," *Grocery Headquarters,* May 1, 1999, 36 (italics added).

27. Manuel, *Prophets of Paris,* 75; Godwin, *Thoughts on Man,* 77; Edward M. East, *Mankind at the Crossroads* (New York: Charles Scribner's Sons, 1924), 346–47; W. H. Forbes, "What Will India Eat Tomorrow?" *Atlantic Monthly* (August 1951), 36, 40; David Pimentel and Marcia Pimentel, "Land, Energy and Water: The Constraints Governing Ideal U.S. Population Size," *NPG Forum,* spring 1991, accessed May 14, 2003, from http://dieoff.org/page136.htm.

28. Ronald Walter Greene, *Malthusian Worlds: U.S. Leadership and the Governing of the Population Crisis* (New York: Westview Press, 1999), 33–38; Malthus, *Population,* 115–16. On British attitudes toward "offals," see Stephen Mennell, *All Manners of Food: Eating and Taste in England and France from the Middle Ages to the Present* (Urbana: University of Illinois Press, 1996), 310–16.

29. Malthus, *Population*, 117. As a slight corrective to Malthus, Sucheta Mazumdar argues that that Chinese population boomed only after the sixteenth-century importation of the American sweet potato—a much more prolific and more easily cultivated source of calories than grain. "The Impact of New World Food Crops on the Diet and Economy of China and India, 1600–1900," in *Food in Global History*, ed. Raymond Grew (Boulder: Westview Press, 1999), 66–68. For radical perspectives on China and India's food problems, see Mike Davis, *Late Victorian Holocausts: El Niño Famines and the Making of the Third World* (London: Verso, 2001); Vandana Shiva, *The Violence of the Green Revolution: Third World Agriculture, Ecology, and Politics* (London: Zen Books, 1991); Frances Moore Lappé and Joseph Collins, *World Hunger: Twelve Myths* (New York: Grove Press, 1986); Robert Shaffer, "Pearl S. Buck and the Politics of Food," *Proteus* 17 (spring 2000): 9–14.

30. "Was Malthus Right?" *World's Work*, December 1928, 130; Paul S. Henshaw, "80,000 Hungry Mouths a Day," *Saturday Review*, August 13, 1955, 31; Marvin Harris, "The Cultural Ecology of India's Sacred Cattle," *Current Anthropology* 7 (1966): 51–66; Rifkin, *Beyond Beef*, 34–40.

31. Ronald Takaki, *Strangers from a Different Shore: A History of Asian Americans* (New York: Penguin, 1989), 230–73; Donna Gabaccia, *We Are What We Eat: Ethnic Food and the Making of Americans* (Cambridge, MA: Harvard University Press, 1998), 104; Mary P. Ryan, *Democracy and Public Life in the American City during the Nineteenth Century* (Berkeley: University of California Press, 1997), 181–91, 286–92; Roger Daniels, *Coming to America: A History of Immigration and Ethnicity in American Life* (New York: HarperCollins, 1990), 238–50. For a meditation on the dog-eating stereotype, see Frank H. Wu, *Yellow: Race in America beyond Black and White* (New York: Basic Books, 2001), 215–28. "Milk, Living Standards Are Closely Connected," *Science News Letter*, December 26, 1953, 406. On the ideology of milk, see DuPuis, *Nature's Perfect Food*. Shirley Geok-lin Lim, "Boiled Chicken Feet and Hundred-Year-Old Eggs: Poor Chinese Feasting," in *Through the Kitchen Window: Women Writers Explore the Intimate Meanings of Food and Cooking*, ed. Arlene Voski Avakian (Boston: Beacon Press, 1997), 223.

32. Buck quoted in Bentley, *Eating for Victory*, 102; Richard Pillsbury, *No Foreign Food: The American Diet in Time and Place* (Boulder: Westview Press, 1998), 92–93; *American Cookery* (1945), quoted in Jane Stern and Michael Stern, *American Gourmet* (New York: HarperCollins, 1991), 54.

33. Walter B. Pitkin, *Must We Fight Japan?* (New York: Century, 1921), 292–96; Mike Davis, *Ecology of Fear: Los Angeles and the Imagination of Disaster* (New York: Metropolitan Books, 1998), 359, 275–398.

34. Peter N. Stearns, *Fat History: Bodies and Beauty in the Modern West* (New York: New York University Press, 1997), 234–36; Janet Poppendieck, *Sweet Charity? Emergency Food and the End of Entitlement* (New York: Viking, 1998), 43–44; Lappé, *Diet for a Small Planet*, 3; Fairfield Osborn, *The Limits of the Earth* (Boston: Little, Brown, 1953); Harrison Brown, *The Challenge of Man's Future* (New York: Viking Press, 1954); Georg Borgstrom, *The Food and People Dilemma* (North Scituate, MA: Duxbury Press, 1973); "Was Malthus Right?" 131; U. P. Hedrick, "Multiplicity of Crops as a Means of Increasing the Future

Food Supply," *Science*, October 30, 1914, 611–12; Grant Canyon, "Nitrogen Will Feed Us," *Atlantic Monthly*, September 1953, 50. For vivid pictures of Indian famine and crowding, coupled with a classic neo-Malthusian message, see the 1996 documentary *Paul Ehrlich and the Population Bomb*, videocassette, 60 minutes (San Francisco: KQED-TV, 1996).

35. John H. Perkins, *Geopolitics and the Green Revolution: Wheat, Genes, and the Cold War* (New York: Oxford University Press, 1997); "Meat Consumption Soars in the Third World," *The Futurist*, November 1998, 6; Lester R. Brown et al., *Vital Signs 1997* (New York: W. W. Norton, 1997), 20–22, 30; Brown, *Who Will Feed China?*; James L. Watson, ed., *Golden Arches East: McDonald's in East Asia* (Stanford: Stanford University Press, 1997).

36. Gardner and Halweil, *Underfed and Overfed*, 27; Susan Moeller, *Compassion Fatigue: How the Media Sell Disease, Famine, War, and Death* (New York: Routledge, 1999); Robert D. Kaplan, "The Coming Anarchy," *Atlantic*, February 1994, accessed June 4, 2003, available at www.theatlantic.com/politics/foreign/anarchy.htm.

37. Fiddes, *Meat*, 65; Fox, *Deep Vegetarianism*, 23–31, 100–112.

38. Joan Jacobs Brumberg, *Fasting Girls: The History of Anorexia Nervosa* (New York: Plume, 1989), 176; Laura Shapiro, *Perfection Salad: Women and Cooking at the Turn of the Century* (New York: Farrar, Straus and Giroux, 1986), 91–102; Sidney W. Mintz, *Sweetness and Power: The Place of Sugar in Modern History* (New York: Penguin, 1986), 145; Bentley, *Eating for Victory*, 85–102, 155; Deborah Barndt, *Tangled Routes: Women, Work, and Globalization on the Tomato Trail* (Lanham, MD: Rowman and Littlefield, 2002), 82–112. On postwar trends, see also Marjorie L. DeVault, *Feeding the Family: The Social Organization of Caring as Gendered Work* (Chicago: University of Chicago Press, 1991).

39. Ellen Messer, "Food from Peace and Roles of Women," in *Who Will Be Fed in the 21st Century?* ed. Keith Weibe, Nicole Ballenger, and Per Pinstrup-Andersen (Washington, DC: International Food Policy Research Institute, 2001), 64; Peter Atkins and Ian Bowler, *Food in Society: Economy, Culture, Geography* (London: Arnold, 2001), 317.

40. Carole Counihan, *The Anthropology of Food and Power: Gender, Meaning, and Power* (New York: Routledge, 1999), 153, 148; Marie Smyth, "Hedge Nutrition, Hunger, and Irish Identity," in *Through the Kitchen Window: Women Writers Explore the Intimate Meanings of Food and Cooking*, ed. Arlene Voski Avakian (Boston: Beacon Press, 1997), 89; Kathryn Paxton George, "Should Feminists Be Vegetarians?" *Signs* 19 (winter 1994): 405–34.

41. Carolyn Merchant, *Ecological Revolutions: Nature, Gender, and Science in New England* (Chapel Hill: University of North Carolina Press, 1989), 82; Pilcher, *Que Vivan Los Tamales!*, 25–43; Jane Tompkins, *West of Everything: The Inner Life of Westerns* (New York: Oxford University Press, 1992), 117; Vandana Shiva, "Development as a New Project of Western Patriarchy," in *Reweaving the World: The Emergence of Ecofeminism*, ed. Irene Diamond and Gloria Feman Orenstein (San Francisco: Sierra Club Books, 1990), 189–200; Atkins and Bowler, *Food in Society*, 315–17; Barndt, *Tangled Routes*; Mary Neth, *Preserving the Family Farm: Women, Community, and the Foundations of Agribusi-*

ness in the Midwest, 1900–1940 (Baltimore: Johns Hopkins University Press, 1995). For a general elaboration of how new household technologies increased women's work, see Ruth Schwartz Cowan, *More Work for Mother: The Ironies of Household Technology from the Open Hearth to the Microwave* (New York: Basic Books, 1983).

TWO. THE DEBATE

1. Betty Barclay Franks, "Futurists and the American Dream: A History of Contemporary Futurist Thought" (D.Arts diss., Carnegie-Mellon University, 1985), 266.

2. Frank E. Manuel, *The Prophets of Paris: Turgot, Condorcet, Saint-Simon, Fourier, and Comte* (New York: Harper Torchbooks, 1965), 56; Marquis de Condorcet, "The Future Progress of the Human Mind," in *Esquisse d'un Tableau Historique des Progres de L'Esprit Humain* (1794); accessed May 21, 2003; available at http://ishi.lib.berkeley.edu/~hist28o/research/condorcet/pages/progress_main.html. For the late eighteenth century's "pride in human capacity," see Asa Briggs, *The Making of Modern England, 1783–1867* (New York: Harper Torchbooks, 1965), 18–19.

3. William Godwin, "Of Body and Mind," in *Thoughts on Man, His Nature, Productions, Discoveries, Interspersed with Some Particulars Respecting the Author* (London: Effingham Wilson, 1831), 28; accessed May 21, 2003; available at http://dwardmac.pitzer.edu/Anarchist_Archives/godwin/thoughts/TMNPDfrontpiece.html. On Godwin's home life, see Miranda Seymour, *Mary Shelley* (New York: Grove Press, 2000), 3–20. For a sardonic sketch of Godwin by an arch-Malthusian, see Garrett Hardin, *Living within Limits: Ecology, Economics, and Population Taboos* (New York: Oxford University Press, 1993), 20–21.

4. Thomas Malthus, *An Essay on the Principle of Population* (1798; London: Penguin, 1985), 136. On Malthus's "serene and happy life," see Antony Flew's introduction to this edition, 16–17; also Robert Heilbroner, *The Worldly Philosophers* (New York: Simon & Schuster, 1961), 58–84. On Franklin and Adams, see Joseph J. Spengler, "Population Prediction in Nineteenth Century America," *American Sociological Review* 1 (1936): 905–6; Fernand Braudel, *The Structures of Everyday Life* (Berkeley: University of California Press, 1992), 105; Heilbroner, *Worldly Philosophers*.

5. Malthus, *Population*, 126, 131, 216; Heilbroner, *Worldly Philosophers*, 63.

6. Arthur Gribben, ed., *The Great Famine and the Irish Diaspora in America* (Amherst: University of Massachusetts Press, 1999); Mike Davis, *Late Victorian Holocausts: El Niño Famines and the Making of the Third World* (London; Verso, 2001), 21–38; Briggs, *Making of Modern England*, 15–60, 184–235.

7. James R. Gibson, Jr., *Americans versus Malthus: The Population Debate in the Early Republic, 1790–1840* (New York: Garland, 1989); Harvey Levenstein, *Revolution at the Table: The Transformation of the American Diet* (New York: Oxford University Press, 1988), 7–9; William H. Brock, *Justus Von Liebig: The Chemical Gatekeeper* (Cambridge: Cambridge University Press, 1997), 145–82; Thomas Vargish, "Why the Person Sitting Next to You Hates Limits to

Growth," *Technological Forecasting and Social Change* 16 (1980): 179–89; Spengler, "Population Prediction," 905–21.

8. Rebecca L. Spang, *The Invention of the Restaurant: Paris and Modern Gastronomic Culture* (Cambridge, MA: Harvard University Press, 2000), 193, 208; Kenneth L. Ames, *Death in the Dining Room and Other Tales of Victorian Culture* (Philadelphia: Temple University Press, 1992), 71, 44–95; Pamela Walker Laird, *Advertising Progress: American Business and the Rise of Consumer Marketing* (Baltimore: Johns Hopkins University Press, 1998), 108–51. For fairs, see part III.

9. William Godwin, *Thoughts on Man, His Nature, Productions, Discoveries, Interspersed with Some Particulars Respecting the Author* (London: Effingham Wilson, 1831), 238, 102–3, 247; accessed May 21, 2003; available at http://dwardmac.pitzer.edu/Anarchist_Archives/godwin/thoughts/TMNPDfrontpiece.html. Flew, introduction to Malthus, *Population*, 35; John Bellamy Foster and Fred Magdoff, "Liebig, Marx, and the Depletion of Soil Fertility: Relevance for Today's Agriculture," in *Hungry for Profit*, ed. Fred Magdoff, John Bellamy Foster, and Frederick Buttel (New York: Monthly Review Press, 2000), 43–60.

10. Richard Hofstadter, *Social Darwinism in American Thought* (Boston: Beacon, 1955); Paul F. Boller, *American Thought in Transition: The Impact of Evolutionary Naturalism, 1865–1900* (New York: Rand McNally, 1969), 46–69; William Graham Sumner, "Sociology," in *American Thought: Civil War to World War I*, ed. Perry Miller (New York: Holt, Rinehart and Winston, 1954), 72–92; Mike Davis, *Ecology of Fear: Los Angeles and the Imagination of Disaster* (New York: Metropolitan Books, 1998), 284; Mary P. Ryan, *Democracy and Public Life in the American City during the Nineteenth Century* (Berkeley: University of California Press, 1997), 181–217.

11. Hofstadter, *Social Darwinism*, 179–201; John Higham, *Strangers in the Land: Patterns of American Nativism, 1860–1925* (New York: Atheneum 1967), 131–93; Harvey Green, *Fit for America: Health, Fitness, Sport, and American Society* (New York: Pantheon, 1986), 101–258; Richard P. Tucker, *Insatiable Appetite: The United States and the Ecological Degradation of the Tropical World* (Berkeley: University of California Press, 2000); Donald Worster, *Nature's Economy: A History of Ecological Ideas* (Cambridge: Cambridge University Press, 1985), 114–87.

12. Davis, *Late Victorian Holocausts*, 23–115; Boller, *American Thought in Transition*, 59–60; Francis A. Walker, "Our Population in 1900," *Atlantic Monthly* (1873), reprinted in Walker, *Discussions in Economics and Statistics* (New York: Henry Holt & Co., 1899), 33.

13. Simon Patten, *The Premises of Political Economy* (Philadelphia: J. B. Lippincott, 1885), 87; Ronald Takaki, *Strangers from a Different Shore: A History of Asian Americans* (New York: Penguin, 1989); John H. Perkins, *Geopolitics and the Green Revolution: Wheat, Genes, and the Cold War* (New York: Oxford University Press, 1997), 1–74; Steven Stoll, *The Fruits of Natural Advantage: Making the Industrial Countryside in California* (Berkeley: University of California Press, 1998), 7–19; Gilbert C. Fite, *American Farmers: The New Minority* (Bloomington: Indiana University Press, 1984), 1–37; Alan Trachtenberg, *The*

Incorporation of American Culture and Society in the Gilded Age (New York: Hill and Wang, 1982).

14. Davis, *Late Victorian Holocausts*, 119–75; W. O. Atwater, "The Food-Supply of the Future," *The Century* 43 (November 1891), 101–12; idem, "What the Coming Man Will Eat," *The Forum*, June 1892, 488–99; J. M. Rusk, "American Farming A Hundred Years Hence," *North American Review*, March 1893, 257–64. For an overview of many estimates, including from the 1890s, see Joel E. Cohen, *How Many People Can the Earth Support?* (New York: W. W. Norton, 1995).

15. Pritchett quoted by W. S. Woytinsky and E. S. Woytinsky, *World Population and Production: Trends and Outlook* (New York: Twentieth Century Fund, 1953), 245; Felix L. Oswald, "National Population under 300 Million," in *Today Then: 1993 as Predicted in 1893*, ed. Dave Walter (Helena, MT: American and World Geographic Publishing, 1992), 65–66; Pearson quoted in Hofstadter, *Social Darwinism*, 185–86; Ravenstein and Marshall quoted in Cohen, *How Many People?* 161–65; Higham, *Strangers in the Land*, 146–47.

16. Joseph S. Davis, "The Specter of Dearth of Food: History's Answer to Sir William Crookes," in *Facts and Factors in Economic History* (Cambridge, MA: Harvard University Press, 1932), 733, 736; Henry J. W. Dam, "Foods in the Year 2000," *McClure's Magazine*, September 1894, 303; Atwater, "The Food-Supply of the Future"; Jeremiah Rusk, "Agriculture Can Meet All Demands," in *Today Then: 1993 as Predicted in 1893*, ed. Dave Walter (Helena, MT: American and World Geographic Publishing, 1992), 71–72.

17. Mary E. Lease, "Improvements So Extraordinary the World Will Shudder," in *Today Then: 1993 as Predicted in 1893*, ed. Dave Walter (Helena, MT: American and World Geographic Publishing, 1992), 178.

18. Fite, *American Farmers*, 30; David B. Danbom, *The Resisted Revolution: Urban America and the Industrialization of Agriculture, 1900–1930* (Ames: Iowa State University Press, 1979); Donald Worster, *Dust Bowl: The Southern Plains in the 1930s* (New York: Oxford University Press, 1979), 80–97; Warren S. Thompson, "Population: A Study in Malthusianism" (Ph.D. diss, Columbia University, 1915), 53–65.

19. Edward S. Martin, "The Population Problem," *Harper's*, November 1924, 802–5; Higham, *Strangers in the Land*, 264–99; Daniel Bluestone, "The Pushcart Evil," in *The Landscape of Modernity: New York City, 1900–1940*, ed. David Ward and Olivier Zunz (Baltimore: Johns Hopkins University, 1992), 287–312; Terry Smith, *Making the Modern: Industry, Art and Design in America* (Chicago: University of Chicago Press, 1993), 1–14.

20. Edward Alsworth Ross, "Population Pressure and War," *Scribner's Magazine*, September 1927, 357; J. M. Keynes, *The Economic Consequences of the Peace* (New York: Harcourt Brace, 1920), 15, 24; Walter B. Pitkin, *Must We Fight Japan?* (New York: Century, 1921); Takaki, *Strangers from a Different Shore*, 197–212.

21. U.S. Department of Agriculture, *Agricultural Yearbook, 1923* (Washington, DC: Government Printing Office, 1924), 481–82, 494; "Agricultural Production and the Population of the United States," *Science News*, October 23, 1925, x; Edward M. East, *Mankind at the Crossroads* (New York: Charles Scrib-

ner's Sons, 1924), 69–70; "Fighting for Food in 1960?" *Literary Digest,* September 5, 1925, 13; Edward M. East, "Our Changing Agriculture," *Scribner's,* March 1924, 304, 301.

22. "Fighting for Food in 1960?" 13; Daniel Hall, "The Relation between Cultivated Area and Population," *Scientific Monthly,* October 1926, 360, 364; George Handley Knibbs, *The Shadow of the World's Future* (London: Ernest Benn, 1928), 26–32. As if this were not enough to worry about, Knibbs also added the concern, later echoed by Lester Brown, that a more prosperous, meat-eating Asia could threaten world grain reserves.

23. Margaret Sanger, ed., *Proceedings of the World Population Conference at Salle Centrale, Geneva, 1927* (London: Edward Arnold, 1927), 93; Jeffrey Charles, "Searching for Gold in Guacamole: California Growers Market the Avocado, 1910–1994," in *Food Nations: Selling Taste in Consumer Societies,* ed. Warren Belasco and Phillip Scranton (New York: Routledge, 2002), 143; Edward Alsworth Ross, *Standing Room Only?* (New York: Century Co., 1927), 115–16; East, *Mankind at the Crossroads,* 346–47.

24. Carole McCann, *Birth Control Politics in the United States, 1916–1945* (Ithaca: Cornell University Press, 1994); Daniel J. Kevles, *In the Name of Eugenics: Genetics and the Uses of Human Heredity* (New York: Knopf, 1985).

25. Alonzo E. Taylor, "Agricultural Capacity and Population Increase," in *Population Problems in the United States and Canada,* ed. Louis Dublin (Boston: Houghton Mifflin, 1926), 107, 110.

26. Raymond Pearl, "The Biology of Death," *Atlantic Monthly,* September 1921, 201; idem, *The Nation's Food: A Statistical Study of a Physiological and Social Problem* (Philadelphia: W. B. Saunders, 1920), 17.

27. East, *Mankind at the Crossroads,* viii, 56–57, 68–70, 160–68.

28. John C. Burnham, *How Superstition Won and Science Lost: Popularizing Science and Health in the United States* (New Brunswick: Rutgers University Press, 1987); Edwin E. Slosson, *Creative Chemistry* (New York: Century Co., 1919), 10; idem, "The Expansion of Chemistry," *Industrial and Engineering Chemistry,* May 1924, 447–50; Crookes quoted in Davis, "The Specter of Dearth of Food," 754; anonymous, "The Future of America: A Biological Forecast," *Harper's Magazine,* April 1928, 533; ACS president quoted in "The Chemist and the Food Supply," *Science-Supplement,* August 10, 1928, xii.

29. Levenstein, *Revolution at the Table,* 147–60; Jack R. Kloppenburg, *First the Seed: The Political Economy of Plant Biotechnology, 1492–2000* (Cambridge: Cambridge University Press, 1988), 153; Vernon Kellogg, "When Cabbages Are Kings," *World's Work,* May 1925, 53; J. Russell Smith, *The World's Food Resources* (New York: Henry Holt, 1919), 177.

30. Worster, *Dust Bowl,* 91–92, 187; Davis, "The Specter of Dearth of Food," 740; Stoll, *Fruits of Natural Advantage,* 158; Donald Worster, *Rivers of Empire: Water, Aridity, and the Growth of the American West* (New York: Pantheon, 1985); 191–256; Carey McWilliams, *Factories in the Fields: The Story of Migratory Farm Labor in California* (Berkeley: University of California Press, 2000), 185–200; Fite, *American Farmers,* 66–79.

31. Wheeler McMillen, *Too Many Farmers: The Story of What Is Here and Ahead in Agriculture* (New York: William Morrow, 1929), 332; Kloppenburg,

First the Seed, 87; Baker quoted in Stoll, *Fruits of Natural Advantage*, 157; Davis, "The Specter of Dearth of Food," 752; Oliver Baker, "The Trend of Agricultural Production in North America," in *Population*, ed. Corrado Gini et al. (Chicago: University of Chicago Press, 1930), 280.

32. Enid Charles, *Twilight of Parenthood: A Biological Study of the Decline of Population Growth* (London: Watts & Co., 1934), 105; Winston Churchill, "Fifty Years Hence," *Popular Mechanics*, March 1932, 396; Oliver E. Baker, "The Population Prospect," *Scientific Monthly*, August 1934, 167–68; National Resources Board, *A Report on National Planning and Public Works in Relation to Natural Resources and including Land Use and Water Resources* (Washington, DC: Government Printing Office, 1934), 8–9. For egalitarian politics, see Elmer Leslie McDowell, "The American Standard of Living," *North American Review*, January 1934, 71–75; Harvey Levenstein, *Paradox of Plenty: A Social History of Eating in Modern America* (New York: Oxford University Press, 1993), 53–63; Janet Poppendieck, *Sweet Charity? Emergency Food and the End of Entitlement* (New York: Viking, 1998), 13–14, 143–47; Peter Eisinger, *Toward an End to Hunger in America* (Washington, DC: Brookings Institution, 1998), 42.

33. Oliver E. Baker, Ralph Borsodi, and M. L. Wilson, *Agriculture in Modern Life* (New York: Harper, 1939), 151; Paul B. Sears, *Deserts on the March*, 3rd ed. (Norman: University of Oklahoma Press, 1959), 7–9; Carl Sauer, "The Prospect for Redistribution of Population," in *Limits of Land Settlement*, ed. Isaiah Bowman (New York: Council on Foreign Relations, 1937), 16; J. Russell Smith and M. Ogden Phillips, *North America: Its People and the Resources, Development, and Prospects of the Continent as the Home of Man* (New York: Harcourt Brace and World, 1940), 957; Worster, *Dust Bowl*, 186.

34. Paul K. Conkin, *Tomorrow a New World: The New Deal Community Program* (Ithaca: Cornell University Press, 1959); Baker, Borsodi, and Wilson, *Agriculture in Modern Life*, 5.

35. C. C. Furnas, *America's Tomorrow: An Informal Excursion into the Era of the Two-Hour Working Day* (New York: Funk & Wagnalls, 1932), 47–48; William J. Hale, *The Farm Chemurgic: Farmward the Star of Destiny Lights Our Way* (Boston: Stratford, 1934), iii; idem, *Chemistry Triumphant: The Rise and Reign of Chemistry in a Chemical World* (Baltimore: Williams & Wilkins, 1932). For other corporate rationalists, see O. W. Willcox, *Reshaping Agriculture* (New York: W. W. Norton, 1934); Harold Pinches, "Engineering's Biggest Job," *Yale Review* 27 (spring 1938): 496–515.

36. First Earl of Birkenhead [Frederick Edward Smith], *The World in 2030 AD* (London: Hodder & Stoughton, 1930), 18–20; Churchill, "Fifty Years Hence," 397.

37. Smith, *Making the Modern;* William E. Akin, *Technocracy and the American Dream* (Berkeley: University of California Press, 1977); George W. Gray, *The Advancing Front of Science* (New York: McGraw-Hill, 1937); Roger Burlingame, *Engines of Democracy: Inventions and Society in Mature America* (New York: Charles Scribner's Sons, 1940); Robert W. Rydell, *World of Fairs: The Century-of-Progress Expositions* (Chicago: University of Chicago Press, 1993); Worster, *Dust Bowl*, 182–230.

38. Worster, *Dust Bowl*, 182; John D. Black, *Food Enough* (Lancaster, PA:

Jacques Cattell Press, 1943); Joseph J. Spengler, "The World's Hunger—Malthus, 1948," *Food: Proceedings of the Academy of Political Science* 23 (January 1949): 67; M. K. Bennett, "Population and Food Supply: The Current Scare," *Scientific Monthly* (January 1949), 17; Warren S. Thompson, *Population Problems,* 3rd ed. (New York: McGraw-Hill, 1942). As British Lord Simon of Wythenshawe put it, "These extra mouths may be a danger for the future comparable to the danger of the hydrogen bomb." See "The Population Bomb," *Population Bulletin,* July 1954, 67. For general background on postwar food and population jitters, see Perkins, *Geopolitics and the Green Revolution,* 118–48.

39. Joseph S. Davis, *The Population Upsurge in the United States,* War-Peace Pamphlet no. 12 (Stanford: Stanford University Food Research Institute, December 1949), 18, 37, 67. For similar uncertainties, see Harold Dorn, "Pitfalls in Population Forecasts and Projections," *Journal of the American Statistical Association* 45 (September 1950): 311–34.

40. William Vogt, *Road to Survival* (New York: William Sloane Associates, 1948); Fairfield Osborn, *Our Plundered Planet* (Boston: Little, Brown & Co., 1948), 31. For a taste of 1948, in addition to Osborn and Vogt, see Halbert L. Dunn, "Are There Too Many People in the World?" *Hygeia,* February 1948, 114–41; C. Lester Walker, "Too Many People," *Harper's,* February 1948, 97–104; "Coming: A Hungry 25 Years," *Life,* April 26, 1948, 30; William L. Laurence, "Population Outgrows Food, Scientists Warn the World," *New York Times,* September 15, 1948, 1.

41. On the "beefsteak election," see Levenstein, *Paradox of Plenty,* 98–100; Vogt, *Road to Survival,* 63, 286.

42. Frank A. Pearson and Floyd A. Harper, *The World's Hunger* (Ithaca: Cornell University Press, 1945), 69, 61; Whelpton quoted in Walker, "Too Many People," 102.

43. Frederick J. Stare, "Fiasco in Food," *Atlantic,* January 1948, 21; Frank G. Boudreau, "Nutrition as a World Problem," *Transactions of the New York Academy of Sciences,* series 2, v. 8 (January 1946): 119; "Coming: A Hungry 25 Years," 30.

44. Robert M. Salter, "World Soil and Fertilizer Resources in Relation to Food Needs," *Science,* May 23, 1947, 533–38; John Donald Black and Maxine Enlow Kiefer, *Future Food and Agriculture Policy: A Program for the Next Ten Years* (New York: McGraw-Hill, 1948), 66–67; Edgar Taschdjian, "Problems of Food Production," *Bulletin of the Atomic Scientists,* August 1951, 210; *A Water Policy for the American People; The Report of the President's Water Resources Policy Commission* (Washington, DC: Government Printing Office, December 1950), 149–64; *Grain Market Features,* August 25, 1948, quoted in M. K. Bennett, "Population and Food Supply," 17.

45. Vogt, *Road to Survival,* 284, 194, 35, 279, 209.

46. Eisenhower quoted in Bennett, "Population and Food Supply," 17–19; Conrad Taeuber, "Some Sociological Problems in the Work of the FAO," *American Sociological Review* 13 (December 1948): 653–59; John Boyd-Orr, *The White Man's Dilemma: Food and the Future* (London: George Allen and Unwin, 1953), 1–51. On postwar famine concerns, see Amy Bentley, *Eating for Victory:*

NOTES TO PAGES 42-43 / 279

Food Rationing and the Politics of Domesticity (Urbana: University of Illinois Press, 1998), 143–70.

47. Marjorie Van de Water, "More Mouths Than Food," *Science News Letter,* October 18, 1947, 250; Sir Gladwyn Jebb (1950) quoted by Guy Irving Burch, "A Winning Program for Democracy," *Population Bulletin,* November 1950, 3; *Senior Scholastic* (1951) quoted by John R. Wilmoth and Patrick Ball, "The Population Debate in American Popular Magazines, 1946–1990," *Population and Development Review* 18 (December 1992): 646. On birth control advocacy during the Cold War, see Wilmoth and Ball, "The Population Debate"; James Reed, *The Birth Control Movement and American Society: From Private Vice to Public Virtue* (Princeton: Princeton University Press, 1978), 281–88; Phyllis Tilson Piotrow, *World Population Crisis: The United States Response* (New York: Praeger, 1973); Richard Symonds and Michael Carder, *The United Nations and the Population Question, 1945–1970* (New York: McGraw-Hill, 1973); Allan Chase, *The Legacy of Malthus: The Social Costs of the New Scientific Racism* (New York: Knopf, 1977); Linda Gordon, *Woman's Body, Woman's Right: A Social History of Birth Control in America* (New York: Penguin, 1977), 391–402. It is a telling indicator of how little notice had been paid to food history that food insecurity is barely mentioned in any of these early works.

48. H. H. Bennett quoted by Donald Worster, *The Wealth of Nature: Environmental History and the Ecological Imagination* (New York: Oxford University Press, 1993), 77; "Better Grass Will Give More Food for Defense," *Science News Letter,* June 9, 1951, 360; Weaver quoted by Perkins, *Geopolitics and the Green Revolution,* 138.

49. Sir Henry Tizard quoted in "Famine Danger Foreseen," *Science News Letter,* September 18, 1948, 179.

50. Examples of this optimistic conservatism are M. K. Bennett, "Population and Food Supply"; Black and Kiefer, *Future Food and Agricultural Policy;* E. C. Stakman, "Science in the Service of Agriculture," *Scientific Monthly,* February 1949, 75–83; U.S. Bureau of Agricultural Economics, *Long-Range Agricultural Policy* (Washington, DC: Government Printing Office, 1948); U.S. Department of Agriculture, *Crops in Peace and War: Yearbook of Agriculture 1950–1951* (Washington, DC: Government Printing Office, 1950); John D. Black, "Population and Scarce Food Resources," in *Studies in Population,* ed. George R. Mair (Princeton: Princeton University Press, 1949), 51–65.

51. Jan Hasbrouck, "A Hungry World Looks to the U.S. Wheatbowl," *New Republic,* August 25, 1947, 13–14; Jan Hasbrouck, "Planning an Ever Normal Diet," *New Republic,* October 27, 1947, 13–15; H. E. Babcock, "Surplus Food? There's No Such Animal," *Saturday Evening Post,* July 19, 1947, 28–29; USDA, *Yearbook, 1950–51,* 1–48; Ernest Havemann, "The Great Glut," *Life,* March 20, 1950, 116–24; "Too Much," *New Republic,* July 17, 1950, 8; Levenstein, *Paradox of Plenty,* 144–59.

52. Bennett, "Population and Food Supply," 25; Boyd-Orr, *White Man's Dilemma,* 79; Egon Glesinger, *The Coming Age of Wood* (New York: Simon and Schuster, 1949), 133. Turning wood pulp into feed and food was, indeed, a favorite theme of USDA yearbooks, although the USDA's motives were often more

short-term—to find marketable uses for waste and surpluses, see, for example, USDA, *Yearbook, 1950–51,* 886.

53. Jacob Rosin and Max Eastman, *The Road to Abundance* (New York: McGraw-Hill, 1953), 9, 57; "Go Deep for Food," *Science News Letter,* November 4, 1950, 291. For more on this subject, see part III.

54. Will Durant, *The Story of Philosophy* (New York: Simon and Schuster, 1926), 142; Brittain, *Let There Be Bread* (New York: Simon and Schuster, 1952), 219–29; E. C. Stakman, "Science in the Service of Agriculture," *Scientific Monthly,* February 1949, 83; Victor Cohn, *1999: Our Hopeful Future* (Indianapolis: Bobbs-Merrill, 1956), 168.

55. Whitney R. Cross, "The Road to Conservation," *Antioch Review* 8 (December 1948): 437.

56. William Vogt, "No Bread, No Circuses," *Saturday Review,* March 13, 1954, 13; Warren S. Thompson, "Some Reflections on World Population and Food Supply during the Next Few Decades," in *Studies in Population,* ed. George R. Mair (Princeton: Princeton University Press, 1949), 84–85, 81, 92.

57. Harrison Brown, *The Challenge of Man's Future* (New York: Viking Press, 1954), 147, 219.

58. Stakman, "Science in the Service of Agriculture," 78; A Richard Crabb, *The Hybrid Corn-Makers: Prophets of Plenty* (New Brunswick: Rutgers University Press, 1947); Kloppenburg, *First the Seed,* 5–6, 91–129; Jack Doyle, *Altered Harvest: Agriculture, Genetics, and the Fate of the World's Food Supply* (New York: Penguin, 1986), 32–45; *A Water Policy for the American People,* 157; H. R. Trolley, "Population and Food Supply," in *Freedom from Want: A Survey of the Possibilities of Meeting the World's Food Needs,* ed. E. E. DeTurk (New York: Chronica Botanica, 1948), 218–20.

59. "Antibiotics in the Barnyard," *Fortune,* March 1952, 139; Albert Abarbanel, "Out of the Test Tube," *Science Digest,* June 1952, 1–5; "Special Protein Wanted," *Science News Letter,* August 28, 1954, 142; "Meatless Diet Adequate," *Science News Letter,* February 2, 1952, 70.

60. T. C. Byerly, "Role of Genetics in Adapting Animals to Meet Changing Requirements for Human Food," *Scientific Monthly,* November 1954, 323; "A Triumph and an Obligation," *Life,* January 3, 1955, 2.

61. Symonds and Carder, *The United Nations and the Population Question,* 79; P. V. Sukhatme, "The World's Hunger and Future Needs in Food Supplies," *Journal of the Royal Statistical Society* 124 (1961): 499; Edgar Ansel Mowrer, "Sawdust, Seaweed, and Synthetics; The Hazards of Crowding," *Saturday Review,* December 8, 1956, 11 ff; Harrison Brown, James Bonner, and John Weir, *The Next Hundred Years* (New York: Viking Press, 1957), 69; P. K. Whelpton (interview), "Too Many People in the World?" *U.S. News and World Report,* July 13, 1956, 80.

62. Mowrer, "Sawdust," 54; Piotrow, *World Population Crisis,* 36–42; Peter J. Donaldson, *Nature against Us: The United States and the World Population Crisis, 1965–1990* (Chapel Hill: University of North Carolina Press, 1990), 23–25.

63. Harrison Brown, "The Next Ninety Years," in *The Next Ninety Years: Proceedings of a Conference Sponsored by the Office for Industrial Associates*

at the California Institute of Technology, March 7–8, 1967 (Pasadena: California Institute of Technology, 1967), 8–9; James Bonner, "The Next Ninety
Years," in The Next Ninety Years, 37, 41. Compare this with Bonner's relative
optimism in 1957 in Brown, Bonner, and Weir, The Next Hundred Years, 70–81.

64. William Paddock and Paul Paddock, Famine—1975! America's Decision:
Who Will Survive? (Boston: Little, Brown & Co., 1967), 7–39, 56, 209, 211. For
a taste of the looming apocalypse, see Wilmoth and Ball, "Population Debate,"
648; Abe Peck, Uncovering the Sixties: The Life and Times of the Underground
Press (New York: Pantheon Books, 1985); Todd Gitlin, The Sixties: Years of Hope,
Days of Rage (New York: Bantam, 1987); David Caute, The Year of the Barri-
cades: A Journey through 1968 (New York: Perennial, 1988). For how this influ-
enced countercultural food practices, see Warren Belasco, Appetite for Change:
How the Counterculture Took on the Food Industry (Ithaca: Cornell University
Press, 1993), 1–108.

65. Paul R. Ehrlich, "Eco-Catastrophe!" in The Environmental Handbook,
ed. Garrett De Bell (New York: Ballantine Books, 1970), 161–76; idem, The Population Bomb (New York: Ballantine Books, 1968); Michael Smith, "The Short
Life of a Dark Prophecy: The Rise and Fall of the 'Population Bomb' Crisis," in
Fear Itself: Enemies Real and Imagined in American Culture, ed. Nancy Lusignan Schultz (West Lafayette: Purdue University Press, 1999), 343; Wilmoth and
Ball, "Population Debate," 636–37; "A Thoughtful New Student Cause: Crusade
against Too Many People," Life, April 17, 1970, 31 ff.

66. Lester R. Brown, Seeds of Change: The Green Revolution and Development in the 1970s (New York: Praeger, 1970), x; Luther R. Carter, "World Food
Supply: Problems and Prospects," Science, January 6, 1967, 56–57; Rex F. Daly,
"Food Enough for the U.S.? A Crystal Ball Look Ahead," in Food for Us All:
The Yearbook of Agriculture 1969 (Washington, DC: Government Printing Office,
1969), 87–90; Donella H. Meadows et al., The Limits to Growth: A Report of
the Club of Rome's Project on the Predicament of Mankind (New York: Universe Books, 1972).

67. National Academy of Sciences—National Research Council, Committee
on Resources and Man, Resources and Man (San Francisco: W. H. Freeman,
1969), 1–19.

68. Norman Borlaug, "The Green Revolution, Peace and Humanity," Nobel
Peace Prize acceptance lecture, Oslo, Norway, December 11, 1970, quoted in
Derek Tribe, Feeding and Greening the World: The Role of International Agri-
cultural Research (Oxford: CAB International, 1994), 16; Brown, Seeds of
Change, 12.

69. Herman Kahn et al., The Next 200 Years: A Scenario for America and
the World (New York: William Morrow, 1976), 106–35; Barbara Ford, Future
Food: Alternative Protein for the Year 2000 (New York: William Morrow, 1978),
28, 167–87.

70. Edward Fried and Charles Schultz, eds., Higher Oil Prices and the World
Economy: The Adjustment Problem (Washington, DC: Brookings Institution,
1975), 1–2; Fite, American Farmers, 201–3; Greg Critser, Fat Land: How Americans Became the Fattest People in the World (New York: Houghton Mifflin,
2003), 7–29.

71. Meadows et al., *The Limits to Growth;* Cohen, *How Many People?* 121–22, 68, 179, 183–90, 41; Donaldson, *Nature against Us,* 26; Paul Ehrlich and John P. Holdren, "8,000,000,000 People: We'll Never Get There," *Development Forum,* April 1976, reprinted in *The Feeding Web: Issues in Nutritional Ecology,* ed. Joan Dye Gussow (Palo Alto: Bull Publishing, 1978), 35–38.

72. Cohen, *How Many People?* 68; Wilmoth and Ball, "The Population Debate," 635, 661; Worldwatch Institute, *Vital Signs 2003* (New York: W. W. Norton, 2003), 29, 31.

73. Susan D. Moeller, *Compassion Fatigue: How the Media Sell Disease, Famine, War and Death* (New York: Routledge, 1999), 1–53, 97–155.

74. Thomas Hine, *Populuxe: The Look and Life of America in the '50s and '60s, from Tailfins and TV Dinners to Barbie Dolls and Fallout Shelters* (New York: Knopf, 1990). See part III for a more extended discussion of this theme.

75. David Pimentel and Mario Giampieto, "Food, Land, Population and the U.S. Economy," (Washington, DC: Carrying Capacity Network, November 21, 1994), accessed July 22, 2003, from http://dieoff.org/page40.htm; David Pimentel and Marcia Pimentel, "Land, Energy and Water: The Constraints Governing Ideal U.S. Population Size," *NPG Forum,* spring 1991, accessed May 14, 2003, from http://dieoff.org/page136.htm; Henry W. Kindall and David Pimentel, "Constraints on the Expansion of the Global Food Supply," *Ambio* 23 (May 1994), accessed July 22, 2003, from http://dieoff.org/page36.htm; David Pimentel and Marcia Pimentel, "Population Growth, Environmental Resources and the Global Availability of Food," *Social Research* 66 (winter 1998): 426.

76. Lester R. Brown and Hal Kane, *Full House: Reassessing the Earth's Population Carrying Capacity* (New York: W. W. Norton, 1994), 23, 202; Lester R. Brown, *Who Will Feed China? Wake-Up Call for a Small Planet* (New York: W. W. Norton, 1995).

77. Frances Moore Lappé, Joseph Collins, and Peter Rosset, *World Hunger: Twelve Myths,* 2nd updated and revised edition (New York: Grove Press, 1998), 58–84, 164–65; Peter Rosset et al., "Myths and Root Causes: Hunger, Population, and Development," *Food First Backgrounder* 1 (fall 1994): 8.

78. Paul E. Waggoner, *How Much Land Can Ten Billion People Spare for Nature?* (Ames, IA: Council for Agricultural Science and Technology, 1994).

79. Joseph F. Coates, John B. Mahaffie, and Andy Hines, *2025: Scenarios of US and Global Society Reshaped by Science and Technology* (Greensboro, NC: Oakhill Press, 1997), 361–99.

80. Norman Myers and Julian Simon, *Scarcity or Abundance? A Debate on the Environment* (New York: W. W. Norton, 2002), 13, 124, 174; Ed Regis, "The Doomslayer," *Wired Archive,* February 1997, accessed July 22, 2003, from www.wired.com/wired/archive/5.02/ffsimon_pr.html; Julian Simon, *The State of Humanity* (Boston: Basil Blackwell, 1995).

THREE. THE DEEP STRUCTURE OF THE DEBATE

1. Donald Worster, *Nature's Economy: A History of Ecological Ideas* (Cambridge: Cambridge University Press, 1985), 345; I. F. Clarke, *The Pattern of Expectation, 1644–2001* (New York: Basic Books, 1979); Howard E. McCurdy,

Space and the American Imagination (Washington, DC: Smithsonian Institution Press, 1997), 1–6; John Boyd-Orr, *The White Man's Dilemma: Food and the Future* (London: George Allen and Unwin, 1953), 29. Similarly, John Wilmoth and Patrick Ball cite enduring "argumentative frames" in their content analysis of the population debate, "The Population Debate in American Popular Magazines, 1946–1990," *Population and Development Review* 18 (December 1992): 639.

2. Thomas Malthus, *An Essay on the Principle of Population* (1798; London: Penguin, 1985), 78; Frank E. Manuel, *The Prophets of Paris: Turgot, Condorcet, Saint-Simon, Fourier, and Comte* (New York: Harper Torchbooks, 1965), 66–67; J. M. Keynes, *The Economic Consequences of the Peace* (New York: Harcourt Brace, 1920), 15.

3. William Vogt, *Road to Survival* (New York: William Sloane Associates, 1948), 285, 63; Edward M. East, *Mankind at the Crossroads* (New York: Charles Scribner's Sons, 1924), 64; William Paddock and Paul Paddock, *Famine—1975! America's Decision: Who Will Survive?* (Boston: Little, Brown & Co., 1967), 9–11; Lester R. Brown, *Tough Choices: Facing the Challenge of Food Scarcity* (New York: W. W. Norton, 1996), 44–45.

4. Will Durant, *The Story of Philosophy* (New York: Simon and Schuster, 1926), 123; Harrison Brown interview with Bernard Kalb, *Saturday Review,* March 20, 1954, 14; Kirk S. Smith et al., *Earth and the Human Future: Essays in Honor of Harrison Brown* (Boulder: Westview, 1986).

5. William H. Brock, *Justus Von Liebig: The Chemical Gatekeeper* (Cambridge: Cambridge University Press, 1997). For the writings of other futurists mentioned in this paragraph in the chapter, see earlier notes and bibliography.

6. Brock, *Justus Von Liebig;* Joseph S. Davis, "The Specter of Dearth of Food: History's Answer to Sir William Crookes," in *Facts and Factors in Economic History* (Cambridge, MA: Harvard University Press, 1932), 733–36; Josue De Castro, *The Geography of Hunger* (Boston: Little, Brown and Co., 1952); Boyd-Orr, *White Man's Dilemma,* 79; Garrett Hardin, *Living within Limits: Ecology, Economics, and Population Taboos* (New York: Oxford University Press, 1993), 15.

7. Harvey Brooks, "Technology-Related Catastrophes: Myth and Reality," in *Visions of Apocalypse: End or Rebirth?* ed. Saul Friedlander et al. (New York: Holmes and Meier, 1985), 109. The professional-activist distinction comes from Phyllis Tilson Piotrow's discussion of birth control activists in *World Population Crisis: The United States Response* (New York: Praeger, 1973), xiv. For how hunger activists use the word "emergency" to gain public attention, see Janet Poppendieck, *Sweet Charity? Emergency Food and the End of Entitlement* (New York: Penguin, 1998), 96–98.

8. J. R. Smith, "Shall the World Starve?" *Country Gentleman,* June 9, 1917, 3–4; Paul B. Sears, *Deserts on the March,* 3rd ed. (Norman: University of Oklahoma Press, 1959); John Boyd-Orr, *The White Man's Dilemma: Food and the Future* (London: George Allen and Unwin, 1953); Karl Sax, *Standing Room Only: The Challenge of Overpopulation* (Boston: Beacon Press, 1953); Lester Brown, Christopher Flavin, and Sandra Postel, *Saving the Planet: How to Shape an Environmentally Sustainable Global Economy* (New York: W. W. Norton, 1991); Lester Brown and Hal Kane, *Full House: Reassessing the Earth's Population Car-*

rying Capacity (New York: W. W. Norton, 1994); Lester Brown, *Who Will Feed China? Wake-Up Call for a Small Planet* (New York: W. W. Norton, 1995); idem, *Tough Choices: Facing the Challenge of Food Scarcity* (New York: W. W. Norton, 1996).

9. O. E. Baker, "Land Utilization in the United States: Geographical Aspects of the Problem," *Geographical Review* 13 (January 1923): 1, 4. Frank Manuel writes that the great cornucopian "crisis philosophers" of the eighteenth and nineteenth centuries—Turgot, Condorcet, Saint-Simon, and Comte—invariably "saw mankind at the crossroads" and their moment as "the instant of the great divide." Manuel, *The Prophets of Paris,* 5–6.

10. David Pimentel and Marcia Pimentel, "U.S. Food Production Threatened by Rapid Population Growth," October 30, 1997, accessed July 24, 2003, at www.ecofuture.org/pop/reports.html#usfoodpimentel; East, *Mankind at the Crossroads,* 167; Paul R. Ehrlich, "Eco-Catastrophe!" in *The Environmental Handbook,* ed. Garrett De Bell (New York: Ballantine Books, 1970), 167; Brock, *Justus Von Liebieg,* 178; Edwin Teale, "New Foods from the Test Tube," *Popular Science Monthly,* July 1934, 13, 112.

11. Vogt, *Road to Survival,* 78; Derek Tribe, *Feeding and Greening the World: The Role of International Agricultural Research* (Oxford: CAB International, 1994), 25. See also Gordon Conway, *The Doubly Green Revolution: Food for All in the 21st Century* (Ithaca: Cornell University Press, 1998); Marion Nestle, *Safe Food: Bacteria, Biotechnology, and Bioterrorism* (Berkeley: University of California Press, 2003), 139–66; Daniel Charles, *Lords of the Harvest: Biotech, Big Money, and the Future of Food* (Cambridge, MA: Perseus Publishing, 2001), 262–82.

12. Joel E. Cohen, *How Many People Can the Earth Support?* (New York: W. W. Norton, 1995), 164, 172; William Reville, "Is There a World Population Crisis?" *Irish Times,* August 10, 1998, 5; Peter Vitousek, Paul R. Ehrlich, Anne H. Ehrlich, and Pamela Matson, "Human Appropriation of the Products of Photosynthesis," *BioScience* 36 (June 1986), accessed July 24, 2003, from http://dieoff .org/page83.htm; Joseph A. Amato, *Dust: A History of the Small and the Invisible* (Berkeley: University of California Press, 2000), 108, 142.

13. Garrett Hardin, *Living within Limits* (New York: Oxford University Press, 1993), 18; Robert Heilbroner, *The Worldly Philosophers* (New York: Simon & Schuster, 1961), 61–72; Lester R. Brown, "Facing Food Scarcity," *World Watch,* November/December 1995, 10–20; "Will the World Starve?" *The Economist,* November 16, 1996, 21–23; "Environmental Scares: Plenty of Gloom," *The Economist,* December 20, 1997, 19–21. The best overall critique of these statistical fallacies is Cohen, *How Many People?*; also, Vaclav Smil, *Feeding the World: A Challenge for the Twenty-First Century* (Cambridge, MA: MIT Press, 2000), 1–21.

14. Peter Eisinger, *Toward an End to Hunger in America* (Washington, DC: Brookings Institution, 1998), 80; Donald Worster, *Nature's Economy* (Cambridge: Cambridge University Press, 1985), 291–315. For the pitfalls of recent famine coverage, see Susan Moeller, *Compassion Fatigue: How the Media Sell Disease, Famine, War, and Death* (New York: Routledge, 1999). On nineteenth-century press attention, see Mike Davis, *Late Victorian Holocausts: El Niño Famines and the Making of the Third World* (London: Verso, 2001).

15. Peter Eisinger, *Toward an End to Hunger in America*, 80; Norman Myers and Julian Simon, *Scarcity or Abundance? A Debate on the Environment* (New York: W. W. Norton, 1994), 120, 136; Peter Weber, *Abandoned Seas: Reversing the Decline of the Oceans*, Worldwatch Paper 116 (Washington, DC: Worldwatch Institute, November 1993); Lester R. Brown, Gary Gardner, and Brian Halweil, *Beyond Malthus: Sixteen Dimensions of the Population Problem*, Worldwatch Paper 143 (Washington, DC: Worldwatch Institute, September 1998); Raymond Pearl, "The Population Problem," *Geographical Review* 12 (October 1922), 636–45; Edwin E. Slosson, "The Expansion of Chemistry," *Industrial and Engineering Chemistry*, May 1924, 447–50.

16. Joseph S. Davis, "The Specter of Dearth of Food: History's Answer to Sir William Crookes," in *Facts and Factors in Economic History* (Cambridge, MA: Harvard University Press, 1932), 736–37; Jeffrey M. Pilcher, *Que Vivan los Tamales! Food and the Making of Mexican Identity* (Albuquerque: University of New Mexico Press, 1998); Larry Zuckerman, *The Potato: How the Humble Spud Rescued the Western World* (New York: North Point Press, 1998); E. Melanie DuPuis, *Nature's Perfect Food: How Milk Became America's Drink* (New York: New York University Press, 2002).

17. M. K. Bennett, "Population and Food Supply: The Current Scare," *Scientific Monthly*, January 1949, 17–26; T. T. Poleman, "World Food: A Perspective," *Science*, May 9, 1975, 510–18; J. C. Waterlow, "Needs for Food: Are We Asking Too Much?" in *Feeding a World Population of More Than Eight Billion People*, ed. J. C. Waterlow et al. (New York: Oxford University Press, 1998), 3–15. On the politics of hunger, see Harvey Levenstein, *Paradox of Plenty: A Social History of Eating in Modern America* (New York: Oxford University Press, 1993), 144–59. On changing dietary advice, Marion Nestle, *Food Politics: How the Food Industry Influences Nutrition and Health* (Berkeley: University of California Press, 2002).

18. Sidney W. Mintz, *Sweetness and Power: The Place of Sugar in Modern History* (New York: Penguin, 1986), 190–91; Cohen, *How Many People?* 171, 161–236. For an excellent commodity chain audit, see Brian Halweil, *Eat Here: Reclaiming Homegrown Pleasures in a Global Supermarket* (New York: W. W. Norton, 2004).

19. John Bongaarts, "Population: Ignoring Its Impact," *Scientific American*, January 2002, 67; East, *Mankind at the Crossroads*, 68–70; Hardin, *Living within Limits*, 122–23, 208; Cohen, *How Many People?* 354–55.

20. Hardin, *Living within Limits*, 264; Edward Alsworth Ross, *Standing Room Only?* (New York: Century Co., 1927), 116.

21. Cohen, *How Many People?* 261–96 (italics added).

22. Smil, *Feeding the World*, 1–6.

23. East, *Mankind at the Crossroads*, 172; USDA, *Agricultural Yearbook, 1923* (Washington, DC: Government Printing Office, 1924), 467; Gilbert C. Fite, *American Farmers: The New Minority* (Bloomington: Indiana University Press, 1984), 115, 185; Jonathan Harris, *World Agriculture and the Environment* (New York: Garland Publishing, 1990), 10; Brown, Gardner, and Hallweil, *Beyond Malthus*, 13; "Environmental Scares," 20.

24. Jevons 1865 quoted in Hardin, *Living within Limits*, 134; Robert J. Mc-

Fall, "Is Food the Limiting Factor in Population Growth?" *Yale Review* 15 (January 1926): 297; "Predictors of Global Famine Have Had to Eat Their Words," *Sacramento Bee,* June 18, 1995, FO6; "Will the World Starve?" *The Economist,* June 10, 1995, 39; "Environmental Scares," 19; "Will the World Starve?" *The Economist,* November 16, 1996, 21-23; "A Raw Deal for Commodities," *The Economist,* April 17, 1999, 76; Myers and Simon, *Scarcity or Abundance?* 123.

25. Malthus, *Population,* 107, 241; Raymond Pearl, "The Biology of Death," *Atlantic Monthly,* September 1921, 210; Ross, *Standing Room Only?* vii; Vogt, *Road to Survival,* 208; Georg Borgstrom, *The Food and People Dilemma* (North Scituate, MA: Duxbury Press, 1973), 3; Fernand Braudel, *The Structures of Everyday Life* (Berkeley: University of California Press, 1992), 49; Hardin, *Living within Limits,* 17.

26. H. P. Armsby, "The Food Supply of the Future," *Science,* December 10, 1909, 818; East, *Mankind at the Crossroads,* 9, 54; idem, "Oversea Politics and the Food Supply," *Scribner's,* January 1924, 114; Vogt, *Road to Survival,* 150; Ehrlich (1970), quoted in Wilmoth and Ball, "The Population Debate in American Popular Magazines, 1946-1990," 650.

27. Malthus, *Population,* 74-93; Arthur Herman, *The Idea of Decline in Western History* (New York: Free Press, 1997), 27-28; "The Future of America: A Biological Forecast," *Harper's,* April 1928, 539; Vogt, *Road to Survival,* 151; Hardin, *Living within Limits,* 119. See also Jared Diamond, *Collapse: How Societies Choose to Fail or Succeed* (New York: Viking, 2005).

28. Henry J. W. Dam, "Foods in the Year 2000," *McClure's Magazine,* September 1894, 303-12.

29. Paddock and Paddock, *Famine—1975!* 95; Bland, quoted in Ross, *Standing Room Only,* 197.

30. Marquis de Condorcet, "The Future Progress of the Human Mind," in *Esquisse d'un Tableau Historique des Progres de L'Esprit Humain* (1794), accessed May 21, 2003 at http://ishi.lib.berkeley.edu/~hist280/research/condorcet/pages/progress_main.html; Scott Nearing, "Race Suicide vs. Overpopulation," *Popular Science Monthly,* January 1911, 83; Linda Gordon, *Woman's Body, Woman's Right: A Social History of Birth Control in America* (New York: Penguin, 1977); Frances Moore Lappé, Joseph Collins, and Peter Rosset, *World Hunger: Twelve Myths,* 2nd updated and revised edition (New York: Grove Press, 1998).

31. Frank Notestein, "The Needs of World Population," *Bulletin of the Atomic Scientists,* April 1951, 99-101; Irene B. Taeuber, "Culture, Technology, and Population Change," *Bulletin of the Atomic Scientists,* August 1951, 206-8; Frank Notestein, "Population," *Scientific American,* September 1951, 28-35.

32. Malthus, *Population,* 69; Edgar Ansel Mowrer, "Sawdust, Seaweed, and Synthetics: The Hazards of Crowding," *Saturday Review,* December 8, 1956, 11, 56; Pearl, "The Population Problem," 636-45.

33. "Warning to Mankind," *Science News Letter,* January 5, 1963, 3; *Time* (1964), cited in Wilmoth and Ball, "Population Debate," 649; Halbert L. Dunn, "Are There Too Many People in the World?" *Hygeia,* February 1948, 114; William Alexander McClung, *Landscapes of Desire: Anglo Mythologies of Los Angeles* (Berkeley: University of California Press, 2000), 51; Mike Davis, *Ecology of Fear: Los Angeles and the Imagination of Disaster* (New York: Metropolitan Books,

1998), 275–355; Worster, *Nature's Economy*, 320–21; Charlotte Perkins Gilman, *Herland* (1915; New York: Pantheon, 1979), 67.

34. McClung, *Landscapes of Desire*, 55; Borgstrom, *Food and People Dilemma*, 72; Julian Huxley, "World Population," *Scientific American*, March 1956, 66; Alan Gregg, "Is Man a Biological Cancer?" *Population Bulletin*, August 1955, 77; Hardin, *Living within Limits*, 175–77; Paul R. Ehrlich and Anne H. Ehrlich, "The Population Explosion," *Amicus Journal*, winter 1990, 29.

35. Mary P. Ryan, *Democracy and Public Life in the American City during the Nineteenth Century* (Berkeley: University of California Press, 1997), 181, 217, 214–15; Daniel Bluestone, "The Pushcart Evil," in *The Landscape of Modernity: New York City, 1900–1940*, ed. David Ward and Olivier Zunz (Baltimore: Johns Hopkins University, 1992), 287–312; Amato, *Dust*, 116; A. L. Melander, "Fighting Insects with Powder and Lead," *Scientific Monthly*, January 1933, 168–73; Irish "scalp" depicted in *Illustrated London News*, December 22, 1849, accessed July 29, 2003, from http://vassun.vassar.edu/~sttaylor/FAMINE/.

36. Enid Charles, *Twilight of Parenthood: A Biological Study of the Decline of Population Growth* (London: Watts & Co., 1934), 35; Norris Dodd, "Forward," in *Freedom from Want*, ed. E. E. DeTurk (New York: Chronica Botanica, 1948), 212. For a very sharp critique, see Allan Chase, *The Legacy of Malthus: The Social Costs of the New Scientific Racism* (New York: Knopf, 1977). Don Hinrichson, "Putting the Bite on Planet Earth: Rapid Human Population Growth Is Devouring Global Natural Resources," *International Wildlife*, September/October 1994, accessed July 29, 2003, at http://dieoff.org/page120.htm.

37. James R. Gibson, Jr. *Americans versus Malthus: The Population Debate in the Early Republic, 1790–1840* (New York: Garland, 1989), 224; Robert Brittain, *Let There Be Bread* (New York: Simon and Schuster 1952), 9, 182; Myers and Simon, *Scarcity or Abundance?* 133.

38. Condorcet, "The Future Progress of the Human Mind"; William Godwin, *Thoughts on Man, His Nature, Productions, Discoveries, Interspersed with Some Particulars Respecting the Author* (London: Effingham Wilson, 1831), 28, 77, accessed May 21, 2003 at http://dwardmac.pitzer.edu/Anarchist_Archives/godwin/thoughts/TMNPDfrontpiece.html; Lappé, Collins, and Rosset, *World Hunger*, 23, 178; Worster, *Nature's Economy*, 152, 125–29; McCurdy, *Space and the American Imagination*, 229–32; Boulding quoted in Hardin, *Living within Limits*, 58.

39. W. O. Atwater, "The Food-Supply of the Future," *The Century* 43 (November 1891): 111; J. Russell Smith, *The World's Food Resources* (New York: Henry Holt, 1919), 6, 517; Myers and Simon, *Scarcity or Abundance?* 198; Lappé, Collins, and Rosset, *World Hunger*, 85–121; W. S. Woytinsky and E. S. Woytinsky, *World Population and Production: Trends and Outlook* (New York: Twentieth Century Fund, 1953); Josue de Castro, *The Geography of Hunger* (Boston: Little, Brown and Co., 1952).

40. Cohen, *How Many People?* 365.

41. Warren S. Thompson, "Some Reflections on World Population and Food Supply during the Next Few Decades," in *Studies in Population*, ed. George R. Mair (Princeton: Princeton University Press, 1949), 83; Vogt, *Road to Survival*, 72; Harrison Brown, *The Challenge of Man's Future* (New York: Viking Press,

1954), 220; USDA, *Agricultural Yearbook, 1923,* 465; Paddock and Paddock, *Famine 1975!.*

42. Vogt, *Road to Survival,* 146. Smith, *World's Food Resources,* 592; William G. Paddock, "Can We Make the Earth Feed Us All?" *Saturday Evening Post,* October 18, 1952, 44 ff; Frank Ligett McDougall, *Food and Population* (New York: Carnegie Endowment for International Peace, 1952); Woytinsky and Woytinsky, *World Population;* Tribe, *Feeding and Greening the World;* Conway, *Doubly Green Revolution.* For a strong critique of neo-Malthusian racism, see Chase, *Legacy of Malthus.* For egalitarians, see Vandana Shiva, *The Violence of the Green Revolution: Third World Agriculture, Ecology, and Politics* (London: Zen Books, 1991); Frances Moore Lappé and Anna Lappé, *Hope's Edge: The Next Diet for a Small Planet* (New York: Jeremy P. Tarcher/Putnam, 2002); Roberto J. Gonzalez, *Zapotec Science: Farming and Food in the Northern Sierra of Oaxaca* (Austin: University of Texas Press, 2001).

43. Davis, *Late Victorian Holocausts,* 332; Shiva, *Violence of the Green Revolution;* Conway, *Doubly Green Revolution;* Angus Wright, "Innocents Abroad: American Agricultural Research in Mexico," in *Meeting the Expectations of the Land,* ed. Wes Jackson et al. (San Francisco: North Point, 1984), 135–51; David Orr, "Food Alchemy and Sustainable Agriculture," in *Ecological Literacy* (Albany: SUNY Press, 1992), 167–79; Gene Logsdon, *At Nature's Pace: Farming and the American Dream* (New York: Pantheon Books, 1994); Gonzalez, *Zapotec Science;* Gary Paul Nabhan, *Enduring Seeds: Native American Agriculture and Wild Plant Conservation* (San Francisco: North Point, 1989); Vandana Shiva, *Stolen Harvest: The Hijacking of the Global Food Supply* (Cambridge, MA: South End Press, 2000). That some of the alleged "dumbness" of poor farmers may have been deliberate resistance to modernization is suggested in John R. Stilgoe, "Plugging Past Reform: Small-Scale Farming Innovation and Big-Scale Research," in *Scientific Authority of Twentieth-Century America,* ed. Ronald G. Walters (Baltimore: Johns Hopkins University Press, 1997), 119–47.

44. Falk (1976) quoted in Joan Dye Gussow, *The Feeding Web: Issues in Nutritional Ecology* (Palo Alto: Bull Publishing, 1978), 56.

45. Brittain, *Let There Be Bread,* v; East, *Mankind at the Crossroads,* 345.

46. Guy Irving Burch and Elmer Pendell, *Human Breeding and Survival: Population Roads to Peace or War* (New York: Penguin, 1947), 23; Vogt, *Road to Survival,* 284; John McPhee, *Encounters with the Archdruid: Narratives about a Conservationist and Three of His Natural Enemies* (New York: Farrar, Straus and Giroux, 1971), 82; East, *Mankind at the Crossroads,* 186; Sandra Postel, "Carrying Capacity: Earth's Bottom Line," *State of the World 1994,* ed. Lester R. Brown et al. (New York: W. W. Norton, 1994), 4–21.

47. Ross, *Standing Room Only,* 196, 114.

48. Malthus, *Population,* 131, 201; East, *Mankind at the Crossroads,* 160, 168; Harrison Brown, *The Human Future Revisited: The World Predicament and Possible Solutions* (New York: W. W. Norton, 1978), 249; Worster, *Nature's Economy,* 246–47; Wright, "Innocents Abroad," 151.

49. Brittain, *Let There Be Bread,* 9, 223; Warren Weaver, "People, Energy, and Food," *Scientific Monthly,* June 1954, 362; Tribe, *Feeding and Greening the*

World, 54; Edward Bellamy, *Looking Backward* (1888; New York: Signet, 1960), 208, 50.

50. Eisinger, *Toward an End to Hunger in America,* 3–5; Robert Costanza, "Four Visions of the Century Ahead," *Futurist,* February 1999, 23; Thomas Vargish, "Why the Person Sitting Next to You Hates Limits to Growth," *Technological Forecasting and Social Change* 16 (1980): 179–89; Elise Boulding, "Education for Inventing the Future" (1977), quoted in Vargish, "Why the Person Sitting Next to You Hates Limits to Growth," 180.

51. As Joseph Corn and Brian Horrigan observe in *Yesterday's Tomorrows: Past Visions of the American Future,* the history of the future "is essentially a history of people attempting to project the values of the past and the present into an idealized future. It is a history of conservative action in the guise of newness" (Baltimore: Johns Hopkins University Press, 1984), 135.

52. "When the World Gets Overcrowded," *Literary Digest,* November 18, 1922, 25–26. Walter Truett Anderson, "Food without Farms: The Biotech Revolution in Agriculture," *The Futurist,* January-February 1990, 16–17; Cohen, *How Many People?* 153. Regarding the appearance of certainty: Leo Tolstoy's Prince Bagratian "tried to make it appear that everything done by necessity, by accident, or by the will of a subordinate commander was done, if not by his direct command, at least in accord with his intentions." *War and Peace* (New York: Simon and Schuster, 1942), 193.

53. Conway, *Doubly Green Revolution;* Monsanto's web page: www.monsanto.com.

54. Andy Hines, "A Checklist for Evaluating Forecasts," *Futurist,* November–December 1995, 24; Hazel Henderson, comments during debate on "The Global Environment: Megaproblem or Not?" World Futurist Society annual meeting, Washington, DC, July 18, 1996; Kathrin Day Lassila, review of *The Betrayal of Science and Reason,* by Paul Ehrlich and Anne Ehrlich, *Amicus Journal* (fall 1996): 46; Holdren's remarks in Smith, *Earth and the Human Future,* 74.

55. Archer Daniels Midland home page, accessed August 5, 2003, at www.admworld.com/; Food First home page, accessed August 5, 2003, at www.foodfirst.org.

56. Malthus, *Population,* 217.

FOUR. THE UTOPIAN CAVEAT

1. Donald Worster, *Nature's Economy: A History of Ecological Ideas* (Cambridge: Cambridge University Press, 1985), 30, 336.

2. For an introduction to the study of science fiction audiences, see Camille Bacon-Smith, *Science Fiction Culture* (Philadelphia: University of Pennsylvania Press, 2000).

3. Jean Pfaelzer, *The Utopian Novel in America: 1886–1896* (Pittsburgh: University of Pittsburgh Press, 1984), 25; Carol Farley Kessler, "Consider Her Ways: The Cultural Work of Charlotte Perkins Gilman's Pragmatorian Stories, 1908–1913," in *Utopian and Science Fiction by Women: Worlds of Difference,* ed. Jane L. Donawerth and Carol A. Kolmerten (Syracuse: Syracuse University

Press, 1994), 126–28; W. H. G. Armytage, *Yesterday's Tomorrows: A Historical Survey of Future Societies* (London: Routledge, 1968), 95; Kobe Abe, *Inter Ice Age 4* (New York: Knopf, 1970), 228; Lifton quoted in Saul Friedlander, introduction to *Visions of Apocalypse: End or Rebirth?* ed. Saul Friedlander et al. (New York: Holmes and Meier, 1985), 16; Harold L. Berger, *Science Fiction and the New Dark Age* (Bowling Green, OH: Popular Press, 1976), 202.

4. Howard E. McCurdy, *Space and the American Imagination* (Washington, DC: Smithsonian Institution Press, 1997); Jeffrey L. Meikle, *Twentieth Century Limited: Industrial Design in America, 1925–1939* (Philadelphia: Temple University Press, 1979), 185–86; Thomas Hine, *Populuxe: The Look and Life of America in the '50s and '60s, from Tailfins and TV Dinners to Barbie Dolls and Fallout Shelters* (New York: Knopf, 1990); Paul K. Conkin, *Tomorrow a New World: The New Deal Community Program* (Ithaca: Cornell University Press, 1959).

5. Pfaelzer, *Utopian Novel in America*, 6–7.

6. Kenneth Roemer, *The Obsolete Necessity: America in Utopian Writing, 1888–1900* (Kent, OH: Kent State University Press, 1976), 179; Daphne Patai, "Beyond Defensiveness: Feminist Research Strategies," in *Women and Utopia: Critical Interpretations,* ed. Marleen Barr and Nicholas Smith (Lanham, MD: University Press of America, 1983), 152; Pfaelzer, *Utopian Novel in America,* 158.

7. This summary of utopian and dystopian conventions owes much to Pfaelzer, *Utopian Novel in America;* Roemer, *Obsolete Necessity;* Armytage, *Yesterday's Tomorrows;* I. F. Clarke, *The Pattern of Expectation, 1644–2001* (New York: Basic Books, 1979); Berger, *Science Fiction;* Jane L. Donawerth and Carol A. Kolmerten, eds., *Utopian and Science Fiction by Women: Worlds of Difference* (Syracuse: Syracuse University Press, 1994); Helen Parker, *Biological Themes in Modern Science Fiction* (Ann Arbor: University of Michigan Press, 1984); Marleen Barr and Nicholas Smith, eds., *Women and Utopia: Critical Interpretations* (Lanham, MD: University Press of America, 1983); W. Warren Wagar, *Terminal Visions: The Literature of Last Things* (Bloomington: Indiana University Press, 1982); Eric Rabkin, Martin Greenberg, and Joseph Olander, eds., *The End of the World* (Carbondale: Southern Illinois Press, 1983).

8. Wagar, *Terminal Visions,* 65–67, 72.

9. Harvey Green, *Fit for America: Health, Fitness, Sport, and American Society* (New York: Pantheon, 1986); James C. Whorton, *Inner Hygiene: Constipation and the Pursuit of Health in Modern Society* (New York: Oxford University Press, 2000), 22.

10. Mike Davis, *Ecology of Fear: Los Angeles and the Imagination of Disaster* (New York: Metropolitan Books, 1998), 283–90; Clarke, *Pattern of Expectation,* 47, 157; Saul Friedlander, "Themes of Decline and End in Nineteenth-Century Imagination," in *Visions of Apocalypse: End or Rebirth?* ed. Saul Friedlander et al. (New York: Holmes and Meier, 1985), 80.

11. Clarke, *Pattern of Expectation,* 149–50; William Morris, *News from Nowhere* (1891; New York: Penguin, 1993), 53–54; Carol J. Adams, *The Sexual Politics of Meat: A Feminist-Vegetarian Critical Theory* (New York: Continuum, 1990), 108–19.

12. Roemer, *Obsolete Necessity;* Neil Harris, "Utopian Fiction and Its Discontents," in *Cultural Excursions* (Chicago: University of Chicago Press, 1990), 150–79. See also Howard P. Segal, *Technological Utopianism in American Culture* (Chicago: University of Chicago Press, 1985); Carol Farley Kessler, introduction to *Daring to Dream: Utopian Stories by U.S. Women, 1836–1919* (Boston: Pandora Press, 1984), 7–14; Clarke, *Pattern of Expectation,* 149; Pfaelzer, *Utopian Novel in America,* 72. On Howells, see Daniel Aaron, *Men of Good Hope: A Story of American Progressives* (New York: Oxford University Press, 1951), 172–207.

13. For key utopian themes of balance and unity, see Segal, *Technological Utopianism,* 16; Roemer, *Obsolete Necessity,* 134–52.

14. Anne Mendelsohn, "The Decline of the Apple," in *The New Agrarianism,* ed. Eric T. Freyfogle (Washington, DC: Shearwater Books, 2002), 111–27; Kevin Starr, *Inventing the Dream: California through the Progressive Era* (New York: Oxford University Press, 1985), 45–100; Steven Stoll, *The Fruits of Natural Advantage: Making the Industrial Countryside in California* (Berkeley: University of California Press, 1998), 7–31. For a classic analysis of American pastoralism, see, of course, Leo Marx, *The Machine in the Garden: Technology and the Pastoral Ideal in America* (New York: Oxford University Press, 1964).

15. Donald C. Burt, "The Well-Manicured Landscape: Nature in Utopia," in *America as Utopia,* ed. Kenneth M. Roemer (New York: Burt Franklin, 1981), 175–85; A. P. Russell, *Sub-Coelum: A Sky-Built Human World* (Boston: Houghton Mifflin, 1893), 91, 36.

16. Carl J. Guarneri, *The Utopian Alternative: Fourierism in Nineteenth-Century America* (Ithaca: Cornell University Press, 1991), 133, 107–8, 123.

17. Charlotte Perkins Gilman, *Herland* (1915; New York: Pantheon Books, 1979), 79–80. For other examples, see Milan C. Edson, *Solaris Farm: A Story of the 20th Century* (Washington, DC: by the author, 1900); Alex Craig, *Ionia: Land of Wise Men and Fair Women* (Chicago: E. A. Weeks, 1898). Lyman Tower Sargent uses "technological utopianism" to suggest the utopian desire to be liberated from drudgery while still living in close contact with nature. See Sargent, "A New Anarchism: Social and Political Ideas in Some Recent Feminist Eutopias," in *Women and Utopia: Critical Interpretations,* ed. Marleen Barr and Nicholas Smith (Lanham, MD: University Press of America, 1983), 31.

18. Arthur Bird, *Looking Forward* (1899; New York: Arno, 1971), 180; Burt, "Well-Manicured Landscape"; Rosalind Williams, *Notes on the Underground: An Essay on Technology, Society, and the Imagination* (Cambridge, MA: MIT Press, 1990).

19. Mary E. Bradley Lane, *Mizora: A Prophecy* (1880; Boston: Gregg Press, 1975), 19–20, 43, 21, 26; Kristin Anderson, introduction to *Mizora: A Prophecy,* by Mary E. Bradley Lane, xii–xiii (Boston: Gregg Press, 1975).

20. Edward Bellamy, *Looking Backward* (1888; New York: Signet, 1960), 131, 80–84, 107–10; Lane, *Mizora,* 50–56; Mary Griffith, "Three Hundred Years Hence" (1836), reprint in *Daring to Dream: Utopian Stories by U.S. Women, 1836–1919,* ed. Carol Farley Kessler (Boston: Pandora Press, 1984), 32–33.

21. Griffith, "Three Hundred Years Hence," 33–34; Mauricio Borrero, "Food and the Politics of Scarcity in Urban Soviet Russia, 1917–1941," in *Food*

Nations: Selling Taste in Consumer Societies, ed. Warren Belasco and Phillip Scranton (New York: Routledge, 2002), 258–76.

22. Jane Sophia Appleton, "Sequel to the Vision of Bangor in the 20th Century" (1848), reprint in *Daring to Dream: Utopian Stories by U.S. Women, 1836–1919*, ed. Carol Farley Kessler (Boston: Pandora Press, 1984), 56–58; Annie Denton Cridge, "Man's Rights; Or How Would You Like It?" (1870), reprint in *Daring to Dream: Utopian Stories by U.S. Women, 1836–1919*, ed. Carol Farley Kessler (Boston: Pandora Press, 1984), 79–88.

23. Dolores Hayden, *The Grand Domestic Revolution: A History of Feminist Designs for American Homes, Neighborhoods, and Cities* (Cambridge, MA: MIT Press. 1981), 135–36, 183–205, 231; Polly Wynn Allen, *Building Domestic Liberty: Charlotte Perkins Gilman's Architectural Feminism* (Amherst: University of Massachusetts Press, 1988), 63–71, 106–10; Gilman, *Herland*, 68–71.

24. Cridge, "Man's Rights," 78; Bradford Peck, *The World a Department Store: A Twentieth Century Utopia* (Lewiston, ME: by the author, 1900), 225, 228; Bellamy, *Looking Backward*, 113–15; Harvey Levenstein, *Revolution at the Table: The Transformation of the American Diet* (New York: Oxford University Press, 1988), 60–72; also James Harvey Sweetland, "American Utopian Fiction, 1798–1926" (Ph.D. diss., University of Notre Dame, 1976), 117–42.

25. Clarke, *Pattern of Expectation*, 156.

26. On the New Nutrition, see Levenstein, *Revolution at the Table*, 30–108; Bellamy, *Looking Backward*, 112.

27. Lane, *Mizora*, 74; Gilman, *Herland*, 47–48. Herman Hine Brinsmade, *Utopia Achieved: A Novel of the Future* (New York: Broadway Publishing Co., 1912), 15, 25, 69–71. On Fletcher, see Levenstein, *Revolution at the Table*, 87–92.

28. Warren Belasco, "Food, Morality, and Social Reform," in *Morality and Health*, ed. Allan M. Brandt and Paul Rozin (New York: Routledge, 1997), 190–92; Rebecca L. Spang, *The Invention of the Restaurant: Paris and Modern Gastronomic Culture* (Cambridge, MA: Harvard University Press, 2000), 48.

29. John Jacob Astor, *A Journey in Other Worlds* (New York: D. Appleton and Co., 1894), 46; Jules Verne, "In the Twenty-Ninth Century: The Day of an American Journalist in 2889," in *Yesterday and Tomorrow* (1889; reprint, London: Arco, 1965), 111; Hugo Gernsback, *Ralph 124C 41+* (1911; reprint, Lincoln: University of Nebraska Press, 2000), 84–87.

30. Jane L. Donawerth, "Science Fiction by Women in the Early Pulps, 1926–1930," in *Utopian and Science Fiction by Women: Worlds of Difference*, ed. Jane L. Donawerth and Carol A. Kolmerten (Syracuse: Syracuse University Press, 1994), 138–39.

31. Lane, *Mizora*, 26, vi, 47.

32. Bird, *Looking Forward*, 184–85; Mary E. Lease, "Improvements So Extraordinary the World Will Shudder," in *Today Then: America Best Minds Look 100 Years into the Future on the Occasion of the 1893 World's Columbian Exposition*, ed. Dave Walter (Helena, MT: American & World Geographic Publishing, 1992), 178; Anna Bowman Dodd, *The Republic of the Future or, Socialism a Reality,* 1887, excerpted in *The Land of Contrasts, 1880–1901*, ed. Neil Harris (New York: George Brazillier, 1970), 199; Donawerth, "Science Fiction by

Women," 138; Joseph J. Corn and Brian Horrigan, *Yesterday's Tomorrows: Past Visions of the American Future* (Baltimore: Johns Hopkins University Press, 1984), 15.

33. Dodd, *Republic of the Future,* 195, 199.

34. L. Frank Baum, *The Magic of Oz* (Chicago: Reilly & Lee Co., 1919), 236–37. On Baum's political satire, see Henry M. Littlefield, "The Wizard of Oz: Parable on Populism," *American Quarterly* 16 (spring 1964): 47–58.

FIVE. DYSTOPIAS

1. W. Warren Wagar, *The Next Three Futures: Paradigms of Things to Come* (New York: Praeger Publishers, 1991), 15–17; Edward Cornish, *The Study of the Future* (Bethesda, MD: World Future Society, 1993), 68–70.

2. H. G. Wells, *The Time Machine* (1895; reprint, New York: Penguin, 2000), 41, 32, 24, 27, 30, 78, 77, 14; Rosalind Williams, *Notes on the Underground: An Essay on Technology, Society, and the Imagination* (Cambridge, MA: MIT Press, 1990), 125.

3. H. G. Wells, *The War of the Worlds* (1898; reprint, New York: Berkley, 1964), 121.

4. H. G. Wells, *When the Sleeper Wakes* (1899, reprint in *Three Prophetic Science Fiction Novels of H. G. Wells* (New York: Dover Publications, 1960), 17, 97–98.

5. Ibid., 142–43, 97.

6. H. G. Wells, *The Food of the Gods* (1904; reprint, New York: Airmont Publishing, 1965), 73. I am especially grateful to my research assistant, Tara Tucker, for her notes on this book.

7. Ibid., 70, 99, 98.

8. Ibid., 97, 99.

9. I. F. Clarke, *The Pattern of Expectation, 1644–2001* (New York: Basic Books, 1979), 277.

10. These contrasts are highlighted in Aldous Huxley's 1958 reassessment, *Brave New World Revisited* (New York: Harper and Row, 1958).

11. Aldous Huxley, *Brave New World* (1932; reprint, New York: Perennial, 1969), 48.

12. Ibid., 48, 99, 138, 118, 167, 136. On the modern vitamin craze, see Rima Apple, *Vitamania: Vitamins in American Culture* (New Brunswick, NJ: Rutgers University Press, 1996).

13. Ibid., 174, 140, 83, 167, 152.

14. Ibid., 32–33, 161, 153.

15. Harold L. Berger, *Science Fiction and the New Dark Age* (Bowling Green, OH: Popular Press, 1976), x.

16. Ward Moore, *Greener Than You Think* (New York: William Sloan, 1947), 4, 5, 165. Thanks to Tara Tucker for assistance with this book.

17. George Orwell, *1984* (New York: Signet, 1950), 5, 19, 58, 7, 40–41, 47, 108, 144–45, 225.

18. Berger, *Science Fiction,* 44; Isaac Asimov, "Satisfaction Guaranteed," in *Earth Is Room Enough,* 95–108 (New York: Bantam Books, 1957); idem, "The

Last Trump," in *Earth Is Room Enough*, 108–23; Disch cited in W. Warren Wagar, "The Rebellion of Nature," in *The End of the World,* ed. Eric S. Rabkin, Martin H. Greenberg, and Joseph D. Olander (Carbondale: Southern Illinois University Press, 1983), 13–72; "To Serve Man," *Twilight Zone,* March 2, 1962. Thanks much to Angela Hughes and Tara Tucker for help with these stories.

19. Isaac Asimov, "Living Space," in *Earth Is Room Enough*, 80–94; Gary Westphal, "For Tomorrow We Dine: The Sad Gourmet at the Scientificafe," in *Foods of the Gods: Eating and the Eaten in Fantasy and Science Fiction,* ed. Gary Westphal, George Slusser, and Eric S. Rabkin (Athens: University of Georgia Press, 1996), 214–18.

20. Berger, *Science Fiction,* 159–60, 188–90; Howard E. McCurdy, *Space and the American Imagination* (Washington, DC: Smithsonian Institution Press, 1997), 103; Michael Smith, "The Short Life of a Dark Prophecy: The Rise and Fall of the 'Population Bomb,'" in *Fear Itself: Enemies Real and Imagined in American Culture,* ed. Nancy Lusignan Schultz (West Lafayette, IN: Purdue University Press, 1999), 331.

21. Berger, *Science Fiction,* 155–58.

22. Kobe Abe, *Inter Ice Age 4* (New York: Knopf, 1970); Berger, *Science Fiction,* 156–59.

23. Frederick Pohl and C. M. Kornbluth, *The Space Merchants,* 1952, collected in *Venus, Inc.* (Garden City, NJ: Doubleday, 1984), 8, 4, 24, 15, 63, 69.

24. Ibid., 74, 14, 16; Frederick Pohl, *The Merchants' War* (New York: St. Martin's Press, 1984).

25. Isaac Asimov, *Caves of Steel* (New York: Signet, 1953), 100–102, 150–52. On the "localization" of globalized fast food cuisine, see James L. Watson, ed., *Golden Arches East: McDonald's in East Asia* (Stanford: Stanford University Press, 1997).

26. Harry Harrison, *Make Room! Make Room!* (1966; reprint, New York: Berkeley Medallion, 1967), 3, 131, 10, 173.

27. John Brunner, *Stand on Zanzibar* (New York: Ballantine, 1968), 616.

28. John Brunner, *The Sheep Look Up* (New York: Ballantine, 1972), 97, 38–40, 67, 128.

29. Ibid., 43, 96, 182, 82, 216. Review by James John Bell, June 21, 2003, Diverse Books, accessed August 27, 2003 at http://news.diversebooks.com/reviews/03/07/15/1121233.shtml.

30. John G. Mitchell, "On the Spoor of the Slide Rule," in *Ecotactics: The Sierra Club Handbook for Environment Activists,* ed. John G. Mitchell (New York: Pocket Books, 1970), 24, 21; Berger, *Science Fiction,* 31; Warren Belasco, *Appetite for Change: How the Counterculture Took on the Food Industry* (Ithaca: Cornell University Press, 1993); John Case and Rosemary C. R. Taylor, eds., *Co-Ops, Communes, and Collectives: Experiments in Social Change in the 1960s and 1970s* (New York: Pantheon Books, 1979).

31. Ernest Callenbach, *Ecotopia: The Novel of Your Future* (New York: Bantam, 1975), 9–11, 15–17, 21–29, 53, 82–86, 104.

32. Ibid., 29, 82–85, 194, 198.

33. Marge Piercy, *Woman on the Edge of Time* (New York: Fawcett Crest, 1976), 23, 29, 10, 34, 183, 54, 354.

34. Ibid., 68–70, 73.

35. Ibid., 128–29, 100, 124. For a restatement of Piercy's principles of an alternative food system, see Jack Kloppenburg Jr., John Hendrickson, and G. W. Stevenson, "Coming into the Foodshed," *Agriculture and Human Values* 13:3 (summer 1996): 33–42.

36. Piercy, *Woman*, 226, 97.

37. Ibid., 76, 56, 172. Mike Davis, *Ecology of Fear: Los Angeles and the Imagination of Disaster* (New York: Metropolitan Books, 1998), 316–18.

38. Piercy, *Woman*, 368.

39. Ibid., 368, 300, 297, 296, 275. For more of the same, see Marge Piercy, *He, She, and It* (New York: Knopf, 1991), 202.

40. Dorothy Bryant, *The Kin of Ata Are Waiting* (New York: Random House, 1971). Many thanks to Tara Tucker's unpublished research paper, "*The Kin of Ata Are Waiting*: Uses of Pastoral Utopianizing and Femtopianism in Modern Utopian Literature" (University of Maryland Baltimore County, 1996).

41. Davis, *Ecology of Fear*, 275; Starhawk, *The Fifth Sacred Thing* (New York: Bantam Books, 1993).

42. Starhawk, *The Fifth Sacred Thing*, 18.

43. Octavia E. Butler, *Parable of the Sower* (New York: Four Walls Eight Windows, 1993), 289, 295.

44. Davis, *Ecology of Fear*, 278.

45. T. C. Boyle, *A Friend of the Earth* (New York: Viking Books, 2000), 271.

SIX. THE CLASSICAL FUTURE

1. "The Optimism Gap Grows" (Washington, DC: Pew Research Center for the People and the Press, January 17, 1997), accessed on September 3, 2003, from http://people-press.org/reports/display.php3?ReportID=115; Bjorn Lomborg, *The Skeptical Environmentalist: Measuring the Real State of the World* (Cambridge: Cambridge University Press, 2001), 34–42. When it comes to people's perception of crime, however, the gap may narrow. As George Gerbner suggests in his famous study of the "mean world syndrome," heavy viewers of television tend to *over*estimate their personal vulnerability to violent attack. George Gerbner, Michael Morgan, and Nancy Signorielli, "The Scary World of Media Violence" (1994), accessed September 4, 2003, from www.mediaed.org/videos/CommercialismPoliticsAndMedia/TheKillingScreens/studyguide/html.

2. Warren Belasco, *Appetite for Change: How the Counterculture Took on the Food Industry* (Ithaca: Cornell University Press, 1993), 63.

3. See chapter 8 for further explanation of my use of the term "recombinant."

4. J. Russell Smith, *The World's Food Resources* (New York: Henry Holt, 1919), 3, 6–13.

5. Ibid., 594, 613 (italics added).

6. Robert W. Rydell, *All the World's a Fair: Visions of Empire at American International Expositions, 1876–1916* (Chicago: University of Chicago Press, 1984), 4; idem, *World of Fairs: The Century-of-Progress Expositions* (Chicago: University of Chicago Press, 1993), 21, 15.

7. Rydell, *All the World's a Fair*, 2, 10–37; idem, *World of Fairs*, 1; Asa Briggs,

The Making of Modern England, 1783–1867 (New York: Harper Torchbooks, 1965), 398; Curtis Hinsley, "The World as Marketplace: Commodification of the Exotic at the World's Columbian Exposition," in *Exhibiting Cultures: The Poetics and Politics of Museum Display,* ed. Ivan Karp and Steven D. Lavine (Washington, DC: Smithsonian Institution Press, 1991), 345.

8. Robert W. Rydell, "The Culture of Imperial Abundance: World's Fairs in the Making of American Culture," in *Consuming Visions: Accumulation and Display of Goods in America, 1880–1920,* ed. Simon T. Bronner (New York: Norton, 1989), 192.

9. John G. Cawelti, "America on Display: The World's Fairs of 1876, 1893, 1933," in *The Age of Industrialism in America,* ed. Frederic C. Jaher (New York: Free Press, 1968), 317–63; James Gilbert, *Perfect Cities: Chicago's Utopias of 1893* (Chicago: University of Chicago Press, 1991), 22; Trumbull White and William Igleheart, *The World's Columbian Exposition, Chicago 1893* (Philadelphia: P. W. Ziegler, 1893), 168.

10. J. W. Buel, *The Magic City: A Massive Portfolio of Original Photographic Views of the Great World's Fair* (St. Louis: Historical Publishing Co., 1894), n.p; Leslie Prosterman, *Ordinary Life, Festival Days: Aesthetics in the Midwestern County Fair* (Washington, DC: Smithsonian Institution Press, 1995); John Elfreth Watkins Jr., "What May Happen in the Next Hundred Years," *Ladies' Home Journal,* December 1900, reprinted in *The 1990s & Beyond,* ed. Edward Cornish (Bethesda, MD: World Future Society, 1990), 150–55.

11. Reid Badger, *The Great American Fair: The World's Columbian Exposition and American Culture* (Chicago: Nelson Hall, 1979), 103; Burton Benedict, *The Anthropology of World's Fairs: San Francisco's Panama-Pacific International Exposition of 1915* (Berkeley: Scolar Press, 1983), 16; Marian Shaw, *World's Fair Notes: A Woman Journalist Views Chicago's 1893 Columbian Exposition* (Chicago: Pogo Press, 1992), 33, 17.

12. Shaw, *Woman Journalist,* 16, 33; Buel, *Magic City,* n.p.

13. Shaw, *Woman Journalist,* 34; Rossiter Johnson, ed., *A History of the World's Columbian Exposition,* vol. 3: *Exhibits* (New York: D. Appleton, 1898), 5–6, 10; Neil Harris, ed., *The Land of Contrasts, 1880–1901* (New York: George Braziller, 1970), 297.

14. Shaw, *Woman Journalist,* 54; Johnson, *History,* 105; Mrs. Mark Stevens, *Six Months at the World's Fair* (Detroit: Detroit Free Press Printing Co., 1895), 171, 182. On the overselling of California fruit farming, see Steven Stoll, *The Fruits of Natural Advantage: Making the Industrial Countryside in California* (Berkeley: University of California Press, 1998).

15. Shaw, *Woman Journalist,* 25, 15, 56–61; Rydell, *All the World's a Fair,* 67; Hinsley, "World as Marketplace," 345.

16. Rydell, *All the World's a Fair,* 65; Buel, *Magic City,* n.p.; "The Great Fair," *World's Columbian Exposition Illustrated,* July 1891, 2; James W. Loewen, *Lies My Teacher Told Me: Everything Your American History Textbook Got Wrong* (New York: New Press, 1995), 154–62; Doris Witt, *Black Hunger: Food and the Politics of U.S. Identity* (New York: Oxford University Press, 1999), 33. On the symbolic significance of Victorian appetites and etiquette, see John F. Kasson, "The Rituals of Dining: Table Manners in Victorian America," in *Dining in Amer-*

ica, 1850–1900, ed. Kathryn Grover (Amherst: University of Massachusetts Press, 1987), 127–29.

17. Badger, *Great American Fair,* 104; Witt, *Black Hunger,* 36, 21–53; Susan Strasser, *Satisfaction Guaranteed: The Making of the American Mass Market* (New York: Pantheon, 1989), 183–84; Kenneth W. Goings, *Mammy and Uncle Mose: Black Collectibles and American Stereotyping* (Bloomington: Indiana University Press, 1994), 28–31.

18. Dorothy Daniels Birk, *The World Came to St. Louis: A Visit to the 1904 World's Fair* (St. Louis: Bethany Press, 1979), 64; Rydell, *All the World's a Fair,* 167–83, 196.

19. Rydell, *All the World's a Fair,* 196; Kasson, "Rituals of Dining," 139.

20. Rebecca L. Spang, "All the World's a Restaurant: On the Global Gastronomics of Tourism and Travel," in *Food in Global History,* ed. Raymond Grew (Boulder: Westview, 1999), 82, 86; idem, *The Invention of the Restaurant: Paris and Modern Gastronomic Culture* (Cambridge, MA: Harvard University Press, 2000), 193; Russell Lewis, "Everything under One Roof: Fairs and Department Stores in Paris and Chicago," *Chicago History* 12 (fall 1983): 28–47; Bradford Peck, *The World a Department Store: A Twentieth Century Utopia* (Lewiston, ME: by the author, 1900).

21. John A. Jakle and Keith A. Sculle, *Fast Food: Roadside Restaurants in the Automobile Age* (Baltimore: Johns Hopkins University Press, 1999), 99; Waverly Root and Richard de Rochemont, *Eating in America: A History* (New York: William Morrow, 1976), 428; Shaw, *Woman Journalist,* 340; Jeanne Madeline Weimann, *The Fair Women* (Chicago: Academy Chicago Press, 1981), 459. For more on the historic role of corn, as well as its ingenious display at cornucopian festivals, see Betty Fussell, *The Story of Corn* (New York: North Point Press, 1992).

22. Roland Marchand and Michael L. Smith, "Corporate Science on Display," in *Scientific Authority and Twentieth-Century America,* ed. Ronald G. Walters (Baltimore: Johns Hopkins University Press, 1997), 174–82; *Official Guide Book of the New York World's Fair 1939* (New York: Exposition Publications, 1939), 106, 104; Jane Stern and Michael Stern, *American Gourmet* (New York: HarperCollins, 1991), 133; Root and de Rochemont, *Eating in America,* 355.

23. Michael L. Smith, "Representations of Technology at the 1964 World's Fair," in *The Power of Culture: Critical Essays in American History,* ed. Richard Wrightman Fox and T. J. Jackson Lears (Chicago: University of Chicago Press, 1993), 237. Marchand and Smith, "Corporate Science on Display," 173, 178, 181.

24. Hasia Diner, *Hungering for America: Italian, Irish, and Jewish Foodways in the Age of Migration* (Cambridge, MA: Harvard University Press, 2001), 63, xv–xii; William Dean Howells, *The Altrurian Romances: Through the Eye of the Needle* (Bloomington: Indiana University Press, 1968), 309.

25. Chester Liebs, *Main Street to Miracle Mile: American Roadside Architecture* (Baltimore: Johns Hopkins University Press, 1995), 48–49. Roland Marchand makes a similar point about the "heroic proportions" of product displays in *Advertising the American Dream: Making Way for Modernity, 1920–1940* (Berkeley: University of California Press, 1985), 265–67; see also Clifford E. Clark Jr.,

"Ranch-House Suburbia: Ideals and Realities," in *Recasting America: Culture and Politics in the Age of Cold War,* ed. Lary May (Chicago: University of Chicago Press, 1989), 171–91.

26. Smith, *World's Food Resources,* 215, 234–39.

27. Jan Whitaker, *Tea at the Blue Lantern Inn: A Social History of the Tea Room Craze in America* (New York: St. Martin's Press, 2002).

SEVEN. THE MODERNIST FUTURE

1. Bevis Hillier, *The Style of the Century 1900–1980* (New York: E. P. Dutton, 1983), 70. For the progressive, liberating nature of culinary modernism, see Rachel Laudan, "A Plea for Culinary Modernism," *Gastronomica* 1:1 (February 2001): 36–44; James Watson, ed. *Golden Arches East: McDonald's in East Asia* (Stanford: Stanford University Press, 1997).

2. Rosalind Williams, *Notes on the Underground: An Essay on Technology, Society, and the Imagination* (Cambridge, MA: MIT Press, 1990), 103; David E. Nye, *Electrifying America: Social Meanings of a New Technology, 1880–1940* (Cambridge, MA: MIT Press, 1990), 33–34.

3. Merle Curti, "America at the World Fairs, 1851–1893," in *Probing Our Past* (New York: Harper, 1955), 255–63; Reid Badger, *The Great American Fair: The World's Columbian Exposition and American Culture* (Chicago: Nelson Hall, 1979), 3–15; Robert F. Dalzell Jr., *American Participation in the Great Exhibition of 1851* (Amherst, MA: Amherst College Press, 1960); Robert C. Post, "Reflections of American Science and Technology at the New York Crystal Palace Exhibition of 1853," *Journal of American Studies* 17 (1983): 337–56.

4. Rossiter Johnson, ed., *A History of the World's Columbian Exposition,* vol. 3: *Exhibits* (New York: D. Appleton, 1898), 19; Trumbull White and William Igleheart, *The World's Columbian Exposition, Chicago 1893* (Philadelphia: P. W. Ziegler, 1893), 168; Frederik A. Fernald, "Household Arts at the World's Fair," *Popular Science Monthly* (October 1893), 806–7; Daniel T. Miller, "The Columbian Exposition of 1893 and the American National Character," *Journal of American Culture* 10:2 (summer 1987): 18.

5. Harvey Levenstein, *Revolution at the Table: The Transformation of the American Diet* (New York: Oxford University Press, 1988), 49, 72–85; Laura Shapiro, *Perfection Salad: Women and Cooking at the Turn of the Century* (New York: Farrar, Straus and Giroux, 1986), 158, 78–79, 152; Dolores Hayden, *The Grand Domestic Revolution: A History of Feminist Designs for American Homes, Neighborhoods, and Cities* (Cambridge, MA: MIT Press, 1981), 151–55.

6. Jeanne Madeline Weimann, *The Fair Women* (Chicago: Academy Chicago Press, 1981), 258, 463; Shapiro, *Perfection Salad,* 156, 90–94; Jeanne Madeline Weimann, "A Temple to Women's Genius: The Woman's Building of 1893," *Chicago History* 6:1 (spring 1977): 32; Fernald, "Household Arts," 803–12; Maud Howe Elliott, ed., *Art and Handicraft in the Women's Building of the World's Columbian Exposition* (New York: Goupil and Co., 1893), 42.

7. Elliott, *Art and Handicraft,* 41; Ben C. Truman, *History of the World's Fair* (Philadelphia: H. W. Kelley, 1893), 189; Dolores Hayden, *The Grand Domestic Revolution: A History of Feminist Designs for American Homes, Neigh-*

borhoods, and Cities (Cambridge, MA: MIT Press, 1981), 189; Marian Shaw, *World's Fair Notes: A Woman Journalist Views Chicago's 1893 Columbian Exposition* (Chicago: Pogo Press, 1992), 61.

8. Richard D. Mandell, *Paris 1900: The Great World's Fair* (Toronto: University of Toronto Press, 1967), 81–87; David R. Francis, *The Universal Exposition of 1904* (St. Louis: Louisiana Purchase Exposition Company, 1913), 455. William Winget, *A Tour in America and a Visit to the St. Louis Exposition* (Torquay, UK: n.p., 1904), 26–29; Levenstein, *Revolution at the Table,* 130–31, 39–40; E. Melanie DuPuis, *Nature's Perfect Food: How Milk Became America's Drink* (New York: New York University Press, 2002), 73–89; Dorothy Daniels Birk, *The World Came to St. Louis: A Visit to the 1904 World's Fair* (St. Louis: Bethany Press, 1979), 76; Susan Strasser, *Satisfaction Guaranteed: The Making of the American Mass Market* (New York: Pantheon, 1989), 255–60; Francis, *Universal Exposition,* 457.

9. Joseph A. Amato, *Dust: A History of the Small and the Invisible* (Berkeley: University of California Press, 2000), 111; Roland Marchand, *Advertising the American Dream: Making Way for Modernity, 1920–1940* (Berkeley: University of California Press, 1985); Martha Banta, *Taylored Lives: Narrative Productions in the Age of Taylor, Veblen, and Ford* (Chicago: University of Chicago Press, 1993).

10. Shapiro, *Perfection Salad,* 83, 100, 214; Levenstein, *Revolution at the Table,* 152–53; John H. Girdner, "The Food We Eat," *Munsey's Magazine,* November 1902, 188–90.

11. Levenstein, *Revolution at the Table,* 188; Philip Langdon, *Orange Roofs, Golden Arches: The Architecture of American Chain Restaurants* (New York: Alfred A. Knopf, 1986), 11, 14; H. G. Wells, *When the Sleeper Wakes* (1899), reprint in *Three Prophetic Science Fiction Novels of H. G. Wells* (New York: Dover Publications, 1960), 143.

12. Langdon, *Orange Roofs,* 14–21. See also Jeffrey L. Meikle, *American Plastic: A Cultural History* (New Brunswick: Rutgers University Press, 1997), 63–90.

13. Thomas Alva Edison, "Inventions of the Future," *The Independent,* January 6, 1910, 18; idem, "The Woman of the Future," *Good Housekeeping,* October 19, 1912, 436; Susan Strasser, *Never Done: A History of American Housework* (New York: Pantheon, 1982), 81; Edwin E. Slosson, "Electric Farming," *Scientific Monthly,* August 1926, 185; Nye, *Electrifying America,* 287–335; Strasser, *Never Done,* 67–84.

14. Strasser, *Satisfaction Guaranteed,* 252–85; Chester H. Liebs, *Main Street to Miracle Mile: American Roadside Architecture* (Baltimore: Johns Hopkins University Press, 1995), 117–35; Tracey Deutsch, "Untangling Alliances: Social Tensions Surrounding Independent Grocery Stores and the Rise of Mass Retailing," in *Food Nations: Selling Taste in Consumer Societies,* ed. Warren Belasco and Philip Scranton (New York: Routledge, 2002), 166, 169.

15. Richard Tedlow, *New and Improved: The Story of Mass Marketing in America* (New York: Basic Books, 1990), 187–258; Liebs, *Main Street to Miracle Mile,* 126–30.

16. Jeffrey L. Meikle, *Twentieth Century Limited: Industrial Design in America, 1925–1939* (Philadelphia: Temple University Press, 1979), 173.

17. Wheeler McMillen, *Too Many Farmers: The Story of What Is Here and Ahead in Agriculture* (New York: William Morrow, 1929), 303, 305–6; "America in the Year 2500: A Political Forecast," *Harper's*, May 1928, 685–93; J. B. S. Haldane, *Daedalus* (London: Kegan Paul, 1924), 39.

18. Henry Ford, "Henry Ford on Farm and Factory," *Literary Digest*, June 25, 1932, 51; McMillen, *Too Many Farmers*, 154. Anne B. W. Effland, "'New Riches from the Soil': The Chemurgic Ideas of Wheeler McMillen," *Agricultural History* 69:2 (spring 1995): 288–97; David E. Wright, "Agricultural Editors Wheeler McMillen and Clifford V. Gregory and the Farm Chemurgic Movement," *Agricultural History* 69:2 (spring 1995): 272–87.

19. John Elfreth Watkins Jr. "What May Happen in the Next Hundred Years," *Ladies' Home Journal*, December 1900, reprinted in *The 1990s & Beyond*, ed. Edward Cornish (Bethesda: World Future Society, 1990), 154; Robert West Howard, *The Vanishing Land* (New York: Ballantine Books, 1985), 169; A. Richard Crabb, *The Hybrid Corn-Makers: Prophets of Plenty* (New Brunswick: Rutgers University Press, 1947), 318; Jack Doyle, *Altered Harvest: Agriculture, Genetics, and the Fate of the World's Food Supply* (New York: Penguin, 1986), 32–45; Jack R. Kloppenburg, Jr., *First the Seed: The Political Economy of Plant Biotechnology, 1492–2000* (Cambridge: Cambridge University Press, 1988).

20. Daniel J. Kevles, *In the Name of Eugenics: Genetics and the Uses of Human Heredity* (New York: Knopf, 1985). On the rise of the grain-fed fast-food chicken industry, see William Boyd, "Making Meat: Science, Technology, and American Poultry Production," *Technology and Culture* 42:4 (2001): 631–64.

21. Robert W. Rydell, *World of Fairs: The Century-of-Progress Expositions* (Chicago: University of Chicago Press, 1993), 49, 38–58; Watkins, "What May Happen," 153; Boyd, "Making Meat," 652–53. On the eugenics–animal breeding connection, see F. R. Marshall, "The Relation of Biology to Agriculture," *Popular Science Monthly*, June 1911, 539–53.

22. Edwin E. Slosson, "The Expansion of Chemistry," *Industrial and Engineering Chemistry*, May 1924, 449; Winston Churchill, "Fifty Years Hence," *Popular Mechanics*, March 1932, 390–97; Aldous Huxley, *Brave New World* (1932; reprint, New York: Perennial, 1969), 4.

23. Ray Stannard Baker, "The Scientist and the Food Problem," *Harper's Monthly Magazine*, November 1903, 932–37; F. G. Cottrell, "Fertilizers from the Air," *Scientific Monthly*, September 1925, 245–49.

24. Elbert W. Rockwood, "The Work of the Chemist in Conservation," *Popular Science Monthly*, March 1911, 296; McMillen, *Too Many Farmers*, 205; Harry A. Curtis, "Our Nitrogen Problem," *Annals of the American Academy of Political and Social Science* 112:201 (March 1924), 173; Joseph S. Davis, "The Specter of Dearth of Food: History's Answer to Sir William Crookes," in *Facts and Factors in Economic History* (Cambridge, MA: Harvard University Press, 1932), 741. A 1945 review of artificial nitrogen fixation noted that the Haber process, while widely used, was still very complicated and expensive. Willard Smith, "New Process Yields Cheap Fertilizers," *Science Digest*, December 1945, 54–56.

25. "Food and Population—in 2027," *Literary Digest*, October 8, 1927, 16; Henry Smith Williams, "The Miracle-Workers: Modern Science in the Industrial World," *Everybody's Magazine*, October 1907, 497–98.

26. "Food from Waste Products," *Literary Digest,* January 4, 1913, 16; Edwin E. Slosson, *Creative Chemistry* (New York: Century Co., 1919), 110–27; Roger W. Babson, "Twenty Ways to Make a Million," *The Forum,* May 1929, 280; Levenstein, *Revolution at the Table,* 152–53; Rima Apple, *Vitamania: Vitamins in American Culture* (New Brunswick: Rutgers University Press, 1996); Edwin Teale, "New Foods from the Test Tube," *Popular Science Monthly,* July 1934, 13–15.

27. Meikle, *American Plastic,* 31; Edwin Slosson, "Food from Shale," *Scientific Monthly,* July 1925, 106; "Food from Waste Products," 16; Babson, "Twenty Ways," 280.

28. Vernon Kellogg, "When Cabbages Are Kings," *World's Work,* May 1925, 53; "U.S. Wheat Yields from the Montana Wheat and Barley Committee," accessed May 25, 2004, from http://wbc.agr.state.mt.us/factsfigs/pt/ptaw.html; Donald Worster, *Nature's Economy: A History of Ecological Ideas* (Cambridge: Cambridge University Press, 1985), 304.

29. Worster, *Nature's Economy,* 313.

30. Carl L. Alsberg, "Progress in Chemistry and the Theory of Population," *Industrial and Engineering Chemistry,* May 1924, 524–26.

31. Ibid., 525–56.

32. Churchill, "Fifty Years Hence," 396; First Earl of Birkenhead [Frederick Edward Smith], *The World in 2030 AD* (London: Hodder & Stoughton, 1930), 19–20.

33. Frank E. Manuel, *The Prophets of Paris: Turgot, Condorcet, Saint-Simon, Fourier, and Comte* (New York: Harper Torchbooks, 1965), 93.

34. Gerald Wendt, *Science for the World of Tomorrow* (New York: W. W. Norton, 1939), 214; Rydell, *World of Fairs.* On Wendt, see Peter J. Kuznick, "Losing the World of Tomorrow: The Battle over the Presentation of Science at the 1939 New York World's Fair," *American Quarterly* 46 (1994): 341–73.

35. Joseph J. Corn and Brian Horrigan, *Yesterday's Tomorrows: Past Visions of the American Future* (Baltimore: Johns Hopkins University Press, 1984), 49; Rydell, *World of Fairs,* 99; Joseph P. Cusker, "The World of Tomorrow: Science, Culture, and Community at the New York World's Fair," in *Dawn of a New Day: The New York World's Fair, 1939/40,* ed. Helen A. Harrison (New York: New York University Press, 1980), 9; Folke T. Kihlstedt, "Utopia Realized: The World's Fairs of the 1930s," in *Imagining Tomorrow: History, Technology, and the American Future,* ed. Joseph J. Corn (Cambridge, MA: MIT Press, 1986), 104.

36. Wendt, *Science for the World of Tomorrow,* 23–24. Henry Wallace, "A New Day for the Farm," *New York Times World's Fair Section,* March 5, 1939, 12.

37. Rydell, *World of Fairs,* 150; Ford B. Bryan, *Beyond the Model T* (Detroit: Wayne State University Press, 1990), 112–13; Meikle, *American Plastic,* 133–35; Stanley Applebaum, ed., *The New York World's Fair, 1939/40* (New York: Dover, 1977), 114.

38. "Food at the World's Fair Plays a Leading Role in the Big Show," *Food Industries,* May 1939, 254; Wendt, *Science for the World of Tomorrow,* 196; Kuznick, "Losing the World of Tomorrow," 353–58; Cusker, "The World of Tomorrow," 13, 94; Helen A. Harrison, ed., *Dawn of a New Day: The New York World's Fair, 1939/40* (New York: New York University Press, 1980), 93.

39. Larry Zim, Mel Lerner, and Herbert Rolfes, *The World of Tomorrow: The New York World's Fair* (New York: Harper and Row, 1988), 125, 109; "Food at the World's Fair," 256.

40. Roland Marchand, "Corporate Imagery and Popular Education: World's Fairs and Expositions in the United States, 1893–1940," in *Consumption and American Culture*, ed. David E. Nye and Carl Pedersen (Amsterdam: VU University Press, 1991), 18–33; Eve Jochnowitz, "Feasting on the Future: Serving Up the World of Tomorrow at the New York World's Fair of 1939–1940" (M.A. thesis, New York University, 1997), 13; *Official Guide Book of the New York World's Fair 1939* (New York: Exposition Publications, 1939), 105; Harrison, *Dawn of a New Day*, 96.

41. Applebaum, *New York World's Fair*, 78; Rydell, *World of Fairs*, 125; Roland Marchand, *Creating the Corporate Soul: The Rise of Public Relations and Corporate Imagery in American Big Business* (Berkeley: University of California Press, 1998), 267; Roland Marchand and Michael L. Smith, "Corporate Science on Display," in *Scientific Authority and Twentieth Century America*, ed. Ronald G. Walters (Baltimore: Johns Hopkins University Press, 1997) 154, 163; "Food at the World's Fair," 257.

42. Jochnowitz, "Feasting on the Future," 13; "What Shows Pulled at the Fair?" *Business Week*, November 4, 1939, 27.

43. Jochnowitz, "Feasting on the Future," 24–25; "Food at the World's Fair," 257, 255; *Official Guide Book*, 115, 109; Marchand and Smith, "Corporate Science on Display," 160.

44. Brian Horrigan, "The Home of Tomorrow, 1927–1945," in *Imagining Tomorrow: History, Technology, and the American Future*, ed. Joseph J. Corn (Cambridge, MA: MIT Press, 1986), 139–40; Rydell, *World of Fairs*, 124.

45. Nye, *Electrifying America*, 357; Jochnowitz, "Feasting on the Future," 41–45; "The Middleton Family at the New York World's Fair," accessed May 26, 2004, at www2.sjsu.edu/faculty/wooda/middleton/middletonelektro.html.

46. Jochnowitz, "Feasting on the Future," 35, 51; Ivan C. Miller, "What Makes a World's Fair Exhibit Click," *Food Industries*, January 1940, 46–47.

47. Gilman quoted by Virginia C. Gildersleeve, "Women's Role," *The New York Times World's Fair Section*, March 5, 1939, 38; Andrew Wood, "The Middleton Film: Romance and Ideology at the New York World's Fair," accessed May 26, 2004, at www2.sjsu.edu/faculty/wooda/middleton/middletonfilm.html; Horrigan, "Home of Tomorrow," 154–59.

48. For an official history of military rations, see the Quartermaster Foundation, accessed May 26, 2004, at www.qmfound.com/; Thomas Hine, *Populuxe: The Look and Life of America in the '50s and '60s, from Tailfins and TV Dinners to Barbie Dolls and Fallout Shelters* (New York: Knopf, 1990), 60, 15.

49. "Sunny Side of the Street," *Life*, September 10, 1951, 3; "Chemists Look into a Bright New World," *Business Week*, September 15, 1951, 19.

50. Richard Tedlow, *New and Improved: The Story of Mass Marketing in America* (New York: Basic Books, 1990), 232; Liebs, *Main Street to Miracle Mile*, 131; E. C. Stakman, "Science in the Service of Agriculture," *Scientific Monthly*, February 1949, 78; "Go Deep for Food," *Science News Letter*, November 4, 1950, 291; Maxwell Reid Grant, "Engineering Better Meat," *Science Digest*, April

1949, 59–60. According to Harvey Levenstein, by 1974 there were 50 percent fewer dairy cows and 85 percent fewer dairy farms than in 1950, but they produced just as much milk—and they did so even without the Rotolactor! Harvey Levenstein, *Paradox of Plenty: A Social History of Eating in Modern America* (New York: Oxford University Press, 1993), 110.

51. William Boyd, "Making Meat: Science, Technology, and American Poultry Production," *Technology and Culture* 42:4 (2001): 657.

52. Ross Holman, "Streamlining the Henhouse," *Science Digest*, May 1955, 53–56.

53. Letitia Brewster and Michael Jacobson, *The Changing American Diet: A Chronicle of American Eating Habits from 1910–1980* (Washington, DC: Center for Science in the Public Interest, 1980), 43.

54. John H. Perkins, *Geopolitics and the Green Revolution: Wheat, Genes, and the Cold War* (New York: Oxford University Press, 1997). See also part I on the Green Revolution.

55. Hine, *Populuxe*, 24, 125, 128; "Revolution in the Kitchen," *U.S. News and World Report*, February 15, 1957, 60; Victor Cohn, "Your Wonderful Future Home," *Science Digest*, January 1957, 39–43; Millard S. Purdy, "Farm Wonders of Today," *Science Digest*, August 1949, 35; Ross Holman, "Pushbutton Rain," *Science Digest*, May 1955, 61–65.

56. Langdon, *Orange Roofs, Golden Arches*, 85–95, 119, 100–101; Hine, *Populuxe*, 26–27. On domestic Cold War culture, see Elaine Tyler May, *Homeward Bound: American Families in the Cold War Era* (New York: Basic Books, 1988), 162–82; Karal Ann Marling, *As Seen on TV: The Visual Culture of Everyday Life in the 1950s* (Cambridge, MA: Harvard University Press, 1994), 242–83; McCurdy, *Space and the American Imagination*.

57. Marling, *As Seen on TV*, 202–40; Jane Stern and Michael Stern, *Square Meals* (New York: Knopf, 1984), 246–319; Laura Shapiro, *Something from the Oven: Reinventing Dinner in 1950s America* (New York: Viking, 2004); Joseph J. Corn, epilogue in *Imagining Tomorrow*, ed. Joseph J. Corn (Cambridge, MA: MIT Press, 1986), 219–29.

58. John A. McWethy, "More Food with Power Farming," *Science Digest*, July 1945, 87–90; A. C. Monahan, "Farming from the Sky," *Science News Letter*, September 15, 1951, 170–71; "When 'Push-Button' Farm Machines Are a Reality," ad in *Fortune*, February 1954, 41.

59. Orville Schell, *Modern Meat: Antibiotics, Hormones, and the Pharmaceutical Farm* (New York: Random House, 1984), 3–27; Ann Ewing, "Chemical Team Spurs Growth," *Science News Letter*, April 14, 1951, 234–35; "Antibiotics for the Starving," *Science News Letter*, November 1, 1952, 275; "Pigs Raised Like Chicks," *Science News Letter*, December 1, 1951, 341; Corn, epilogue in *Imagining Tomorrow*, 221.

60. "Life on the Chemical Newsfront," *Scientific American*, February 1956, 14; Sam Matthews, "Fight Flies for Fly-Free World," *Science News Letter*, July 1, 1950, 10–11; "Weed-Killers Aid Crops," *Science News Letter*, September 11, 1948, 166.

61. Paul Boyer, *By the Bomb's Early Light: American Thought and Culture at the Dawn of the Atomic Age* (New York: Pantheon Books, 1985); Ray Vicker,

"Next: Radiated Foods," *Science Digest,* October 1954, 31; Cohn, *Our Hopeful Future,* 128, 39.

62. Ruth Schwartz Cowan, *More Work for Mother: The Ironies of Household Technology from the Open Hearth to the Microwave* (New York: Basic Books, 1983), 139; Gerry Schremp, *Kitchen Culture: Fifty Years of Food Fads* (New York: Pharos Books, 1991), 57; Ashton J. O'Donnell, "Soon: Irradiated Foods," *Science Digest,* December 1957, 1; Michael Amrine, "Your Life in 1985," *Science Digest,* October 1955, 23–27; Boyer, *By the Bomb's Early Light,* 109, 111; David Dietz, *Atomic Energy in the Coming Era* (New York: Dodd, Mead & Co., 1945), 13, 17.

63. Henry Wallace, "Radioactivity and Plant Growth," *New Republic,* October 13, 1947, 11; Lowell E. Campbell and Leonard G. Schoenleber, "Barnyard Death Rays," *Science Digest,* April 1949, 61; Amrine, "Your Life in 1985," 26; Albert Abarbanel, "Out of the Test Tube," *Science Digest,* June 1952, 5. Perhaps this was the inspiration for Robert Bloch's 1968 dystopian novel, *This Crowded Earth,* in which humans are bioengineered to stand under three feet tall. See Harold L. Berger, *Science Fiction and the New Dark Age* (Bowling Green, OH: Popular Press, 1976), 158–59.

64. William L. Laurence, *Dawn over Zero: The Story of the Atomic Bomb* (New York: Knopf, 1946), 267–68; Gordon Dean, "Atomic Energy for Peace," *Science Digest,* March 1952, 57–61; Edward S. Deevey, Jr., "The Human Crop," *Scientific American,* April 1956, 110.

65. Lester Velie, "Food Pumped from Pipelines," *Collier's,* December 1948, 9–14; Arthur James Larsen, "More Food from Sunlight," *Science Digest,* September 1952, 39–41. Portions of this section appeared previously in Warren Belasco, "Algae Burgers for a Hungry World? The Rise and Fall of Chlorella Cuisine," *Technology and Culture* 38:7 (July 1997): 608–34.

66. William L. Laurence, "Vital Force Found in Plants May Increase World's Food," *New York Times,* December 31, 1949, 1; "Find Key to Photosynthesis," *Science News Letter,* February 17, 1951, 99–100; "Food to Feed 4 Billion," *Chemical and Engineering News,* September 24, 1951, 3940; "World War Avoidable," *Science News Letter,* December 22, 1951, 387; Karl T. Compton, "Science on the March," *Science Digest,* February 1952, 14; Francis Joseph Weiss, "Chemical Agriculture," *Scientific American,* August 1952, 16; Warren Weaver, "People, Energy, and Food," *Scientific Monthly,* June 1954, 364; J. G. Harrar, "Food for the Future," *Science,* August 19, 1955, 313–16.

67. John Boyd-Orr, *The White Man's Dilemma: Food and the Future* (London, 1953), 73–81; see also Boyd-Orr's foreword to *The Geography of Hunger,* by Josue de Castro (Boston: Little, Brown and Co., 1952), ix–xi; Alfred J. Stamm, "Production of Nutritive Substances from Inedible Carbohydrates," *Proceedings of the American Philosophical Society* 95 (February 1951): 68–76; Cohn, *Our Hopeful Future,* 130; Dam, "Foods in the Year 2000," 303–12; "Single Diet for All Life," *Science News Letter,* September 18, 1954, 182.

68. Cohn, *Our Hopeful Future,* 138, 13; Gordon A. Riley, "Food from the Sea," *Scientific American,* October 1949, 16–19; George A. Reay, "The Ocean as a Potential Source of World Food Supply," *Food Technology,* February 1954, 65–69.

69. R. L. Meier, "Industrialization of Photosynthesis and Its Social Effects," *Chemical and Engineering News,* October 24, 1949, 3112–16 ff; H. A. Spoehr, "Chlorella as a Source of Food," *Proceedings of the American Philosophical Society* 95 (February 1951): 62–67; John S. Burlew, "Current Status of the Large-Scale Culture of Algae," in *Algal Culture: From Laboratory to Pilot Plant,* ed. John S. Burlew (Washington, DC: Carnegie Institution, 1953), 3–23.

70. Dean Burk, "Vast Energy from Tiny Plants," *Science Digest,* June 1950, 83–85; Burlew, "Current Status," 4; Harold W. Milner, "Algae as Food," *Scientific American,* October 1953, 31; "Food or Fuel from Algae?" *Science Digest,* April 1954, 65–67; review of *Algal Culture: From Laboratory to Pilot Plant,* ed. John S. Burlew, *Food Technology,* January 1954, 18; Edgar Taschdjian, "Problems of Food Production," *Bulletin of the Atomic Scientists,* August 1951, 211–12; Harrison Brown, *The Challenge of Man's Future* (New York: Viking Press, 1954), 144–45; Laurence, "Vital Force Found in Plants," 26. Note that 65 grams of protein was a generous allowance; many nutritionists today recommend a somewhat lower daily protein intake, although most Americans eat far more.

71. Velie, "Food Pumped from Pipelines," 9–14.

72. Burk, "Vast Energy from Tiny Plants"; "Let Them Eat Kelp," *Fortune,* July 1956, 72; Edgar Ansel Mowrer, "Sawdust, Seaweed, and Synthetics: The Hazards of Crowding," *Saturday Review,* December 8, 1956, 11 ff. On "gee-whiz" stories, see Herbert J. Gans, *Deciding What's News* (New York: Vintage, 1980), 156–57.

73. "Algae to Feed Starving," *Science News Letter,* July 18, 1953, 35; "Future Food Factory?" *Science News Letter,* January 2, 1952, front cover; John E. Despaul [assistant chief, U.S. Military Food Subsistence Laboratory], "Tomorrow's Dinner," *Science News Letter,* September 13, 1958, 170–71; Allan Carpenter, "Weird Crops of the Future," *Science Digest,* November 1951, 52.

74. Francis Joseph Weiss, "The Useful Algae," *Scientific American,* December 1952, 14–17; "Chemists and the World Ahead," *Newsweek,* September 17, 1951, 55; Larsen, "More Food from Sunlight," 39–41; Laurence, "Vital Force Found in Plants," 1; Cohn, *Our Hopeful Future,* 104–11, 123–29.

75. Fairfield Osborn, *Our Plundered Planet* (Boston: Little, Brown, 1948), 29; Samuel H. Ordway, *Resources and the American Dream* (New York: Ronald Press, 1953), 26; Robert C. Cook, "The Population Bomb," *Bulletin of the Atomic Scientists,* October 1956, 298.

76. Spoehr, "Chlorella as a Source of Food," 63; Jacob Rosin and Max Eastman, *The Road to Abundance* (New York: McGraw-Hill, 1953), 5–6; Thomas Stimson, "Algae for Dinner," *Popular Mechanics,* November 1955, 262; Milner, "Algae as Food," 31–35.

77. Meier, "Industrialization of Photosynthesis," 3112–16; Larsen, "More Food from Sunlight," 39–41.

78. Robert Brittain, *Let There Be Bread* (New York: Simon and Schuster 1952), 102; Cohn, *Our Hopeful Future,* 109; Yuji Morimura and Nobuko Tamiya, "Preliminary Experiments in the Use of Chlorella as Human Food," *Food Technology,* April 1954, 179–82; Meier, "Industrialization of Photosynthesis," 3115; Richard L. Meier, *Science and Economic Development: New Patterns of*

Living (Cambridge, MA: MIT Press, 1956), 68–73; Ann Ewing, "Food Gets Super Taste Appeal," *Science News Letter,* July 15, 1950, 42–43; Bonner quoted in Harrison Brown, James Bonner, and John Weit, *The Next Hundred Years* (New York: Viking Press, 1957), 31; Rosin quoted in Cohn, *Our Hopeful Future,* 127.

79. Morimura and Tamiya, "Preliminary Experiments"; A. W. Fisher and John S. Burlew, "Nutritional Value of Microscopic Algae," in *Algal Culture: From Laboratory to Pilot Plant,* ed. John S. Burlew (Washington, DC: Carnegie Institution, 1953), 303–10.

80. This "moderate" view of algae as animal feed was represented by the FAO's John Boyd-Orr *(White Man's Dilemma),* Cal Tech geochemist Harrison Brown *(The Challenge of Man's Future),* FAO official Josue de Castro *(The Geography of Hunger),* and the Rockefeller Foundation's agriculture research director J. G. Harrar ("Food for the Future"), as well as the scientists most closely associated with the Carnegie Institution chlorella project (see Burlew, *Algal Culture).*

81. Stimson, "Algae for Dinner," 264. Other examples of such economic reasoning are Milner, "Algae as Food," 34; Boyd-Orr, foreword to *Geography of Hunger,* by de Castro, xi; Boyd-Orr, *White Man's Dilemma,* 73–80; Compton, "Science on the March," 14.

82. Lester Brown et al., *Vital Signs: The Trends That Are Shaping Our Future* (New York: W. W. Norton, 1994), 29; Lester Brown and Hal Kane, *Full House: Reassessing the Earth's Population Carrying Capacity* (New York: W. W. Norton, 1994), 166, 210. On soybeans, see Jane Stafford, "New Foods from Abroad," *Science News Letter,* November 3, 1951, 282–83.

83. Dean R. Thacker and Harold Babcock, "The Mass Culture of Algae," *Journal of Solar Energy, Science, and Engineering* 1:1 (January 1957): 41; Meier, *Science and Economic Development,* 56; N. W. Pirie, "Orthodox and Unorthodox Methods of Meeting World Food Needs," *Scientific American,* February 1967, 33.

84. Thacker and Babcock, "Mass Culture of Algae," 47; "Program Aims at Chemical Synthesis of Food," *Chemical and Engineering News,* February 21, 1972, 19.

85. Brown, Bonner, and White, *The Next Hundred Years,* 77; A. Watson Shaw, *Aquaculture and Algae Culture* (Park Ridge, NJ: Noyes Data Corp., 1979), 242–47.

86. Thacker and Babcock, "Mass Culture of Algae," 50.

87. "Space Food Harvest May Be Speeded Up," *Science News Letter,* March 16, 1963, 169; "Algae Farm Tested," *Science News Letter,* December 14, 1963, 370; "Current U.S. Patents," *Science News Letter,* August 14, 1965, 109; Meier, *Science and Economic Development,* 77; "Sewage Treatment in Space," *Science Digest,* April 1967, 37; Herbert J. Coleman, "U.S., Russian Scientists View Algae as Principal Space Food," *Aviation Week and Space Technology,* August 14, 1967, 88–89; B. Mandrovsky, *Aerospace Life Support Systems* (Washington, DC: Library of Congress, 1968); Shaw, *Aquaculture and Algae Culture,* 204–65; "Program Aims at Chemical Synthesis of Food," 19; Gedeliah Shelef and Carl J. Soeder, eds., *Algae Biomass: Production and Use* (Amsterdam: Elsevier, 1980), v–viii.

88. L. V. Venkataraman and E. W. Becker, *Biotechnology and Utilization of Algae—The Indian Experience* (New Delhi: Department of Science and Tech-

nology, 1985), 2; Dhyana Bewicke and Beverly A. Potter, *Chlorella: The Emerald Food* (Berkeley: Ronin Publishing, 1984), 16–58; Patrick Echlin, "The Blue-Green Algae," *Scientific American*, June 1966, 75–81; National Academy of Sciences, *Underexploited Tropical Plants with Promising Value* (Washington, DC: National Academy of Sciences, 1975),162–68; Larry Switzer, *Spirulina: The Whole Food Revolution* (Berkeley: Earthrise, 1984), 2.

89. Robert Henrikson, *Earth Food Spirulina* (Laguna Beach, CA: Ronore Enterprises, 1989), 9; Switzer, *Spirulina;* Bewicke and Potter, *Chlorella;* Ripley D. Fox, "Spirulina: The Alga That Can End Malnutrition," *The Futurist*, February 1985, 30–35; W. J. Oswald, "Algal Production—Problems, Achievements, and Potential," in *Algal Biomass*, ed. Gedaliah Shelef and Carl J. Soeder (Amsterdam: Elsevier, 1980), 2; Venkataraman and Becker, *Biotechnology;* Julie Ann Miller, "Diet for a Blue Planet," *Science News*, April 6, 1985, 220–22.

90. Jochnowitz, "Feasting on the Future," 50–52; "What Shows Pulled at the Fair?" 22–28; Miller, "What Makes a World's Fair Exhibit Click," 44–45; "Reality Replaces Symbolism," *Food Industries,* July 1940, 63; "Food Manufacturers' Exhibits Will Again Dominate at World's Fair," *Food Industries,* May 1940, 42–43; "The Talk of the Industry," *Food Industries,* November 1940, 25; Lewis Mumford, "Closing Statement," in *Future Environments of North America,* ed. F. Fraser Darling and John P. Milton (Garden City, NY: Natural History Press, 1966), 724–25.

91. Hine, *Populuxe*, 80; Horrigan quoted in Nye, *Electrifying America,* 360; Adrian Forty, *Objects of Desire: Design and Society from Wedgwood to IBM* (New York: Pantheon Books, 1986), 182–221; Nye, *Electrifying America,* 238–86; Warren Belasco, *Americans on the Road: From Autocamp to Motel* (Cambridge, MA: MIT Press, 1979); David B. Danbom, *The Resisted Revolution: Urban America and the Industrialization of Agriculture, 1900–1930* (Ames: Iowa State University Press, 1979). John R. Stilgoe argues that the "pluggers" who questioned the "progressive" farming agenda of the USDA and its corporate allies constitute the premodern knowledge base of today's sustainable agriculture movement. See John R. Stilgoe, "Plugging Past Reform: Small-Scale Farming Innovation and Big-Scale Research," in *Scientific Authority of Twentieth-Century America,* ed. Ronald G. Walters (Baltimore: Johns Hopkins University Press, 1997), 119–47. On popular resistance to modernist design, see Genevieve Bell and Joseph Kaye, "Designing Technology for Domestic Spaces: A Kitchen Manifesto," *Gastronomica* 2:2 (spring 2002): 46–62.

92. James J. Delaney, "Peril on Your Food Shelf," *Science Digest*, October 1951, 3–6; "DDT Not Sickness Cause," *Science News Letter,* December 22, 1951, 386; "Chemicals in Food Are Nothing New," *Science Digest,* April 1952, 60; Frank Graham Jr., *Since Silent Spring* (Greenwich, CT: Fawcett Crest, 1970), 30–31; John Lear, "Food and Cancer: The Suspicious Chemicals in Your Marketbasket," *Saturday Review,* October 6, 1956, 57–69.

93. Amrine, "Your Life in 1985," 25; Vicker, "Next: Radiated Foods," 32; Mowrer, "Sawdust," 55; Harrison Brown, *The Challenge of Man's Future,* 219.

94. Hine, *Populuxe,* 127; "Revolution in the Kitchen," 67; Alvin Toffler, *Future Shock* (New York: Bantam, 1970), 222. Laura Shapiro elaborates this theme elegantly in *Something from the Oven.*

95. Hine, *Populuxe,* 128, 133; "Fat in Diet Protects from Radiation Damage" and "Pills Protect from Rays," *Science News Letter,* April 18, 1953, 245.

96. Mumford, "Closing Statement," 724–25. This theme is developed at length in Warren Belasco, "Future Notes: The Meal-in-a-Pill," *Food and Foodways* 8:4 (2000): 253–71.

EIGHT. THE RECOMBINANT FUTURE

1. Todd Gitlin, *Inside Prime Time* (New York: Pantheon Books, 1983), 78. Denizens of cultural studies may note that "recombinant" seems to correspond roughly with "postmodern." As the latter term is much overused and confused, I have chosen to give it a rest here.

2. J. B. Priestly, "A Mistake about the Future," *Harper's Magazine,* June 1927, 115–17.

3. Priestly, "A Mistake," 117; H. G. Wells, *Anticipations of the Reaction of Mechanical and Scientific Progress upon Human Life and Thought* (London: Chapman & Hall, 1902), 116; idem, *Anticipations* (Mineola, NY: Dover Publications, 1999), 65, 109, 77, 95, 77–78; Jan Whitaker, *Tea at the Blue Lantern Inn: A Social History of the Tea Room Craze in America* (New York: St. Martin's Press, 2002).

4. First Earl of Birkenhead (Frederick Edward Smith], *The World in 2030 AD* (London: Hodder & Stoughton, 1930), 20; Wells, *Anticipations* (Dover ed.), 78–70.

5. Daniel J. Boorstin, *The Americans: The National Experience* (New York: Vintage, 1965), 134–47.

6. William Cronon, *Nature's Metropolis: Chicago and the Great West* (New York: W. W. Norton, 1991), 344; Neil Harris, "Great Fairs and American Cities: The Role of Chicago's Columbian Exposition," in *Cultural Excursions* (Chicago: University of Chicago Press, 1990), 120–26; Curtis Hinsley, "The World as Marketplace: Commodification of the Exotic at the World's Columbian Exposition," in *Exhibiting Cultures: The Poetics and Politics of Museum Display,* ed. Ivan Karp and Steven D. Lavine (Washington, DC: Smithsonian Institution Press, 1991), 356; James Gilbert, *Perfect Cities: Chicago's Utopias of 1893* (Chicago: University of Chicago Press, 1991), 130, 72, 78; Brooks Landon, "Ain't No Fiber in Cyberspace: A Metonymic Menu for a Paratactic Potpourri," in *Foods of the Gods: Eating and the Eaten in Fantasy and Science Fiction,* ed. Gary Westphal, George Slusser, and Eric S. Rabkin (Athens: University of Georgia Press, 1996), 230; Trumbull White and William Igleheart, *The World's Columbian Exposition, Chicago 1893* (Philadelphia: P. W. Ziegler, 1893), 600.

7. Warren J. Belasco, "Toward a Culinary Common Denominator: The Rise of Howard Johnson's, 1925–1940," *Journal of American Culture* 2:3 (fall 1979): 503–18; Philip Langdon, *Orange Roofs, Golden Arches: The Architecture of American Chain Restaurants* (New York: Alfred A. Knopf, 1986), 24–25.

8. Oscar Tschirky, "Promise for the Epicure," *New York Times World's Fair Section,* March 5, 1939, 67; Elsie-Jean Stein, *Fun at the Fair: A Trip to the New York World's Fair of 1940 with Bobby and Betty* (New York: Dodge Publishing, 1940), 30, 62, 108; *Official Guide Book of the New York World's Fair 1939* (New York: Exposition Publications, Inc., 1939), 21–23.

9. Thomas Hine, *Populuxe: The Look and Life of America in the '50s and '60s, from Tailfins and TV Dinners to Barbie Dolls and Fallout Shelters* (New York: Knopf, 1990), 167–68; Harris, "Great Fairs," 130; Jane Stern and Michael Stern, *American Gourmet* (New York: HarperCollins, 1991), 62.

10. Stern and Stern, *American Gourmet,* 142–44; "Festival of Gas Pavilion," accessed June 8, 2004, from www.nywf64.com/fesgas07.html.

11. William Alexander McClung, *Landscapes of Desire: Anglo Mythologies of Los Angeles* (Berkeley: University of California Press, 2000), 170. The classic, most savage critique of the Disney formula is Richard Schickel's *The Disney Version: The Life, Times, Art and Commerce of Walt Disney* (New York: Avon, 1969). See also Stephen M. Fjellman, *Vinyl Leaves: Walt Disney World and America* (Boulder: Westview, 1992).

12. "Entertainment + Involvement = Education at Kraft's The Land," *Food Technology,* July 1983, 78.

13. Diana Maria Henry, "Future Food? The Disney Vision, Brought to You by Kraft," *Southern Exposure,* November/December 1983, 22–26; Alexander Wilson, *The Culture of Nature: North American Landscape from Disney to the Exxon Valdez* (Cambridge, MA: Blackwell, 1992), 185; John M. Gerber, "Hydroponics" (Urbana-Champaign: University of Illinois Cooperative Extension Service, April 1985, photocopied); "Entertainment + Involvement," 82.

14. Mike Wallace, *Mickey Mouse History, and Other Essays on American Memory* (Philadelphia: Temple University Press, 1996), 153; Ron Ruggless, "Disney's Brain Trust Lures Best, Brightest," *Nation's Restaurant News,* November 23, 1992, 70; "Aquaculture at The Land," undated EPCOT handout; Peter O. Keegan, "Walt Disney Let Imagination Be His Guide," *Nation's Restaurant News,* November 23, 1992, 94; "Sunshine Season Food Fair," accessed June 21, 2004, at http://allearsnet.com/menu/men_ssff.htm.

15. Bill Carlino, "Directing Food Operations at MGM Theme Park," *Nation's Restaurant News,* November 23, 1992, 74; "Be Our Guest, Be Our Guest," *Nation's Restaurant News,* November 23, 1992, 93.

16. Wallace, *Mickey Mouse History,* 145; Henry, "Future Food?" 24–25; Wilson, *Culture of Nature,* 189; "Food Rocks," accessed June 21, 2004, at www.csis.gvsu.edu/~willbraj/epcotjason/food_rocks_and_kitchen_kabaret.html; Michael Sorkin, *Variations on a Theme Park* (New York: Farrar, Straus & Giroux, 1992), 225.

17. Joseph J. Corn and Brian Horrigan, *Yesterday's Tomorrows: Past Visions of the American Future* (Baltimore: Johns Hopkins University Press, 1984), 82–83; "Yesterland," accessed June 21, 2004, at www.yesterland.com/yester.html; Howard E. McCurdy, *Space and the American Imagination* (Washington, DC: Smithsonian Institution Press, 1997), 41–43; "General Electric Carousel of Progress," accessed June 21, 2004, at www.yesterland.com/progress.html.

18. Seth Schiesel, "Once Visionary, Disney Calls Future a Thing of the Past," *New York Times,* February 23, 1997, 24; Ferren quoted in David Remnick, "Future Perfect: The Next Magic Kingdom," *New Yorker,* October 20, 1997, 217; William Booth, "Planet Mouse: At Disney's Tomorrowland, the Future Is a Timid Creature," *Washington Post,* June 24, 1998, D1, 8.

19. Booth, "Planet Mouse," D8. On Celebration, Florida, see Schiesel,

"Once Visionary"; official Celebration website, accessed June 22, 2004, at www
.celebrationfl.com/. See also Wells, *Anticipations* (Dover ed.), 65, 77–78.

20. Booth, "Planet Mouse," D8.

21. McCurdy, *Space and the American Imagination,* 27.

22. Ibid., 9–82; "Outpost 101," accessed June 22, 2004, at http://library
.thinkquest.org/11356/.

23. McCurdy, *Space and the American Imagination,* 84, 211; NASA Facts,
"Food for Space Flight," accessed June 22, 2004, at www.nasa.gov/lb/audience/
forstudents/postsecondary/features/F_Food_for_Space_Flight.html; Tom Wolfe,
The Right Stuff (New York: Bantam, 1980); "History of Food in Space," accessed
June 22, 2004, at http://liftoff.msfc.nasa.gov/academy/astronauts/food-history
.html.

24. Rick Weiss, "Moonstruck: Cosmic Cuisine," *Washington Post,* April 1,
1998, E11; "Outpost 101."

25. "Archive of Center for Research on Controlled Ecological Life Support
Systems (CELSS) at Purdue University 1990–1995," accessed June 22, 2004, at
www.cyanosite.bio.purdue.edu/nscort/homepage.html; Patricia Picone Mitchell,
"Can Food Be Made from Coal?" *Washington Post,* May 27, 1984, M1–2; Gerald K. O'Neill, "Space Colonies: The High Frontier," in *1999: The World of Tomorrow,* ed. Edward Cornish (Washington, DC: World Future Society, 1978),
66–74; McCurdy, *Space and the American Imagination,* 151.

26. McCurdy, *Space and the American Imagination,* 211–12; Lori Valigra,
"Recipes for Beyond a Small Planet," MSNBC, February 18, 1998, accessed February 24, 1998, at www.msnbc.com; Jane Brody, "The Restaurant at the Edge
of the Universe," NYTimes.com, May 19, 1998, accessed December 4, 1998, at
www.NYTimes.com; NASA Facts, "Food for Space Flight."

27. Glen Golightly, "The View's Great—and the Food's Not Bad Either,"
Space.com, February 20, 2000, accessed April 13, 2001, at www.space.com/news/
spaceshuttles/sts99_food.html; Lisa J. Huriash, "For Astronaut, Keeping Kosher
Is His Mission," *Washington Post,* May 13, 2001, A12. For kosher recombinant
trends, see Marilyn Halter, *Shopping for Identity: The Marketing of Ethnicity*
(New York: Shocken Books, 2000), 115; Philip Chien, "Space Food Has Come a
Long Way," *Amarillo Globe-News,* June 1, 1999, accessed April 13, 2001, at http://
weather.amarillonet.com/stories/060199/new_come.shtml; "Extraterrestrial Cuisine Is Cooking in Cornell Lab," Cornell University news release, January 19,
1998, accessed April 13, 2001, at www.news.cornell.edu; Weiss, "Moonstruck,"
E11; Brody, "The Restaurant at the Edge of the Universe"; Valigra, "Recipes for
Beyond a Small Planet"; Judy Peet, "NASA Tries for Space Food with the Flavors of Home," seattletimes.com, January 19, 1999, accessed April 13, 2001, at
http://seattletimes.nwsource.com; "Archive of Center for Research on Controlled
Ecological Life Support Systems (CELSS) at Purdue University 1990–1995";
Wendy Wolfson, "Raising the Steaks," *New Scientist,* December 21, 2002, 60;
Richard Stenger, "Lab-Grown Fish Chunks Could Feed Space Travelers," CNN,
March 22, 2002, accessed March 27, 2002, at CNN.com.

28. Weiss, "Moonstruck"; Brody, "Restaurant at the Edge of the Universe";
Karen Springen, "'Houston, We Have a Recipe': What's Cooking in Outer Space,"
Newsweek, November 9, 1998, 10; Valigra, "Recipes for Beyond a Small Planet";

Golightly, "The View's Great"; Diane Toops, "What's Cooking in Space?" *Food Processing,* December 1997, 64; Alan Crawford, "Pizza Hut Breaks the Final Frontier as Its Name Goes into Space," *The Scotsman,* July 12, 2000, 5. On similar developments in military cuisine, see "Combat Food," *The Osgood File (CBS Radio Network),* June 29, 1999, accessed January 24, 2003, from www.acfnewsource.org.

29. Sylvia Carter, "Fields of Genes," *Newsday Our Future,* 1999, accessed June 22, 2004, from http://future.newsday.com/3/ftopo328.htm; Bruce Livesey, "Strange Fruit," *Eye* (Toronto), April 22, 1999, 11–12; Steve Rhodes, "Friendly Farming: How Green Is My Acre," *Newsweek,* December 26, 1994, 113–14; Leticia Mancini, "Food Technology's Excellent Adventure," *Food Engineering,* January 1992, 76; Phyllis Hanes, "Attention, Future Food Shoppers!" *Christian Science Monitor,* June 20, 1991, 14; Liz Brody, "Future Food: What You'll Be Eating When You Live Next Door to the Jetsons," *Men's Health,* June 1991, 62; "Forecasting Future Food," *Supermarket Business,* July 1991, 10; Sarah Fritschner, "A Look Ahead to the Year 2000," *Louisville Courier-Journal,* February 16, 1999, 9a; Charlyne Varkonyi, "Previewing Foods of Tomorrow," *Los Angeles Times,* January 18, 1990, H44.

30. Phyllis Richman, "What's Old Is New," *Washington Post,* March 22, 1989, E1; Joan Nathan, "Food of the Future Is Ethnic and Fast," *Washington Post,* March 8, 1989, C4; Ryan Matthews, "Dawn of the Traditionalists," *Grocery Marketing,* June 1989, 38.

31. Bobbi Ignelzi, "Taste Tomorrow: Future Foods Won't Be Unfamiliar, Just Better," *San Diego Union-Tribune,* February 23, 1989, 1; Jonathan Probber, "Future Food: A Look at Eating in the Year 2000," *New York Times,* January 27, 1988, C1; Jack Williams, "Future Foods: Soygurt, Fish Hot Dogs, and Other Stuff That's Good for You," *San Diego Union-Tribune,* October 16, 1987, D1.

32. Michael Rogers, "Marvels of the Future," *Newsweek,* December 25, 1989, 77–78; Edward Dolnick, "Future Schlock," *In Health,* September-October 1990, 22.

33. Varkonyi, "Previewing Foods of Tomorrow." A rare exception is Barbara Ehrenreich, *Nickel and Dimed: On (Not) Getting By in America* (New York: Henry Holt, 2001).

34. Susan Strasser, *Satisfaction Guaranteed: The Making of the American Mass Market* (New York: Pantheon, 1989).

35. The seminal work was Douglas Coupland, *Generation X: Tales for an Accelerated Culture* (New York: St. Martin's Press, 1992).

36. Marcia Mogelonsky, "The Aging of a New Generation," Food Channel, 1997, accessed June 25, 1997 at www.foodchannel.com; Sylvia Carter, "Who Will Do the Cooking?" *Newsday Our Future,* 1999, accessed June 28, 1999, at http://future.newsday.com/3/ffodo331.htm.

37. For an excellent illustration of the three-world scenario, see Joseph F. Coates, John B. Mahaffie, and Andy Hines, *2025: Scenarios of US and Global Society Reshaped by Science and Technology* (Greensboro, NC: Oakhill Press, 1997). For a contemporary critique of the same, see Christopher Lasch, "Is Progress Obsolete?" *Time: The Millennium,* fall 1992, 71.

38. Take, for example, an article about functional foods: Carole Sugarman,

"Magic Bullets: Pumped-Up Foods Promise to Make Us Happier and Healthier. We'll See," *Washington Post*, October 21, 1998, E1. For a critique of "cleverness," see David W. Orr, "What Is Education For?" in *Earth in Mind: On Education, Environment, and the Human Prospect* (Washington, DC: Island Press, 1994), 7–15.

39. Thomas Hayden, "O Brave New Farm, Tilled by Satellite and Robot," *Newsweek*, November 24, 1997, 14; "Precision Farming," *The Futurist*, November–December 1993, 56; "Robotic Farmers Boost Productivity," *The Futurist,* November 1998, 2; Coates, Mahaffie, and Hines, *2025,* 361.

40. Coates, Mahaffie, and Hines, *2025, 375*; Andy Hines, "Ever-Smarter Farmers Keep Food Abundant," *Futurist* November-December 1997, 18; Paul E. Waggoner, *How Much Land Can Ten Billion People Spare for Nature?* (Ames, IA: Council for Agricultural Science and Technology, 1994); "Precision Farming"; Christine Lutton, "Cyberfarm," *Forbes,* July 15, 1996, 86–87.

41. Laurie Petersen, "21st Century Supermarket Shopping," *Adweek's Marketing Week*, March 9, 1992, 9; Evan I. Schwartz, "The Progressive Grocer," *Wired*, September 1997, 147; Jan Howells, "Recipe for Success—the Kitchen of the Future," May 4, 2004, accessed June 22, 2004, from www.vnunet.com/features/601712; Coates, Mahaffie, and Hines, *2025, 379*.

42. Coates, Mahaffie, and Hines, *2025,* 29–31; Carter, "Who Will Do the Cooking?"; Howells, "Recipe for Success"; Genevieve Bell and Joseph Kaye, "Designing Technology for Domestic Spaces: A Kitchen Manifesto," *Gastronomica* 2:2 (spring 2002): 46–62.

43. Carter, "Who Will Do the Cooking?"; "Hot Bytes," Internet Food Channel, March 7, 1996, accessed December 4, 1996, and June 30, 1997, accessed July 9, 1997, both from www.foodchannel.com; Alvin Toffler, *Future Shock* (New York: Bantam 1970), 222. The "psychic cake mix" insight supposedly dates back to market researcher Ernest Dichter, who urged processors to require 1950s bakers to add an egg as a way to give them a sense of creative participation. For a scholarly refinement of the "egg theory," see Laura Shapiro, *Something from the Oven: Reinventing Dinner in 1950s America* (New York: Viking, 2004), 74–78.

44. Christopher Lasch, *Haven in a Heartless World: The Family Besieged* (New York: Basic Books, 1977); Harvey Green, *The Light of the Home* (New York: Pantheon Books, 1983); Kenneth L. Ames, *Death in the Dining Room and Other Tales of Victorian Culture* (Philadelphia: Temple University Press, 1992); Carter, "Who Will Do the Cooking?"; Kendall Hamilton, "Oh, Give Me a Home Where the Monitors Roam," *Newsweek*, February 24, 1997, 12. For Wells, see *Anticipations* (Dover ed.). Amy Bentley, "Martha's Food: Whiteness of a Certain Kind," *American Studies* 42:2 (summer 2001): 89–100. On resistance to socialized housekeeping, see Ruth Schwartz Cowan, *More Work for Mother: The Ironies of Household Technology from the Open Hearth to the Microwave* (New York: Basic Books, 1983), 103–99. For one exception, see Brian J. Ford, *The Future of Food* (New York: Thames and Hudson, 2000), 114–15.

45. Petersen, "21st Century Supermarket Shopping," 9; "Hot Bytes," Food Channel, June 20, 1998, accessed June 23, 1998, at www.foodchannel.com; Paul Moomaw, "The Evolution of Home Meal Replacement," Food Channel, April 15, 1996, accessed December 4, 1996, from www.foodchannel.com; Sylvia

Carter, "Tired of Shopping? Bag It," *Newsday Our Future,* 1999, accessed June 28, 1999, from http://future.newsday.com/3/fmono329.htm.

46. "Taste of Tomorrow," 42; Coates, Mahaffie, and Hines, *2025,* 379, 383–84, 436–40.

47. Coates, Mahaffie, and Hines, *2025,* 386–87.

48. "Hot Bytes," Food Channel, June 20, 1998, and June 30, 1998, both accessed July 14, 1998, from www.foodchannel.com; "Hot Bytes," Food Channel, April 15, 1997, accessed June 25, 1997, from www.foodchannel.com; "Hot Bytes," Food Channel, December 31, 1997, accessed January 27, 1998, from www.foodchannel.com.

49. Coates, Mahaffie, and Hines, *2025,* 380–81.

50. "Hot Bytes," Food Channel, September 30, 1998, accessed October 21, 1998, from www.foodchannel.com.

51. Jennifer Tanaka, "From Soup to Nuts," *Newsweek,* March 16, 1998, 77–79; "Hot Bytes," Food Channel, February 16, 1999, accessed July 1, 1999, from www.foodchannel.com.

52. Carter, "Who Will Do the Cooking?"; Tanaka, "From Soup to Nuts," 79.

53. "The Future Poll: Food Shopping," *Newsday Our Future,* 1999, accessed June 28, 1999, from http://future.newsday.com/3/fgpoll29.htm; Schwartz, "Progressive Grocer," 147; Carter, "Tired of Shopping?"; Tanaka, "From Soup to Nuts," 77; Fritschner, "Look Ahead," 9a; John L. Stanton and Richard J. George, "21 Food Trends for the 21st Century," *Grocery Marketing,* September 1996, 62; John Kessler, "Cooking: Young Adults Fueling Revival," *AccessAtlanta,* July 9, 1998, accessed July 14, 1998, from www.accessatlanta.com; Susan Mills, "A Guide to Success in 2010," *Restaurants USA Online,* September 1999, accessed January 17, 2003, from www.restaurant.org/research; Anthony Floreno, "Flavors Taste Brave New World," *Chemical Marketing Reporter,* June 24, 1996, SR30; Sean Poulter, "Darling, Your Dinners Are in the Microwaves," *Daily Mail,* June 9, 1992, 18; Phil Lempert, "The Food Consumer in 2003: A Shopper with No Time and No Cooking Skills," *Supermarket Guru,* October 27, 2002, accessed January 16, 2003, from http://supermarketguru.com.

54. "Hot Bytes," Food Channel, March 31, 1997, accessed June 25, 1997, from www.foodchannel.com; Karen Springen, "Candy and Coffee Are the New Health Foods? We Wish," *Newsweek,* May 25, 1998, 14; Lee Aschoff, "Future Food to be Healthier, Tastier, and Longer-Lasting," *Milwaukee Journal Sentinel,* April 11, 1999, 1.

55. Sugarman, "Magic Bullets," E3; Nanci Hellmich, "Future Food Could Lengthen Your Life," *USA Today Hot Line,* January 4, 1999, accessed June 28, 1999, from www.usatoday/com; "Hot Bytes," Food Channel, April 15, 1998, accessed December 4, 1996, from www.foodchannel.com.

56. Warren Belasco, *Appetite for Change: How the Counterculture Took on the Food Industry* (Ithaca: Cornell University Press, 1993), 185–99; Sugarman, "Magic Bullets," E6.

57. "Hot Bytes," Food Channel, September 25, 1996, accessed December 4, 1996, and "Hot Bytes," Food Channel, September 15, 1997, accessed September 24, 1997, both from www.foodchannel.com; Springen, "Candy and Coffee," 14; "Hot Bytes," Food Channel, June 20, 1998, accessed June 23, 1998, from

www.foodchannel.com; Marissa Fox, "Brave New Foods," *Women's Sports & Fitness,* June 2000, 104; Anne Underwood, "A Prescriptive Palette," *Newsweek,* December 6, 1999, 91–92; "A Taste of Tomorrow," 42.

58. Marion Nestle, *Food Politics: How the Food Industry Influences Nutrition and Health* (Berkeley: University of California Press, 2002), 1–28.

59. Ibid., 315, 320–21; Underwood, "Prescriptive Palate," 91–92; Sally Squires, "Designer Foods Take Off," *Washington Post Health,* May 18, 1999, 12–15; Jeremy Rifkin, "God in a Labcoat," *Utne Reader,* May-June 1999, 66–71; "In the Mood for New Food Ideas," *Food Manufacture,* July 2001, 16; "Hot Bytes," Food Channel, September 15, 1997, accessed September 24, 1997, from www.foodchannel.com; "Hot Bytes," Food Channel, November 15, 1996, accessed December 4, 1996, and September 15, 1998, accessed October 21, 1998, both from www.foodchannel.com; David Stipp, "Engineering the Future of Food," *Fortune,* September 28, 1998, 128 ff.

60. Sugarman, "Magic Bullets," E1; "The Rise of Nutraceuticals," *Science News Online,* February 15, 1997, accessed June 23, 1998, from www.sciencenews .org; Coates, Mahaffie, and Hines, 2025, 384; Ann Toner, "Cooking Illiterates Drive Future of Food Trends," *Omaha World Herald,* March 7, 1996, 43.

61. Stipp, "Engineering," 128; Squires, "Designer Foods," 14–15; Nestle, *Food Politics,* 315–37.

62. "Health, Wellness Categories Likely to Offer Significant Growth Opportunities," *Food Chemical News,* June 21, 1999, 17; Stipp, "Engineering," 128; Andrew Pollack, "New Ventures Aim to Put Farms in Vanguard of Drug Production," *New York Times,* May 14, 2000, accessed May 22, 2000, from www.biotech-info.net/new_ventures.html; idem, "Vaccine Delivered by Fork, Not Needle," *New York Times,* May 14, 2000, accessed May 22, 2000, from www .biotech-info/fork_vaccine.html; Rick Weiss, "Replacing Needles with Nibbles to Put a Bite on Disease," *Washington Post,* May 4, 1998, A3.

63. Springen, "Candy and Coffee," 14; Sugarman, "Magic Bullets," E1, E3, E6; Nestle, *Food Politics,* 336.

64. Sugarman, "Magic Bullets," E1; "Hot Bytes," Food Channel, January 30, 1999, accessed July 1, 1999, from www.foodchannel.com; Belasco, *Appetite for Change,* 237–42; "Hot Bytes," *Food Channel,* January 15, 1996, accessed December 4, 1996, from www.foodchannel.com.

65. Joanna Glasner, "Food: the Final E-Frontier," *Wired News,* January 20, 2000, accessed July 9, 2002, from www.wired.com/news; Daniel McGinn, "I'll Help Myself," *Newsweek,* April 29, 2002, 52.

66. John Frederick Moore, "Why Peapod Is Thriving: First-Failure Advantage," *Business 2.0,* August 14, 2001, accessed July 9, 2002, from www.business2 .com; Keith Regan, "More Troubles for Peapod," *E-Commerce Times,* October 26, 2000, accessed July 9, 2002, from www.ecommercetimes.com; "Grocers Find Profitable Growth in the Darndest Places," *Hoover's Online,* June 10, 2002, accessed July 9, 2002, from http://hoovnews.hoovers.com; Phil Lempert, "From E-Revolution to E-Evolution," *Supermarket Guru,* October 8, 2001, accessed January 16, 2003, from http://supermarketguru.com.

67. Matthew Herper, "'Smart' Kitchens a Long Way Off," Forbes.com, December 21, 2001, accessed January 17, 2003, from www.forbes.com; Beth

Panitz, "Smart Kitchens: Science Fiction or High-Tech Reality?" *Restaurants USA,* October 2000, accessed January 17, 2003, from www.restaurant.org; Suzanne Smalley, "Taking a Swipe at the Problem of Coupons," *Newsweek,* April 29, 2002, 47–48; Tim Johnson, "'Functional' Food Trend Brings a Host of Local Companies to the Table," *Kemper City Business,* July 13, 1998, accessed July 14, 1998, from www.amcity.com/twincities/stories/current/story4.html; Barbara Hoover, "Food Cures What Ails You," *Detroit News,* March 24, 1998, accessed April 7, 1998, from http://detnews.com; "The Future of Food," *Beverage Industry,* May 2001, 53; John Gregerson, "The 31st Annual Top R&D Survey," *Food Processing,* September 1, 2002, accessed January 8, 2003, from www.foodprocessing .com; "Foodservice 2010," accessed January 8, 2003, from www.fdi.org.

68. David Orr, "Prices and the Life Exchanged: Costs of the U.S. Food System," in *Earth in Mind: On Education, Environment, and the Human Prospect* (Washington, DC: Island Press, 1994), 172, 175. In addition to Orr, particularly lyrical and influential successors of Thoreau include Alan Thein Durning, *This Place on Earth: Home and the Practice of Permanence* (Seattle: Sasquatch Books, 1996); Joan Dye Gussow, *This Organic Life: Confessions of a Suburban Homesteader* (White River Junction, VT: Chelsea Green, 2001); Gary Paul Nabhan, *Coming Home to Eat: The Pleasures and Politics of Local Foods* (New York: W. W. Norton, 2002). For a taste of the radical critique of globalization and biotechnology, see Vandana Shiva, *Stolen Harvest: The Hijacking of the Global Food Supply* (Cambridge, MA: South End Press, 2000); Miguel Altieri, *Genetic Engineering in Agriculture: The Myths, Environmental Risks, and Alternatives* (Oakland: Food First, 2001); Marc Lappé and Britt Bailey, *Against the Grain: Biotechnology and the Corporate Takeover of Your Food* (Monroe, ME: Common Courage Press, 1998); Brian Halweil, "The Emperor's New Crops," *World Watch,* July/August 1999, 21–29. For a sweeping overview of alternative "globalization from below," see Frances Moore Lappé and Anna Lappé, *Hope's Edge: The Next Diet for a Small Planet* (New York: Jeremy P. Tarcher/Putnam, 2002).

69. Christopher Wolf, "A Taste of Tomorrow's Foods," *The Futurist,* May–June 1994, 17; Marion Nestle, *Safe Food: Bacteria, Biotechnology, and Bioterrorism* (Berkeley: University of California Press, 2003), 139–248; Belasco, *Appetite for Change,* 142–44; "Hot Bytes," Food Channel, December 30, 1998, and November 30, 1998, accessed January 20, 1999, from www.foodchannel.com; on GM labels, see, for example, Rick Weiss, "British Report: Label Gene-Modified Food," *Washington Post,* May 18, 1999, A2; "Genetically Modified Food," *The Economist,* June 19, 1999, 19–21; John Burgess, "Trade Rules Set on Food Genetics," *Washington Post,* January 30, 2000, A1; Paul Jacobs, "Cornucopia of Biotech Food Awaits Labeling," *Los Angeles Times,* January 31, 2000, 1.

POSTSCRIPT

1. Victor Cohn, *1999: Our Hopeful Future,* 1956, quoted in Laura Lee, *Bad Predictions: 2000 Years of the Best Minds Making the Worst Forecasts* (Rochester Hills, MI: Elsewhere Press, 2000), 28; Russell quoted in Lee, *Bad Predictions,* 27; "Your Life in 1985," *Science Digest,* 1955, quoted in Lee, *Bad Predictions,* 28.

2. Bill Gates, 1981: "640K ought to be enough for anybody," quoted in Lee,

Bad Predictions, 108; Thomas Watson, 1958: "I think there is a world market for maybe five computers," quoted in Lee, *Bad Predictions,* 106; Richard Manning, "Super Organics," *Wired,* May 2004, 176–80 ff; Michael Pollan, "The Great Yellow Hype," *New York Times Magazine,* March 4, 2001, 15.

3. Researchers at RAND developed the Delphi technique in the early 1960s as a way to come up with an intensive "group forecast." Edward Cornish, *The Study of the Future* (Bethesda, MD: World Future Society, 1993), 85–86.

4. William Thompson, Lord Kelvin, quoted in Lee, *Bad Predictions,* 136, 113; Ehrlich, *Population Bomb,* 1968, quoted in Lee, *Bad Predictions,* 30.

5. For an enlightening set of meditations by professional futurists on this theme of multiple futures, see Michael Marien and Lane Jennings, eds., *What I Have Learned: Thinking about the Future Then and Now* (Westport, CT: Greenwood, 1987).

6. Gordon Conway, *The Doubly Green Revolution: Food for All in the 21st Century* (Ithaca: Cornell University Press, 1998); Archer Daniels Midland homepage, accessed July 16, 2004, at www.admworld.com/eng/; Syngenta homepage, accessed July 16, 2004, at www.zeneca.com/en/index.aspx; Monsanto homepage, accessed July 16, 2004, at www.monsanto.com.

SELECTED BIBLIOGRAPHY

Aaron, Daniel. *Men of Good Hope: A Story of American Progressives.* New York: Oxford University Press, 1951.

Abe, Kobe. *Inter Ice Age 4.* New York: Knopf, 1970.

Adams, Carol J. *The Sexual Politics of Meat: A Feminist-Vegetarian Critical Theory.* New York: Continuum, 1990.

Akin, William E. *Technocracy and the American Dream.* Berkeley: University of California Press, 1977.

Alcott, William A. "The World Is a Mighty Slaughterhouse and Flesh-Eating and Human Decimation." In *Ethical Vegetarianism: From Pythagoras to Peter Singer,* ed. Kerry S. Walters and Lisa Portmess. Albany: State University of New York Press, 1999.

Aldiss, Brian W. *Greybeard.* New York: Harcourt, Brace, and World, 1964.

Allen, Polly Wynn. *Building Domestic Liberty: Charlotte Perkins Gilman's Architectural Feminism.* Amherst: University of Massachusetts Press, 1988.

Altieri, Miguel. *Genetic Engineering in Agriculture: The Myths, Environmental Risks, and Alternatives.* Oakland: Food First, 2001.

Amato, Joseph A. *Dust: A History of the Small and the Invisible.* Berkeley: University of California Press, 2000.

Ames, Kenneth L. *Death in the Dining Room and Other Tales of Victorian Culture.* Philadelphia: Temple University Press, 1992.

Anderson, Walter Truett. "Food without Farms: The Biotech Revolution in Agriculture." *The Futurist,* January–February 1990, 16–21.

Apple, Rima. *Vitamania: Vitamins in American Culture.* New Brunswick: Rutgers University Press, 1996.

Applebaum, Stanley, ed. *The New York World's Fair, 1939/40.* New York: Dover, 1977.

Appleton, Jane Sophia. "Sequel to the Vision of Bangor in the 20th Century." 1848.

Reprinted in *Daring to Dream: Utopian Stories by U.S. Women, 1836–1919,* ed. Carol Farley Kessler. Boston: Pandora Press, 1984.

Armytage, W. H. G. *Yesterday's Tomorrows: A Historical Survey of Future Societies.* London: Routledge, 1968.

Asimov, Isaac. *Caves of Steel.* New York: Signet, 1953.

———. "The Last Trump." In Isaac Asimov, *Earth Is Room Enough.* New York: Bantam Books, 1957.

———. "Living Space." In Asimov, *Earth Is Room Enough.*

———. "Satisfaction Guaranteed." In Asimov, *Earth Is Room Enough.*

Astor, John Jacob. *A Journey in Other Worlds.* New York: D. Appleton and Co., 1894.

Atkins, Peter, and Ian Bowler. *Food in Society: Economy, Culture, Geography.* London: Arnold, 2001.

Avineri, Shlomo, ed. *Karl Marx on Colonialism.* New York: Anchor, 1969.

Bacon-Smith, Camille. *Science Fiction Culture.* Philadelphia: University of Pennsylvania Press, 2000.

Badger, Reid. *The Great American Fair: The World's Columbian Exposition and American Culture.* Chicago: Nelson Hall, 1979.

Ballard, J. G. "Billenium." 1961. Reprinted in *Science Fiction: Contemporary Mythology,* ed. Patricia Warrick, Martin Henry Greenberg, and Joseph Olander. New York: Harper and Row, 1978.

Barr, Marleen, and Nicholas Smith, eds. *Women and Utopia: Critical Interpretations.* Lanham, MD: University Press of America, 1983.

Belasco, Warren. "Algae Burgers for a Hungry World? The Rise and Fall of Chlorella Cuisine." *Technology and Culture* 38:7 (July 1997): 608–34.

———. *Americans on the Road: From Autocamp to Motel.* Cambridge, MA: MIT Press, 1979.

———. *Appetite for Change: How the Counterculture Took on the Food Industry.* Ithaca: Cornell University Press, 1993.

———. "Food Matters: Perspectives on an Emerging Field." In *Food Nations: Selling Taste in Consumer Societies,* ed. Warren Belasco and Philip Scranton. New York: Routledge, 2002.

———. "Food, Morality, and Social Reform." In *Morality and Health,* ed. Allan M. Brandt and Paul Rozin. New York: Routledge, 1997.

———. "Future Notes: The Meal-in-a-Pill." *Food and Foodways* 8:4 (2000): 253–71.

———. "Toward a Culinary Common Denominator: The Rise of Howard Johnson's, 1925–1940." *Journal of American Culture* 2:3 (fall 1979): 503–18.

Belasco, Warren, and Philip Scranton, eds. *Food Nations: Selling Taste in Consumer Societies.* New York: Routledge, 2002.

Bellamy, Edward. *Looking Backward.* 1888. Reprint, New York: Signet, 1960.

Benedict, Burton. *The Anthropology of World's Fairs: San Francisco's Panama-Pacific International Exposition of 1915.* Berkeley: Scolar Press, 1983.

Bentley, Amy. *Eating for Victory: Food Rationing and the Politics of Domesticity.* Urbana: University of Illinois Press, 1998.

Berger, Harold L. *Science Fiction and the New Dark Age.* Bowling Green, OH: Popular Press, 1976.

Bird, Arthur. *Looking Forward: A Dream of the United States of the Americas in 1999*. 1899. New York: Arno, 1971.

Birk, Dorothy Daniels. *The World Came to St. Louis: A Visit to the 1904 World's Fair*. St. Louis: Bethany Press, 1979.

Birkenhead, First Earl of [Frederick Edward Smith]. *The World in 2030 AD*. London: Hodder & Stoughton, 1930.

Black, John D. *Food Enough*. Lancaster, PA: Jacques Cattell Press, 1943.

Black, John Donald, and Maxine Enlow Kiefer. *Future Food and Agriculture Policy: A Program for the Next Ten Years*. New York: McGraw-Hill, 1948.

Blish, James. "We All Die Naked." In *Three for Tomorrow*, ed. Robert Silverberg. New York: Dell, 1969.

Bonner, James. "The Next Ninety Years." In *The Next Ninety Years: Proceedings of a Conference Sponsored by the Office for Industrial Associates at the California Institute of Technology, March 7–8, 1967*. Pasadena: California Institute of Technology, 1967.

Boorstin, Daniel J. *The Americans: The National Experience*. New York: Vintage, 1965.

Borgstrom, Georg. *The Food and People Dilemma*. North Scituate, MA: Duxbury Press, 1973.

Boyd-Orr, John. *The White Man's Dilemma: Food and the Future*. London: George Allen and Unwin, 1953.

Boyer, Paul. *By the Bomb's Early Light: American Thought and Culture at the Dawn of the Atomic Age*. New York: Pantheon Books, 1985.

Boyle, T. C. *A Friend of the Earth*. New York: Viking Books, 2002.

Brandt, Allan M., and Paul Rozin, eds. *Morality and Health*. New York: Routledge, 1997.

Braudel, Fernand. *The Structures of Everyday Life*. Berkeley: University of California Press, 1992.

Brewster, Letitia, and Michael Jacobson. *The Changing American Diet: A Chronicle of American Eating Habits from 1910–1980*. Washington, DC: Center for Science in the Public Interest, 1980.

Brinsmade, Herman Hine. *Utopia Achieved: A Novel of the Future*. New York: Broadway Publishing Co., 1912.

Brittain, Robert. *Let There Be Bread*. New York: Simon and Schuster, 1952.

Brock, William H. *Justus Von Liebig: The Chemical Gatekeeper*. Cambridge: Cambridge University Press, 1997.

Brooks, Harvey. "Technology-Related Catastrophes: Myth and Reality." In *Visions of Apocalypse: End or Rebirth?* ed. Saul Friedlander et al. New York: Holmes and Meier, 1985.

Brown, Harrison. *The Challenge of Man's Future*. New York: Viking Press, 1954.

———. *The Human Future Revisited: The World Predicament and Possible Solutions*. New York: W. W. Norton, 1978.

———. "The Next Ninety Years." In *The Next Ninety Years: Proceedings of a Conference Sponsored by the Office for Industrial Associates at the California Institute of Technology, March 7–8, 1967*. Pasadena: California Institute of Technology, 1967.

Brown, Harrison, James Bonner, and John Weir. *The Next Hundred Years.* New York: Viking Press, 1957.

Brown, Lester R. *Seeds of Change: The Green Revolution and Development in the 1970s.* New York: Praeger, 1970.

———. *Tough Choices: Facing the Challenge of Food Scarcity.* New York: W. W. Norton, 1996.

———. *Who Will Feed China? Wake-Up Call for a Small Planet.* New York: W. W. Norton, 1995.

Brown, Lester R., Christopher Flavin, and Sandra Postel. *Saving the Planet: How to Shape an Environmentally Sustainable Global Economy.* New York: W. W. Norton, 1991.

Brown, Lester R., Gary Gardner, and Brian Halweil. *Beyond Malthus: Sixteen Dimensions of the Population Problem.* Worldwatch Paper 143. Washington, DC: Worldwatch Institute, September 1998.

Brown, Lester R., and Hal Kane. *Full House: Reassessing the Earth's Population Carrying Capacity.* New York: W. W. Norton, 1994.

Brunner, John. *The Sheep Look Up.* New York: Ballantine, 1972.

———. *Stand on Zanzibar.* New York: Ballantine, 1968.

Bryant, Dorothy. *The Kin of Ata Are Waiting.* New York: Random House, 1971.

Buel, J. W. *The Magic City: A Massive Portfolio of Original Photographic Views of the Great World's Fair.* St. Louis: Historical Publishing Co., 1894.

Burch, Guy Irving, and Elmer Pendell. *Human Breeding and Survival: Population Roads to Peace or War.* New York: Penguin, 1947.

Burgess, Anthony. *The Wanting Seed.* New York: Ballantine, 1964.

Burlew, John S. "Current Status of the Large-Scale Culture of Algae." In *Algal Culture: From Laboratory to Pilot Plant,* ed. John S. Burlew. Washington, DC: Carnegie Institution, 1953.

Burt, Donald C. "The Well-Manicured Landscape: Nature in Utopia." In *America as Utopia,* ed. Kenneth M. Roemer. New York: Burt Franklin, 1981.

Butler, Octavia E. *Parable of the Sower.* New York: Four Walls Eight Windows, 1993.

Callenbach, Ernest. *Ecotopia: The Novel of Your Future.* New York: Bantam, 1975.

Canto, Christophe, and Odile Faliu. *The History of the Future: Images of the 21st Century.* Paris: Flammarion, 1993.

Cawelti, John G. "America on Display: The World's Fairs of 1876, 1893, 1933." In *The Age of Industrialism in America,* ed. Frederic C. Jaher. New York: Free Press, 1968.

Charles, Daniel. *Lords of the Harvest: Biotech, Big Money, and the Future of Food.* Cambridge, MA: Perseus Publishing, 2001.

Charles, Enid. *Twilight of Parenthood: A Biological Study of the Decline of Population Growth.* London: Watts & Co., 1934.

Chase, Allan. *The Legacy of Malthus: The Social Costs of the New Scientific Racism.* New York: Knopf, 1977.

Christopher, John. *No Blade of Grass.* New York: Avon Books, 1956,

Clarke, I. F. *The Pattern of Expectation, 1644–2001.* New York: Basic Books, 1979.

Coates, Joseph F., John B. Mahaffie, and Andy Hines. *2025: Scenarios of US and Global Society Reshaped by Science and Technology*. Greensboro, NC: Oakhill Press, 1997.

Cohen, Joel E. *How Many People Can the Earth Support?* New York: W. W. Norton, 1995.

Cohn, Victor. *1999: Our Hopeful Future*. Indianapolis: Bobbs-Merrill, 1956.

Condorcet, Marquis de. "The Future Progress of the Human Mind." In *Esquisse d'un Tableau Historique des Progres de L'Esprit Humain*. 1794. Accessed May 21, 2003. Available at http://ishi.lib.berkeley.edu/~hist280/research/condorcet/pages/progress_main.html.

Conkin, Paul K. *Tomorrow a New World: The New Deal Community Program*. Ithaca: Cornell University Press, 1959.

Conway, Gordon. *The Doubly Green Revolution: Food for All in the 21st Century*. Ithaca: Cornell University Press, 1998.

Cook, J. Gordon. *The Fight for Food*. New York: Dial Press, 1957.

Corn, Joseph J., ed. *Imagining Tomorrow: History, Technology, and the American Future*. Cambridge, MA: MIT Press, 1986.

Corn, Joseph J., and Brian Horrigan. *Yesterday's Tomorrows: Past Visions of the American Future*. Baltimore: Johns Hopkins University Press, 1984.

Cornish, Edward. *The Study of the Future*. Bethesda, MD: World Future Society, 1993.

Cowan, Ruth Schwartz. *More Work for Mother: The Ironies of Household Technology from the Open Hearth to the Microwave*. New York: Basic Books, 1983.

Crabb, A. Richard. *The Hybrid Corn-Makers: Prophets of Plenty*. New Brunswick: Rutgers University Press, 1947.

Craig, Alex. *Ionia: Land of Wise Men and Fair Women*. Chicago: E. A. Weeks, 1898.

Cridge, Annie Denton. "Man's Rights; Or How Would You Like It?" 1870. Reprinted in *Daring to Dream: Utopian Stories by U.S. Women, 1836–1919*, ed. Carol Farley Kessler. Boston: Pandora Press, 1984.

Cusker, Joseph P. "The World of Tomorrow: Science, Culture, and Community at the New York World's Fair." In *Dawn of a New Day: The New York World's Fair, 1939/40*, ed. Helen A. Harrison. New York: New York University Press, 1980.

Dalzell, Robert F., Jr. *American Participation in the Great Exhibition of 1851*. Amherst, MA: Amherst College Press, 1960.

Davis, Joseph S. *The Population Upsurge in the United States*, War-Peace Pamphlet no. 12. Stanford: Stanford University Food Research Institute, December 1949.

———. "The Specter of Dearth of Food: History's Answer to Sir William Crookes." In *Facts and Factors in Economic History*. Cambridge, MA: Harvard University Press, 1932.

Davis, Mike. *Ecology of Fear: Los Angeles and the Imagination of Disaster*. New York: Metropolitan Books, 1998.

———. *Late Victorian Holocausts: El Niño Famines and the Making of the Third World*. London: Verso, 2001.

de Castro, Josue. *The Geography of Hunger.* Boston: Little, Brown and Co., 1952.

Devereux, Stephen. *Famine in the Twentieth Century.* Brighton, UK: Institute of Development Studies, 2000.

Diamond, Jared. *Collapse: How Societies Choose to Fail or Succeed.* New York: Viking, 2005.

Dietz, David. *Atomic Energy in the Coming Era.* New York: Dodd, Mead & Co., 1945.

Diner, Hasia. *Hungering for America: Italian, Irish, and Jewish Foodways in the Age of Migration.* Cambridge, MA: Harvard University Press, 2001.

Dodd, Anna Bowman. *The Republic of the Future or, Socialism a Reality.* 1887. Excerpted in *The Land of Contrasts, 1880–1901,* ed. Neil Harris. New York: George Brazilier, 1970.

Dodd, Norris. "Forward." In *Freedom from Want,* ed. E. E. DeTurk. New York: Chronica Botanica, 1948.

Donaldson, Peter J. *Nature against Us: The United States and the World Population Crisis, 1965–1990.* Chapel Hill: University of North Carolina Press, 1990.

Donawerth, Jane L. "Science Fiction by Women in the Early Pulps, 1926–1930." In *Utopian and Science Fiction by Women,* ed. Jane L. Donawerth and Carol A. Kolmerten. Syracuse: Syracuse University Press, 1994.

Donawerth, Jane L., and Carol A. Kolmerten, eds. *Utopian and Science Fiction by Women: Worlds of Difference.* Syracuse: Syracuse University Press, 1994.

Doyle, Jack. *Altered Harvest: Agriculture, Genetics, and the Fate of the World's Food Supply.* New York: Penguin, 1986.

Drewnowski, Adam. "Fat and Sugar in the Global Diet: Dietary Diversity in the Nutrition Transition." In *Food in Global History,* ed. Raymond Grew. Boulder: Westview Press, 1999.

Durning, Alan Thein. *This Place on Earth: Home and the Practice of Permanence.* Seattle: Sasquatch Books, 1996.

East, Edward M. *Mankind at the Crossroads.* New York: Charles Scribner's Sons, 1924.

Edson, Milan C. *Solaris Farm: A Story of the 20th Century.* Washington, DC: by the author, 1900.

Ehrlich, Paul R. "Eco-Catastrophe!" In *The Environmental Handbook,* ed. Garrett De Bell. New York: Ballantine Books, 1970.

———. "Mankind's Inalienable Rights." In *The Environmental Handbook,* ed. Garrett De Bell. New York: Ballantine Books, 1970.

———. *The Population Bomb.* New York: Ballantine Books, 1968.

Ehrlich, Paul, and John P. Holdren. "8,000,000,000 People: We'll Never Get There." *Development Forum,* April 1976. Reprinted in *The Feeding Web: Issues in Nutritional Ecology,* ed. Joan Dye Gussow. Palo Alto: Bull Publishing, 1978.

Elliott, Maud Howe, ed. *Art and Handicraft in the Women's Building of the World's Columbian Exposition.* New York: Goupil and Co., 1893.

Fisher, A. W., and John S. Burlew. "Nutritional Value of Microscopic Algae." In *Algal Culture: From Laboratory to Pilot Plant,* ed. John S. Burlew. Washington, DC: Carnegie Institution, 1953.

Fite, Gilbert C. *American Farmers: The New Minority.* Bloomington: Indiana University Press, 1984.

Fjellman, Stephen M. *Vinyl Leaves: Walt Disney World and America.* Boulder: Westview, 1992.

Ford, Barbara. *Future Food: Alternative Protein for the Year 2000.* New York: William Morrow, 1978.

Ford, Brian J. *The Future of Food.* New York: Thames and Hudson, 2000.

Francis, David R. *The Universal Exposition of 1904.* St. Louis: Louisiana Purchase Exposition Company, 1913.

Frank, George, ed. *Science Fact: Astounding and Exciting Developments That Will Transform Your Life.* New York: Sterling Publishing, 1978.

Franks, Betty Barclay. "Futurists and the American Dream: A History of Contemporary Futurist Thought." D.Arts diss., Carnegie-Mellon University, 1985.

Friedlander, Saul. Introduction to *Visions of Apocalypse: End or Rebirth?* ed. Saul Friedlander et al. New York: Holmes and Meier, 1985.

———. "Themes of Decline and End in Nineteenth-Century Imagination." In *Visions of Apocalypse: End or Rebirth?* ed. Saul Friedlander, et al. New York: Holmes and Meier, 1985.

Furnas, C. C. *America's Tomorrow: An Informal Excursion into the Era of the Two-Hour Working Day.* New York: Funk & Wagnalls, 1932.

Fussell, Betty. *The Story of Corn.* New York: North Point Press, 1992.

Gabaccia, Donna. *We Are What We Eat: Ethnic Food and the Making of Americans.* Cambridge, MA: Harvard University Press, 1998.

Gardner, Gary, and Brian Halweil. *Underfed and Overfed: The Global Epidemic of Malnutrition.* Worldwatch Paper 150. Washington, DC: Worldwatch Institute, March 2000.

Gearhart, Sally Miller. *Wanderground.* Boston: Alyson Publications, 1978.

Gernsback, Hugo. *Ralph 124C 41+.* 1911. Reprint, Lincoln: University of Nebraska Press, 2000.

Gibson, James R., Jr. *Americans versus Malthus: The Population Debate in the Early Republic, 1790–1840.* New York: Garland, 1989.

Gilbert, James. *Perfect Cities: Chicago's Utopias of 1893.* Chicago: University of Chicago Press, 1991.

Gilman, Charlotte Perkins. *Herland.* 1915. Reprint, New York: Pantheon Books, 1979.

Gitlin, Todd. *Inside Prime Time.* New York: Pantheon Books, 1983.

Glesinger, Egon. *The Coming Age of Wood.* New York: Simon and Schuster, 1949.

Godwin, William. *Of Population.* London: Longman, Hurst, Rees, and Brown, 1820. Accessed May 21, 2003. Available at http://dwardmac.pitzer.edu/Anarchist_Archives/godwin/population/chapter3.html.

———. *Thoughts on Man, His Nature, Productions, Discoveries, Interspersed with Some Particulars Respecting the Author.* London: Effingham Wilson, 1831. Accessed May 21, 2003. Available at http://dwardmac.pitzer.edu/Anarchist_Archives/godwin/thoughts/TMNPDfrontpiece.html.

Greene, Ronald Walter. *Malthusian Worlds: U.S. Leadership and the Governing of the Population Crisis.* New York: Westview Press, 1999.

Griffith, Mary. "Three Hundred Years Hence." 1836. Reprinted in *Daring to Dream: Utopian Stories by U.S. Women, 1836–1919,* ed. Carol Farley Kessler. Boston: Pandora Press, 1984.

Guarneri, Carl J. *The Utopian Alternative: Fourierism in Nineteenth-Century America.* Ithaca: Cornell University Press, 1991.

Gussow, Joan Dye, ed. *The Feeding Web: Issues in Nutritional Ecology.* Palo Alto: Bull Publishing, 1978.

———. *This Organic Life: Confessions of a Suburban Homesteader.* White River Junction, VT: Chelsea Green, 2001.

Haldane, J. B. S. *Daedalus.* London: Kegan Paul, 1924.

Hale, William J. *Chemistry Triumphant: The Rise and Reign of Chemistry in a Chemical World.* Baltimore: Williams & Wilkins, 1932.

———. *Eat Here: Reclaiming Homegrown Pleasures in a Global Supermarket.* New York: W. W. Norton, 2004.

———. *The Farm Chemurgic: Farmward the Star of Destiny Lights Our Way.* Boston: Stratford, 1934.

Hardin, Garrett. *Living within Limits: Ecology, Economics, and Population Taboos.* New York: Oxford University Press, 1993.

Harris, Neil. "Great Fairs and American Cities: The Role of Chicago's Columbian Exposition." In *Cultural Excursions.* Chicago: University of Chicago Press, 1990.

———. "Utopian Fiction and Its Discontents." In *Cultural Excursions.* Chicago: University of Chicago Press, 1990.

Harrison, Harry. *Make Room! Make Room!* 1966. Reprint, New York: Berkeley Medallion, 1967.

Harrison, Helen A., ed. *Dawn of a New Day: The New York World's Fair, 1939/40.* New York: New York University Press, 1980.

Hayden, Dolores. *The Grand Domestic Revolution: A History of Feminist Designs for American Homes, Neighborhoods, and Cities.* Cambridge, MA: MIT Press. 1981.

Hazell, Peter B. R., and C. Ramasamy. *The Green Revolution Reconsidered: The Impact of High-Yielding Rice Varieties in South India.* Baltimore: Johns Hopkins University Press, 1991.

Heilbroner, Robert. *The Worldly Philosophers.* New York: Simon & Schuster, 1961.

Hine, Thomas. *Populuxe: The Look and Life of America in the '50s and '60s, from Tailfins and TV Dinners to Barbie Dolls and Fallout Shelters.* New York: Knopf, 1990.

Hinsley, Curtis. "The World as Marketplace: Commodification of the Exotic at the World's Columbian Exposition." In *Exhibiting Cultures: The Poetics and Politics of Museum Display,* ed. Ivan Karp and Steven D. Lavine. Washington, DC: Smithsonian Institution Press, 1991.

Hofstadter, Richard. *Social Darwinism in American Thought.* Boston: Beacon, 1955.

Howells, William Dean. *The Altrurian Romances: Through the Eye of the Needle.* Bloomington: Indiana University Press, 1968.

Hughes, Angela. "Dystopian Themes and *The Parable of the Sower.*" Unpublished research paper. University of Maryland Baltimore County, 1995.

Huxley, Aldous. *Ape and Essence.* 1948. Reprint, New York: Bantam, 1958.
———. *Brave New World.* 1932. Reprint, New York: Perennial, 1969.
———. *Brave New World Revisited.* New York: Harper and Row, 1958.
———. *Island.* 1962. Reprint, New York: Perennial, 1972.
Jochnowitz, Eve. "Feasting on the Future: Serving Up the World of Tomorrow at the New York World's Fair of 1939–1940." M.A. thesis, New York University, 1997.
Johnson, Rossiter, ed. *A History of the World's Columbian Exposition.* Vol. 3: *Exhibits.* New York: D. Appleton, 1898.
Kahn, Herman, et al. *The Next 200 Years: A Scenario for America and the World.* New York: William Morrow, 1976.
Kasson, John F. "The Rituals of Dining: Table Manners in Victorian America." In *Dining in America, 1850–1900,* ed. Kathryn Grover. Amherst: University of Massachusetts Press, 1987.
Kennedy, Paul. *Preparing for the Twenty-First Century.* New York: Random House, 1993.
Kermode, Frank. "Apocalypse and the Modern." In *Visions of Apocalypse: End or Rebirth?* ed. Saul Friedlander et al. New York: Holmes and Meier, 1985.
Kessler, Carol Farley. "Consider Her Ways: The Cultural Work of Charlotte Perkins Gilman's Pragmatorian Stories, 1908–1913." In *Utopian and Science Fiction by Women: Worlds of Difference,* ed. Jane L. Donawerth and Carol A. Kolmerten. Syracuse: Syracuse University Press, 1994.
———, ed. *Daring to Dream: Utopian Stories by U.S. Women, 1836–1919.* Boston: Pandora Press, 1984.
Keynes, J. M. *The Economic Consequences of the Peace.* New York: Harcourt Brace, 1920.
Kihlstedt, Folke T. "Utopia Realized: The World's Fairs of the 1930s." In *Imagining Tomorrow: History, Technology, and the American Future,* ed. Joseph J. Corn. Cambridge, MA: MIT Press, 1986.
Kloppenburg, Jack R., Jr. *First the Seed: The Political Economy of Plant Biotechnology, 1492–2000.* Cambridge: Cambridge University Press, 1988.
Kloppenburg, Jack, Jr., John Hendrickson, and G. W. Stevenson. "Coming in to the Foodshed." *Agriculture and Human Values* 13:3 (summer 1996): 33–42.
Knibbs, George Handley. *The Shadow of the World's Future.* London: Ernest Benn, 1928.
Laird, Pamela Walker. *Advertising Progress: American Business and the Rise of Consumer Marketing.* Baltimore: Johns Hopkins University Press, 1998.
Landon, Brooks. "Ain't No Fiber in Cyberspace: A Metonymic Menu for a Paratactic Potpourri." In *Foods of the Gods: Eating and the Eaten in Fantasy and Science Fiction,* ed. Gary Westphal, George Slusser, and Eric S. Rabkin. Athens: University of Georgia Press, 1996.
Lane, Mary E. Bradley. *Mizora: A Prophecy.* 1880. Reprint, Boston: Gregg Press, 1975.
Langdon, Philip. *Orange Roofs, Golden Arches: The Architecture of American Chain Restaurants.* New York: Alfred A. Knopf, 1986.
Lappé, Frances Moore. *Diet for a Small Planet.* New York: Ballantine Books, 1971.

————. *Diet for a Small Planet: 10th anniversary edition.* New York: Ballantine Books, 1982.

Lappé, Frances Moore, and Anna Lappé. *Hope's Edge: The Next Diet for a Small Planet.* New York: Jeremy P. Tarcher/Putnam, 2002.

Lappé, Frances Moore, and Joseph Collins. *World Hunger: Twelve Myths.* New York: Grove Press, 1986.

Lappé, Frances Moore, Joseph Collins, and Peter Rosset. *World Hunger: Twelve Myths.* 2nd updated and revised edition. New York: Grove Press, 1998.

Lappé, Marc, and Britt Bailey. *Against the Grain: Biotechnology and the Corporate Takeover of Your Food.* Monroe, ME: Common Courage Press, 1998.

Lee, Laura. *Bad Predictions: 2000 Years of the Best Minds Making the Worst Forecasts.* Rochester Hills, MI: Elsewhere Press, 2000.

Levenstein, Harvey. *Paradox of Plenty: A Social History of Eating in Modern America.* New York: Oxford University Press, 1993.

————. *Revolution at the Table: The Transformation of the American Diet.* New York: Oxford University Press, 1988.

Logsdon, Gene. *At Nature's Pace: Farming and the American Dream.* New York: Pantheon Books, 1994.

Lomborg, Bjorn. *The Skeptical Environmentalist: Measuring the Real State of the World.* Cambridge: Cambridge University Press, 2001.

McClung, William Alexander. *Landscapes of Desire: Anglo Mythologies of Los Angeles.* Berkeley: University of California Press, 2000.

McCurdy, Howard E. *Space and the American Imagination.* Washington, DC: Smithsonian Institution Press, 1997.

McMillen, Wheeler. *Too Many Farmers: The Story of What Is Here and Ahead in Agriculture.* New York: William Morrow, 1929.

Malthus, Thomas. *An Essay on the Principle of Population.* 1798. London: Penguin, 1985.

Mandrovsky, B. *Aerospace Life Support Systems.* Washington, DC: Library of Congress, 1968.

Manuel, Frank E. *The Prophets of Paris: Turgot, Condorcet, Saint-Simon, Fourier, and Comte.* New York: Harper Torchbooks, 1965.

Marchand, Roland. *Advertising the American Dream: Making Way for Modernity, 1920–1940.* Berkeley: University of California Press, 1985.

————. "Corporate Imagery and Popular Education: World's Fairs and Expositions in the United States, 1893–1940." In *Consumption and American Culture,* ed. David E. Nye and Carl Pedersen. Amsterdam: VU University Press, 1991.

————. *Creating the Corporate Soul: The Rise of Public Relations and Corporate Imagery in American Big Business.* Berkeley: University of California Press, 1998.

Marchand, Roland, and Michael L. Smith. "Corporate Science on Display." In *Scientific Authority and Twentieth Century America,* ed. Ronald G. Walters. Baltimore: Johns Hopkins University Press, 1997.

Marien, Michael, and Lane Jennings, eds. *What I Have Learned: Thinking about the Future Then and Now.* Westport, CT: Greenwood, 1987.

Meikle, Jeffrey L. *American Plastic: A Cultural History.* New Brunswick: Rutgers University Press, 1997.

———. *Twentieth Century Limited: Industrial Design in America, 1925–1939.* Philadelphia: Temple University Press, 1979.

Meier, Richard L. *Science and Economic Development: New Patterns of Living.* Cambridge, MA: MIT Press, 1956.

Messer, Ellen. "Food from Peace and Roles of Women." In *Who Will Be Fed in the 21st Century?* ed. Keith Weibe, Nicole Ballenger, and Per Pinstrup-Andersen. Washington, DC: International Food Policy Research Institute, 2001.

Mintz, Sidney W. *Sweetness and Power: The Place of Sugar in Modern History.* New York: Penguin, 1986.

Mirzoeff, Nicholas. "Transculture: From Kongo to the Congo." In *An Introduction to Visual Culture.* London: Routledge, 1999.

Moore, Ward. *Greener Than You Think.* New York: William Sloan, 1947.

Morris, William. *News from Nowhere.* 1891. New York: Penguin, 1993.

Myers, Norman and Julian Simon. *Scarcity or Abundance? A Debate on the Environment.* New York: W. W. Norton, 1994.

Nabhan, Gary Paul. *Coming Home to Eat: The Pleasure and Politics of Local Foods.* New York: W. W. Norton, 2002.

NASA Facts. "Food for Space Flight." Accessed June 22, 2004, at http://www.nasa.gov/lb/audience/forstudents/postsecondary/features/F_Food_for_Space_Flight.html.

National Academy of Sciences—National Research Council, Committee on Resources and Man. *Resources and Man.* San Francisco: W. H. Freeman, 1969.

National Resources Board. *A Report on National Planning and Public Works in Relation to Natural Resources and including Land Use and Water Resources.* Washington, DC: Government Printing Office, 1934.

Nestle, Marion. *Food Politics: How the Food Industry Influences Nutrition and Health.* Berkeley: University of California Press, 2002.

———. *Safe Food: Bacteria, Biotechnology, and Bioterrorism.* Berkeley: University of California Press, 2003.

O'Neill, Gerald K. "Space Colonies: The High Frontier." In *1999: The World of Tomorrow,* ed. Edward Cornish. Washington, DC: World Future Society, 1978.

Ordway, Samuel H. *Resources and the American Dream.* New York: Ronald Press, 1953.

Orr, David. *Earth in Mind: On Education, Environment, and the Human Prospect.* Washington DC: Island Press, 1994.

———. "Food Alchemy and Sustainable Agriculture." In *Ecological Literacy.* Albany: State University of New York Press, 1992.

Orwell, George. *1984.* New York: Signet, 1950.

Osborn, Fairfield. *The Limits of the Earth.* Boston: Little, Brown, 1953.

———. *Our Plundered Planet.* Boston: Little, Brown, 1948.

Paddock, William, and Paul Paddock. *Famine—1975! America's Decision: Who Will Survive?* Boston: Little, Brown & Co., 1967.

Pearl, Raymond. *The Nation's Food: A Statistical Study of a Physiological and Social Problem.* Philadelphia: W. B. Saunders, 1920.

Pearson, Frank A., and Floyd A. Harper. *The World's Hunger.* Ithaca: Cornell University Press, 1945.

Peck, Bradford. *The World a Department Store: A Twentieth Century Utopia.* Lewiston, ME: by the author, 1900.

Perkins, John H. *Geopolitics and the Green Revolution: Wheat, Genes, and the Cold War.* New York: Oxford University Press, 1997.

Pfaelzer, Jean. *The Utopian Novel in America: 1886–1896.* Pittsburgh: University of Pittsburgh Press, 1984.

Piercy, Marge. *Woman on the Edge of Time.* New York: Fawcett Crest, 1976.

Piotrow, Phyllis Tilson. *World Population Crisis: The United States Response.* New York: Praeger, 1973.

Pitkin, Walter B. *Must We Fight Japan?* New York: Century, 1921.

Pohl, Frederick. *The Merchants' War.* New York: St. Martin's Press, 1984.

Pohl, Frederick, and C. M. Kornbluth. *The Space Merchants.* 1952. Collected in *Venus, Inc.* Garden City: Doubleday, 1984.

Postel, Sandra. "Carrying Capacity: Earth's Bottom Line." In *State of the World 1994,* ed. Lester R. Brown et al. New York: W. W. Norton, 1994.

Pyke, Magnus. *Synthetic Food.* London: John Murray, 1970.

Rabkin, Eric, Martin Greenberg, and Joseph Olander, eds. *The End of the World.* Carbondale: Southern Illinois Press, 1983.

Reed, James. *The Birth Control Movement and American Society: From Private Vice to Public Virtue.* Princeton: Princeton University Press, 1978.

Rifkin, Jeremy. *Beyond Beef: The Rise and Fall of the Cattle Culture.* New York: Plume, 1992.

Roemer, Kenneth. *The Obsolete Necessity: America in Utopian Writing, 1888–1900.* Kent, OH: Kent State University Press, 1976.

Rosin, Jacob, and Max Eastman. *The Road to Abundance.* New York: McGraw-Hill, 1953.

Ross, Edward Alsworth. *Standing Room Only?* New York: Century Co., 1927.

Russell, A. P. *Sub-Coelum: A Sky-Built Human World.* Boston: Houghton Mifflin, 1893.

Rydell, Robert W. *All the World's a Fair: Visions of Empire at American International Expositions, 1876–1916.* Chicago: University of Chicago Press, 1984.

———. "The Culture of Imperial Abundance: World's Fairs in the Making of American Culture." In *Consuming Visions: Accumulation and Display of Goods in America, 1880–1920,* ed. Simon T. Bronner. New York: Norton: 1989.

———. *World of Fairs: The Century-of-Progress Expositions.* Chicago: University of Chicago Press, 1993.

Sargent, Lyman Tower. "A New Anarchism: Social and Political Ideas in Some Recent Feminist Eutopias." In *Women and Utopia,* ed. Marleen Barr and Nicholas Smith. Lanham, MD: University Press of America, 1983.

Sax, Karl. *Standing Room Only: The Challenge of Overpopulation.* Boston: Beacon Press, 1953.

Schremp, Gerry. *Kitchen Culture: Fifty Years of Food Fads.* New York: Pharos Books, 1991.

Sears, Paul B. *Deserts on the March.* 3rd ed. Norman: University of Oklahoma Press, 1959.

Segal, Howard P. *Technological Utopianism in American Culture*. Chicago: University of Chicago Press, 1985.

Shapiro, Laura. *Perfection Salad: Women and Cooking at the Turn of the Century*. New York: Farrar, Straus and Giroux, 1986.

———. *Something from the Oven: Reinventing Dinner in 1950s America*. New York: Viking, 2004.

Shaw, Marian. *World's Fair Notes: A Woman Journalist Views Chicago's 1893 Columbian Exposition*. Chicago: Pogo Press, 1992.

Shepard, Ward. *Food or Famine: The Challenge of Erosion*. New York: Macmillan, 1945.

Shiva, Vandana. *Stolen Harvest: The Hijacking of the Global Food Supply*. Cambridge, MA: South End Press, 2000.

———. *The Violence of the Green Revolution: Third World Agriculture, Ecology, and Politics*. London: Zen Books, 1991.

Simon, Julian. *The State of Humanity*. Boston: Basil Blackwell, 1995.

Slosson, Edwin E. *Creative Chemistry*. New York: Century Co., 1919.

Smil, Vaclav. *Feeding the World: A Challenge for the Twenty-First Century*. Cambridge, MA: MIT Press, 2000.

Smith, J. Russell. *The World's Food Resources*. New York: Henry Holt, 1919.

Smith, J. Russell, and M. Ogden Phillips. *North America: Its People and the Resources, Development, and Prospects of the Continent as the Home of Man*. New York: Harcourt Brace and World, 1940.

Smith, Kirk S., et al. *Earth and the Human Future: Essays in Honor of Harrison Brown*. Boulder: Westview, 1986.

Smith, Michael. "The Short Life of a Dark Prophecy: The Rise and Fall of the 'Population Bomb' Crisis." In *Fear Itself: Enemies Real and Imagined in American Culture*, ed. Nancy Lusignan Schultz. West Lafayette: Purdue University Press, 1999.

Smith, Michael L. "Representations of Technology at the 1964 World's Fair." In *The Power of Culture: Critical Essays in American History*, ed. Richard Wrightman Fox and T. J. Jackson Lears. Chicago: University of Chicago Press, 1993.

Sobal, Jeffery. "Food System Globalization, Eating Transformations, and Nutrition Transitions." In *Food in Global History*, ed. Raymond Grew. Boulder: Westview Press, 1999.

Spang, Rebecca L. *The Invention of the Restaurant: Paris and Modern Gastronomic Culture*. Cambridge, MA: Harvard University Press, 2000.

Starhawk. *The Fifth Sacred Thing*. New York: Bantam Books, 1993.

Stevens, Mrs. Mark. *Six Months at the World's Fair*. Detroit: Detroit Free Press Printing Co., 1895.

Stoll, Steven. *The Fruits of Natural Advantage: Making the Industrial Countryside in California*. Berkeley: University of California Press, 1998.

Strasser, Susan. *Never Done: A History of American Housework*. New York: Pantheon, 1982.

———. *Satisfaction Guaranteed: The Making of the American Mass Market*. New York: Pantheon, 1989.

Sturgeon, Theodore. *Venus Plus X*. New York: Pyramid, 1960.

Sweetland, James Harvey. "American Utopian Fiction, 1798–1926." Ph.D. diss., University of Notre Dame, 1976.

Symonds, Richard, and Michael Carder. *The United Nations and the Population Question, 1945–1970*. New York: McGraw-Hill, 1973.

Takaki, Ronald. *Strangers from a Different Shore: A History of Asian Americans*. New York: Penguin, 1989.

Thompson, Warren S. "Population: A Study in Malthusianism." Ph.D. diss., Columbia University, 1915.

———. *Population Problems*. 3rd ed. New York: McGraw-Hill, 1942.

———. "Some Reflections on World Population and Food Supply during the Next Few Decades." In *Studies in Population*, ed. George R. Mair. Princeton: Princeton University Press, 1949.

Toffler, Alvin. *Future Shock*. New York: Bantam 1970.

Tribe, Derek. *Feeding and Greening the World: The Role of International Agricultural Research*. Oxford: CAB International, 1994.

Trolley, H. R. "Population and Food Supply." In *Freedom from Want: A Survey of the Possibilities of Meeting the World's Food Need*, ed. E. E. DeTurk. New York: Chronica Botanica, 1948.

Truman, Ben C. *History of the World's Fair*. Philadelphia: H. W. Kelley, 1893.

Tucker, Richard P. *Insatiable Appetite: The United States and the Ecological Degradation of the Tropical World*. Berkeley: University of California Press, 2000.

Tucker, Tara L. "*The Kin of Ata Are Waiting*: Uses of Pastoral Utopianizing and Femtopianism in Modern Utopian Literature." Unpublished research paper, University of Maryland Baltimore County, 1996.

U.S. Department of Agriculture. *Agricultural Yearbook, 1923*. Washington, DC: Government Printing Office, 1924.

Verne, Jules. "In the Twenty-Ninth Century: The Day of an American Journalist in 2889." In *Yesterday and Tomorrow*. 1889. London: Arco, 1965.

Vogt, William. *Road to Survival*. New York: William Sloane Associates, 1948.

Wackernagel, Mathis, and William Rees. *Our Ecological Footprint: Reducing Human Impact on the Earth*. Gabriola Island, BC: New Society Publishers, 1996.

Wagar, W. Warren. *The Next Three Futures: Paradigms of Things to Come*. New York: Praeger Publishers, 1991.

———. "The Rebellion of Nature." In *The End of the World*, ed. Eric S. Rabkin, Martin H. Greenberg, and Joseph D. Olander. Carbondale: Southern Illinois University Press, 1983.

———. *Terminal Visions: The Literature of Last Things*. Bloomington: Indiana University Press, 1982.

Waggoner, Paul E. *How Much Land Can Ten Billion People Spare for Nature?* Ames, IA: Council for Agricultural Science and Technology, 1994.

Wallace, Mike. *Mickey Mouse History, and Other Essays on American Memory*. Philadelphia: Temple University Press, 1996.

Walter, Dave, ed. *Today Then: 1993 as Predicted in 1893*. Helena MT: American and World Geographic Publishing, 1992.

Walters, Kerry S., and Lisa Portmess, eds. *Ethical Vegetarianism: From Pythagoras to Peter Singer*. Albany: State University of New York Press, 1999.

Waterlow, J. C., et al., eds. *Feeding a World Population of More than Eight Billion People*. New York: Oxford University Press, 1998.

Watkins, John Elfreth Jr. "What May Happen in the Next Hundred Years." *Ladies' Home Journal*. December 1900. Reprinted in *The 1990s & Beyond*, ed. Edward Cornish. Bethesda, MD: World Future Society, 1990.

Weimann, Jeannne Madeline. *The Fair Women*. Chicago: Academy Chicago Press, 1981.

Wells, H. G. *Anticipations of the Reaction of Mechanical and Scientific Progress upon Human Life and Thought*. London: Chapman & Hall, 1902.

———. *Anticipations*. Mineola, NY: Dover Publications, 1999.

———. *Food of the Gods*. 1904. Reprint, New York: Airmont Publishing, 1965.

———. *The Time Machine*. 1895. Reprint, New York: Penguin, 2000.

———. *The War of the Worlds*. 1898. Reprint, New York: Berkley, 1964.

———. *When the Sleeper Wakes*. 1899. Reprinted in *Three Prophetic Science Fiction Novels of H. G. Wells*. New York: Dover Publications, 1960.

Wendt, Gerald. *Science for the World of Tomorrow*. New York: W. W. Norton, 1939.

Westphal, Gary. "For Tomorrow We Dine: The Sad Gourmet at the Scientificafe." In *Foods of the Gods: Eating and the Eaten in Fantasy and Science Fiction*, ed. Gary Westphal, George Slusser, and Eric S. Rabkin. Athens: University of Georgia Press, 1996.

White, Trumbull, and William Igleheart. *The World's Columbian Exposition, Chicago 1893*. Philadelphia: P. W. Ziegler, 1893.

Willcox, O. W. *Reshaping Agriculture*. New York: W. W. Norton, 1934.

Williams, Rosalind. *Notes on the Underground: An Essay on Technology, Society, and the Imagination*. Cambridge, MA: MIT Press, 1990.

Winget, William. *A Tour in America and a Visit to the St. Louis Exposition*. Torquay, U.K.: n.p., 1904.

Worster, Donald. *Dust Bowl: The Southern Plains in the 1930s*. New York: Oxford University Press, 1979.

———. *Nature's Economy: A History of Ecological Ideas*. Cambridge: Cambridge University Press, 1985.

Woytinsky, W. S., and E. S. Woytinsky. *World Population and Production: Trends and Outlook*. New York: Twentieth Century Fund, 1953.

Wright, Angus. "Innocents Abroad: American Agricultural Research in Mexico." In *Meeting the Expectations of the Land*, ed. Wes Jackson et al. San Francisco: North Point, 1984.

Wu, Frank H. *Yellow: Race in America beyond Black and White*. New York: Basic Books, 2001.

Zim, Larry, Mel Lerner, and Herbert Rolfes. *The World of Tomorrow: The New York World's Fair*. New York: Harper and Row, 1988.

ACKNOWLEDGMENTS

If it takes a village to raise a child, it takes a whole world to write a book. Thanks first of all to that wondrous global data depot, the Library of Congress, which once again overwhelmed me with more sources than I could possibly handle. The University of Maryland Baltimore County gave me several semesters off, some research and travel support, and myriad classroom opportunities to try out half-baked ideas on innocent undergraduates. Many other organizations and institutions provided similar venues, particularly the American Film Institute (Silver Spring, Maryland); California Academy of Sciences; Cornell University; Culinary Historians of Washington; Greenbelt Library; Hagley Museum and Library; New York University's Department of Nutrition, Food, Studies, and Public Health; Silver Spring Library; Smithsonian Institution; United States Department of Agriculture; University of Delaware's History Department; University of Maryland Baltimore County's Humanities and Social Science Forums; University of Michigan; and the annual meetings of the American Historical Association, American Society for Environmental History, American Studies Association, Association for the Study of Food and Society, Organization of American Historians, Society for the History of Technology, and World Futurist Society. Earlier versions of this research also appeared in *Technology and Culture, Culture and Agriculture,* and *Food and Foodways.*

Working in the exciting new fields of food studies and futurism, I have had many important conversations and interchanges with a host of scholars and writers, including Ken Albala, Gary Allen, Keith Allen, Rima Apple, Arlene Avakian, Deborah Barndt, Amy Bentley, Jenny Berg, Charlotte Biltekoff, Dorothy Blair, Danny Block, Alessandro Bonanno, Allan Brandt, Martin Bruegel, Joan Jacobs Brumberg, Elisabeth Castleman, Shirley Cherkasky, Janet Chrzan, Kate Clancy, Doug Constance, Joseph Corn, Carole Counihan, Ken Dahlberg, Mitchell Davis, Netta Davis, Laura DeLind, Jon Deutsch, Hasia Diner, Adam Drewnowski, Jane Dusselier, Gail Feenstra, Marcie Cohen Ferris, Gary Fine, Claude Fischler, Deborah Fitzgerald, Harriet Friedmann, Donna Gabaccia, Darra Goldstein, Rayna Green, Ray Grew, Joan Dye Gussow, Kolleen Guy, Barbara Haber, Michael Hamm, Annie Hauck-Lawson, Lisa Heldke, Carol Helstosky, Roger Horowitz, Michael Jacobson, Nancy Jenkins, Virginia Jenkins, Eve Jochnowitz, Alice Julier, Steve Kaplan, Solomon Katz, Barbara Kirshenblatt-Gimblett, Jack Kloppenburg, Jeremy Korr, Peter Kuznick, Rachel Laudan, Harvey Levenstein, Walter Levy, Laura Lindenfeld, Lucy Long, Lisa Markowitz, Karal Ann Marling, Donna Maurer, Jim McDonald, Alex McIntosh, Sidney Mintz, Arwen Mohun, Anne Murcott, Joan Nathan, Marion Nestle, Jackie Newman, Marion Newman, Fabio Parasecoli, Gabriella Petrick, Jeff Pilcher, Tracy Poe, Elaine Power, Krishnendu Ray, Alice Ross, Paul Rozin, Faith Davis Ruffins, Philip Scranton, Laura Shapiro, Terry Sharrer, Barbara Shortridge, Andy Smith, Jeff Sobal, Audrey Spindler, Bill Staggs, Susan Strasser, Helen Tangires, Paul Thomas, Carolyn Thomas de la Pena, Kyla Wazana Tompkins, Katie Leonard Turner, Margaret Visser, Bill Whit, Merry White, Rick Wilk, Jennifer Wilkins, Psyche Williams-Forson, Doris Witt, Christopher Wolf, Rafia Zafar, and Wilbur Zelinsky.

Having taught at the University of Maryland Baltimore County for more years than I can count, I am deeply gratified to have many fine colleagues who have supported, inspired, and encouraged my work in so many ways: Guenet Abraham, Drew Alfgren, Jo Ann Argersinger, Peter Argersinger, Joe Arnold, Ken Baldwin, Tom Beck, Robert Deluty, Tony Farquhar, Jonathan Finkelstein, Guisseppi Forgionne, Jay Freyman, Marilyn Goldberg, Sue Hahn, Doug Hamby, Carol Harmon, Keith Harries, Daphne Harrison, Freeman Hrabowski, John Jeffries, Art Johnson, Bill Johnson, Carolyn Koehler, Joan Korenman, Phil Landon, Patricia Lanoue, Larry Lasher, Doug MacLean, Ken Maton, David Mitch, Franc Nunoo-Quarcoo, Sandy Parker, Art Pittenger, Bob Platt, Mary Rivkin, Pat Scully, Simmona Simmons-Hodo, Bob Sloan, Jerry Stephany, John Titchener, Tom Vargish, Liz Walton, Carl Weber, Rick Welch, Victor Wexler, Larry Wilt, and Ka-Che Yip. And special credit goes to my American Studies Department colleagues, past and present, who have shared my interests, raised the right issues, cheered my weird courses, and tolerated my incessant worrying about food and the future: John Bloom, Kathy Bryan, Wendy Kozol, Jason Loviglio, Mike Hummel, Carole McCann, Pat McDermott, Greg Metcalf, Ed Orser, Kathy Peiss, Leslie Prosterman, Dabrina Taylor, Kendra Wallace, and Joshua Woodfork. I also remain deeply indebted to past mentors who helped me to shape my written voice—Phil Church, Bill Freehling, Kenneth Jenkins, Gerry Linderman, Bob Sklar, and Wendy Wolf. And at University of California Press, editor Sheila Levine and California Studies in Food and Culture editor Darra Goldstein provided just the right amount of feedback right when I needed it.

Much of this work was developed collaboratively with my students at the University of Maryland Baltimore County, who asked tough questions, slipped me pertinent cartoons and clippings, pestered their friends and relatives for me, critiqued seminal texts (especially *Brave New World, Looking Backward,* and *Woman on the Edge of Time*), wrote wonderful scenarios, plied me with sustainable snacks, and were kind enough not to sleep during the more boring parts of my courses. Of the many wonderful student scholars who have come my way, I remember these most gratefully: Marco Alva, Jennifer Arrington, Trevor Blank, Elisabeth Castleman, Ed Conley, Barbara Cunningham, Kevin Daugherty, Brad Engel, Sharon Faircloth, Adrienne Finley, Jean Flanagan, Alicia Gabriel, Rachel Gunde, Ian Haupt, Andy Hershberger, Angela Hughes, Eric Hughes, Ed Kapuscinski, Chrissy Keen, Karen Keys, Aaron Krebeck, David Landgren, Jon Ledford, Karen Lewis, Tracie McClintic, Pat McGann, Michael McLaurin, Ryan Moschell, Jack Moyer, Jamie Peck, Phuong Pham, Amy Poff, Brock Posner-Smuck, Mary Potorti, Rachel Raffel, Suzanne Rogers-White, Michael Rund, Rob Savillo, Tony Sclafani, Kelly Scott, Karen Siegrist, Sutton Stokes, Nancy Swartz, Tara Tucker, Paul Turley, David Wright, Suzanne Wright, Rebecca Yingling, and Samantha Zline.

Good friends and an astonishingly utopian family kept me going during the slow times. Ana and John Stayton, Clare and Dave Heidtke, Leni Fried and Mike Augspurger, Hal Fried and Betty Daniel, and Harvey and Susie Edwards all offered rural refuge and sympathetic ears when the writing dried up. For over twenty-five years, my grower friends at the Takoma Park Farmers' Market have supplied me with the edible results of the organic life. Brett Williams's infectious enthusiasm, curiosity, and sense of outrage has sustained my own. Important conversations with Anne Murcott sharpened my critical sensibilities, and Joan Dye Gussow continued to show me what a life devoted to scholarship, activism, and gardening looks like. My parents, Shirley Belasco, Max Desfor, and Joyce and Ed Fried, nourished me with a healthy diet of family meals, kind words, good jokes, and friendly clippings. As always, my life partner, Amy Belasco, walked and talked me through every stage of the project. No, she didn't type the final manuscript, but her keenly analytical approach to everything toughened me up. And my children, Sonia and Nathaniel, watched and discussed countless sci-fi films with me, forgave my grumpy spells, and, most important, showed me why the future matters.

INDEX

Soule, Henri, 162
South Beach Beverages, 252–53
Soviet Union, 53, 231
Soylent Green (film; 1973), 51, 53, 57, 96, 134
soy/soybeans: classical future and, 152; in dystopian fiction, 133; price of, and algae cultivation, 209; as protein-rich substitute, 30
Space and the American Imagination (McCurdy), 61–62, 97
space colonies, 233
Space.com, 234
space farming, 233
space food, ix, 230–35
The Space Merchants (Pohl and Kornbluth), 131–33, 195
space program, 82, 97, 196–97, 220, 230–35
Space Shuttle, 233–34
Spang, Rebecca, 23, 113, 160
species extinction, 59
"speed scratch" cuisine, 244, 255
Spengler, Joseph, 38
Spielberg, Steven, 248–49
spirulina, 212. *See also* algae
Spoehr, H. A., 181
sprawl, 79–80
Standard Brands, 190
Standing Room Only? (Ross), 30–31
Standing Room Only (Sax), 65
Stand on Zanzibar (Brunner), 135
Stanford University Food Research Institute, 43, 182, 203
Starbucks, 254
Stare, Frederick, 40
Starhawk, 141–42, 143–44, 145
Star Trek (films), 99
Star Trek (TV program; 1967–69), 131, 235
statistics, use of: in food policy debate, 56–57, 59, 67–69, 81; in utopian fiction, 137–38
Steinbeck, John, 37
Stevenson, Robert Louis, 102
Stewart, Martha, 244–45
Stilgoe, John R., 307n91
St. Louis, 154, 159, 170, 196–97
Stollweick Brothers, 155
Strasser, Susan, 170
streamline moderne style, 175
streamlining: automation and, 191–93; hybridization and, 176–79, 195; of industrial agriculture, 175–76, 194; nuclear power and, 200–1; of photosynthesis, 181–82, 183–84, 185, 201, 222; and reduction in biodiversity,

194–96; rhetoric of, 182–83; space farming and, 233; synthetic fertilizers and, 179–80; synthetic food and, 180–83; at world's fairs, 185–88
Stuckert, Mrs. Coleman, 169–70
Sub-Coelum (Russell), 105
subsistence farming, 85
subsistence homesteads, 35, 37, 97
suburbia, 163–64, 196, 200–1, 215
Sugar Research Foundation, 47
Sumner, William Graham, 25
Sun Microsystems, 249
superhighways, 185, 194
supermarkets, ix, 174–75, 194, 195, 242–43
supplements, 251–52, 255, 256
survivalism, gourmet, 141–42
sustainability: biotechnology and, 91, 241; at Disney theme parks, 227; Malthusianism and, 57, 77, 87; meat consumption and, 12. *See also* carrying capacity, global
sustainable agriculture movement, 87, 307n91
Swift, Gustavus, 154, 167–68
Swift, Jonathan, 86, 130
Swift & Company, 190
synthetic chemistry, 43–44, 92
synthetic fertilizers, 179–80
synthetic food: class and, 213; conservative food habits and, 52–53, 85; cornucopian promotion of, 32, 36–37, 171; in dystopian fiction, 57, 102, 130–35; food policy debate and, 91; historical precedents for, 77; inaccurate predictions about, 263; streamlining and, 180–83; in utopian fiction, 107, 114–15; women's liberation and, 27–28; at world's fairs, 27, 168. *See also* algae; meals-in-a-pill
synthetic protein, 36–37

Tang, 229, 230, 233, 256
Taylor, Alonzo, 31
Taylor, Frederick Winslow, 116
Taza (restaurant; Chicago), 248
technocracy, 88, 131–33, 142–43
technological utopianism, 89, 118, 124, 181, 237, 291n17
technology: metaphors for, 85–87; modernist future and, 171–75, 199–201; negative side effects of, 84–85, 90, 126–28; "smart," 239–46; transfer of, 84; in utopian fiction, 106–7, 111–12, 117–18, 139–41; world's fair displays of, 167–68, 188–90

CALIFORNIA STUDIES IN FOOD AND CULTURE

Darra Goldstein, Editor

Text:	10/13 Sabon
Display:	Franklin Gothic
Compositor:	Integrated Composition Systems
Printer and Binder:	Sheridan Books, Inc.